*The Rise of Islam and the
Bengal Frontier, 1204–1760*

Comparative Studies on Muslim Societies
General Editor, Barbara D. Metcalf

The Rise of Islam and the Bengal Frontier, 1204–1760

RICHARD M. EATON

University of California Press

BERKELEY   LOS ANGELES   LONDON

This book is a print-on-demand volume. It is manufactured
using toner in place of ink. Type and images may be less
sharp than the same material seen in traditionally printed
University of California Press editions.

The publisher gratefully acknowledges the contribution provided by the
General Endowment Fund of the Associates of the University of California Press.

University of California Press
Berkeley and Los Angeles, California

University of California Press, Ltd.
London, England

First Paperback Printing 1996

Library of Congress Cataloging-in-Publication Data

Eaton, Richard Maxwell.
    The rise of Islam and the Bengal frontier, 1204–1760 / Richard
M. Eaton.
        p.   cm.—(Comparative studies on Muslim societies ; 17)
    Includes bibliographical references (p.   ) and index.
    ISBN 0-520-20507-3 (alk. paper)
    1. Bengal (India)—History.   2. Islam—India—Bengal—History.
I. Title.   II. Series.
DS485.B46E16   1993
954'.14—dc20   92-34002
                                                          CIP

Printed in the United States of America

To Clio
2 P.M., 15 November 1978

Contents

Illustrations

Tables

Note on Translation and Transliteration

The author is responsible for all translations in this study except for those otherwise credited in the notes. The system of transliteration for Persian words when italicized, or when forming a book or manuscript title, is that of F. Steingass, *A Comprehensive Persian-English Dictionary* (Beirut: Librairie du Liban, 1970), with the following exceptions: the fourth letter of the Persian alphabet, *thā*, is rendered "th"; the eleventh letter, *żāl*, is rendered "ż"; the nineteenth letter, *ṭā*, is rendered "ṭ"; and the twentieth letter, *ẓā*, is rendered "ẓ". Bengali and Sanskrit names or terms, when italicized, are given in the conventional system of transcribing the Devanagari to the Roman script.

Acknowledgments

I am deeply grateful to the many people who over the past decade or so have given me valuable assistance during the various stages of preparing the present work. The idea of the book took shape in early 1980, when I was a fellow at the National Humanities Center at Research Triangle Park, North Carolina. In fall 1981 and spring 1982 a fellowship with the American Institute of Indian Studies and a Fulbright-Hays Training Grant, administered through the American Cultural Center in Dhaka, enabled me to undertake exploratory field research in India and Bangladesh. Thanks to a University of Arizona Humanities grant, in fall 1984 I returned to Bangladesh for more research, and in spring 1985 I began analyzing data while a fellow with the Institute for Advanced Studies in Jerusalem. In spring 1987 I was able to work on the manuscript while at the Ecole des Hautes Etudes en Sciences Sociales, Paris, and a sabbatical leave of absence from the University of Arizona in 1988–89 enabled me to complete the bulk of the writing. For funding my travel, facilitating my support, and opening the doors of my research generally, I wish to thank all the then directors and officers of the above institutions—in particular P. R. Mehendiratta and Tarun Mitra of the American Institute of Indian Studies, Ahmed Mustafa of the American Cultural Center, William Bennett of the National Humanities Center, Nehemia Levtzion of the Institute for Advanced Studies, and Marc Gaborieau of the Ecole des Hautes Etudes en Sciences Sociales.

I could never have undertaken this project without the generous assistance of the many librarians and staff at institutions whose holdings provide the book's documentary basis. Special thanks go to the British Library and the India Office Library, London; the Bodleian Library, Oxford; the Bibliothèque Nationale, Paris; the National Archives of India, New Delhi;

the Aligarh Muslim University Library; the Khuda Bakhsh Oriental Public Library, Patna; the National Library, the Asiatic Society, and the West Bengal Secretariat, Calcutta; the Varendra Research Museum, Rajshahi; the Dhaka University Library and the Bangla Academy, Dhaka; the Chittagong University Museum; and the Muslim Sahitya Samsad, Sylhet. I am especially indebted to Qazi Jalaluddin Ahmed, secretary of the Bangladesh Ministry of Education, for facilitating my research and making it possible for me to examine Mughal documents preserved in the various District Collectorates.

For supplying me with photographs used in the book, I wish to thank Catherine Asher (fig. 6) and the Smithsonian Institution and its photographer, Charles Rand (fig. 1). For granting permission to make my own photographs, I thank G. S. Farid of the Asiatic Society in Calcutta (figs. 2, 3, 11), Shamsul Husain of the Chittagong University Museum (figs. 16, 17), and Omar Farooq and A. R. Khan of the Chittagong District Collectorate (figs. 22, 23, 24).

Many of the themes in this book were first proposed in lectures I presented at various stages in the book's evolution. These took place at Duke University, Calcutta University, the Asiatic Society of Bangladesh, the University of Pennsylvania, Ohio State University, the University of Arizona, Rutgers University, Utrecht University, Leiden University, the Centre d'Etudes de l'Inde et de l'Asie du Sud in Paris, Heidelberg University, Cornell University, the University of Wisconsin, the University of Texas at Austin, the University of Washington, Arizona State University, Pomona College, and the University of Chicago. I wish to express my gratitude to all the learned colleagues who attended those lectures and who generously offered comments and suggestions. I am also indebted to the many colleagues with whom I have privately exchanged views on various themes in this book, and from whom I profited much. In particular, I would mention Will Bateson, Elaine Scarry, Peter Bertocci, Ralph Nicholas, Muzaffar Alam, Shireen Moosvi, Paul Jackson S.J., Rajat Ray, Gautam Bhadra, Jagadish Narayan Sarkar, M. R. Tarafdar, Sirajul Islam, Perween Hasan, Kamalakanta Gupta, Thérèse Blanchet, France Bhattacharya, Dale Eickelman, André Wink, Anupam Sen, Abdul Karim, John Voll, Yohanan Friedmann, David Shulman, Marc Gaborieau, Sushil Chaudhury, Asim Roy, Marilyn Waldman, Tony Stewart, Carl Ernst, the late S. H. Askari, the late Sukumar Sen, and the late Hitesranjan Sanyal. My thanks also go to friends and colleagues who took the time to read through drafts of all or parts of the manuscript, and who made valuable comments and suggestions. These include Mimi Klaiman, Callie Williamson, Norman Yoffee, Margaret Case, Rafiuddin Ahmed, Carol Salomon, Dharma Kumar, and Barbara Metcalf.

For whatever shortcomings may remain in the study, however, I alone bear responsibility.

Numerous other friends supported me in nonacademic ways, and to them I acknowledge my sincere gratitude. Among these I am pleased to mention Father G. M. Tourangeau and Joseph Sarkar of the Oriental Institute, Barisal, who introduced me to the language, culture, and society of Lower Bengal; Jim and Naomi Novak, who gave hearty welcome and kind hospitality whenever I turned up in Dhaka; Jan "Van" Paxton, who bravely persevered in transcribing my early handwritten drafts; and Tad Park, who more than once rescued me from extremely stressful computer crises. Finally, I record my thanks to Pushpo (née Blossom), a canine friend who, curled at my feet, faithfully and supportively accompanied the writing of the following chapters.

Introduction

Sometime in 1243–44, residents of Lakhnauti, a city in northwestern Bengal, told a visiting historian of the dramatic events that had taken place there forty years earlier. At that time, the visitor was informed, a band of several hundred Turkish cavalry had ridden swiftly down the Gangetic Plain in the direction of the Bengal delta. Led by a daring officer named Muhammad Bakhtiyar, the men overran venerable Buddhist monasteries in neighboring Bihar before turning their attention to the northwestern portion of the delta, then ruled by a mild and generous Hindu monarch. Disguising themselves as horse dealers, Bakhtiyar and his men slipped into the royal city of Nudiya. Once inside, they rode straight to the king's palace, where they confronted the guards with brandished weapons. Utterly overwhelmed, for he had just sat down to dine, the Hindu monarch hastily departed through a back door and fled with many of his retainers to the forest hinterland of eastern Bengal, abandoning his capital altogether.[1]

This coup d'état inaugurated an era, lasting over five centuries, during which most of Bengal was dominated by rulers professing the Islamic faith.

---

1. Maulana Minhaj-ud-Din Abu'l-'Umar-i-'Usman, *Ṭabaḳāt-i-Nāṣirī: A General History of the Muhammadan Dynasties of Asia, Including Hindustan (810–1260)*, trans. H. G. Raverty (Calcutta: Asiatic Society of Bengal, 1881; reprint, New Delhi: Oriental Books Reprint, 1970), 1: 557–58. This account by Minhaj is the earliest narrative we have of this important event. It is likely that some of the historian's informants had been eyewitnesses to the events they described; some may well have participated in them.

Nudiya is probably identifiable with Naudah, a village several miles northeast of Rohanpur railway station in western Rajshahi District. See Abul Kalam Muhammad Zakariah, "Muhammad Bakhtiyar's Conquest of Nudiah," *Journal of the Varendra Research Museum* 6 (1980–81): 57–72.

In itself this was not exceptional, since from about this time until the eighteenth century, Muslim sovereigns ruled over most of the Indian subcontinent. What was exceptional, however, was that among India's interior provinces only in Bengal—a region approximately the size of England and Scotland combined—did a majority of the indigenous population adopt the religion of the ruling class, Islam. This outcome proved to be as fateful as it is striking, for in 1947 British India was divided into two independent states, India and Pakistan, on the basis of the distribution of Muslims. In Bengal, those areas with a Muslim majority would form the eastern wing of Pakistan—since 1971, Bangladesh—whereas those parts of the province with a Muslim minority became the state of West Bengal within the Republic of India. In 1984 about 93 million of the 152 million Bengalis in Bangladesh and West Bengal were Muslims, and of the estimated 96.5 million people inhabiting Bangladesh, 81 million, or 83 percent, were Muslims; in fact, Bengalis today comprise the second largest Muslim ethnic population in the world, after the Arabs.[2]

How can one explain this development? More particularly, why did such a large Muslim population emerge in Bengal—so distant from the Middle East, from which Islam historically expanded—and not in other regions of India? And within Bengal, why did Islamization occur at so much greater a rate in the east than in the west? Who converted and why? At what time? What, if anything, did "conversion" mean to contemporary Bengalis? And finally, between the thirteenth and eighteenth centuries, in what ways did different generations and different social classes of Muslims in Bengal understand, construe, or even construct, Islamic civilization? In seeking answers to these questions, this study explores processes embedded in the delta's premodern history that may cast light on the evolution of Bengal's extraordinary cultural geography.

Bengal's historical experience was extraordinary not only in its widespread reception of Islam but also in its frontier character. In part, the thirteenth-century Turkish drive eastward—both to Bengal and within Bengal—was the end product of a process triggered by political convulsions in thirteenth-century Inner Asia. For several centuries before and after the Mongol irruption into West Asia, newly Islamicized Turks from Central Asia and the Iranian Plateau provided a ready supply of soldiers, both as slaves and as free men, for commanders such as Muhammad Bakhtiyar. Once within Bengal's fertile delta, these men pushed on until stopped only by geographical barriers. Surrounded on the north and east by moun-

2. Richard V. Weekes, ed., *Muslim Peoples: A World Ethnographic Survey,* 2d ed. (Westport, Conn.: Greenwood Press, 1984), 1: 137.

tains, and to the south by the sea, Bengal was the terminus of a continentwide process of Turko-Mongol conquest and migration. It was, in short, a frontier zone.

In reality, Bengal in our period possessed not one but several frontiers, each moving generally from west to east. One of these was the political frontier, which defined the territories within which the Turks and their successors, the Bengal sultans and governors of the Mughal Empire, minted coins, garrisoned troops, and collected revenue. A second, the agrarian frontier, divided settled agricultural communities from the forest, Bengal's natural state before humans attacked it with ax and plow. A third was the Islamic frontier, which divided Muslim from non-Muslim communities. A porous phenomenon, as much mental as territorial in nature, this last was the frontier that proved so fateful in 1947. Finally, all three frontiers were superimposed on a much older one, a frontier defined by the long-term eastward march of Sanskritic civilization in the Bengal delta. Characterized either by an egalitarian agrarian society organized around Buddhist monastic institutions or by a hierarchically ordered agrarian society presided over by Brahman priests, Sanskritic civilization in both its Buddhist and its Brahmanic forms had moved down the Gangetic Plain and into the Bengal delta many centuries before Muhammad Bakhtiyar's coup of 1204.

After the establishment of Muslim power in Bengal, the political frontier was extended as the new rulers and their successors overpowered or won over centers of entrenched agrarian interests. As aliens occupying the country by force of arms, Muslim soldiers and administrators were generally concentrated in garrison settlements located in or near pre-conquest urban centers. This was natural in those parts of the delta where the conquerors encountered developed agrarian communities, for by controlling the cities they could control the agriculturally rich hinterland, linked to cities by markets and revenue-paying networks. The Turkish occupation of Bengal thus followed the settlement pattern found throughout the early Delhi sultanate, anticipating in this respect the cantonment city employed by the British in their occupation of India in the nineteenth century.

Of a very different nature was Bengal's agrarian frontier, which divided the delta's cultivated terrain from the wild forests or marshlands that were as yet unpenetrated, or only lightly penetrated, by plow agriculture and agrarian society. Whereas the political frontier was man-made and subject to rapid movement, the agrarian frontier was more stable, slower-moving, and shaped by natural as well as human forces. Prominent among these natural forces was the historic movement of Bengal's rivers, which in the

long run caused the northwestern and western delta to decay as their channels shifted increasingly eastward. As new river systems gave access to
new tracts of land and deposited on them the silt necessary to fertilize their
soil, areas formerly covered by dense forest were transformed into rice
fields, providing the basis for new agrarian communities. Yet, although
driven by natural forces, the movement of Bengal's agrarian frontier was
also a human phenomenon, since it necessarily involved the arduous work
of colonizing and settling new lands.

Our understanding of the third frontier, the cultural one, should not be
biased by early Persian histories of the Turkish conquest, which typically
speak of a stark, binary opposition between "Islam" and "infidelity" (*kufr*).
Use of these terms has often given the impression that the rise of Muslim
communities in Bengal was a corollary to, or simply a function of, the
expansion of Turkish arms. In fact, however, the terms "Islam" and "infidelity" as used in these sources simply refer to the rulers and the ruled—
that is, Persianized Turks who were assumed to be Muslim, and Bengali
subjects who were assumed to be non-Muslim. Since large numbers of
Bengali Muslims did not emerge until well after the conquest was completed, for the first several centuries after Muhammad Bakhtiyar's invasion, the political and cultural frontiers remained quite distinct geographically.

Each of Bengal's frontiers thus moved by its own dynamics: the Sanskritic frontier by the growth of Buddhist- or Brahman-ordered communities; the political frontier by the force of arms and the articulation and
acceptance of the Muslim regime's legitimate authority; the agrarian frontier by the twin processes of riverine movement and colonization; and the
Islamic frontier by the gradual incorporation of indigenous communities
into a Muslim-oriented devotional life. Having their own laws of motion,
these frontiers overlapped one another in various ways. For example, after
having established a base in the northwestern corner of the delta, which
for four hundred years remained the epicenter of its rule in Bengal, Turkish power moved swiftly to the revenue-rich southwest. There, where the
rulers encountered a dense agrarian society, conquest by Turks did not
involve the physical extension of the arable land, but simply the capture
of the local revenue structure. On the other hand, in much of the eastern
and southern delta, where field agriculture had not yet replaced thick forests, the political and agrarian frontiers collapsed into one. There, the territorial reach of Turkish domination normally stopped at the edge of forests,
only penetrating further when the forest itself was cleared. Hence in the
east, the expanding Turkish movement involved not only the incorporation

of indigenous peoples into a new political system but the physical transformation of the land from marsh or forest into rice fields.

The interaction between the delta's Sanskritic, political, agrarian, and Islamic frontiers thus forms one of the great themes of Bengal's history, and it constitutes a central concern of this study. The theme is pursued in both of the book's chronologically distinct divisions. Part I treats the establishment and evolution of Indo-Islamic civilization from the early thirteenth century to the late sixteenth, for most of which time the delta region was ruled by kings of the independent Bengal sultanate. Chapter 1 sketches Bengal's cultural, political, and economic profile prior to the advent of Islamic rule. Chapter 2 explores how Central Asian conquerors, informed by medieval Perso-Islamic conceptions of political legitimacy, established themselves amidst a society that had inherited very different political and cultural traditions. Chapter 3 follows the activities of the earliest Sufis—Muslim mystics and holy men—who settled in the delta and reconstructs their own various encounters with Bengali culture. Chapter 4 examines the delta's economy and the sociocultural basis of Muslim and Hindu communities that crystallized under the sultanate. Since this discussion sets the stage for analysis of the origin of mass Muslim society, the following chapter, Chapter 5, steps out of the narrative and reviews past and present debates concerning "conversion" to Islam, both in medieval India generally and in Bengal particularly.

Part II explores the sociocultural transformations that took place between the late sixteenth and the mid-eighteenth centuries, when Bengal was incorporated into the Mughal Empire. Paradoxically, a substantial majority of Bengal's Muslim population emerged under a regime that did not, as a matter of policy, promote the conversion of Bengalis to Islam. This part of the book seeks resolution of this apparent paradox. Chapter 6 describes the rise and consolidation of the Mughals' authority in Bengal, while Chapter 7 reconstructs the ideological basis of their rule, exploring the place of Bengali culture and the Islamic religion in Mughal imperial culture. As the book moves from the sixteenth and seventeenth centuries to the eighteenth, the perspective becomes increasingly local in nature, with the result that political figures and events familiar to students of early- or mid-eighteenth-century history—Murshid Quli Khan, Aliverdi Khan, the rise of the East India Company, the battle of Plassey, the "Black Hole" of Calcutta, and so on—receive little or no mention at all. Attention is focused instead on the institutions through which provincial Mughal officials deepened the roots of their authority in the countryside at a time when power in Delhi, the Mughal capital, was steadily diminishing.

Imperial expansion on the Mughal periphery during imperial decline at the center thus constitutes the second apparent paradox with which Part II is concerned. Yet the principal emphasis of this part, as with the first, is on culture change, and in particular the growth of Islamic institutions and Muslim society. Thus Chapter 8 examines the political and cultural implications of agrarian growth in the Mughal period, and both Chapter 8 and Chapter 9 explore the role played by village mosques and shrines in the diffusion of Mughal authority and Islamic values in the region. Finally, in contrast to these two chapters, which analyze the politicoeconomic correlates of culture change, Chapter 10 examines the specifically religious dimensions of Islamization in premodern Bengal.

As to the periodization indicated in the book's title, one may legitimately ask why a cultural study ends with a political date—1760, the year the English East India Company became paramount in the Bengal region. For one thing, historians are always constrained by the chronological scope of their sources, and the intrusion of Englishmen into Bengal's revenue system abruptly ended the Persian documentation that forms the data base for the book's later chapters. A further reason for ending this study in 1760 is the demise of a patronage system that had played a decisive role in the articulation of both Mughal political culture and Islamic institutions. Although many of the social and cultural processes examined in these chapters continued into the later eighteenth century and even the nineteenth, the disappearance of imperial patronage as a principal motor behind them makes the year 1760 a convenient stopping point.

This book is written with several audiences in mind. For South Asians who understand Islamic history in the subcontinent in terms of an unassimilated "foreign" intrusion, the study explores how this religion, together with the Perso-Turkic civilization that carried it into the subcontinent, became indigenized in the cultural landscape of premodern Bengal. For Middle Easterners who understand Islam's historical and cultural center of gravity as lying between the Nile and the Oxus rivers, the book examines how and why Islamic civilization in the late medieval period became at least as vibrant and creative on the Bengali "periphery" as in the Middle Eastern "heartland." It also addresses the issue of why so many more Muslims reside outside the Middle East, especially in South Asia, than within it. Finally, this study seeks to reach Western readers for whom Islam's significant expansion was in the direction of Europe—a confrontation that, among other things, bequeathed to Europe and its cultural offshoots an image of Islam as a "militant" religion. I argue that Islam's more significant expansion lay in the direction of India, where Muslims encountered civilizations far more alien than those they met with in the European or Judeo-Christian worlds. Their responses to that encounter, moreover, proved far more creative; and in Bengal, at least, the meeting of Islamic and indigenous cultures led to an exceptional demographic development: the emergence of the world's second-largest Muslim ethnic community. This book is concerned with the nature of that encounter and its extraordinary outcome.

PART 1

BENGAL UNDER THE SULTANS

1   Before the Turkish Conquest

[The Sylhet region of East Bengal] was outside the pale of
human habitation, where there is no distinction between
natural and artificial, infested by wild animals and poisonous
reptiles, and covered with forest out-growths.
                    Lokanatha copper plate (seventh century A.D.)

Bengal in Prehistory

Physically, the Bengal delta is a flat, low-lying floodplain in the shape of
a great horseshoe, its open part facing the Bay of Bengal to the south.
Surrounding its rim to the west, north, and east are disconnected hill systems, out of which flow some of the largest rivers in southern Asia — the
Ganges, the Brahmaputra, and the Meghna. Wending their way slowly
over the delta's flat midsection, these rivers and their tributaries deposit
immense loads of sand and soil, which over millennia have gradually built
up the delta's land area, pushing its southern edge ever deeper into the bay.
In historical times, the rivers have been natural arteries of communication
and transportation, and they have defined Bengal's physical and ancient
cultural subregions — Varendra, the Bhagirathi-Hooghly basin, Vanga, Samatata, and Harikela (see map 1).[1]

   The delta was no social vacuum when Turkish cavalrymen entered it in

1. Situated in the northwestern delta north of the Padma River, Varendra included
the territories now constituting the districts of Malda, Pabna, Rajshahi, Bogra, Dinajpur, and Rangpur. The Bhagirathi-Hooghly basin included several ancient cultural subregions—Suhma, Vardhamana, Radha, and Gauda—corresponding to the
modern districts of Midnapur, Howrah, Hooghly, Burdwan, Birbhum, and Murshidabad. Ancient Vanga, or Central Bengal, included the area corresponding to
the modern districts of Dhaka, Faridpur, Jessore, Bakarganj, Khulna, Nadia, and
Twenty-four Parganas. Samatata included the hilly region east of the Meghna
River in the southeastern delta, corresponding to modern Comilla, Noakhali, and
Chittagong. Harikela referred to the delta's northeastern hinterland, including
modern Mymensingh and Sylhet. On the ancient subregions of Bengal, see Barrie
M. Morrison, *Political Centers and Cultural Regions in Early Bengal* (Tucson:
University of Arizona Press, 1970), esp. ch. 4, and Susan L. Huntington, *The "Pala-
Sena" Schools of Sculpture* (Leiden: Brill, 1984), 171. For a discussion of Bengal's
physical subregions, see O. H. K. Spate and A. T. A. Learmonth, *India and Paki-*

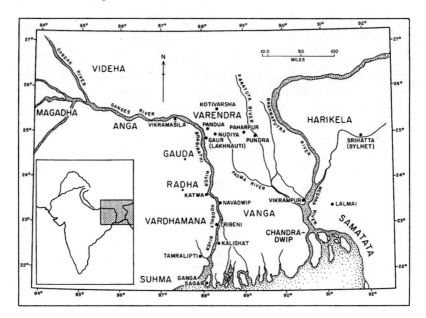

Map 1. Cultural regions of early Bengal

the thirteenth century. In fact, it had been inhabited long before the earliest appearance of dated inscriptions in the third century B.C. In ancient North Bengal, Pundra (or Pundranagara, "city of the Pundras"), identifiable with Mahasthan in today's Bogra District, owed its name to a non-Aryan tribe mentioned in late Vedic literature.[2] Similarly, the Radha and Suhma peoples, described as wild and churlish tribes in Jain literature of the third century B.C.,[3] gave their names to western and southwestern Bengal respectively, as the Vanga peoples did to central and eastern Bengal.[4] Archaeological evidence confirms that already in the second millennium B.C., rice-cultivating communities inhabited West Bengal's Burdwan District. By the eleventh century B.C., peoples in this area were living in systematically aligned houses, using elaborate human cemeteries, and making copper ornaments and fine black-and-red pottery. By the early part of the

stan: A General and Regional Geography, 3d ed. (London: Methuen, 1967), 571–73.

2. *Aitareya Brāhmaṇa* 7.6, cited in S. K. Chatterji, *Origin and Development of the Bengali Language* (Calcutta: University of Calcutta Press, 1926), 1: 62.

3. These include the *Āyāraṃa Sutta* and *Gaina Sūtras*, cited in Chatterji, *Origin and Development*, 1: 71.

4. Chatterji, *Origin and Development*, 1: 67.

first millennium B.C., they had developed weapons made of iron, probably smelted locally alongside copper.[5] Rather than permanent field agriculture, which would come later, these peoples appear to have practiced shifting cultivation; having burned patches of forest, they prepared the soil with hoes, seeded dry rice and small millets by broadcast or with dibbling sticks, and harvested crops with stone blades, which have been found at excavated sites.[6] These communities could very well have been speakers of "Proto-Munda," the Austroasiatic ancestor of the modern Munda languages, for there is linguistic evidence that at least as early as 1500 B.C., Proto-Munda speakers had evolved "a subsistence agriculture which produced or at least knew grain—in particular rice, two or three millets, and at least three legumes."[7]

In the sixth and fifth centuries B.C., dramatic changes that would permanently alter Bengal's cultural history took place to the immediate west of the delta, in the middle Gangetic Plain, where the practice of shifting cultivation gradually gave way to settled farming, first on unbunded permanent fields and later on bunded, irrigated fields. Moreover, whereas the earlier forms of rice production could have been managed by single families, the shift to wet rice production on permanent fields required substantial increases in labor inputs, the use of draft animals, some sort of irrigation technology, and an enhanced degree of communal cooperation.[8] As the

---

5. P. C. Das Gupta, *The Excavations at Pandu Rajar Dhibi* (Calcutta: Directorate of Archaeology, West Bengal, 1964), 14, 18, 22, 24, 31. The site is located on the southern side of the Ajay River, six miles from Bhedia. The archaeological record reveals prehistoric rice-cultivating communities living all along the middle Gangetic Plain. Excavations in the Belan Valley south of Allahabad have found peoples cultivating rice (*Oryza sativa*) as early as the middle of the seventh millennium B.C., which is the earliest-known evidence of rice cultivation in the world. G. R. Sharma and D. Mandal, *Excavations at Mahagara, 1977–78 (a Neolithic Settlement in the Belan Valley)*, vol. 6 of *Archaeology of the Vindhyas and the Ganga Valley*, ed. G. R. Sharma (Allahabad: University of Allahabad, 1980), 23, 27, 30.
6. Ram Sharan Sharma, *Material Culture and Social Formations in Ancient India* (New Delhi: Macmillan India, 1983), 118.
7. See Arlene R. K. Zide and Norman H. Zide, "Proto-Munda Cultural Vocabulary: Evidence for Early Agriculture," in *Austroasiatic Studies*, ed. Philip N. Jenner, Laurence C. Thompson, and Stanley Starosta, pt. 2 (Honolulu: University Press of Hawaii, 1976), 1324. The authors show that Munda terms for uncooked, husked rice (*Oryza sativa*) have clear cognates in the language's sister Austroasiatic branch, Mon-Khmer. They also conclude that "the agricultural technology included implements which presuppose the knowledge and use of such grains and legumes as food, since, the specific and consistent meanings for 'husking pestle' and 'mortar' go back, at least in one item, to Proto-Austroasiatic."
8. Te-Tzu Chang, "The Impact of Rice on Human Civilization and Population Expansion," *Interdisciplinary Science Reviews* 12, no. 1 (1987): 65.

middle Gangetic Plain receives over fifty inches of rainfall annually, over double that of the semi-arid Punjab,[9] the establishment of permanent rice-growing operations also required the clearing of the marshes and thick monsoon forests that had formerly covered the area. Iron axes, which began to appear there around 500 B.C., proved far more efficient than stone tools for this purpose.[10] Iron plowshares, which also began to appear in the middle Ganges region about this time, were a great improvement over wooden shares and vastly increased agricultural productivity in this region's typically hard alluvial soil.[11] The adoption of the technique of transplanting rice seedings, a decisive step in the transition from primitive to advanced rice cultivation, also occurred in the middle Ganges zone around 500 B.C.[12]

Early Indo-Aryan Influence in Bengal

These changes were accompanied by the intrusion of immigrants from the north and west, the Indo-Aryans, who brought with them a vast corpus of Sanskrit sacred literature. Their migration into the Gangetic Plain is also associated with the appearance of new pottery styles. Both kinds of data show a gradual eastward shift in centers of Indo-Aryan cultural production: from the twelfth century B.C. their civilization flourished in the East Punjab and Haryana area (Kuru), from the tenth to the eighth centuries in the western U.P. area (Panchala), and from the seventh to the sixth centuries B.C. in the eastern U.P. and northern Bihar region (Videha).[13] Literature produced toward the end of this migratory process reveals a hierarchically ordered society headed by a hereditary priesthood, the Brahmans, and sustained by an ideology of ritual purity and pollution that conferred a pure status on Indo-Aryans while stigmatizing non-Aryans as impure "barbarians" (*mleccha*). This conceptual distinction gave rise to a moving cultural frontier between "clean" Indo-Aryans who hailed from points to the west, and "unclean" Mlecchas already inhabiting regions in the path

9. Spate and Learmonth, *India and Pakistan*, 47.
10. Romila Thapar, *From Lineage to State: Social Formations in the Mid-First Millennium B.C. in the Ganga Valley* (Bombay: Oxford University Press, 1984), 68. Although fire could have been used for clearing forests of their cover, permanent field agriculture required the removal of tree stumps, for which the use of iron axes and spades would have been necessary. Sharma, *Material Culture*, 92.
11. Sharma, *Material Culture*, 92–96.
12. Ibid., 96–99.
13. Michael Witzel, "On the Localisation of Vedic Texts and Schools," in *India and the Ancient World: History, Trade and Culture before A.D. 650*, ed. Gilbert Pollet (Leuven: Departement Oriëntalistiek, 1987), 173–213; and id., "Tracing the Vedic Dialects," in *Dialectes dans les littératures Indo-Aryennes*, ed. Colette Caillat (Paris: Collège de France, Institut de civilisation indienne, 1989), 97–265.

of the Indo-Aryan advance. One sees this frontier reflected in a late Vedic text recording the eastward movement of an Indo-Aryan king and Agni, the Vedic god of fire. In this legend, Agni refuses to cross the Gandak River in Bihar since the areas to the east—eastern Bihar and Bengal—were considered ritually unfit for the performance of Vedic sacrifices.[14] Other texts even prescribe elaborate expiatory rites for the purification of Indo-Aryans who had visited these ritually polluted regions.[15]

Despite such taboos, however, Indo-Aryan groups gradually settled the upper, the middle, and finally the lower Ganges region, retroactively justifying each movement by pushing further eastward the frontier separating themselves from tribes they considered ritually unclean.[16] As this occurred, both Indo-Aryans and the indigenous communities with which they came into contact underwent considerable culture change.[17] For example, in the semi-arid Punjab the early Indo-Aryans had been organized into lineages led by patrilineal chiefs and had combined pastoralism with wheat and barley agriculture. Their descendants in the middle Ganges region were organized into kingdoms, however, and had adopted a sedentary

14. Romila Thapar, "The Image of the Barbarian in Early India," *Comparative Studies in Society and History* 13, no. 4 (October 1971): 417. The text is the *Śatapatha Brāhmaṇa*.
15. These include the *Mārkaṇḍeya Purāṇa* and the *Yajñavalkya Smṛti* 3.292. Cited in Thapar, "Image," 417.
16. For example, the eastern frontier of Indo-Aryan country in the *Ṛg Veda* was the Yamuna River; in the *Paippalāda Saṁhitā*, it was Kasi (Benares region); in the *Saunakīya Saṁhitā*, it was Anga (eastern Bihar); and in the *Aitareya Brāhmaṇa* (7.18), it was Pundra, or northern Bengal. See Witzel, "Localisation," 176, 187.
17. Today modern Bengali, an Indo-Aryan language, is surrounded on all sides by a number of non-Indo-Aryan language groups—Austroasiatic, Dravidian, Sino-Tibetan—suggesting that over the past several millennia the non-Indo-Aryan speakers of the delta proper gradually lost their former linguistic identities, while those inhabiting the surrounding hills retained theirs. On the other hand, the survival of non-Indo-Aryan influences in modern standard Bengali points to the long process of mutual acculturation that occurred between Indo-Aryans and non-Indo-Aryans in the delta itself. Such influences include a high frequency of retroflex consonants, an absence of grammatical gender, and initial-syllable word stress. As M. H. Klaiman observes, "descendants of non-Bengali tribals of a few centuries past now comprise the bulk of Bengali speakers. In other words, the vast majority of the Bengali linguistic community today represents present or former inhabitants of the previously uncultivated and culturally unassimilated tracts of eastern Bengal." M. H. Klaiman, "Bengali," in *The World's Major Languages*, ed. Bernard Comrie (New York: Oxford University Press, 1990), 499, 511. See also Chatterji, *Origin and Development*, 1: 79, 154; and F. B. J. Kuiper, "Sources of the Nahali Vocabulary," in *Studies in Comparative Austroasiatic Linguistics*, ed. Norman H. Zide (Hague: Mouton, 1966), 64. For a map showing the modern distribution of the Bengali and non-Indo-Aryan languages in the delta region, see Joseph E. Schwartzberg, ed., *A Historical Atlas of South Asia* (Chicago: University of Chicago Press, 1978), 100.

life based on the cultivation of wet rice. Moreover, although the indigenous peoples of the middle and lower Ganges were regarded as unclean barbarians, Indo-Aryan immigrants merged with the agrarian society already established in these regions and vigorously took up the expansion of rice agriculture in what had formerly been forest or marshland. Thus the same Vedic text that gives an ideological explanation for why Videha (northern Bihar) had not previously been settled—that is, because the god Agni deemed it ritually unfit for sacrifices—also provides a material explanation for why it was deemed fit for settlement "now": namely, that "formerly it had been too marshy and unfit for agriculture."[18] The Indo-Aryans' adoption of peasant agriculture is also seen in the assimilation into their vocabulary of non-Aryan words for agricultural implements, notably the term for "plow" (*lāṅgala*), which is Austroasiatic in origin.[19]

By 500 B.C. a broad ideological framework had evolved that served to integrate kin groups of the two cultures into a single, hierarchically structured social system.[20] In the course of their transition to sedentary life, the migrants also acquired a consciousness of private property and of political territory, onto which their earlier lineage identities were displaced. This, in turn, led to the appearance of state systems, together with monarchal government, coinage, a script, systems of revenue extraction, standing armies, and, emerging very rapidly between ca. 500 and 300 B.C., cities.[21] Initially, these sweeping developments led to several centuries of rivalry and warfare between the newly emerged kingdoms of the middle Gangetic region. Ultimately, they led to the appearance of India's first empire, the Mauryan (321–181 B.C.).

All these developments proved momentous for Bengal. In the first place, since the Mauryas' political base was located in Magadha, immediately

18. Cited in Witzel, "Localisation," 195.

19. Colin P. Masica, "Aryan and Non-Aryan Elements in North Indian Agriculture," in *Aryan and Non-Aryan in India*, ed. Madhav M. Deshpande and Peter E. Hook (Ann Arbor: University of Michigan, 1979), 132.

20. This is not to say that anything resembling today's caste system suddenly appeared at this early date, although the ideological antecedents for that system are clearly visible in this framework.

21. See Thapar, *From Lineage to State*, chs. 2 and 3. Some of the new cities and states included Campa of Anga, Rajghat of Kasi, Rajgir of Magadha, and Kausambi of Vatsa. It has been suggested that the new urbanized areas appeared so suddenly because of competition among former Indo-Aryan lineage groups for wealth and power, which in turn created a need for centralized political systems that could sustain war efforts. See George Erdosy, "The Origin of Cities in the Ganges Valley," *Journal of the Economic and Social History of the Orient* 28, no. 1 (February 1985): 96–103.

west of the delta, Bengal lay on the cutting edge of the eastward advance of Indo-Aryan civilization. Thus the tribes of Bengal certainly encountered Indo-Aryan culture in the context of the growth of this empire, and probably during the several centuries of turmoil preceding the rise of the Mauryas. The same pottery associated with the diffusion of Indo-Aryan speakers throughout northern India between 500 and 200 B.C. — Northern Black Polished ware — now began to appear at various sites in the western Bengal delta.[22] It was in Mauryan times, too, that urban civilization first appeared in Bengal. Pundra (or Pundranagara), a city named after the powerful non-Aryan people inhabiting the delta's northwestern quadrant, Varendra, became the capital of the Mauryas' easternmost province. A limestone tablet inscribed in Aśokan Brahmi script, datable to the third century B.C., records an imperial edict ordering the governor of this region to distribute food grains to people afflicted by a famine.[23] This suggests that by this time the cultural ecology of at least the Varendra region had evolved from shifting cultivation with hoe and dibble stick to a higher-yielding peasant agriculture based on the use of the plow, draft animals, and transplanting techniques.

Contact between Indo-Aryan civilization and the delta region coincided not only with the rise of an imperial state but also with that of Buddhism, which from the third century B.C. to the seventh or eighth century A.D. experienced the most expansive and vital phase of its career in India. In contrast to the hierarchical vision of Brahmanism, with its pretensions to social exclusion and ritual purity, an egalitarian and universalist ethic permitted Buddhists to expand over great distances and establish wide, horizontal networks of trade among ethnically diverse peoples. This ethic also suited Buddhism to large, cross-cultural political systems, or empires. Aśoka (ca. 273–236 B.C.), India's first great emperor and the third ruler of the Mauryan dynasty, established the religion as an imperial cult. Positive evidence of the advance of Buddhism in Bengal, however, is not found until the second century B.C., when the great stupa at Sanchi (Madhya Pradesh) included Bengalis in its lists of supporters. In the second or third century A.D., an inscription at Nagarjunakhonda (Andhra Pradesh) mentioned Ben-

22. Northern Black Polished ware has been discovered in Chandraketugar in the Twenty-four Parganas, Tamluk in Midnapur, Bangarh and Gaur in Malda, Mahasthan in Bogra, and Khadar Pather Mound and Sitakot in Dinajpur. See Clarence Maloney, "Bangladesh and Its People in Prehistory," *Journal of the Institute of Bangladesh Studies* 2 (1977): 17.
23. Ramaranjan Mukherji and Sachindra Kumar Maity, *Corpus of Bengal Inscriptions Bearing on History and Civilization of Bengal* (Calcutta: Firma K. L. Mukhopadhyay, 1967), 39–40.

gal as an important Buddhist region,[24] and in A.D. 405–11, a visiting Chinese pilgrim counted twenty-two Buddhist monasteries in the city of Tamralipti (Tamluk) in southwestern Bengal, at that time eastern India's principal seaport.[25]

Yet Buddhism in eastern India, as it evolved into an imperial cult patronized by traders and administrators, became detached from its roots in non-Aryan society. Rather than Buddhists, it was Brahman priests who, despite taboos about residing in "unclean" lands to the east, seized the initiative in settling amidst Bengal's indigenous peoples from at least the fifth century A.D. on.[26] What perhaps made immigrant Brahmans acceptable to non-Aryan society was the agricultural knowledge they offered, since the technological and social conditions requisite for the transition to peasant agriculture, already established in Magadha, had not yet appeared in the delta prior to the Mauryan age.[27] All of this contributed to a long-term process—well under way in the fifth century A.D. but still far from complete by the thirteenth—by which indigenous communities of primitive cultivators became incorporated into a socially stratified agrarian society based on wet rice production.[28]

In the middle of the eighth century, large, regionally based imperial systems emerged in Bengal, some of them patronizing Buddhism, others

24. Gayatri Sen Majumdar, *Buddhism in Ancient Bengal* (Calcutta: Navana, 1983), 11.
25. R. C. Majumdar, *History of Ancient Bengal* (Calcutta: G. Bharadwaj & Co., 1971), 522–23. See Schwartzberg, ed., *Historical Atlas*, 18, 19.
26. Puspa Niyogi, *Brahmanic Settlements in Different Subdivisions of Ancient Bengal* (Calcutta: R. K. Maitra, 1967), 4, 19–20.
27. As D. D. Kosambi noted, Brahman rituals were accompanied by "a practical calendar, fair meteorology, and sound-working knowledge of agricultural technique unknown to primitive tribal groups which never went beyond the digging-stock or hoe." D. D. Kosambi, "The Basis of Ancient Indian History," *Journal of the American Oriental Society* 75, pt. 1 (1955): 36. See also ibid., pt. 4, 236n. Kosambi was the first to observe that "the major historical change in ancient India was not between dynasties but in the advance of agrarian village settlements over tribal lands, metamorphosing tribesmen into peasant cultivators or guild craftsmen." Ibid., 38.
28. A similar process has been noted for neighboring Assam. Analyzing inscriptions of the fifth to thirteenth centuries, Nayanjot Lahiri notes "an irresistible correlation between the peasant economy and the principles involved in the caste structure in Assam. There is no group of tribesmen in this region which has not involved itself in the caste structure in some form or the other after the adoption of wet rice cultivation. In the process of detribalisation and their inclusion in the traditional Hindu fold the Brahmins were extremely significant. Detribalization involved, among other things, a renunciation of tribal forms of worship and the acceptance of traditional Hindu gods and goddesses." Nayanjot Lahiri, "Landholding and Peasantry in the Brahmaputra Valley c. 5th–13th centuries A.D.," *Journal of the Economic and Social History of the Orient* 33, no. 2 (June 1990): 166.

a revitalized Brahmanism. The first and most durable of these was the powerful Pala Empire (ca. 750–1161), founded by a warrior and fervent Buddhist named Gopala. From their core region of Varendra and Magadha, the early kings of this dynasty extended their sway far up the Gangetic Plain, even reaching Kanauj under their greatest dynast, Dharmapala (775–812).[29] It was about this time, too, that a regional economy began to emerge in Bengal. In 851 the Arab geographer Ibn Khurdadhbih wrote that he had personally seen samples of the cotton textiles produced in Pala domains, which he praised for their unparalleled beauty and fineness.[30]

A century later another Arab geographer, Mas'udi (d. 956), recorded the earliest-known notice of Muslims residing in Bengal.[31] Evidently long-distance traders involved in the overseas export of locally produced textiles, these were probably Arabs or Persians residing not in Pala domains but in Samatata, in the southeastern delta, then ruled by another Bengali Buddhist dynasty, the Chandras (ca. 825–1035). What makes this likely is that kings of this dynasty, although much inferior to the Palas in power, and never contenders for supremacy over all of India like their larger neighbors to the west, were linked with Indian Ocean commerce through their control of the delta's most active seaports. Moreover, while the Palas used cowrie shells for settling commercial transactions,[32] the Chandras maintained a silver coinage that was more conducive for participation in international trade.[33]

29. Although most Pala copper plates from ca. 750 to ca. 950 were issued from Magadha in modern Bihar, literary sources place the dynasty's original home in Varendra, over which the Palas continued to exercise authority until the mid twelfth century. Majumdar, *History of Ancient Bengal*, 99, 159.

30. *Ahbar as-Sin wa l-Hind: Relations de la Chine et de l'Inde*, trans. Jean Sauvaget (Paris: Société d'édition "Les Belles Lettres," 1948), 13.

31. Mas'udi, *Les Prairies d'or* [*Murūj al-dhahab*], trans. Barbier de Meynard and Pavet de Courteille, corrected by Charles Pellat (Paris: Société asiatique, 1962), 1: 155. "Dans le royaume du Dharma [i.e., Pala], les transactions commerciales se font avec des cauris (*wada'*), qui sont la monnaie du pays. On y trouve le bois d'aigle (*'ūd*), l'or et l'argent; on y fabrique des étoffes d'une finesse et d'une délicatesse inégalées. . . . Les Indiens mangent sa [i.e., the elephant's] chair, et ils sont imités par les Musulmans qui habitent ce pays, parce qu'il est de la même espèce que les boeufs et les buffles."

32. Sauvaget, *Ahbar as-Sin wa l-Hind*, 13; Mas'udi, *Prairies* 1: 155.

33. M. R. Tarafdar, "Trade and Society in Early Medieval Bengal," *Indian Historical Review* 4, no. 2 (January 1978): 277. The evidence for Chandra coinage is based on a horde of about 200 silver coins discovered at Mainamati "in a level," writes A. H. Dani, "which clearly belongs to the time of the Buddhist Chandra rulers of East Bengal, who had their capital at Vikramapura." The mint-place given on some of these coins is Pattikera, the name of a village still extant in Comilla District. See Dani, "Coins of the Chandra Kings of East Bengal," *Journal of the Numismatic Society of India* 24 (1962): 141; Abdul Momin Chowdhury, *Dynastic History of*

Under the patronage of the Palas and various dynasties in Samatata, Buddhism received a tremendous lift in its international fortunes, expanding throughout maritime Asia as India's imperial cult par excellence. Dharmapala himself patronized the construction of two monumental shrine-monastery complexes—Vikramaśila in eastern Bihar, and Paharpur in Bengal's Rajshahi district[34]—and between the sixth and eleventh centuries, royal patrons in Samatata supported another one, the Salban Vihara at Lalmai.[35] As commercially expansive states rose in eastern India from the eighth century on, Buddhism as a state cult spread into neighboring lands—in particular to Tibet, Burma, Cambodia, and Java—where monumental Buddhist shrines appear to have been modeled on prototypes developed in Bengal and Bihar.[36] At the same time, Pala control over Magadha, the land of the historical Buddha, served to enhance that dynasty's prestige as the supreme patrons of the Buddhist religion.[37]

Mas'udi's remark about Muslims residing in Pala domains is significant in the context of these commercially and politically expansive Buddhist states, for by the tenth century, when Bengali textiles were being absorbed into wider Indian Ocean commercial networks, two trade diasporas overlapped one another in the delta region. One, extending eastward from the Arabian Sea, was dominated by Muslim Arabs or Persians; the other, ex-

Bengal, c. 750–1200 A.D. (Dacca: Asiatic Society of Pakistan, 1967), 163 and n. 5. See also Bela Lahiri, "A Survey of the Pre-Muhammadan Coins of Bengal," *Journal of the Varendra Research Museum* 7 (1981–82): 77–84.

34. Frederick M. Asher, *The Art of Eastern India, 300–800* (Minneapolis: University of Minneapolis Press, 1980), 91.

35. Barrie M. Morrison, *Lalmai, a Cultural Center of Early Bengal: An Archaeological Report and Historical Analysis* (Seattle: University of Washington Press, 1974), 27. For a discussion of Buddhist civilization in ancient Samatata, see Puspa Niyogi, "Buddhism in the Mainamati-Lalmai Region (with Reference to the Land Grants of S.E. Bengal)," *Journal of the Varendra Research Museum* 7 (1981–82): 99–109.

36. Haroun er Rashid, "Some Possible Influences from Bengal and Bihar on Early Ankor Art and Literature," *Journal of the Asiatic Society of Bangladesh* 22, no. 1 (April 1977): 9–19.

37. For example, Dharmapala's son Devapala (812–50) received an envoy from the Buddhist king of Srivijaya in Java-Sumatra, who requested the Pala king to grant a permanent endowment to a Buddhist monastery at Nalanda. Similarly, during the reign of Ramapala (1072–1126), the ruler of the Pagan Empire in Burma, Kyansittha (d. ca. 1112), sent a considerable quantity of jewels by ship to Magadha for the purpose of restoring the Buddhist shrines in Bodh Gaya. Hirananda Shastri, "The Nalanda Copper-Plate of Devapaladeva," *Epigraphia Indica* 17 (1924): 311–17. Janice Stargardt, "Burma's Economic and Diplomatic Relations with India and China from Early Medieval Sources," *Journal of the Economic and Social History of the Orient* 14, no.1 (April 1971): 57.

tending eastward from the Bay of Bengal, by Buddhist Bengalis.[38] The earliest presence of Islamic civilization in Bengal resulted from the overlapping of these two diasporas.

The Rise of Early Medieval Hindu Culture

Even while Indo-Buddhist civilization expanded and flourished overseas, however, Buddhist institutions were steadily declining in eastern India. Since Buddhists there had left life-cycle rites in the hands of Brahman priests, Buddhist monastic establishments, so central for the religion's institutional survival, became disconnected from the laity and fatally dependent on court patronage for their support. To be sure, some Bengali dynasties continued to patronize Buddhist institutions almost to the time of the Muslim conquest. But from as early as the seventh century, Brahmanism, already the more vital tradition at the popular level, enjoyed increasing court patronage at the expense of Buddhist institutions.[39] By the eleventh century even the Palas, earlier such enthusiastic patrons of Buddhism, had begun favoring the cults of two gods that had emerged as the most important in the newly reformed Brahmanical religion—Śiva and Vishnu.[40]

38. On the Arab trade diaspora, traceable in the Indian Ocean to the first century A.D. and especially evident by the tenth century, see André Wink, *Al-Hind: The Making of the Indo-Islamic World*, vol. 1: *Early Medieval India and the Expansion of Islam, 7th–11th Centuries* (Leiden: Brill, 1990), 65–86.

39. Notes by Chinese pilgrims in Bengal attest to the drop in the number of Buddhist monasteries there, and also to the emergence of Brahmanic temples. Writing in the early fifth century, Fa-hsien counted twenty-two monasteries in Tamralipti. Two centuries later, Hsüan-tsang counted just ten monasteries there, compared with fifty Brahmanic temples. By 685, the number of monasteries in Tamralipti had dropped to just five or six, as recorded by the pilgrim I-ching. A similar pattern held in North Bengal (Varendra), where Hsüan-tsang counted twenty monasteries and a hundred Brahmanic temples, and in southeast Bengal (Samatata), where he counted thirty monasteries and a hundred temples. The decline in court patronage of monasteries might not have been so serious, however, had there been a fervent and supportive Bengali Buddhist laity. But what is conspicuously absent in the history of East Indian Buddhism as recorded by Taranatha, a Tibetan monk who wrote in 1608, is any evidence of popular enthusiasm for the religion. Rather, the author seems to have identified the fate of Buddhism with that of its great monasteries. The withdrawal of court patronage for such institutions thus proved fatal for the religion generally. See *Chinese Accounts of India: Translated from the Chinese of Hiuen Tsiang*, trans. Samuel Beal (Calcutta: Susil Gupta, 1958), 4: 403, 407, 408; *A Record of the Buddhist Religion as Practiced in India and the Malay Archipelago* (A.D. 671–695) by I-ching, trans. J. Takakasu (Delhi: Munshiram Manoharlal, 1966), xxxiii; and *Taranatha's History of Buddhism in India*, ed. Debiprasad Chattopadhyaya (Calcutta: K. P. Bagchi & Co., 1980), xiii–xiv.

40. Huntington, *"Pala-Sena" Schools*, 179, 201. Most of the art patronized by Pala kings of the eleventh and twelfth centuries was Brahmanic in subject matter, with Vaishnava themes outnumbering the rest three to one. Ibid., 155.

These trends are seen most clearly in the later Bengali dynasties — the Varmans (ca. 1075–1150) and especially the Senas (ca. 1097–1223), who dominated all of Bengal at the time of the Muslim conquest. The kings of the Sena dynasty were descended from a warrior caste that had migrated in the eleventh century from South India (Karnataka) to the Bhagirathi-Hooghly region, where they took up service under the Palas. As Pala power declined, eventually evaporating early in the twelfth century, the Senas first declared their independence from their former overlords, then consolidated their base in the Bhagirathi-Hooghly area, and finally moved into the eastern hinterland, where they dislodged the Varmans from their capital at Vikrampur. Moreover, since the Senas had brought from the south a fierce devotion to Hindu culture (especially Śaivism), their victorious arms were accompanied everywhere in Bengal by the establishment of royally sponsored Hindu cults.[41] As a result, by the end of the eleventh century, the epicenter of civilization and power in eastern India had shifted from Bihar to Bengal, while royal patronage had shifted from a primarily Buddhist to a primarily Hindu orientation. These shifts are especially evident in the artistic record of the period.[42]

Behind these political developments worked deeper religious changes, occurring throughout India, that served to structure the Hindu religion as it evolved in medieval times and to distinguish it from its Vedic and Brahmanical antecedents. As Ronald Inden has argued, the ancient Vedic sacrificial cult (ca. 1000–ca. 300 B.C.) experienced two major historical transformations.[43] The first occurred in the third century B.C., when the Mauryan emperor Aśoka established Buddhism as his imperial religion. At that time the Vedic sacrifice, which was perceived by Buddhists as violent and selfish, was replaced by gift-giving (*dāna*) in the form either of offerings to Buddhist monks by the laity or of gifts of land bestowed on Buddhist institutions by Buddhist rulers. In response to these developments, Brahman priests began reorienting their own professional activities from performing bloody animal sacrifices to conducting domestic life-cycle rites for non-Brahman householders. At the same time, they too became recipients of gifts in the form of land donated by householders or local elites, as began occurring in Bengal from the fifth century A.D. This first transformation of the Vedic sacrifice did not, however, cause a rupture be-

41. H. C. Ray, *The Dynastic History of Northern India (Early Medieval Period)*, 2d ed. (New Delhi: Munshiram Manoharlal, 1973), 1: 354–58.
42. Huntington, *"Pala-Sena" Schools*, 179, 201.
43. Ronald Inden, "The Ceremony of the Great Gift (Mahādāna): Structure and Historical Context in Indian Ritual and Society," in Marc Gaborieau and Alice Thorner, *Asie du sud: Traditions et changements* (Paris: Centre national de la recherche scientifique, 1979), 131–36.

tween Buddhism and Brahmanism. In fact, the two religions coexisted quite comfortably, the former operating at the imperial center, the latter at the regional periphery.[44]

The second transformation of the Vedic sacrifice occurred in the seventh and eighth centuries, when chieftains and rulers began building separate shrines for the images of deities. The regenerative cosmic sacrifice of Vedic religion, which Buddhists had already transformed into rites of gift-giving to monks, was now transformed into a new ceremony, that of the "Great Gift" (*mahādāna*), which consisted of a king's honoring a patron god by installing an image of him in a monumental temple. These ideas crystal-lized toward the end of the eighth century, when, except for the Buddhist Palas, the major dynasties vying for supremacy over all of India—the Pratiharas of the north, the Rashtrakutas of the Deccan, and the Pandyas and Pallavas of the south—all established centralized state cults focusing on Hindu image worship. Instead of worshiping Vedic gods in a general or collective sense, each dynasty now patronized a single deity (usually Vishnu or Śiva), understood as that dynasty's cosmic overlord, whose earthly representative was the gift-giving king. These conceptions were physically expressed in monumental and elaborately carved temples that, like Buddhist stupas, were conceptually descended from the Vedic sacrifi-cial fire altar.[45] Brahmans, meanwhile, evolved into something much grander than domestic priests who merely tended to the life-cycle rituals of their non-Brahman patrons. Now, in addition to performing such ser-vices, they became integrated into the ritual life of Hindu courts, where they officiated at the kings' "Great Gift" and other state rituals.

Copper-plate inscriptions issued from the tenth through the twelfth centuries show how these ideas penetrated the courts of Bengal. Detailed lists of state officers found in inscriptions of the major dynasties of the post-tenth-century period—Pala, Chandra, Varman, and Sena—all show an elaboration of centralized state systems, increasing social stratification, and bureaucratic specialization.[46] Moreover, donations in land became at this time a purely royal prerogative, while the donations themselves (at least those in the northern and western delta) consisted of plots of agricul-tural land whose monetary yields were known and specified, indicating a rather thorough peasantization of society. And, except in the case of Sama-tata, recipients of these grants were Brahmans who received land not only

44. Ibid., 133.
45. Ibid., 134. See also Ronald Inden, "Hierarchies of Kings in Early Medieval India," *Contributions to Indian Sociology* 15, nos. 1–2 (1981): esp. 121–25.
46. Swapna Bhattacharya, *Landschenkungen und staatliche Entwicklung im früh-mittelalterlichten Bengalen* (Wiesbaden: Franz Steiner Verlag, 1985), 165.

for performing domestic rituals, as had been the case in earlier periods, but for performing courtly rituals.[47] Indeed, the granting of land to Brahmans who officiated at court rituals had become a kingly duty, a necessary component of the state's ideological legitimacy.

In these centuries, then, the ideology of medieval Hindu kingship became fully elaborated in the delta. The earliest Sena kings, it is true, had justified their establishment of power in terms of their victorious conquests,[48] and in this respect they differed little from their own conquerors, the Turks of the early Delhi sultanate. Yet the Senas' political theory was based on a religious cosmology fundamentally different from that of their Muslim conquerors. In the Islamic conception, the line separating the human and superhuman domains was stark and unbridgeable; neither humans nor superhumans freely moved or could move from one domain to the other. In the Sena conception, however, as in medieval Hindu thought generally, the line between human and superhuman was indistinct. Since it was the king's performance of royally sponsored rituals that served to uphold *dharma*—that is, cosmic, natural, and human order as understood in classical Indian thought—movement between the two domains could be actuated by the intervention of the king's ritual behavior. "He was never tired of offering sacrifices," one inscription boasts of Vijaya Sena (ca. 1095–1158),

> and through his power Dharma [*dharma*], though she had become one-legged in the course of time, could move about on the earth, quickly taking the help of the rows of sacrificial pillars. That sacrificer [the king] calling down the immortals from the slopes of [the cosmic mountain] Meru full of the enemies killed by himself, brought about an interchange of the inhabitants of heaven and earth. (For) by (the construction of) lofty "houses of gods" (i.e. temples) and by (the excavation of) extensive lakes the areas of both heaven and earth were reduced and thus they were made similar to one another.[49]

By ritually bringing about "an interchange of the inhabitants of heaven and earth," the king symbolically erased the distinction between the human and superhuman domains.

Like Hindu kings elsewhere in eleventh- and twelfth-century India, the Senas projected their vision of the cosmos and their own proper place in it through the medium of architecture, specifically the monumental royal temple. By replicating cosmic order in the medium of stone monuments,

47. Morrison, *Political Centers*, 108.
48. See Nani Gopal Majumdar, *Inscriptions of Bengal*, vol. 3 (Rajshahi: Varendra Research Society, 1929), 52–53.
49. Ibid., 54.

in which they placed an image of their patron overlord, and by placing themselves and their temples at the center of the earthly stage, these kings mimicked the manner in which their patron overlord presided over cosmic order. Thus Vijaya Sena proclaimed:

> [The king] built a lofty edifice of Pradyumneśvara, the wings, and plinth and the main structure of which occupied the several quarters, and the middle and the uppermost parts stretched over the great oceanlike space—(it is) the midday mountain of the rising and setting Sun who touches the Eastern and Western mountains, the supporting pillar of the house which is the three worlds and the one that remains of the mountains. . . . If the creator would make a jar, turning on the wheel of the earth Sumeru like a lump of clay, then that would be an object with which could be compared the golden jar placed by him (i.e., the king) on (the top of) this (temple).[50]

The Sena kings also expressed their kingly authority by performing the "Great Gift" ceremony in honor of their patron overlord, who under the last pre-conquest king, Lakshmana Sena, was Vishnu. Although this great god was the ritualized recipient of the "Great Gift," its effective recipients were officiating Brahman priests.[51]

The Diffusion of Bengali Hindu Civilization

By the time of the Muslim conquest, then, the official cult of a cosmic overlord, monumental state temples, and royally patronized Brahman priests had all emerged as central components of the Senas' religious and political ideology. It was not the case, however, that by that time early Indo-Aryan civilization and its later Hindu offshoot had penetrated all quarters of the Bengal delta evenly. Rather, the evidence indicates that Bengal's northwestern and western subregions were far more deeply influenced by Indo-Aryan and Hindu civilization than was the eastern delta, which remained relatively less peasantized and less Hinduized. This is seen, for example, in pre-thirteenth-century land use and settlement patterns. A seventh-century grant of land on the far eastern edge of the delta,

---

50. Today, unfortunately, only a few architectural fragments remain of what must have been a magnificent edifice, situated at Deopara some seven miles northwest of Rajshahi town, on a road leading to Godagari. Ibid., 42, 54–55.
51. Thus we read that Lakshmana Sena had made a donation of cultivated, tax-free lands "as fee for the ceremony of the Great Gift in which a golden horse and chariot were given away, on this auspicious day, after duly touching water and in the name of the illustrious god Narayana [Vishnu], for the merit and fame of my parents as well as myself, for as long as the moon, sun and the earth endure, according to the principle of *Bhumichchhidra* [tax-exempt status], to Iśvaradevaśarmman, who officiated as the *Acharya* [priest] in the 'Great Gift of gold horse and chariot.'" Ibid., 104.

in modern Sylhet, describes the donated territory as lying "outside the pale of human habitation, where there is no distinction between natural and artificial; infested by wild animals and poisonous reptiles, and covered with forest out-growths."[52] In such regions, grants of uncultivated land were typically made in favor of groups of Brahmans or to Buddhist monasteries with a view to colonizing the land and bringing it into cultivation.[53] One plate issued by a tenth-century Chandra king granted an enormous area of some one thousand square miles in Sylhet to the residents of eight monasteries; it also settled about six thousand Brahmans on the land.[54]

But in the west the situation was different. In the Bhagirathi-Hooghly region, most land grants were made to individual Brahmans and were typically small in size. After the ninth century, royal donations in this area aimed not at pioneering new settlements but at supporting Brahmans on lands already brought under the plow. These grants typically gave detailed measurements of arable fields, specified their revenue yields, and instructed villagers to pay their taxes in cash and kind to the donees.[55] Such terms and conditions point to a far greater intensity of rice cultivation, a higher degree of peasantization, and a greater population density in the Bhagirathi-Hooghly region than was the case in the relatively remote and more forested eastern delta.

Differences between east and west are also seen in patterns of urbanization. Using archaeological data, Barrie Morrison has made comparative calculations of the total area of ancient Bengal's six principal royal palaces.[56]

Pundranagara	22,555,000 sq. ft.
Pandua	13,186,800 sq. ft.
Gaur	10,000,000 sq. ft.
Kotivarsha	2,700,000 sq. ft.
Vikrampur	810,000 sq. ft.
Devaparvata (at Lalmai)	360,000 sq. ft.

The four largest of these were located in cities of Varendra, or northwestern Bengal, whereas the palace sites of Vikrampur and Devaparvata, located in the east and southeast (at Lalmai) respectively (see map 1), were many times smaller. In part, this reflects the political importance of Varendra, always a potential player in struggles over the heartland of Indo-

---

52. Cited in Niyogi, *Brahmanic Settlements,* 41.
53. Bhattacharya, *Landschenkungen,* 168.
54. Morrison, *Political Centers,* 98.
55. Ibid., 17, 99. Bhattacharya, *Landschenkungen,* 168.
56. Morrison, *Lalmai,* 124.

Aryan civilization owing to its contiguity with neighboring Magadha and the middle Gangetic Plain. Yet the data on palace size also indicate a greater degree of urbanization and a higher population density in the delta's northwestern sector than was the case in the south and east. With larger cities, too, went greater occupational specialization and social stratification, for in Bengal as in ancient Magadha, the core areas of Indo-Aryan civilization spread with the advance of city life.

There are several reasons for the greater penetration of Indo-Aryan culture in the western delta than in the east. One has to do with persistent facts of climate. Moving down the Gangetic Plain, the monsoon rainfall increases as the delta is approached, and within the delta it continues to increase as one crosses to its eastern side. The Bhagirathi-Hooghly region, comprising most of today's West Bengal, gets about fifty-five inches of rain annually, whereas central and eastern Bengal get between sixty and ninety-five inches, with the mouth of the Meghna receiving from one hundred to one hundred and twenty and eastern Sylhet about one hundred and fifty inches.[57] If this climatic pattern held in ancient times, the density of vegetation in the deltaic hinterland, formerly covered with thick forests, mainly of *śāl* (*Shorea robusta*),[58] would have increased as one moved eastward. Cutting it would have required much more labor and organization, even with the aid of iron implements, than in the less densely forested westerly regions.

Also at work here were patterns of Brahman immigration to and within Bengal. West Bengal was geographically contiguous to the upper and middle Gangetic zone, long established as the heartland of Indo-Aryan civilization. Hence, when from the ninth century an increasing number of scholarly and ritually pure Brahmans migrated from this area into Bengal, most received fertile lands in the western delta. On the other hand recipients of lands further to the east, in the modern Comilla and Chittagong area, tended to be local Brahmans or migrants from neighboring parts of the delta.[59] This suggests an eastward-sloping gradient of ritual status, with higher rank associated with the north and west, and lower rank with the less-settled east.

Finally, the different degree of Aryanization in the eastern and western delta was related to ancient Bengal's sacred geography, and in particular to the association of the Ganges River with Brahmanically defined ritual pu-

57. Spate and Learmonth, *India and Pakistan*, 575.
58. Ibid., 63; Anil Rawat, "Life, Forests and Plant Sciences in Ancient India," in *History of Forestry in India*, ed. Ajay S. Rawat (New Delhi: Indus Publishing Co., 1991), 246.
59. Bhattacharya, *Landschenkungen*, 167–68.

rity. This river was already endowed with great sanctity when Indo-
Aryans entered the delta,[60] and for centuries thereafter Hindus made pilgrimage sites of towns along its banks in western Bengal—for example,
Navadwip, Katwa, Tribeni, Kalighat, and Ganga Sagar. With reference to
the eastern delta, on the other hand, the geographer S. C. Majumdar notes
that "no such sanctity attaches to the Padma below the Bhagirathi offtake
nor is there any place of pilgrimage on her banks."[61] This was because from
prehistoric times through the main period of Brahman settlement in the
delta, the principal channel of the Ganges flowed down the delta's west-
ernmost corridor through what is now the Bhagirathi-Hooghly channel.
It did not divert eastward into the Padma until the sixteenth century, long
after the Turkish conquest. As a result, the river's sanctity lingered on
in West Bengal—even today the Bhagirathi-Hooghly River is sometimes
called the Adi-Ganga, or "original Ganges"—while the eastern two-thirds
of the delta, cut off from the Ganges during the formative period of Bengal's encounter with Indo-Aryan civilization, remained symbolically disconnected from Upper India, the heartland of Indo-Aryan sanctity and
mythology.

By the thirteenth century, then, most of Bengal west of the Karatoya
and along the Bhagirathi-Hooghly plain had become settled by an agrarian
population well integrated with the Hindu social and political values es-
poused by the Sena royal house. There, too, indigenous tribes had become
rather well assimilated into a Brahman-ordered social hierarchy. But in the
vast stretches of the central, eastern, and northeastern delta, the diffusion
of Indo-Aryan civilization was far less advanced. In the Dhaka area, the
city of Vikrampur, though an important administrative center, from which
nearly all of Bengal's copper-plate inscriptions were issued in the tenth
through twelfth centuries, shrank before its neighbors to the west in both
size and sacredness. And in the extreme southeast, the impressive urban
complex at Lalmai-Mainamati, with its distinctive artistic tradition,[62] its
extensive history of Buddhist patronage, and its cash-nexus economy, ap-

60. The Ganges cult is of great antiquity, and the associations of water with life,
fertility, and the Goddess are traceable to the Indus Valley civilization. We know
from the *Arthaśāstra* (4.3), composed between the fourth century B.C. and the third
century A.D., that prayers were offered to the Ganges as a remedy for drought. By
the sixth century, figures of the goddess Ganga figured prominently as guardians
on temples of the Gupta dynasty (ca. 300–550 A.D.). Steven G. Darian, *The Ganges
in Myth and History* (Honolulu: University Press of Hawaii, 1978), 88.
61. S. C. Majumdar, *Rivers of the Bengal Delta* (Calcutta: University of Calcutta
Press, 1942), 66. See also Surinder Mohan Bhardwaj, *Hindu Places of Pilgrimage
in India* (Berkeley and Los Angeles: University of California Press, 1973), 36–37,
81; Schwartzberg, ed., *Historical Atlas*, 34.
62. Asher, *Art of Eastern India*, 99. Huntington, *"Pala-Sena" Schools*, 200.

pears somewhat disconnected from the Gangetic culture to the west, looking outward to wider Indian Ocean commercial networks.

In sum, although the eastern delta had certainly begun to be peasantized, especially along the valleys of the larger river systems, such as at Vikrampur and Lalmai, the process had not advanced there to the extent that it had in the west and northwest of Bengal. East of the Karatoya and south of the Padma lay a forested and marshy hinterland, inhabited mainly by non-Aryan tribes not yet integrated into the agrarian system that had already revolutionized Magadha and most of western Bengal. As a result, in 1204, when Muhammad Bakhtiyar's Turkish cavalry captured the western Sena city of Nudiya, it was to this eastern hinterland that King Lakshmana Sena and his retainers fled. It was also in this region that subsequent generations of pioneers would concentrate their energies as Bengal's economic and cultural frontiers continued to migrate eastward.

2 The Articulation of Political Authority

The world is a garden, whose gardener is the state.
                    Fakhr al-Din Razi (d. 1209)

We arrived before the Sultan. He was seated on a large gilt sofa covered with different-sized cushions, all of which were embedded with a smattering of precious stones and small pearls. We greeted him according to the custom of the country—hands crossed on our chests and heads as low as possible.
                    A Portuguese official in Bengal (1521)

The geographic expansion of Muslim power in premodern Bengal is easy enough to reconstruct. In any given area of the delta, as in the premodern Muslim world generally, the erection of mosques, shrines, colleges, or other buildings, civil or military, usually presupposed control by a Muslim state. Epigraphic data testifying to the construction of such buildings thus form one kind of evidence for political expansion. The same is true of coinage. Since reigning kings jealously claimed the right to strike coins as a token of their sovereignty, the growth of mint towns also reflects the expanding territorial reach of Muslim states. These two kinds of sources, epigraphic and numismatic, thus permit a visual reconstruction of the growth of Muslim political authority in Bengal through time and space, as depicted in map 2.

It is more challenging, however, to reconstruct the changing meaning of that authority, both to the rulers and to the subject population. All political behavior derives its meaning through the prism of culture. Equally, invocations of political symbols most effectively confer authority on rulers when they and their subjects share a common political culture.[1] But what happened in the cases of "conquest dynasties," as in Bengal, where the con-

1. Here it is useful to distinguish between the terms *authority* and *power*. Max Weber defined the latter as "the probability that one actor within a social relationship will be in a position to carry out his own will despite resistance, regardless of the basis on which this probability rests." By analyzing the articulation of culturally contextualized political symbols, the present chapter focuses on what Weber understood as the basis "on which this probability rests"—that is, political authority. Max Weber, *The Theory of Social and Economic Organization*, ed. and trans.

quering class was of a culture fundamentally different from that of the subject population? How did rulers in such circumstances remain in effective control without resorting to the indefinite and prohibitively costly use of coercive force? To raise these questions is to suggest that the political frontier in Bengal may be understood not only as a moving line of garrisons, mint towns, and architectural monuments. Also involved was the more subtle matter of accommodation, or the lack of it, between a ruling class and a subject population that, as of 1204, adhered to fundamentally different notions of legitimate political authority. The transformation of these concepts of legitimacy over time—their divergence from or convergence with one another—constitutes a political frontier far less tangible than a military picket line, but one ultimately more vital to understanding the dynamics of Bengal's premodern history.

Perso-Islamic Conceptions of Political Authority, Eleventh–Thirteenth Centuries

By the time Muhammad Bakhtiyar conquered northwestern Bengal in 1204, Islamic political thought had already evolved a good deal from its earlier vision of a centralized, universal Arab caliphate. In that vision the caliph was the "successor" (Ar., *khalīfa*) to the Prophet Muhammad as the combined spiritual and administrative leader of the worldwide community of Muslims. In principle, too, the caliphal state, ruled from Baghdad since A.D. 750, was merely the political expression of the worldwide Islamic community. But by the tenth century that state had begun shrinking, not only in its territorial reach, but, more significantly, in its capacity to provide unified political-spiritual leadership. This was accompanied, between the ninth and eleventh centuries, by the movement of clans, tribes, and whole confederations of Turkish-speaking peoples from Inner Asia to the caliphate's eastern provinces. Coming as military slave-soldiers recruited to shore up the flagging caliphal state, as migrating pastoral nomads, or as armed invaders, these Turks settled in Khurasan, the great area embracing today's northeastern Iran, western Afghanistan, and Central Asia south of the Oxus River. As Baghdad's central authority slackened, Turkish military might provided the military basis for new dynasties—some Iranian, some Turkish—that established themselves as de facto rulers in Khurasan.

Important cultural changes coincided with these demographic and political developments. Khurasan was not only Inner Asia's gateway to the Iranian Plateau and the Indian subcontinent. It was also the principal region

A. M. Henderson and Talcott Parsons (New York: Oxford University Press, 1947), 152.

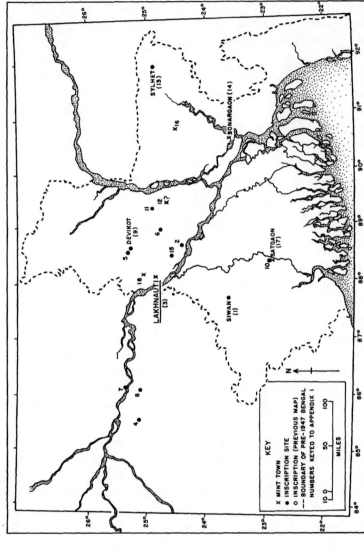

Map 2. Growth of
Muslim rule,
1204–1760

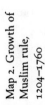

(a) 1204–1342: governors, Balbani rulers, Shams al-Din Firuz, and successors (1204–81; 1281–1300; 1301–22; 1322–42)

KEY

X MINT TOWN
● INSCRIPTION SITE
○ INSCRIPTION (PREVIOUS MAP)
--- BOUNDARY OF PRE-1947 BENGAL
NUMBERS KEYED TO APPENDIX I

MILES
10 0   50   100

N

SYLHET● (13)

X 16

SONARGAON (14) X

DEVIKOT (9) ●●
5 ●   ● 6   12
                  11   X?
        ● 15   2

10 ●/SATGAON (17)

18 X
LAKHNAUTI X
(3)

SIWAN ● (1)

7 ●
● 8

● 4

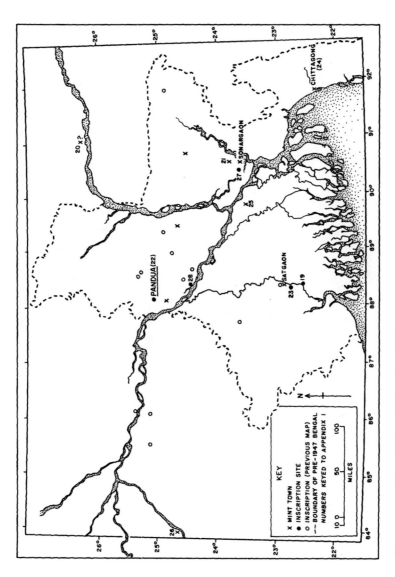

KEY

X MINT TOWN
● INSCRIPTION SITE
O INSCRIPTION (PREVIOUS MAP)
-- BOUNDARY OF PRE-1947 BENGAL
   NUMBERS KEYED TO APPENDIX I

MILES

(b) 1342–1433: Ilyas Shahi and Raja Ganesh dynasties (1342–1414; 1415–33)

Map 2 (*continued*)

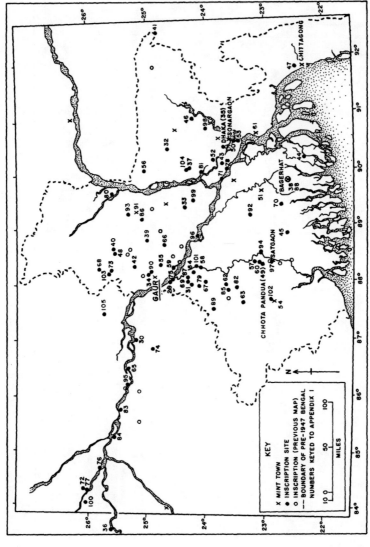

(c) 1433–1538: restored Ilyas Shahis, Abyssinian kings, and Husain Shahis (1433–86; 1486–93; 1493–1538)

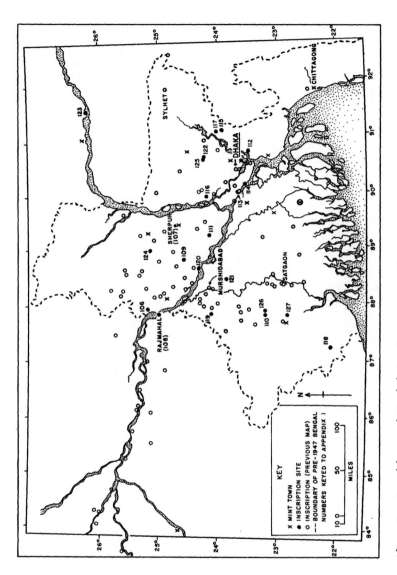

(d) 1538–1760: Afghans and Mughals (1538–75; 1575–1760)

where Iran's rich civilization, largely submerged in the early centuries of Arab-Islamic rule, was being revitalized in ways that creatively synthesized Persian and Arab Islamic cultures. The product, Perso-Islamic civilization, was in turn lavishly patronized by the several dynasties that arose in this area—notably the Tahirids, the Saffarids, the Samanids, and the Ghaznavids—at a time when Baghdad's authority in its eastern domains was progressively weakening. Although themselves ethnic Turks, the Ghaznavids (962–1186) promoted the revival of Persian language and culture by attracting to their regional courts the brightest "stars" on the Persian literary scene, such as Iran's great epic poet Firdausi (d. 1020). Ghaznavid rulers used the Persian language for public purposes, adopted Persian court etiquette, and enthusiastically promoted the Persian aesthetic vision as projected in art, calligraphy, architecture, and handicrafts. They also accepted the fiction of having been "appointed" by the reigning Abbasid caliph in Baghdad. Indeed, as recent Muslim converts themselves, Turkish soldiers in Ghaznavid service became avid partisans, defenders, and promoters of Sunni Islam.[2]

It was the Ghaznavids, too, who first carried Perso-Islamic civilization to India. Pressed from behind by the Seljuqs, a more powerful Turkish confederation, to whom in 1040 they lost any claim to Khurasan, Ghaznavid armies pushed ever eastward toward the subcontinent—first to eastern Afghanistan, and finally to Lahore in the Punjab. Toward the end of the twelfth century, however, the Ghaznavids were themselves overrun by another Turkish confederation, the chiefs of Ghur, located in the hills of central Afghanistan. In 1186 Muhammad Ghuri seized Lahore, extinguished Ghaznavid power there, and seven years later established Muslim rule in Delhi. A decade after that, Muhammad Bakhtiyar, operating in Ghurid service, swept down the lower Gangetic Plain and into Bengal.

The political ideas inherited by Muhammad Bakhtiyar and his Turkish followers had already crystallized in Khurasan during the several centuries preceding their entry into Bengal in 1204. This was a period when Iranian jurists struggled to reconcile the classical theory of the unitary caliphal state with the reality of upstart Turkish groups that had seized control over the eastern domains of the declining Abbasid empire. What emerged was a revised theory of kingship that, although preserving the principle that caliphal authority encompassed both spiritual and political affairs, justified a de facto separation of church and state. Whereas religious authority continued to reside with the caliph in Baghdad, political and administrative

2. Marilyn Robinson Waldman, *Toward a Theory of Historical Narrative: A Case Study in Perso-Islamicate Historiography* (Columbus: Ohio State University Press, 1988), 30.

authority was invested in those who wielded the sword. Endeavoring to make the best of a bad situation, the greatest theologian of the time, Abu Hamid al-Ghazali (d. 1111), concluded that *any* government was lawful so long as its ruler, or *sultān*, made formal acknowledgement of the caliph's theoretical authority in his domain. A sultan could do this, Ghazali maintained, by including the reigning caliph's name in public prayers (*khuṭba*) and on his minted coins (*sikka*).³ In short, a sultan's authority rested, not on any sort of divine appointment or ethnic inheritance, but on his ability to maintain state security and public order.⁴

In this way pre-Islamic Persian ideals of kingship—especially those focusing on society's inherent need for a strong monarch and, reciprocally, on the monarch's duty to rule with justice—were assimilated by the sultanates that sprang up within the caliphate's eastern domains.⁵ One of the clearest statements of this political vision was given by Fakhr al-Din Razi (d. 1209) of Herat, a celebrated Iranian scholar and jurist who served several Khurasani princes, in particular those of the Ghurid dynasty of Turks. Inasmuch as Razi was at the height of his public career when his own patrons conquered North India (1193) and Bengal (1204) and had even been sent once on a mission to northwestern India himself (ca. 1184), it is probable that his political thought was familiar to the Ghurid conquerors of Bengal. Certainly, Razi and Muhammad Bakhtiyar inherited a shared tradition of political beliefs and symbols current in thirteenth-century Khurasan and the Perso-Islamic world generally. In his *Jāmiʿ al-ʿulūm* Razi formulated the following propositions:

> The world is a garden, whose gardener is the state [*dawlat*];
> The state is the sultan whose guardian is the Law [*sharīʿa*];

3. Ann K. S. Lambton, *State and Government in Medieval Islam* (New York: Oxford University Press, 1981), 106–29. See also Erwin I. J. Rosenthal, *Political Thought in Medieval Islam: An Introductory Outline* (Cambridge: Cambridge University Press, 1962), 42–43.

4. Nizam al-Mulk (d. 1092), the Iranian prime minister to the Seljuq sultans, even counseled his Turkish patrons to establish an elaborate network of state spies. His great work, the *Siyāsat-nāma* ("Book of Government"), represents the efforts of an experienced Persian administrator to assimilate the new Turkish rulers into the autocratic tradition of pre-Muslim Persian kingship. See *The Book of Government, or Rules for Kings: The Siyar al-Muluk or Siyasat-nama of Nizam al-Mulk*, trans. Hubert Darke, 2d ed. (London: Routledge & Kegan Paul, 1978).

5. A good discussion of these ideas may be found in A. K. S. Lambton, "Justice in the Medieval Persian Theory of Kingship," *Studia Islamica* 17 (1962): 91–119. See also Waldman, *Toward a Theory*, 99; *A Mirror for Princes: "The Qābūs Nāma" by Kai Kāʾūs ibn Iskandr, Prince of Gurgān*, trans. Reuben Levy (New York: Dutton, 1951), 213; and Cornell H. Fleischer, "Royal Authority, Dynastic Cyclism, and 'Ibn Khaldūnism' in Sixteenth-Century Ottoman Letters," *Journal of Asian and African Studies* 18 (1983): 201–3.

> The Law is a policy, which is protected by the kingdom [*mulk*];
> The kingdom is a city, brought into being by the army [*lashkar*];
> The army is made secure by wealth [*māl*];
> Wealth is gathered from the subjects [*ra'īyat*];
> The subjects are made servants by justice ['*adl*];
> Justice is the axis of the prosperity of the world ['*ālam*].[6]

Far from mere platitudes about how kings ought to behave, these propositions present a unified theory of a society's moral, political, and economic basis—a worldview at once integrated, symmetrical, and closed. One notes in particular the omission of any reference to God; it is royal justice, not the Deity, that binds together the entire structure. Islamic Law, though included in the system, appears as little more than a prop to the sultanate. And the caliph, though implicit in the scheme, is not mentioned at all.

This ideology of monarchal absolutism was not, however, the only vision of worldly authority inherited by Muhammad Bakhtiyar and his Muslim contemporaries. By the thirteenth century there had also appeared in Perso-Islamic culture an enormous lore, written and oral, that focused on the spiritual and worldly authority of Sufis, or Muslim holy men. Their authority sometimes paralleled, and sometimes opposed, that of the courts of kings. For Turks, moreover, Sufi models of authority were especially vivid, since Central Asian Sufis had been instrumental in converting Turkish tribes to Islam shortly before their migrations from Central Asia into Khurasan, Afghanistan, and India.[7] This model of authority is seen in the oldest Persian treatise on Sufism, the *Kashf al-maḥjūb* of 'Ali Hujwiri (d. ca. 1072). Written in Lahore in Ghaznavid times and subsequently read widely in India, this treatise summarized Sufi doctrines and practices as understood in the eastern Muslim world in the eleventh century. It also served to shape the contours of Sufism as a complete system of Islamic piety, especially in the Indo-Muslim world. Writing on the place of Sufi saints in the Muslim universe, Hujwiri asserted that God "has made the Saints the governors of the universe; they have become entirely devoted to His business, and have ceased to follow their sensual affections. Through the blessing of their advent the rain falls from heaven, and through the purity of their lives the plants spring up from the earth, and through their spiritual influence the Moslems gain victories over the unbelievers."[8]

6. Fakhr al-Din Razi, *Jāmi' al-'ulūm*, ed. Muhammad Khan Malik al-Kuttab (Bombay, A.H. 1323 [A.D. 1905]), 207. In the "Mirror for Princes" literary genre so popular in Razi's day, such maxims were often attributed to Alexander the Great.
7. See W. Barthold, *Turkestan Down to the Mongol Invasion*, 3d ed. (London: Luzac, 1968), 160, 255, 376; J. Spencer Trimingham, *The Sufi Orders in Islam* (Oxford: Clarendon Press, 1971), 51–54.
8. 'Ali Hujwiri, *The Kashf al-mahjub*, trans. Reynold A. Nicholson, 2d ed. (reprint, London: Luzac, 1970), 213.

Such a vision, in which all things in God's creation are dependent on a hierarchy of saints, would appear irreconcilable with the courtly vision of the independent sultan and his dependent "herd," the people. And indeed there is a long history of conflict between these two visions of authority. Yet it is also true that the discourse of authority found in Sufi traditions often overlapped and even converged with that found in courtly traditions. For example, both Sufi and courtly literatures stressed the need to establish authority over a *wilāyat*, or a territorially defined region. The Arabic term *walī*, meaning "one who establishes a *wilāyat*," meant in one tradition "governor" or "ruler" and in the other "saint" or "friend of God." Again, in courtly discourse the Persian term *shāh* meant "king"; yet Sufis used it as the title of a powerful saint. In the same way, in royal discourse the *dargāh* referred to the court of a king, while for Sufis it referred to the shrine of a powerful saint. And as a symbol of legitimate authority the royal crown (*tāj*) used in the coronation ceremonies of kings closely paralleled the Sufi's turban (*dastār*), used in rituals of succession to Sufi leadership.

These considerations would suggest that in the Perso-Islamic world of this period sultans did not exercise sole authority, or even ultimate authority. They certainly possessed effective power, reinforced by all the pomp and glitter inherited from their pre-Islamic Persian imperial legacy. Courtly sentiments like that expressed by Razi—"The world is a garden, whose gardener is the state"—indeed saw the world as a mere plaything of the state—that is, the sultan. Yet in a view running counter to this, both historical and Sufi works repeatedly hinted that temporal rulers had only been entrusted with a temporary lease of power through the grace (*baraka*) of this or that Muslim saint. For, it was suggested, since such saints possessed a special nearness to God, in reality it was they, and not princes or kings, who had the better claim as God's representatives on earth. In the opinion of their followers, such powerful saints could even make or unmake kings and kingdoms.[9] So, while sultans formally acknowledged the caliph as the font of their authority, many people, and sometimes sultans too, looked to spiritually powerful Sufis for the ultimate source of that authority. From a village perspective, after all, kings or caliphs were as politically abstract as they were geographically distant; and after the Mongol destruction of Baghdad in 1258, caliphs all but ceased to exist even in name. Sufi saints, by contrast, were by definition luminous, vivid, and very much near at hand.

Thus, by the thirteenth century, when Bengal was conquered by Mus-

9. Simon Digby, "The Sufi Shaikh as a Source of Authority in Mediaeval India," in *Puruṣārtha*, vol. 9, *Islam et société en Asie du sud*, ed. Marc Gaborieau (Paris: Ecole des Hautes études en sciences sociales, 1986), 62.

lim Turks, sultans and Sufis had both inherited models of authority that, though embedded in a shared pool of symbols, made quite different assumptions about the world and the place that God, kings, and saints occupied in it. Moreover, both models differed radically from the ideas of political legitimacy current among the Hindu population formerly ruled by kings of the conquered Sena dynasty. For in Islamic cosmology, as communicated, for example, in Muslim Bengali coinage, the human and superhuman domains were sharply distinct, with both the sultanate and the caliphate occupying a political space beneath the ultimate authority of God, who alone occupied the superhuman world. Consequently the sultan's proper role, in theory at least, was limited to merely implementing the *shariʿa*, Sacred Law. On the other hand, Sena ideology posited no such rigid barrier between human and superhuman domains; movement between the two was not only possible but achievable through a king's ritual behavior. And far from being under an abstract Sacred Law, the Senas understood religion itself, or *dharma*, as dependent on the king's ritual performances. Hence the Senas had not seen themselves as implementing divine order; they sought rather to replicate that order on earth, and even to summon down the gods to reside in royally sponsored temples.

How, then, did people subscribing to these contrasting political ideologies come to terms with one another once it was understood that Muhammad Bakhtiyar and his successors intended to remain in Bengal?

A Province of the Delhi Sultanate, 1204–1342

The only near-contemporary account of Muhammad Bakhtiyar's 1204 capture of the Sena capital is that of the chronicler Minhaj al-Siraj, who visited Bengal forty years after the event and personally collected oral traditions concerning it.[10] "After Muhammad Bakhtiyar possessed himself of that territory," wrote Minhaj,

10. The date of conquest, although not specified by Minhaj, can be inferred from numismatic evidence. In the year 601 A.H., corresponding to A.D. 1204–5, the conqueror himself issued a gold coin (fig. 1) bearing the legend *Gauḍa vijaye*, "On the conquest of Gaur" (i.e., Bengal). But the date A.H. 601 stamped on this coin evidently refers to the coin's date of issue and not to the date of conquest. For, several years after the conquest, the governor of the province, ʿAli Mardan, declared his independence from Delhi and began issuing coins in his own name, one of which was dated Ramazan 600 A.H., or May 1204 A.D. (fig. 2). Since ʿAli Mardan did not declare his sovereignty until 1210, the date on the coin was evidently intended to refer to the date of conquest, and not to the coin's issue date. This interpretation is further supported by the exactness of the coin's date—Ramazan 600. As Indo-Muslim coins were normally stamped only with the year of issue and not the month, such precision would seem to refer to an extraordinary event, which the conquest of Bengal certainly was. See John Deyell, *Living without Silver: The*

> he left the city of Nudiah in desolation, and the place which is (now)
> Lakhnauti he made the seat of government. He brought the different
> parts of the territory under his sway, and instituted therein, in every
> part, the reading of the *khutbah*, and the coining of money; and,
> through his praiseworthy endeavours, and those of his Amirs, *masjids*
> [mosques], colleges, and monasteries (for Dervishes), were founded in
> those parts.[11]

The passage clearly reveals the conquerors' notion of the proper instruments of political legitimacy: reciting the Friday sermon, striking coins, and raising monuments for the informal intelligentsia of Sufis and the formal intelligentsia of scholars, or *'ulamā*.

Both their coins and their monuments reveal how the rulers viewed themselves and wished to be viewed by others. Both, moreover, were directed at several different audiences simultaneously. One of these consisted of the conquered Hindus of Bengal, who, having never heard a *khuṭba*, seen a Muslim coin, or set foot in a mosque, were initially in no position to accord legitimate authority either to these symbols or to their sponsors. But for a second audience—the Muslim world generally, and more immediately, the rulers of the Delhi sultanate, the parent kingdom from which Bengal's new ruling class sprang—the *khuṭba*, the coins, and the building projects possessed great meaning. It is important to bear in mind these different audiences when "reading" the political propaganda of Bengal's Muslim rulers.

Militarily, Muhammad Bakhtiyar's conquest was a blitzkrieg; his cavalry of some ten thousand horsemen had utterly overwhelmed a local population unaccustomed to mounted warfare.[12] After the conquest, Bakhtiyar and his successors continued to hold a constant and vivid symbol of their power—their heavy cavalry—before the defeated Bengalis. In the year 1204–5 (601 A.H.), Bakhtiyar himself struck a gold coin in the name of his overlord in Delhi, Sultan Muhammad Ghuri, with one side depicting a Turkish cavalryman charging at full gallop and holding a mace in hand (fig. 1). Beneath this bold emblem appeared the phrase *Gauḍa vijaye*, "On the conquest of Gaur" (i.e., Bengal), inscribed not in Arabic but in San-

---

Monetary History of Early Medieval North India (Delhi: Oxford University Press, 1990), 364, coin no. 298.

11. Minhaj-ud-Din Abu'l-'Umar-i-'Usman, *Ṭabakāt-i-Nāṣirī: A General History of the Muhammadan Dynasties of Asia, Including Hindustan (810–1260)*, trans. H. G. Raverty (Calcutta: Asiatic Society of Bengal, 1881; reprint, New Delhi: Oriental Books Reprint Corp., 1970), 1: 559–60.

12. Bakhtiyar's band of two hundred cavalrymen, with which he surprised Lakshmana Sena in Nudiya, was but an advance detachment from his main force of ten thousand.

Fig. 1. Gold coin of Muham-
mad Bakhtiyar, struck in
A.H. 601 (A.D. 1204–5) in
Bengal in the name of Sul-
tan Muhammad Ghuri. Ob-
verse and reverse. Photo by
Charles Rand, Smithsonian
Institution.

skrit.[13] On the death of the Delhi sultan six years later, the governor of
Bengal, 'Ali Mardan, declared his independence from North India and began issuing silver coins that also bore a horseman image (fig. 2).[14] And
when Delhi reestablished its sway over Bengal, coins minted there in the
name of Sultan Iltutmish (1210–35) continued to bear the image of the
horseman (fig. 3).[15] For neither Muhammad Bakhtiyar, 'Ali Mardan, nor
Sultan Iltutmish was there any question of seeking legitimacy within the
framework of Bengali Hindu culture or of establishing any sense of continuity with the defeated Sena kingdom. Instead, the new rulers aimed at

13. Nicholas W. Lowick, "The Horseman Type of Bengal and the Question of Commemorative Issues," *Journal of the Numismatic Society of India* 35 (1973): 196–
208; P. L. Gupta, "Nagari Legend on Horseman Tankah of Muhammad bin Sam,"
ibid.: 209–12. See too P. L. Gupta, "On the Date of the Horseman Type Coin of
Muhammad bin Sam," ibid. 38 (1976): 81–87.
14. G. S. Farid, "Hitherto Unknown Silver Tankah of Sultan Alauddin Ali Mardan
Khilji, 607–610 A.H.," *Journal of the Asiatic Society* 18, nos. 1–4 (1976): 104–6.
According to Farid, this coin is dated 610 A.H. (1213–14 A.D.). But the coin published
by him, depicted in figure 2, is worn on the place where the date is normally given.
Another copy of the same coin reproduced by John Deyell clearly reveals the date
Ramazan 600 A.H., evidently referring to the date of the Turkish conquest of
Bengal. See Deyell, *Living without Silver*, 364, coin no. 298.
15. Lowick, "Horseman Type," 200.

Fig. 2. Silver coin of 'Ali Mardan (ca. 1208–13), commemorating the conquest of Bengal in A.H. Ramazan 600 (A.D. May 1204). Obverse only.

Fig. 3. Silver coin of Sultan Iltutmish (1210–35), struck in Bengal. Obverse only.

communicating a message of brute force. As Peter Hardy aptly puts it, referring to the imposition of early Indo-Turkish rule generally, "Muslim rulers were there in northern India as rulers because they were there—and they were there because they had won."[16]

Such reliance on naked power, or at least on its image, is also seen in the earliest surviving Muslim Bengali monuments. Notable in this respect is the tower (*mīnār*) of Chhota Pandua, in southwestern Bengal near Cal-

16. Peter Hardy, "The Growth of Authority over a Conquered Political Elite: The Early Delhi Sultanate as a Possible Case Study," in *Kingship and Authority in South Asia*, ed. J. F. Richards (Madison: South Asian Studies, University of Wisconsin, 1978), 207.

Fig. 4. Minar of Chhota Pandua (late thirteenth century).

cutta (fig. 4). Built toward the end of the thirteenth century, when Turkish power was still being consolidated in that part of the delta, the tower of Chhota Pandua doubtless served the usual ritual purpose of calling the faithful to prayer, inasmuch as it is situated near a mosque. But its height and form suggest that it also served the political purpose of announcing victory over a conquered people. Precedents for such a monument, more-

Fig. 5. Mosque of Zafar Khan, Tribeni (1298).

over, already existed in the Turkish architectural tradition.[17] Bengal's earliest surviving mosques also convey the spirit of an alien ruling class simply transplanted to the delta from elsewhere. Constructed (or restored) in 1298 in Tribeni, a formerly important center of Hindu civilization in southwest Bengal, the mosque of Zafar Khan (fig. 5) appears to replicate the aesthetic vision of early Indo-Turkish architecture as represented, for example, in the Begumpur mosque in Delhi (ca. 1343). Clues to the circumstances surrounding the construction (or restoration) of the mosque are found in its dedicatory inscription:

> Zafar Khan, the lion of lions, has appeared
> By conquering the towns of India in every expedition, and by restoring
>   the decayed charitable institutions.
> And he has destroyed the obdurate among infidels with his sword and

17. Examples include the *mīnār* of Bahram Shah in Ghazni (early twelfth century), the *mīnār* of Ghiyath al-Din Muhammad in Jam, located on Afghanistan's Hari Rud River (late twelfth century), and, closest in time and place to Bengal, the Qutb Minar of Delhi (1200–1215), the stupendous and imposing tower that was the first monument built by the Turks on their establishment of permanent rule in North India.

spear, and lavished the treasures of his wealth in (helping) the miserable.[18]

Zafar Khan's claims to have destroyed "the obdurate among infidels" gains some credence from the mosque's inscription tablet, itself carved from materials of old ruined Hindu temples, while the mutilated figures of Hindu deities are found in the stone used in the monument proper.[19] Near Zafar Khan's mosque stands another structure, built in 1313, which is said to be his tomb; its doorways were similarly reused from an earlier pre-Islamic monument, and embedded randomly on its exterior base are sculpted panels bearing Vaishnava subject matter.[20]

How was the articulation of these political symbols received by the several "audiences" to whom they were directed? As late as thirty years after the conquest, pockets of Sena authority continued to survive in the forests beyond the reach of Turkish garrisons. Whenever Turkish forces were out of sight, petty chieftains with miniature, mobile courts would appear before the people in their full sovereign garb—riding elephants in ivory-adorned canopies, wearing bejeweled turbans of white silk, and surrounded by armed retainers—in an apparent effort to continue receiving tribute and administering justice as they had done before.[21] In 1236 a Tibetan Buddhist pilgrim recorded being accosted by two Turkish soldiers on a ferryboat while crossing the Ganges in Bihar. When the soldiers demanded gold of him, the pilgrim audaciously replied that he would report them to the local raja, a threat that so provoked the Turks' wrath as nearly to cost him his life.[22] Clearly, after three decades of alien rule, people continued to view the Hindu raja as the legitimate dispenser of justice.

If Muslim coins and the architecture of this period projected to the subject Bengali population an image of unbridled power, they projected very different messages to the parent Delhi sultanate, and beyond that, the larger Muslim world. Throughout the thirteenth century, governors of Bengal tried whenever possible to assert their independence from the par-

18. Shamsud-Din Ahmed, ed. and trans., *Inscriptions of Bengal*, vol. 4 (Rajshahi: Varendra Research Museum, 1960), 20.
19. Ibid., 19.
20. Catherine B. Asher, "Inventory of Key Monuments," in *The Islamic Heritage of Bengal*, ed. George Michell (Paris: UNESCO, 1984), 136. The basalt pillars of Chhota Pandua's Bari Mosque, most likely dating to the early fourteenth century, were simply reused from pre-Islamic structures; they still bear traces of Hindu or Buddhist images. Ibid., 52.
21. George Roerich, trans., *Biography of Dharmasvamin (Chag lo-tsa-ba Chos-rje-dpal), a Tibetan Monk Pilgrim* (Patna: K. P. Jawaswal Research Institute, 1959), 64–65.
22. Ibid., 98.

ent dynasty in Delhi, and each such attempt was accompanied by bold attempts to situate themselves within the larger political cosmology of Islam. For example, when the self-declared sultan Ghiyath al-Din 'Iwaz asserted his independence from Delhi in 1213, he attempted to legitimize his position by going over the head of the Delhi sultan and proclaiming himself the right-hand defender (*nāṣir*) of the supreme Islamic authority on earth, the caliph in Baghdad.[23] This marked the first time any ruler in India had asserted a direct claim to association with the wellspring of Islamic legitimacy, and it prompted Iltutmish, the Delhi sultan, not only to invade and reannex Bengal but to upstage the Bengal ruler in the matter of caliphal support. After his armies defeated Ghiyath al-Din in 1227, Iltutmish arranged to receive robes of honor from Caliph al-Nasir in Baghdad, one of which he sent to Bengal with a red canopy of state. There it was formally bestowed upon Iltutmish's own son, who was still in Lakhnauti, having just had the erstwhile independent king of Bengal beheaded.[24] By having the investiture ceremony enacted in the capital city of the defeated sultan of Bengal, Iltutmish vividly dramatized his own prior claims to caliphal legitimacy. For the time being, the delta was politically reunited with North India, and for the next thirty years Delhi appointed to Bengal governors who styled themselves merely "king of the kings of the East" (*mālik-i mulūk al-sharq*).[25]

But Delhi was distant, and throughout the thirteenth century the temptation to throw off this allegiance proved irresistible, especially as the imperial rulers were chronically preoccupied with repelling Mongol threats from the Iranian Plateau. So governors rebelled, and each brief assertion of independence was followed by their adoption of ever more exalted titles on their coins and public monuments. In 1281 Sultan Ghiyath al-Din Balban, the powerful sovereign of Delhi, ruthlessly stamped out one revolt by hunting down his rebel governor and publicly executing him. Yet within a week of Balban's death in 1287, his own son, Bughra Khan, whom the father had left behind as his new governor, declared his independence. Bughra's son, who ascended the Bengal throne as Rukn al-Din Kaikaus (1291–1300), then boldly styled himself on one mosque "the great Sultan, master of the necks of nations, the king of the kings of Turks and Persians, the lord of the crown, and the seal," as well as "the right hand of the

23. See Abdul Karim, *Corpus of the Muslim Coins of Bengal, down to* A.D. *1538*, Asiatic Society of Pakistan Publication No. 6 (Dacca: Asiatic Society of Pakistan, 1960), 18.

24. Minhaj-ud-Din 'Usman, *Ṭabaḳāt-i-Nāṣirī*, trans. Raverty, 1: 629–30.

25. Shamsud-Din Ahmed, ed. and trans., *Inscriptions*, 4: 7–8.

viceregent of God"—that is, "helper of the caliph." On another mosque he even styled himself the "shadow of God" (*ẓill Allah*), an exalted title derived from ancient Persian imperial usage.[26]

Exasperated with the wayward province, Delhi for several decades ceased mounting the massive military offensives necessary to keep it within its grip. In fact, the actions of Sultan Jalal al-Din Khalaji (r. 1290–96) betray something more than mere indifference toward the delta. A contemporary historian recorded that on one occasion the sultan rounded up about a thousand criminals ("thugs") and "gave orders for them to be put into boats and to be conveyed into the Lower country to the neighbourhood of Lakhnauti, where they were to be set free. The *thags* would thus have to dwell about Lakhnauti, and would not trouble the neighbourhood (of Dehli) any more."[27] Within a century of its conquest, then, Bengal had passed from being the crown jewel of the empire, whose conquest had occasioned the minting of gold commemorative coins, to a dumping ground for Delhi's social undesirables. Already we discern here the seeds of a North Indian chauvinism toward the delta that would become more manifest in the aftermath of the Mughal conquest in the late sixteenth century.

The Early Bengal Sultanate, 1342–ca. 1400

In 1258 Mongol armies under the command of Hülegü Khan sacked Baghdad and executed the reigning caliph, al-Mustaʿsim, thereby formally extinguishing the ultimate font of Islamic political legitimacy. Nonetheless, for a half century after this disaster, coins struck in India continued to invoke the phrase "in the time of the caliph, al-Mustaʿsim," suggesting the inability of Indo-Muslim rulers to conceive of any legitimizing authority other than that stemming from the titular Abbasid caliph. But finally, in 1320, Qutb al-Din Mubarak, the Delhi sultan, broke from tradition and boldly declared himself to be the caliph of Islam. Although the title did not stick, and was in fact harshly received, the principle was now established that Islam could have multiple caliphs, and that they could reside even outside the Arab world. This revolution in Islamic political thinking occurred just about the time when Bengal again asserted its independence from the Delhi sultanate. In 1342 a powerful noble, Shams al-Din Ilyas Shah (1342–57), wrested Bengal free from Delhi's grip and established the

26. Ibid., 14–15, 17–18.
27. Zia al-Din Barani, *Tārīkh-i Fīrūz Shāhī*, in *The History of India as Told by Its Own Historians*, trans. and ed. H. M. Elliot and John Dowson (Allahabad: Kitab Mahal, 1964), 3: 141. This is the earliest record of the use of the word *thug*.

first of several dynasties that remained independent from North India for the next two and a half centuries. The break with Delhi was marked by a shift of the Ilyas Shahi capital from Lakhnauti, the provincial capital throughout the age of Delhi's hegemony, to the new site of Pandua, located some twenty miles to the north.

Initially, Delhi did not allow Bengal's assertions of independence to go unchallenged. In 1353 Sultan Firuz Tughluq took an enormous army down the Ganges to punish the breakaway kingdom. Although Firuz slew up to 180,000 Bengalis and even temporarily dislodged Shams al-Din Ilyas Shah from his capital at Pandua, he failed to reannex the delta. Six years later, Firuz made another attempt to restore the delta to Delhi's authority, but he was again rebuffed, this time by Shams al-Din's son and successor, Sikandar Shah (r. 1357–89).[28] These inconclusive invasions of Bengal, and the successful tactics of the two Bengali kings to elude the North Indian imperialists by fading into the interior, finally persuaded Firuz and his successors of the futility of trying to hold onto the distant province. After 1359 Bengal was left undisturbed by North Indian armies for nearly two centuries.

In reality, the emergence of the independent Ilyas Shahi dynasty represented the political expression of a long-present cultural autonomy. In the late thirteenth century, Marco Polo made mention of "Bangala," a place he had apparently heard of from his Muslim informants, and which he understood as being a region distinct from India, for he described it as "tolerably close to India" and its people as "wretched Idolaters" who spoke "a peculiar language."[29] Our first indigenous reference to "Bengal" appears in the mid fourteenth century, when the historian Shams-i Siraj 'Afif referred to Shams al-Din Ilyas Shah (1342–57) as the "sultan of the Bengalis" and the "king of Bengal."[30] The coins of this ruler, and the architecture of his son and successor, clearly reflect the new mood of independence. Shams al-Din's coins are inscribed:

[Obverse:] The just sultan, Shams al-dunya va al-din, Abu'l Muzaffar, Ilyas Shah, the Sultan.
[Reverse:] The second Alexander, the right hand of the caliphate, the defender (or helper) of the Commander of the Faithful.[31]

28. Shams-i Siraj 'Afif, *Tārīkh-i Fīrūz Shāhī*, in *The History of India as Told by Its Own Historians*, trans. and ed. H. M. Elliot and John Dowson (Allahabad: Kitab Mahal, 1964), 3: 297, 303–12.
29. *The Book of Ser Marco Polo*, trans. and ed. Henry Yule and Henri Cordier, 3d ed. (Amsterdam: Philo Press, 1975), 2: 115.
30. 'Afif, *Tārīkh*, in Elliot and Dowson, *History of India*, 3:295, 296.
31. Karim, *Corpus*, 42.

Here the sultan not only proclaims an association with the caliphate but lays claim to imperial glory, calling himself "the second Alexander." Though perhaps not measuring up to the accomplishments of Alexander the Great, Shams al-Din certainly did a creditable job of "world-conquering" in the politically dense theater of fourteenth-century India: in addition to resisting repeated invasions from Delhi, he defeated a host of neighboring Hindu rajas, namely those of Champaran, Tirhut, Kathmandu, Jajnagar, and Kamrup (corresponding to modern Bihar, Nepal, Orissa, and Assam).

The most spectacular evidence of the dynasty's imperial pretensions is seen in a single monument built by the founder's son and successor, Sultan Sikandar (r. 1357–89). This is the famous Adina mosque, completed in 1375 in the Ilyas Shahi capital of Pandua (figs. 6 and 7). Although its builders reused a good deal of carved stone from pre-conquest monuments, the mosque does not appear to have been intended to convey a message of political subjugation to the region's non-Muslims, who in any event would not have used the structure. In fact, stylistic motifs in the mosque's prayer niches reveal the builders' successful adaptation, and even appreciation, of late Pala-Sena art.[32] The imposing monument is also likely to have been a statement directed at Sikandar's more distant Muslim audience, his former overlords in Delhi, now bitter rivals. Having successfully defended his kingdom from Sultan Firuz's armies, Sikandar projected his claims of power and independence by erecting a monument greater in size than any edifice built by his North Indian rivals. Measuring 565 by 317 feet externally, and with an immense courtyard (445 by 168 feet) surrounded by a screen of arches and 370 domed bays, the Adina mosque easily surpassed Delhi's Begumpur mosque, the principal mosque of Firuz Tughluq (1351–88), in size.[33] In fact, the Adina remains the largest mosque ever built in the Indian subcontinent.

Its style, moreover, signals a sharp break from the Delhi-based architectural tradition. The western, or Mecca-facing, side of the mosque projects a distinctly imperial mood, reminiscent of the grand style of pre-Islamic

32. Naseem Ahmed Banerji, "The *Mihrabs* in the Adina Mosque at Pandua, India: Evidence of the Reuse of Pala-Sena Remains" (paper read at the twenty-first conference on South Asia, University of Wisconsin, Madison, November 6–8, 1992).
33. Asher, "Inventory," 109–10. See also Yolande Crowe, "Reflections on the Adina Mosque at Pandua," in *The Islamic Heritage of Bengal*, ed. George Mitchell (Paris: UNESCO, 1984), 157. These figures compare with the Begumpur mosque's outer measurements of 328 feet on a side, courtyard measurements of 284 by 273 feet, and a total of 105 domed bays. See Anthony Welch and Howard Crane, "The Tughluqs: Master Builders of the Delhi Sultanate," *Muqarnas* 1 (1983): 130–31.

Fig. 6. Adina Mosque, Pandua (1375). Interior facing western wall, showing collapsed barrel vault. Photo by Catherine Asher.

Fig. 7. Adina Mosque, Pandua (1375). Exterior of western wall, showing façade of barrel vault.

Fig. 8. Taq-i Kisra, Ctesiphon (near Baghdad, third century A.D.). Façade in the late nineteenth century. From Arthur Upham Pope, *A Survey of Persian Art* (Ashiya, Japan: Jay Glück, 1964), vol. 7, pl. 149. Reprinted by permission of Jay Glück.

Iran.[34] This wall is a huge multistoried screen, whose exterior surfaces utilize alternating recesses and projections, both horizontally and vertically, to produce a shadowing effect. Whereas such a wall has no clear antecedent in Indo-Islamic architecture, it does recall the external façade of the famous Taq-i Kisra palace of Ctesiphon (third century A.D.), the most imposing architectural expression of Persian imperialism in Sasanian times (A.D. 225–641) (fig. 8). Even more revealing in this respect is the design of the mosque's central nave. Whereas the sanctuary of the Tughluqs' Begumpur mosque in Delhi was covered with a dome—a feature carried over, together with the four-iwan scheme, from Seljuq Iran (1037–1157) to India in the twelfth and thirteenth centuries[35]—that of the Adina mosque is covered with a barrel vault. Never before used on a monumental scale anywhere in India, this architectural device divided the whole structure into two halves, as did the great barrel vault of the Taq-i Kisra. The mosque thus departed decisively from Delhi's architectural tradition, while drawing on the much earlier tradition of Sasanian Iran. We know that generations

34. As Percy Brown notes, the monument resembled "the forum of some ancient classical city rather than a self-contained Muslim house of prayer, with the high vaulted sanctuary on the western side simulating an imperial approach in the form of a majestic triumphal archway." Brown, *Indian Architecture, Islamic Period*, 5th ed. (Bombay: D. B. Taraporevala, 1968), 36.
35. See Tsukinowa Tokifusa, "The Influence of Seljuq Architecture on the Earliest Mosques of the Delhi Sultanate Period in India," *Acta Asiatica* 43 (1982): 37–60.

Fig. 9. Adina Mosque, Pandua (1375). Royal balcony, interior.

of Iranian architects and rulers had considered the Sasanian Taq-i Kisra palace to be the acme of visual grandiosity and splendor, and a model to be consciously imitated.[36] Thus Sikandar was at least an heir, if not a conscious imitator, of this tradition.

The interior of the Adina mosque also projects an aura of imperial majesty. To the immediate north of the central sanctuary is a raised platform, the so-called "king's throne" (*bādshāh kā takht*), which enabled the sultan and his entourage to pray at a height elevated above the common people (fig. 9).[37] And, while the latter entered the mosque from a gate in the mosque's southeast corner, the "king's throne" could be reached only through a private entranceway that passed through the western wall. This

36. Just over fifty years before construction of the Adina mosque, the Ilkhanid prince 'Ali Shah had built his Jami' mosque in Tabriz with a barrel vault that in width actually surpassed that of the Taq-i Kisra. Since contemporary observers compared the Tabriz mosque with the Taq-i Kisra, it is clear that the great Sasanian palace was on the minds of fourteenth-century Iranians. Donald N. Wilber, *The Architecture of Islamic Iran: The Il Khanid Period* (Princeton: Princeton University Press, 1955), 146–47.

37. A similar structure is found in the Jami' mosque of Ahmedabad, Gujarat, which the Mughal emperor Jahangir (1605–27) described as a caged-in stone platform used by the king and his intimates and courtiers "on account of the crowding of people." Jahangir, *Tūzuk-i-Jahāngīrī*, trans. Alexander Rodgers and Henry Beveridge, 2d ed., 2 vols in 1 (Delhi: Munshiram Manoharlal, 1968), 1: 425.

entire doorway was evidently stripped from some pre-Muslim structure, as can be seen by the defaced Buddhist or Hindu image in its lintel (fig. 10). As if the mosque's imperial architecture did not speak for itself, Sultan Sikandar ordered the following words inscribed on its western facade:

> In the reign of the exalted Sultan, the wisest, the most just, the most liberal and most perfect of the Sultans of Arabia and Persia, who trust in the assistance of the Merciful Allah, Abul Mujahid Sikandar Shah the Sultan, son of Ilyas Shah, the Sultan. May his reign be perpetuated till the Day of Promise (Resurrection).[38]

One word of praise for God, mentioned in passing, and the rest for the sultan!

Both the coinage and the architecture of the early Ilyas Shahi kings, then, indicate a strategy of political legitimization fundamentally different from that of their predecessors. Whereas the governors of thirteenth-century Bengal had merely transplanted Delhi's architectural tradition to the delta, the sultans, having wrested their autonomy from Delhi, asserted their claims of legitimacy by placing state ideology alternately on pan-Islamic and imperial bases. If Sultan Sikandar's architecture and Sultan Shams al-Din's coinage reflect an imperial strategy of legitimation, we see the pan-Islamic approach in the latter's claimed association with the caliph, and in the lavish patronage of the holiest shrines of Islam by Sikandar's son and successor, Sultan Ghiyath al-Din A'zam Shah (r. 1389–1410), who sponsored the construction of Islamic colleges (*madrasas*) in both Mecca and Medina.[39]

Moreover, although the Bengal sultans continued to inscribe most of their monuments and coins in Arabic, from the mid fourteenth century on, they began articulating their claims to political authority in Perso-Islamic terms. They employed Persianized royal paraphernalia, adopted an elaborate court ceremony modeled on the Sasanian imperial tradition, employed a hierarchical bureaucracy, and promoted Islam as a state-sponsored religion, a point vividly and continuously revealed on state coinage. Foreign dignitaries who visited Pandua at its height in the early fifteenth century remarked on a court ceremony that we can recognize as distinctly Persian. "The dwelling of the King," wrote a Ming Chinese ambassador in 1415,

---

38. Shamsud-Din Ahmed, ed. and trans., *Inscriptions*, 4: 38.
39. Ibn Hajar al-'Asqalani, *Inbā' al-ghumr bi-anbā al-'umr* (Cairo: Al-Majlis al-A'lā li-l-Shu'ūn al-Islāmīyah, 1969), 2: 496; Muhammad Sakhavi, *Al-Zau' al-lāmi' li-ahl al-qarn al-tāsi'* (Beirut: Maktabat al-Hayat, 1966), 2: 313. See also Ziauddin Desai, "Some New Data Regarding the Pre-Mughal Muslim Rulers of Bengal," *Islamic Culture* 32 (1958): 199–200.

Fig. 10. Adina Mosque, Pandua (1375). Lintel over royal doorway.

is all of bricks set in mortar, the flight of steps leading up to it is high and broad. The halls are flat-roofed and white-washed inside. The inner doors are of triple thickness and of nine panels. In the audience hall all the pillars are plated with brass ornamented with figures of flowers and animals, carved and polished. To the right and left are long verandahs on which were drawn up (on the occasion of our audience) over a thousand men in shining armour, and on horseback outside, filling the courtyard, were long ranks of (our) Chinese (soldiers) in shining helmets and coats of mail, with spears, swords, bows and arrows, looking martial and lusty. To the right and the left of the King were hundreds of peacock feather umbrellas and before the hall were some hundreds of soldiers mounted on elephants. The king sat cross-legged in the principal hall on a high throne inlaid with precious stones and a two-edged sword lay across his lap.[40]

Clearly dazzled by the ceremony of Pandua's royal court, the ambassador continued: "Two men bearing silver staffs and with turbaned heads came to usher (us) in. When (we) had taken five steps forward (we) made salutation. On reaching the middle (of the hall) they halted and two other men with gold staffs led us forward with some ceremony as previously. The King having returned our salutations, kotowed before the Imperial Mandate, raised it to his head, then opened and read it. The imperial gifts were all spread out on carpets in the audience hall." The ambassador was then treated to a sumptuous banquet, after which the sultan "bestowed on the envoys gold basins, gold girdles, gold flagons, and gold bowls."[41] The peacock feathers, the umbrellas, the files of foot soldiers, the throne inlaid with precious stones, the lavish use of gold—all of these point unmistakably to the kind of paraphernalia typically associated with Perso-Islamic and even Sasanian royalty. Only the presence of elephants recalls the ceremony of traditional Indian courts.

Whether appealing to mainly Islamic symbols of authority, as was typically the case from 1213 to 1342, or to imperial Persian symbols of authority, as was typically the case from 1342 on, the Muslim ruling class sought the basis of its political legitimacy in symbols originating *outside* the area over which they ruled. No more were Bengal's rulers, like the early governors, content with declaring themselves merely first among "kings of the

40. W. W. Rockhill, "Notes on the Relations and Trade of China with the Eastern Archipelago and the Coast of the Indian Ocean during the Fourteenth Century," *T'oung Pao* 16, pt. 2 (1915): 441–42. The first few decades of the fifteenth century witnessed China's brief but significant maritime diaspora under the early Ming dynasty. During two of the seven great expeditions the Ming court sent into the Indian Ocean, Chinese officials, traveling via Chittagong and Sonargaon, reached the Bengali capitals of Pandua (1415) and Gaur (1432).
41. Ibid., 442.

East." On the Adina mosque, Sultan Sikandar proclaimed that he was the most perfect among kings of Arabia and Persia, not even mentioning those of the Indian subcontinent, where he was actually ruling. In the same spirit his son and successor, Sultan Ghiyath al-Din A'zam Shah, tried without success to persuade Hafiz, the great poet of Shiraz, to come and adorn his court at Pandua.[42] The political and cultural referents of these kings lay, not in Delhi or Central Asia, but much further to the west—in Mecca, Medina, Shiraz, and ancient Ctesiphon.

The Rise of Raja Ganesh (ca. 1400–1421)

Protracted over many decades, this campaign of self-legitimization by references external to Bengal was bound to have its effect on that other audience to which the Muslim regime addressed itself—the Bengali population, and especially the Hindu landholding elites whose cooperation was essential for the kingdom's administration. Tensions between the Indo-Turkish ruling class and Hindu Bengali society surfaced toward the end of the fourteenth century when Sufis of the Chishti and Firdausi orders, who vehemently championed a reformed and purified Islam, insisted that the state's foreign and Islamic identity not be diluted by admitting Bengalis into the ruling class. In 1397 Maulana Muzaffar Shams Balkhi (d. 1400), a Sufi of the Firdausi order, complained in a letter to Sultan Ghiyath al-Din A'zam Shah:

> The vanquished unbelievers with heads hanging down, exercise their
> power and authority to administer the lands which belong to them. But
> they have also been appointed (executive) officers over the Muslims in
> the lands of Islam, and they impose their orders on them. Such things
> should not happen.[43]

But such things did happen; indeed, they had to. Bengali nobles constituted a proud and experienced class of administrators who knew the land, the people, and the way local government had traditionally been managed. Even if the Indo-Turkish ruling class had wanted to recruit foreign administrators from Upper India or the Middle East, Bengal's physical isolation from those areas, together with its political isolation from North India, dictated that powerful Hindu Bengali nobles be maintained in positions of

---

42. M. I. Borah, "An Account of the Immigration of Persian Poets into Bengal," *Dacca University Studies* 1 (November 1935): 144.

43. Muzaffar Shams Balkhi, *Maktūbāt-i Muẓaffar Shams Balkhī* (Persian MS., Acc. no. 1859, Khuda Bakhsh Oriental Public Library, Patna), letter 163, p. 509. See also S. H. Askari, "The Correspondence of Two Fourteenth-Century Sufi Saints of Bihar with the Contemporary Sovereigns of Delhi and Bengal," *Journal of the Bihar Research Society* 42, no. 2 (1956): 187. Askari's translation.

local authority. Muzaffar Shams's protest is itself evidence that such had been the policy.

In short, though the sultanate aligned itself ideologically with the Middle East, it was rooted politically in Bengal. This fundamental contradiction shaped the most severe domestic crisis the sultanate faced, an upheaval focusing on the rise of a remarkable noble named Raja Ganesh. Described in a contemporary letter as "a landholder of four hundred years' standing"(*chahār ṣad sāla zamīndār*),[44] this noble was evidently descended from a ruling family prominent since Pala and Sena times. By the opening of the fifteenth century, Raja Ganesh seems to have wielded effective control over the rich lands running along the Ganges between modern Rajshahi and Pabna.[45] He definitely belonged to that class of men to whom Muzaffar Shams referred when he wrote in 1397 of "vanquished unbelievers" exercising political authority over the Muslims of Bengal.

After Ghiyath al-Din's death in 1410, tensions between Turks and Bengalis considerably intensified, and during the second decade of the fifteenth century, the crisis passed quite beyond the government's control. According to the historian Muhammad Qasim Firishta (d. 1623), Raja Ganesh "attained to great power and predominance" during the reign of Sultan Shihab al-Din (1411–14), at which time the Bengali noble became the "master of the treasury and the kingdom." When the sultan died, he wrote, Ganesh, "raising aloft the banner of kingship, seized the throne and ruled for three years and several months."[46] But the historian Nizam al-Din Ahmad (d. 1594) makes no mention of Raja Ganesh having actually usurped the throne, recording only that when Sultan Shihab al-Din Bayazid Shah died, "a *zamīndār* [landholder] of the name of Kans [Ganesh] acquired power and dominion over the country of Bangala," and that his "period of power" [*muddat-i istīlā*'] lasted seven years."[47] The only contemporary

44. Shaikh Nur Qutb-i 'Alam, *Maktūbāt-i Shaikh Nūr Quṭb-i 'Ālam* (Persian MS., Subhan Allah no. 297671/18, Maulana Azad Library, Aligarh Muslim University, Aligarh), letter 9, p. 68. See also Abdul Karim, "Nur Qutb 'Alam's Letter on the Ascendancy of Ganesa," in Muhammad Enamul Haq, *Abdul Karim Sahitya-Visarad Commemoration Volume* (Dacca: Asiatic Society of Bangladesh, 1972), 338.
45. The best treatment of the revolution is found in the study of Ahmad Hasan Dani, "The House of Raja Ganesa of Bengal," *Journal of the Asiatic Society of Bengal: Letters* 18, no. 2 (1952): 121–70.
46. Muhammad Qasim Firishta, *Tārīkh-i Firishta* (Lucknow: Nawal Kishore, 1864–65), 2: 297.
47. Khwajah Nizamuddin Ahmad, *The Ṭabaqāt-i-Akbarī*, trans. Brajendranath De, ed. Baini Prasad (Calcutta: Asiatic Society of Bengal, 1931–39), 3, pt. 1: 430–31; text, ed., B. De and M. Hidayat Hosein (Calcutta: Asiatic Society of Bengal, 1931–35), 3: 265.

references to this episode are by Arab chroniclers, who evidently derived their information from pilgrims or other travelers who had journeyed from Bengal to Arabia. Affirming that the throne had passed from Ghiyath al-Din A'zam Shah to his son Saif al-Din (1410–11), the chroniclers relate that the latter's slave rebelled against Raja Ganesh, captured him, and seized control of the kingdom. But then, the chroniclers stated, the son of Raja Ganesh revolted against the usurper, converted to Islam under the adopted name Muhammad Jalal al-Din, and then himself mounted the throne as sultan of Bengal.[48]

A continuous run of coins minted by Muslim rulers in Bengal indicates that during the height of the turmoil, from 1410 to 1417, Muslim kings continued to hold de jure authority in the delta.[49] This being the case, Nizam al-Din's statement that Raja Ganesh had acquired dominion in the kingdom suggests that the Bengali noble at this time ruled but did not reign, preferring to govern Bengal through a succession of Muslim puppets. Yet Ganesh evidently exerted overwhelming influence over these puppet sultans, for the contemporary Arab chroniclers, and later Firishta too, mistook his de facto rule for de jure sovereignty. In 1415, he took the even bolder step of getting his own son—according to a later source, a lad only twelve years old, named Jadu[50]—installed on the throne of Bengal. Now Raja Ganesh, backed by other Bengali nobles, ruled as regent for his own son.

Despite Raja Ganesh's audacious maneuverings, however, the old guard of Turkish nobles prevented him and his supporters from upsetting the symbolic structure upon which the kingdom's political ideology had rested for over two centuries. For Ganesh's son Jadu did not reign as a Hindu raja; nor was he installed with any of the appropriate symbols of Hindu kingship. Rather, in what appears to have been a compromise formula worked out between political brokers for the Bengali and Turkish factions, he converted to Islam, was renamed Sultan Jalal al-Din Muhammad, and was then allowed to reign as a Muslim king.[51] Immediately upon his accession

48. See Ibn Hajar al-'Asqalani, *Inbā'*, 2: 496; 3: 532. See also Muhammad Sakhawi, *Al-Zau'*, 8: 280.
49. See Karim, *Corpus*, 70–73.
50. Ghulam Hussain Salim, *Riyāzu-s-Salātīn: A History of Bengal*, trans. Abdus Salam (Delhi: Idarah-i Adabiyat-i Delli, 1903), 115.
51. This outcome is suggested by Firishta's statement that after Raja Ganesh's son had declared his intention to become Muslim, but *before* he assumed the throne, the kingdom's nobles unanimously declared, "We follow the king in worldly affairs, but have nothing to do with religion" ("Jamī' ahl-i ḥall va 'aqd muttafiq shuda, goftand: mā tābi'-i pādshāh-īm dar umūr-i dunyawī, ba maẓhab va dīn kārī nīst"). Firishta, *Tārīkh-i Firishta*, 2: 297.

to power in 1415, the new sultan minted coins in his Islamic name. That these coins were issued simultaneously from Pandua and the provincial cities of Chittagong, Sonargaon, and Satgaon suggests a calculated attempt by Raja Ganesh to ensure the acceptance of his son's accession to power as legitimate over *all* of Bengal.

If the Muslim nobility, succumbing to political reality, acquiesced and even participated in these new arrangements, the capital's defenders of Islamic piety, the Sufis, reacted with shock and outrage. "How exalted is God!" exclaimed the most eminent of these, Shaikh Nur Qutb-i 'Alam:

> How exalted is God! He has bestowed, without apparent reasons, the robe of faith on the lad of an infidel and installed him on the throne of the kingdom over his friends. Infidelity has gained predominance and the kingdom of Islam has been spoiled.
>
> Who knows what Divine wisdom ordains
> And what is fated for what individual existence?. . .
>
> Alas, woe to me, the sun of Islam has become obscured and the moon of religion has become eclipsed.[52]

Nur Qutb-i 'Alam even wrote a letter to Ibrahim Sharqi, the sultan of neighboring Jaunpur, imploring him to invade the delta and rid Bengal of the usurping Raja Ganesh. "Why are you sitting calm and happy on your throne," demanded the Sufi, "when the abode of faith of Islam has been reduced to such a condition! Arise and come to the aid of religion, for it is obligatory for you who are possessed of resources."[53] Chronicling the years 1415–20, a Chinese source mentions that a kingdom to the west of Bengal had indeed invaded the delta, but desisted when placated with gold and money.[54] Although Central Asian and Arakanese traditions record somewhat different outcomes of Sultan Ibrahim's invasion,[55] it is nonetheless

52. Shaikh Nur Qutb-i 'Alam, *Maktūbāt*, letter 9, p. 69. See also Abdul Karim, "Nur Qutb 'Alam's Letter," 342–43. Karim's translation.

53. Portions of this letter were reproduced in the correspondence of the contemporary shaikh, Ashraf Jahangir Simnani. See Ashraf Jahangir Simnani, *Maktūbāt-i ashrafī* (Persian MS. no. 27, Aligarh Muslim University History Department, Aligarh), letter 45, fol. 139a. See also S. H. Askari, "New Light on Rajah Ganesh and Sultan Ibrahim Sharqi of Jaunpur from Contemporary Correspondence of Two Muslim Saints," *Bengal Past and Present* 57 (1948): 34. Askari's translation.

54. P. C. Bagchi, "Political Relations between Bengal and China in the Pathan Period," *Visva-Bharati Annals* 1 (1945): 103–4.

55. Around 1442 a diplomat in the service of Shah Rukh, the Timurid ruler of Herat (1405–47), wrote that his master had intervened in the Bengal-Jaunpur crisis at the request of the sultan of Bengal, "directing the ruler of Jaunpur to abstain from attacking the King of Bengal, or to take the consequences upon himself. To which intimation the ruler of Jaunpur was obedient, and desisted from his attacks

clear that the sultan of Jaunpur failed to "liberate" the delta for "Islam" as Nur Qutb-i 'Alam had hoped.

With the capital preoccupied with both internal turmoil and foreign invasion, remnants of various pre-Muslim ruling houses seized the moment to assert their independence from Turkish rule and to reconquer a vast stretch of the eastern and southern delta. For the single year A.H. 820, corresponding to A.D. February 1417–February 1418, no sultanate coins are known to have been issued anywhere in Bengal. On the other hand two successive Hindu kings, Danuja Marddana Deva and his son Mahendra Deva, minted coins during precisely that period from Chittagong, Sonargaon, and "Pāndunagara," an apparent reference to Chhota Pandua in southwestern Bengal.[56] These kings appear to have been descendants of the Deva dynasty of kings of Chandradwip, a kingdom centered in what is now the Barisal area of southeastern Bengal, which had controlled a large area between Sonargaon and Chittagong in the thirteenth century.[57] But Danuja Marddana's and Mahendra's bid to restore the kingdom met with only brief success. In 1418 Sultan Jalal al-Din began issuing coins from what is now Faridpur, indicating that the forces of Raja Ganesh had managed to establish the sultanate's authority in the heart of the southeastern delta.[58] Similar coins issued from Sonargaon and Satgaon in that same year, and from Chittagong in 1420, point to the dramatic reassertion of the sultanate's authority throughout the delta.[59]

---

upon Bengal." 'Abd al-Razzaq, *Matla' al-sa'dain,* in *The History of India as Told by Its Own Historians,* trans. and ed. H. M. Elliot and John Dowson (Allahabad: Kitab Mahal, 1964), 4: 99. On the other hand, a contemporary Arakanese tradition recorded that the forces of Raja Ganesh, then firmly in control of Pandua, had defeated Sultan Ibrahim of Jaunpur in battle. According to this tradition, one of the kings of Arakan, who had been given refuge in Pandua after having been defeated by a Burman monarch in 1406, gave Raja Ganesh the military advice that enabled the Bengalis to defeat Sultan Ibrahim of Jaunpur. A. P. Phayre, *Journal of the Asiatic Society of Bengal* 13 (1844): 44–46, cited in Dani, "House," 135–37. See also A. P. Phayre, *History of Burma* (London: Trubner, 1884), 78.

56. The coins were dated Saka Era 1339 and 1340, corresponding to April 1416 to April 1418. The most thorough examination of the identity and chronology of these two kings is found in Dani, "House," 145–53. Dani links the two kings to the Deva dynasty of kings of Chandradwip in the Barisal area of the southeastern delta on the basis of the testimony of later oral and literary sources that identify Mahendra Deva as the son of Danuja Marddana Deva. As to the identification of "Pāndunagara," since the Deva kings never controlled North Bengal, it is most likely that they attempted to recover from the sultanate only those lands previously under their control, in which case the "Pāndunagara" on their coins would refer not to Hazrat Pandua, the capital, located in northern Bengal, but to the provincial town Chhota Pandua, located in the southwestern delta near the site of modern Calcutta.
57. Dani, "House," 152–53.
58. Ibid., 145.
59. Karim, *Corpus,* table 2, facing 163.

Although the revolt was snuffed out within a year or so, the coinage issued by its leaders tells us much of its ideological basis and of the religious sentiments then prevailing in the Bengal hinterland. On the obverse side of their coins, the Deva kings inscribed the Sanskrit phrase "Śrī Caṇḍī Caraṇa Parāyaṇa," or "devoted to the feet of Goddess Chandi."[60] The phrase corroborates the evidence of writings produced somewhat later that celebrate Chandi as a prominent folk deity and depict her as the protectress of Bengali kingship.[61] Yet, while reflecting a distinct memory of Hindu kingship, these same coins indicate the extent to which Islamic conceptions of political authority had by this time diffused throughout the delta. The inscriptions of the Deva coins are enclosed within various designs—single squares, double squares, plain circles, scalloped circles, triangular rayed circles, squares within circles, or hexagons—all of which had been firmly established in the numismatic tradition of Bengal's Indo-Turkish rulers.[62] This suggests that, even while proclaiming the restoration of Hindu Bengali rule, leaders of the independence movement had to employ Indo-Turkish numismatic formulae to appear legitimate to the general population.

The Raja Ganesh period was a turning point in Bengali history. First, it proved that despite the objections of influential members of the Muslim elite, Bengali Hindus would henceforth be formally integrated into the sultanate's ruling structure. In fact, the political integration of non-Muslims had begun long before the rise of Raja Ganesh, whose own behavior suggests their loyalty to the idea of the sultanate. Immediately upon dealing with the invasion by Sultan Ibrahim of Jaunpur, Ganesh turned his attention to quashing the Deva movements in southern and eastern Bengal, demonstrating his refusal to support explicitly Hindu restorations anywhere in the delta. Only by merging his interests with those of the kingdom as a whole, and by tempering his own power with a policy of conciliation with the powerful Indo-Turkish classes of the capital, did Raja Ganesh retain political influence.[63] Second, the Ganesh episode made telling points respecting the waning power of Hindu political symbolism in the delta. In the capital city, Raja Ganesh did not and could not raise his

---

60. Ibid., 191–93.
61. See France Bhattacharya, "La Déesse et le royaume selon le Kālaketu Upākhyāna du *Caṇḍī Maṅgala*," in *Puruṣārtha*, vol. 5, *Autour de la déesse hindoue*, ed. Madeleine Biardeau (Paris: Ecole des Hautes études en sciences sociales, 1981), 17–53.
62. Karim, *Corpus*, 191–93 and plates 1–6.
63. Firishta explicitly mentions Ganesh's conciliatory policies toward the Indo-Turkish classes in Pandua. "Although Raja Ganesh was not a Muslim," he wrote, "he mixed freely with them and had so much love for them that some Muslims, witnessing to his faith in Islam, wanted to bury him in the Islamic manner." Firishta, *Tārīkh-i Firishta*, 2: 297.

son to the throne as a Hindu; the future Sultan Jalal al-Din could reign only as a Muslim. As a Sufi source later put it, "In order to be sultan, he became Muslim" ("Az ḥasb-i sulṭān Musalmān gasht").[64] In the country's interior, on the other hand, a rebellion raised in the name of Chandi had demonstrated the continued popular association of that goddess with royalty. Yet even here the trappings of Islamic political legitimacy, though not yet its substance, had sunk deep roots, as the coins proclaiming the protection of the goddess were modeled after those of the Bengal sultans. At both royal and popular levels, Bengalis were gradually accommodating themselves to Muslim rule.

Sultan Jalal al-Din Muhammad (1415–32) and His Political Ideology

Surrounded by rebellious Hindus in the interior and by alarmed members of the Muslim elite in the capital, how did the boy-king and Muslim convert Sultan Jalal al-Din assert his own claims to the throne? First, he reversed the policy of his Hindu father respecting the highly influential circle of Chishti Sufis in the capital. Sufi sources, naturally partial to the cause of the shaikhs, depict Raja Ganesh as having systematically persecuted the Sufis of Pandua, even arranging for the murder of one of their next of kin.[65] But Sultan Jalal al-Din broke with this policy by submitting himself to the personal guidance of Pandua's leading Chishti, Shaikh Nur Qutb-i 'Alam. Given the young king's tender age at the time of his accession, it is likely that he had been entrusted to the religious care of the venerable Chishti saint as part of a compromise that Raja Ganesh and influential Indo-Turkish nobles worked out as their price for accepting Ganesh's son as king. In any event, prominent members of the Chishti order clearly emerged as the principal legitimizers of Islamic authority in Bengal, a role they would continue to play for the remainder of the independent sultanate period, and through the Mughal period as well.[66]

---

64. *Mirāt al-asrār* (Persian MS. no. 204, Khuda Bakhsh Library, Patna; compiled in 1654 by 'Abd al-Rahman Chishti, copied in 1806), fol. 517a–b. This interpretation is corroborated by the historian Nizam al-Din Ahmad (d. 1594), who records that Raja Ganesh's son, "owing to his love of rule, became a Muslim, naming himself Sultan Jalal al-Din" ("Pisar-i ū ba-wāsiṭa-yi ḥubb-i riyāsat Musalmān shuda, Sulṭān Jalāl al-Dīn nām-i khūd nihād"). Nizamuddin Ahmad, *Ṭabiqāt-i Akbarī,* text, 3: 266.
65. *Mirāt al-asrār,* fol. 517a. See also Askari, "New Light," 37; Karim, "Nur Qutb 'Alam's Letter," 336–37.
66. Not only did Jalal al-Din and his son and successor Ahmad become disciples of Nur Qutb-i 'Alam, but, the *Mirāt al-asrār* informs us, from then until 1532, twelve more sultans of various ethnic backgrounds ascended the Bengali throne, all of whom were disciples of the line of Chishti shaikhs established in Pandua by Shaikh 'Ala al-Haq (ibid., fol. 517b).

Second, the new monarch sought to legitimize his rule by publicly displaying his credentials as a devout and correct Muslim.[67] Contemporary Arab sources hold that upon his conversion to Islam, Jalal al-Din adopted the Hanafi legal tradition and rebuilt the mosques demolished by his father. Between 1428 and 1431 he also supported the construction of a religious college in Mecca and established close ties with Sultan Ashraf Barsbay, the Mamluk ruler of Egypt. Having plied the latter with gifts, Jalal al-Din requested in return a letter of recognition from the Egyptian sultan, he being the most prestigious Muslim ruler in the Islamic heartlands and the custodian of a remnant line of the Abbasid caliphs. The Mamluk sultan complied with the request, sending the Bengal sultan a robe of honor as well as the letter of recognition.[68] Jalal al-Din also reintroduced on his coins the Muslim confession of faith, which had disappeared from Bengal's coins for several centuries, since the time of Ghiyath al-Din 'Iwaz (r. 1213–27).[69] In fact, he went a good deal further. Perhaps because he could not inscribe on his monuments and coins the usual self-legitimizing formula, "sultan, son of the sultan," in 1427 the king, now a mature man with twelve years' ruling experience, had himself described in one inscription as "the most exalted of the great sultans, the caliph of Allah in the universe."[70] Having tested the reception of his bold statement on a single mosque, he took the bolder step three years later of including "the caliph of Allah" as one of his titles on his coins.[71] For a convert to the religion to claim for himself the loftiest title in the Sunni Muslim world— second only to the Prophet himself—was indeed a monumental leap.[72]

67. Some later historians understood his efforts in this direction as outright bigotry. But there is no contempoary evidence to support the contention—first voiced in the late eighteenth century by Ghulam Hussain Salim and repeated in the late nineteenth century by influential British authorities like James Wise—that Jalal al-Din pursued a policy of forcibly converting his fellow Bengalis to Islam. See Salim, *Riyāzu-s-Salātīn*, 118; Wise, "Muhammadans of Eastern Bengal," 29.

68. Ibn Hajar al-'Asqalani, *Inbā'*, 2: 497; 3: 532; and Muhammad Sakhawi, *Al-Zau'*, 8: 280. See also Ziauddin Desai, "Some New Data Regarding the Pre-Mughal Muslim Rulers of Bengal," *Islamic Culture* 32 (1958): 204.

69. Karim, *Corpus*, 77.

70. "al-Sultān al-a'zam al-mu'azzamīn khalīfat Allah 'alī al-makūnīn Jalāl al-Dunyā w'al-Dīn." Shamsud-Din Ahmed, ed. and trans., *Inscriptions*, 4: 45. This appeared on the mosque of Mandra, in Dhaka District.

71. Karim, *Corpus*, 170. Abdul Karim has argued that Jalal al-Din's use of the inflated title *Khalīfat al-Allah* was "a political stunt to unite the people against his rival Sultan Ibrahim Sharqi of Jaunpur" (ibid., 176). But this hypothesis is untenable, since the Bengal king did not introduce the formula until 1427, and Sultan Ibrahim does not appear to have threatened Bengal after 1420.

72. When the Ilyas Shahi dynasty was restored to power in 1433, its kings, who were Muslims by birth, went further still and styled themselves "the caliph of Allah by proof and testimony" (*khalīfat Allah bi'l-hujjat wa'l-burhān*). By the fifteenth century the symbolism of the caliphate had been exploited so wildly that

Even while strenuously asserting his credentials as a correct Muslim, Jalal al-Din inaugurated a two-century age when the ruling house sought to ground itself in local culture. Reflected in coinage, in patterns of court patronage, in language, in literature, and in architecture, this was by far the most important legacy of Sultan Jalal al-Din's seventeen-year reign. Several undated issues of his silver coins[73] and a huge commemorative silver coin struck in Pandua in 1421 not only lack the Muslim confession of faith but bear the stylized figure of a lion (fig. 11). The numismatist G. S. Farid has explained this unusual motif by arguing that the latter coin— which at 105 grams in weight and 6.7 centimeters in width is perhaps the largest and heaviest coin ever struck in India—was minted for presentation to the emperor of China by Chinese ambassadors and soldiers residing at the Bengal court during the early fifteenth century.[74] Chinese chronicles do indeed record that the Bengal sultans presented silver coins to members of their Bengal mission.[75] But this hypothesis would not explain why the same lion motif is found on the ordinary silver coinage minted by the same sultan. An alternative explanation has been offered by A. H. Dani, who draws attention to Tripura, a small Hindu hill kingdom that managed to maintain a precarious independence on the extreme eastern edge of the delta throughout the sultanate and Mughal periods.[76] Noting that this kingdom depicted lions on its coins, Dani suggests that in addition to re-conquering southern Bengal, Jalal al-Din may also have conquered Tripura, or parts of it, and issued this style of coinage in order to gain the support of its people.[77] However, since the earliest known lion-stamped coin minted by the independent rajas of Tripura did not appear until 1464, or thirty-

its potential for conferring legitimacy on its users seems to have diminished nearly to the vanishing point. Almost anybody could now claim not only association *with* the caliph, but identity *as* the caliph, and even to have "proof and testimony" of the fact. It had become a hollow claim. See Abdul Karim, "'Khalifat Allah' Title in the Coins of Bengal Sultans," *Journal of the Pakistan Historical Society* 8, no. 1 (January 1960): 29.

73. Karim, *Corpus*, 78, 80, pl. 7, no. 1. Another copy of this coin is in the possession of G. S. Farid of the Asiatic Society of Bengal, Calcutta; see Farid, "Rare Lion-Coins of Jalaluddin Mohammad Shah of Bengal Including a Unique Hexagonal Variety," *Journal of the Asiatic Society of Bengal* 16, nos. 1–4 (1974): 151–54.

74. See G. S. Farid, "A New and Unique Ten Tankah Commemorative Coin of Jalaluddin Mohammad Shah of Bengal (818–837 A.H.)," *Journal of the Numismatic Society of India* 38 (1976): 88–95. The coin itself is in Farid's personal collection, Asiatic Society of Bengal, Calcutta.

75. See Fei Hsin, *Hsing ch'a shéng lan* ("Description of the Stary Raft"), in W. W. Rockhill, "Notes on the Relations," *T'oung Pao*, 16, pt. 2, sec. 4 (1915): 442.

76. On Tripura, see D. C. Sircar, *Some Epigraphical Records of the Medieval Period from Eastern India* (New Delhi: Abhinav Publications, 1979), 95–96.

77. The only coins of this type so far discovered were found in Dhaka District, which is adjacent to Tripura. Dani, "House," 164.

Fig. 11. Large commemorative silver coin of Sultan Jalal al-Din Muhammad, struck in 1421.

two years after the death of Sultan Jalal al-Din, the sultan could not have been following the established custom of that kingdom.

On the other hand, one may see the motif of a lion—some species of which are indigenous to India—as a more generalized symbol of political authority in eastern Bengal, not limited to the rajas of Tripura. When the kings of Tripura began striking their own lion-motif coins from 1464 on, they did so as patrons of the Goddess manifested as Durga, whose vehicle (*vāhana*) is a lion.[78] Since the lion is also the vehicle of the Goddess as

78. A. N. Lahiri, "Tripura Coins of Iconographic Interest," *Journal of the Numismatic Society* 29 (1967): 73–75. Somewhat later, beginning with the coinage of Vijayamānika (ca. 1532–ca. 1563), they minted coins bearing a trident (*triśūla*),

Chandi, in whose name a reconstituted Deva dynasty had unsuccessfully rebelled in 1416–18, the sultan possibly intended his lion-motif coins to appeal to deeply rooted sentiments that focused on Goddess-worship generally. Nor did he attempt to disguise his identity as the son of a Hindu chieftain, but instead proclaimed his paternity in Arabic letters, affirming himself to be *bin Kans Rāo*, "son of Raja Ganesh."[79]

Sultan Jalal al-Din, then, was sending different messages to different constituencies in his kingdom. To Muslims, he portrayed himself as the model of a pious sultan, reviving inscription of the Muslim creed on his coinage and even making a claim, unprecedented in Bengal, to be the caliph of Allah. To Hindus, meanwhile, his coins proclaimed a sovereign who was the son of a Hindu king; moreover, they bore an image that, without actually naming Chandi or Durga, would have struck responsive chords among devotees of the Goddess. He also patronized Sanskritic culture by publicly demonstrating his appreciation for scholars steeped in classical Brahmanic scholarship.[80] What is more significant, a contemporary Chinese traveler reported that although Persian was understood by some in the court, the language in universal use there was Bengali.[81] This points to the waning, although certainly not yet the disappearance, of the sort of foreign mentality that the Muslim ruling class in Bengal had exhibited since its arrival over two centuries earlier. It also points to the survival, and now the triumph, of local Bengali culture at the highest level of official society.

The new mood is seen most vividly in the architecture that appeared in the kingdom immediately after the Raja Ganesh episode. Abandoning Middle Eastern or North Indian traditions of religious architecture, Bengali mosques from the reign of Sultan Jalal al-Din on adopted purely indig-

---

unambiguously associated with the god Śiva, depicted at the back of the lion. Later, in 1600, King Yaśodharamānikya began issuing coins with an image of the flute-playing Krishna, with a gopi girl on either side of him, depicted above the image of the lion and trident. This shift toward Vaishnava sentiment in Tripura followed a similar evolution among non-Muslims in Bengal proper. See pp. 109–12.

79. On the smaller coins, he used the Persianized form, *bin Kans Shāh*, or "son of Ganesh Shah." See Karim, *Corpus*, 78. These inscriptional legends also point to Raja Ganesh's renown and even public acceptance, for no sovereign would have linked himself in this way with a hated tyrant.

80. For example, he bestowed six titles on Brhaspati, a deeply learned man of the time, and sponsored a special ceremony when conferring on him the title of "Rāyamukuta." Chintaharan Chakravarti, "Muslim Patronage to Sanskrit Learning," in *B. C. Law Volume*, ed. D. R. Bhandarkar et al., pt. 2 (Poona: Bhandarkar Oriental Research Institute, 1946), 177.

81. Ma Huan, *Ying-yai Sheng-lan: "The Overall Survey of the Ocean's Shores,"* trans. J. V. G. Mills (Cambridge: Cambridge University Press, 1970), 161.

Fig. 12. Eklakhi Mausoleum, Pandua (ca. 1432).

enous motifs and structural traits.[82] Although not itself a mosque, the Eklakhi mausoleum in Pandua (fig. 12), believed to be the sultan's own mausoleum, became the prototype for the subsequent Bengali-style mosque. Here we find all the hallmarks of the new style: square shape, single dome, exclusive use of brick construction in both exterior and interior, massive walls, engaged octagonal corner towers, curved cornice, and extensive terra-cotta ornamentation.[83] The last-mentioned feature, a Bengali tradition dating from at least the eighth century A.D., as in the Buddhist shrine at Paharpur, was now fully reestablished, as witnessed in the façade above the Eklakhi's lintel. A mature example of the new style is seen in the Lattan mosque at Gaur, built ca. 1493–1519 (fig. 13).

Whence came the inspiration for this style of mosque? One source was the familiar thatched bamboo hut found everywhere in the villages of Bengal. Their curved roofs, formed by the natural bend of the bamboo structure under the weight of the thatching, were translated into brick for the first time in the Eklakhi mausoleum, with its gently curved cornice. There-

82. Hitesranjan Sanyal, "Religious Architecture in Bengal (15th–17th Centuries): A Study of the Major Trends," *Indian History Congress, Proceedings*, 32d session (1970), 1: 416. Ahmad Hasan Dani, *Muslim Architecture in Bengal*, Asiatic Society of Pakistan Publication No. 7 (Dacca: Asiatic Society of Pakistan, 1961), 22.
83. Dani, *Muslim Architecture*, 26. Perween Hasan, "Sultanate Mosques and Continuity in Bengal Architecture," *Muqarnas* 6 (1989): 62.

Fig. 13. Lattan Mosque, Gaur (ca. 1493–1519).

after until the end of the sultanate, the thatched hut motif became an essential ingredient of Bengali architecture, whether public or private, Hindu
or Muslim.[84] The art historian Perween Hasan has suggested still another
indigenous source for the Bengali mosque. By comparing sultanate
mosques with Buddhist monuments in Burma dating from the eighth to
eleventh centuries, together with surviving evidence of Buddhist architecture in pre-twelfth-century Bengal, Hasan has come to the conclusion that
Bengal's Buddhist temple tradition directly contributed to the revival of
the square, brick Bengali mosque in the fifteenth century.[85] Drawing on
elements derived both from the rural Bengali thatched hut and from the
pre-Islamic Buddhist temple, then, these structures reflect an essentially
nativist movement, an effort to express an Islamic institution in locally
familiar terms. This style of royal culture became so fixed that it persisted
despite the restoration of the old Ilyas Shahi dynasty in 1433, and despite

84. "Although no mosque ever adopted the typical Hindu *rekhā* or *pirha* towers of
the Pāla period, nor any temple adopt [*sic*] the exterior form of the Islamic dome,
both drew freely on local architectural tradition, so that in spite of widely differing
functions, temple and mosque achieve a certain affinity of design," writes David
McCutchion, who pioneered the study of vernacular architecture in premodern
Bengal. McCutchion, "Hindu-Muslim Continuities in Bengal," *Journal of the Asiatic Society of Pakistan* 13, no. 3 (December 1968): 241.
85. See Hasan, "Sultanate Mosques," 63–66, 69.

the drastic changes in the social composition of the ruling class that took place during the century following Jalal al-Din's death in 1432.[86]

The Indigenization of Royal Authority, 1433–1538

The fifty years after Jalal al-Din's death saw the restoration of the old Ilyas Shahi house and, in a curious throwback to the earliest days of Turkish rule in North India, the appearance of the institution of military slavery. In the 1460s and 1470s, however, instead of Central Asian Turks, black slaves (*habashī*) from Abyssinia in East Africa were recruited for military and civil service.[87] But the influence of these men grew with their numbers, and in time they subverted the very purpose for which they had been imported.[88] In 1486 a coup d'état ended the Ilyas Shahi dynasty for good, plunging the sultanate into seven stormy years of palace intrigues and assassinations as slave after slave attempted to seize the reins of power. Ultimately, 'Ala al-Din Husain, a Meccan Arab who had risen to the office of chief minister under an Abyssinian royal patron, emerged triumphant in another palace coup, which launched the last important ruling house of independent Bengal, the Husain Shahi dynasty.[89]

The reigns of Sultan 'Ala al-Din Husain Shah (1493–1519) and his son Nasir al-Din Nusrat Shah (1519–32) are generally regarded as the "golden age" of the Bengal sultanate.[90] In Husain Shah's reign, for example, Bengali Hindus participated in government to a considerable degree: his chief minister (*vazīr*), his chief of bodyguards, his master of the mint, his governor of Chittagong, his private physician, and his private secretary (*dabīr-i khāṣ*) were all Bengali Hindus.[91] In terms of its physical power and territo-

86. Ziauddin Desai, "Some New Data Regarding the Pre-Mughal Muslim Rulers of Bengal," *Islamic Culture* 32 (1958): 204.
87. Firishta, *Tārīkh*, 2: 298.
88. The last ruler of the Ilyas Shahi dynasty, Sultan Jalal al-Din Fath Shah (1481–1486), "applied the whip of justice to palace eunuchs and Abyssinian slaves who had been gathering in numbers during the reigns of Barbak Shah and Yusuf Shah, and who had achieved the zenith of self-confidence and committed unimaginable [acts of] immoderation," Firishta notes. Ibid., 2: 299.
89. Ibid., 299, 301.
90. This characterization began with the historian Nizam al-Din Ahmad, who in 1594 wrote glowingly of 'Ala al-Din Husain Shah as "an intelligent and able man," who "summoned learned, great and pious men from different parts of the kingdom, and showed kindness to them. He made very great efforts and exertions for enriching and improving the condition of the country. . . . Owing to the auspiciousness of his laudable morals, and pleasing virtues he performed the duties of sovereignty for long years; and all his life was passed in pleasure and enjoyment." Nizamuddin Ahmad, *Ṭabaqāt-i Akbarī*, text, 3: 270; trans., B. De, 3, pt. 1: 443.
91. Jadunath Sarkar, ed., *The History of Bengal*, vol. 2, *Muslim Period, 1200–1757* (1947; Patna: Janaki Prakashan, 1977), 151–2. There is no record of how sixteenth-

rial extent, too, this was the sultanate's high tide. In the second year of his reign, 1494, Sultan Husain Shah extended the kingdom's northern frontiers, invading and annexing both Kuch Bihar ("Kamata") and western Assam ("Kamrup").[92] Writing around 1515, Tome Pires estimated this monarch's armed forces at a hundred thousand cavalrymen. "He fights with heathen kings, great lords and greater than he," wrote the Portuguese official, "but because the king of Bengal is nearer to the sea, he is more practised in war, and he prevails over them."[93] The king thus managed to make a circle of vassals of his neighbors: Orissa to the southwest, Arakan to the southeast, and Tripura to the east.[94]

But the palmy days of independent Bengal were numbered. Even as the Husain Shahi dynasty was taking root, Babur, a brilliant Timurid prince, was rising to prominence in Central Asia and Afghanistan. In 1526, resolving to make a bid for empire in North India, Babur led his cavalry and cannon through the Khyber Pass and overthrew the Lodi dynasty of Afghans, the last rulers of a vastly shrunken and decayed Delhi sultanate. As a result of this triumph, defeated Afghans moved down the Gangetic plain and into the Bengal delta, where they were hospitably received by Nasir al-Din Nusrat Shah.[95] Thus the span of a century from the death of Jalal al-Din Muhammad (d. 1432) to that of Nasir al-Din Nusrat Shah (d. 1532) witnessed a wholesale transformation of Bengal's political fabric. In the reign of the former sultan, descendants of old Turkish families had still formed the kingdom's dominant ruling group. But in the following century the scope of Bengali participation at all levels of government continually widened, while the throne itself passed from Indo-Turks, to East Africans, to an Arab house, and, finally, to Afghans.

How did these changes affect the articulation of state authority? Within the precincts of the court, to be sure, a self-consciously Persian model of political authority was maintained to the end of the sultanate. A member

century Sufis, whose predecessors had decried the appointment of Hindus to high office, felt about these developments.
92. Simon Digby, "The Fate of Daniyal, Prince of Bengal, in the Light of an Unpublished Inscription," *Bulletin of the School of Oriental and African Studies* 36, no. 3 (1973): 593–601.
93. Tome Pires, *Suma Oriental of Tome Pires*, trans. A. Cortesão, 2 vols. (London: Hakluyt Society, 1944), 1: 89.
94. "The rich things there are in Bengal," continues Pires, "are made in these kingdoms, and because they cannot live without the sea, they obey [the Bengal sultan], because he allows them an outlet for their merchandise." Ibid., 89–90.
95. Nusrat Shah not only endowed these Afghan refugees with lands and towns; he also married the daughter of Sultan Ibrahim Lodi, recently defeated by Babur. Firishta, *Tārīkh*, 2: 302.

of a Portuguese mission sent to Nasir al-Din's court in 1521—the earliest-known European mission to Bengal—vividly describes the projection of royal power during his trip to the capital. Ushered into the sultan's court, the writer passed by three hundred bare-chested soldiers bearing swords and round shields, and the same number of archers, on whose shields were painted golden lions with black claws. "We arrived before the [palace's] second gate and were searched as we had been at the first," continues the mission's anonymous interpreter.

> We passed through nine such gates and were searched each time. Be-
> yond the last gate we saw an esplanade as vast as one and a half arena[s]
> and which seemed to be wider than it was long. Twelve horsemen were
> playing polo there. At one end there was a large platform mounted on
> thick sandal-wood supports. The roof supports were thinner and were
> covered in carvings of foliage and small gilded birds. The gilt ceiling was
> also carved and depicted the moon, the sun and a host of stars, all
> gilded.
>   We arrived before the Sultan. He was seated on a large gilt sofa cov-
> ered with different-sized cushions, all of which were embedded with a
> smattering of precious stones and small pearls. We greeted him ac-
> cording to the custom of the country—hands crossed on our chests and
> heads as low as possible.[96]

The polo field at the heart of the court, the royal dais raised on sandal-wood columns, the roof adorned with gilded carvings of birds and heavenly bodies, and the ceremonial etiquette before the sultan—all clearly indicate the survival of Persian political symbols at the sultanate's ritual center. Indeed, this description of the court at Gaur closely compares with that of the court of Pandua given by a Chinese ambassador (see pp. 47–49) a century earlier.

But this political symbolism seems to have been intended for internal use only, as if the court were only reminding itself of its Persian political inheritance.[97] Publicly, the later sultans placed a much greater emphasis

96. *Voyage dans les deltas du Gange et de l'Irraouaddy: Relation portugaise ano-nyme (1521)*, trans. and ed. Genevieve Bouchon and Luis Filipe Thomaz (Paris: Centre culturel portugais, 1988), 321–22.

97. The Husain Shahi sultans also patronized Persian miniature painting traditions. Twenty-six miniature paintings illustrating a copy of Jami's *Yūsuf and Zulaykhā* were apparently produced under the patronage of Sultan 'Ala al-din Husain Shah in 1507–8. There is also an illustrated copy of part of Nizami's *Sikandar-nāma*, dated 1531–32 and dedicated to Sultan Nasir al-Din Nusrat Shah. See Norah M. Titley, *Persian Miniature Painting and Its Influence on the Art of Turkey and India* (London: British Library, 1983), 179, 182–83; Robert Skelton, "The Iskandar Nama of Nusrat Shah," in *Indian Painting: Mughal and Rajput and a Sultanate Manu-script*, ed. Toby Falk, Ellen Smart, and Robert Skelton (London: P. and D. Colnaghi, 1978), 144. Although the subject matter of these works is purely Persian, certain

on merging their interests with local society and culture, as in their public displays of lavish generosity. Wrote the Portuguese diplomat just cited:

> I saw one hundred and fifty cartloads of cooked rice, large quantities of bread, rape, onions, bananas and other fruits of the earth. There were fifty other carts filled with boiled and roasted cows and sheep as well as plenty of cooked fish. All this was to be given to the poor. After the food had been distributed, money was given out, the whole to the value of six hundred thousand of our tangas. . . . I was totally amazed; it had to be seen to be believed. The money was thrown from the top of a platform into a crowd of about four or five thousand people.[98]

While a foreign dignitary was permitted to see a Persianized court with gilded ceilings and sandalwood posts, the common people saw cartloads of cooked rice "and other fruits of the earth."

It was in the late fifteenth and early sixteenth centuries, too, that state-sponsored mosques built in native styles proliferated throughout the delta (see table 1). The court also lent vigorous support to Bengali language and literature. Already in the early fifteenth century, the Chinese traveler Ma Huan observed that Bengali was "the language in universal use."[99] By the second half of the same century, the court was patronizing Bengali literary works as well as Persian romance literature. Sultan Rukn al-Din Barbak (r. 1459–74) patronized the writing of the *Śrī Kṛṣṇa-Vijaya* by Maladhara Basu, and under ʿAla al-Din Husain Shah (1493–1519) and Nasir al-Din Nusrat Shah (1519–32), the court patronized the writing of the *Manasā-Vijaya* by Vipra Das, the *Padma-Purāṇa* by Vijaya Gupta, the *Kṛṣṇa-Maṅ-gala* by Yasoraj Khan, and translations (from Sanskrit) of portions of the great epic *Mahābhārata* by Vijaya Pandita and Kavindra Parameśvara.[100] Sultan Mahmud Shah (1532–38) even dedicated a bridge using a Sanskrit inscription written in Bengali characters, and dated according to the Hindu calendar.[101]

In short, apart from the Persianized political ritual that survived within

---

architectural details depicted in the illustrations appear to be identical with the distinctive features of the Bengali mosque as discussed above—namely, cusped arches, brickwork alternating with polychrome tiles, terra-cotta tiles, and projecting eaves with brackets. See Jeremiah P. Losty, *The Art of the Book in India* (London: British Library, 1982), 68.
98. *Voyage dans les deltas du Gange*, 327.
99. Rockhill, "Notes on the Relations," 437.
100. Niharranjan Ray, "Mediaeval Bengali Culture," *Visva-Bharati Quarterly* 11, no. 2 (August–October 1945): 54; Md. Enamul Haq, *Muslim Bengali Literature* (Karachi: Pakistan Publications, 1957), 38–39.
101. Shamsud-Din Ahmed, ed. and trans., *Inscriptions*, 4: 236–37.

Table 1. Construction of Dated Mosques in Bengal, 1200–1800

	Ordinary	Congregational	Total
1200–1250	2	0	2
1250–1300	3	1	4
1300–1350	2	0	2
1350–1400	4	1	5
1400–1450	5	0	5
1450–1500	52	9	61
1500–1550	28	28	56
1550–1600	15	2	17
1600–1650	7	0	7
1650–1700	17	0	17
1700–1750	8	0	8
1750–1800	4	0	4
Total	147	41	188

Sources: Shamsud-Din Ahmed, ed. and trans., *Inscriptions of Bengal* (Rajshahi: Varendra Research Museum, 1960), 4: 317–38; Qeyamuddin Ahmad, *Corpus of Arabic and Persian Inscriptions of Bihar* (Patna: K. P. Jayaswal Research Institute, 1973); A. H. Dani, *Muslim Architecture in Bengal* (Dacca: Asiatic Society of Pakistan, 1961), 194–95; *Epigraphia Indica, Arabic and Persian Supplement*, 1965: 24; id., 1975: 34–36; *Journal of the Asiatic Society of Pakistan* 2 (1957); id., 11, no. 2 (1966): 143–51; id., 12, no. 2 (1967): 296–303; *Journal of the Asiatic Society of Bangladesh* 28, no. 2 (1983): 83–95; *Journal of the Asiatic Society of Bengal* 6, nos. 1–2 (1964): 15–16; *Journal of the Varendra Research Museum* 2 (1973): 67–70; id., 4 (1975–76): 63–69, 71–80; id., 6 (1980–81): 101–8; id., 7 (1981–82): 184; *Bulletin of the School of Oriental and African Studies* 30, no. 3 (1973): 589; Mohammad Yusuf Siddiq, *Arabic and Persian Texts of the Islamic Inscriptions of Bengal* (Watertown, Mass.: South Asia Press, 1991), 4–123.

the court itself, from the early fifteenth century on, the sultanate articulated its authority through Bengali media. This resulted partly from reassessments made in the wake of the upheavals of the Raja Ganesh period and partly from sustained isolation from North India, which compelled rulers to base their claims of political legitimacy in terms that would attract local support. But royal patronage of Bengali culture was selective in nature. With the apparent aim of broadening the roots of its authority, the court patronized folk architecture as opposed to classical Indian styles, popular literature written in Bengali rather than Sanskrit texts, and Vaishnava Bengali officials instead of Śākta Brahmans. At the same time, Islamic symbolism assumed a measurably lower posture in the projection of state authority. Political pragmatism seems to have dictated the most public of all royal deeds, the minting of coins. Sultan Nasir al-Din Nusrat Shah described himself as "the sultan, son of the sultan, Nasir al-Din Nusrat Shah, the sultan, son of Husain Shah, the sultan."[102] Gone was the bombast of earlier periods, and gone too were references to Greek conquerors or Arab caliphs. Nasir al-Din Nusrat Shah was sultan simply because his father had been; no further justification was deemed necessary. Secure in power, these kings now presented themselves to all Bengalis as indigenous rulers.

It seems, moreover, that this was how contemporary Hindu poets perceived them. In a 1494 work glorifying the goddess Manasa, the poet Vijaya Gupta wove into his opening stanzas praises of the sultan of Bengal that would have flattered any classical Indian raja:

> Sultan Husain Raja, nurturer of the world:
> In war he is invincible; for his opponents he is Yama [god of death].
> In his charity he is like Kalpataru [a fabled wish-yielding tree].
> In his beauty he is like Kama [god of love].
> His subjects enjoy happiness under his rule.[103]

Similarly, in his *Śrī Caitanya Bhāgavat* composed in the 1540s, Vrindavan Das refers to the Bengal king as *rāja*, never using the Arabo-Persian terms *shāh* or *sulṭān*. And in the early 1550s another Vaishnava poet, Jayananda, refers in his *Caitanya-Maṅgala* to the Muslim ruler not only as *rāja* but as *iśvara* ("god"), and even as Indra, the Vedic king of the gods.[104] The use of such titles signals a distinctly Bengali validation of the sultan's authority.

In 1629, shortly after the Mughal conquest of Bengal, and still within living memory of the sultanate, the Augustinian friar Sebastião Manrique visited Bengal and remarked that some of its Muslim kings had been in the habit of sending for water from Ganga Sagar, the ancient holy site where the old Ganges (the modern Hooghly) emptied into the Bay of Bengal. Like Hindu sovereigns of the region, he wrote, these kings would wash themselves in that holy water during ceremonies connected with their installation.[105] This isolated reference, if narrated accurately to the European

102. Karim, *Corpus*, 118. From the accession of Nasir al-Din's son to the end of Bengal's independent monarchy, the inscriptions on both coins and mosques consist of the simple formula "the sultan, son of the sultan." See Ibid., 238, 244, 249.
103. Vijaya Gupta, *Padma-Purāṇa*, ed. Jayanta Kumar Dasgupta (Calcutta: University of Calcutta Press, 1962), 8.
104. J. T. O'Connell, "Vaisnava Perceptions of Muslims in Sixteenth-Century Bengal," in *Islamic Society and Culture: Essays in Honour of Professor Aziz Ahmad*, ed. Milton Israel and N. K. Wagle (New Delhi: Manohar, 1983), 298–302.
105. Sebastião Manrique, *Travels of Fray Sebastien Manrique, 1629–1643*, trans. E. Luard and H. Hosten (Oxford: Hakluyt Society, 1927), 1: 77.

friar, would suggest that balancing the Persian symbols that pervaded their private audiences, the later sultans observed explicitly Indian rites during their coronations, events that were very public and symbolically charged. Contemporary poetic references to these kings as *rāja* or *iśvara* should not, then, be dismissed as mere hyperbole. They had become Bengali kings.

Summary

Having dislodged a Hindu dynasty in Bengal, the earliest Muslim rulers made no attempt on their coins to assert legitimate authority over their conquered subjects, displaying instead a show of coercive power. Their earliest architecture reveals an immigrant people still looking over their shoulders to distant Delhi. In the course of the thirteenth century, however, political rivalry with Delhi compelled Bengal's rulers to adopt a posture of strenuous religious orthodoxy vis-à-vis their former overlords. This they did by associating themselves with the font of all Islamic legitimacy, the office of the caliph in Baghdad. After gaining independence from Delhi in the mid fourteenth century, the sultans of Bengal added to this posture a projection of Persian imperial ideology, reflected in the "Second Alexander" numismatic formula and in Sikandar's grandiose and majestic Adina mosque.

By the early fifteenth century, however, too much emphasis upon either foreign basis of legitimacy—Islamic or imperial Persian—provoked a crisis of confidence among those powerful Bengali nobles upon whose continued political support the minority Muslim ruling class ultimately depended. That crisis, manifested in Raja Ganesh's rise to all but legal sovereignty, in turn provoked a crisis of confidence among the chief Muslim literati, the Sufi elite of the time. These tensions were partially resolved by the conversion of Raja Ganesh's son, Sultan Jalal al-Din, and the latter's attempt to patronize each of the kingdom's principal constituencies—pious Muslims, Sufis of the Chishti order, and devotees of the Goddess—on a separate, piecemeal basis.

But a comprehensive political ideology appealing to all Bengalis only appeared with the restored Ilyas Shahi dynasty and its successors. By evolving a stable, mainly secular modus vivendi with Bengali society and culture, in which mutually satisfactory patron-client relations became politically institutionalized, and in which the state systematically patronized the culture of the subject population, the later Bengal sultanate approximated what Marshall Hodgson has called a "military patronage state."[106]

---

106. Marshall Hodgson, *The Venture of Islam: Conscience and History in a World Civilization* (Chicago: University of Chicago Press, 1974), 3: 25–27.

Dropping all references to external sources of authority, the coins of the later sultans relied instead on a secular dynastic formula of legitimate succession: so-and-so was sultan because his father had been one. And in their public architecture, these kings yielded so much to Bengali conceptions of form and medium that, as the art historian Percy Brown observes, "the country, originally possessed by the invaders, now possessed them."[107]

107. Percy Brown, *Indian Architecture, Islamic Period,* 5th ed. (Bombay: D. B. Taraporevala, 1968), 38.

3 Early Sufis of the Delta

In the country of Bengal, not to speak of the cities, there is no
town and no village where holy saints did not come and settle
down.

Ashraf Jahangir Simnani (ca. 1414)

The Question of Sufis and Frontier Warfare

Bengal's earliest sustained contact with Islamic civilization occurred in the
context of the geopolitical convulsions that had driven large numbers of
Turkish-speaking groups from Central Asia into the Iranian plateau and
India. Whether as military slaves, as adventurers, or as refugees fleeing
before the Mongol advance, Turks gravitated not only to the older centers
of the Islamic world—Baghdad, Cairo, Samarkand—but also to its fringes,
including Bengal. Immigrant groups were often led by a man called *alp* or
alp-eren, identified as "the heroic figure of old Turkic saga, the warrior-
adventurer whose exploits alone justified his way of life."[1] Migrating Turks
also grouped themselves into Islamic mystical fraternities typically organized around Sufi leaders who combined the characteristics of the "heroic
figure of old Turkic saga," the *alp*, and the pre-Islamic Turkish shaman—
that is, a charismatic holy man believed to possess magical powers and to
have intimate contact with the unseen world. It happened, moreover, that
the strict authority structure that had evolved for transmitting Islamic
mystical knowledge from master (*murshid*) to disciple (*murīd*) proved remarkably well suited for binding retainers to charismatic leaders. This, too,
lent force to the Turkish drive to the Bengal frontier.

The earliest-known Muslim inscription in Bengal concerns a group of
such immigrant Sufis. Written on a stone tablet found in Birbhum District
and dated July 29, 1221, just seventeen years after Muhammad Bakhtiyar's
conquest, the inscription records the construction of a Sufi lodge (*khāna-*

---

1. Rudi Paul Lindner, *Nomads and Ottomans in Medieval Anatolia* (Bloomington:
Indiana University, 1983), 24. See also Gerald Clauson, *Etymological Dictionary
of Pre–Thirteenth Century Turkish* (Oxford: Clarendon Press, 1972), 128.

qāh) by a man described as a *faqīr*—that is, a Sufi—and the son of a native of Maragha in northwestern Iran. The building was not meant for this *faqīr* alone, but for a group of Sufis (*ahl-i ṣuffa*) "who all the while abide in the presence of the Exalted Allah and occupy themselves in the remembrance of the Exalted Allah."[2] The tablet appears to have been part of a pre-Islamic edifice before it was put to use for the *khānaqāh*, for on its reverse side is a Sanskrit inscription mentioning the victorious conquests made in this part of the delta by a subordinate of Nayapala, Pala king from ca. A.D. 1035 to 1050. The inscription refers to a large number of Hindu temples in this region, and, despite the Buddhist orientation of the Pala kings, it identifies this subordinate ruler as a devotee of Brahmanic gods.[3] Thus the two sides of the same tablet speak suggestively of the complex cultural history of this part of the delta: Brahmanism had flourished and was even patronized by a state whose official cult was Buddhism; on the other hand, the earliest-known representatives of Islam in this area appear to us in the context of the demolished ruins of Bengal's pre-Muslim past.

But were these men themselves temple-destroying iconoclasts? Can we think of them as *ghāzīs*—that is, men who waged religious war against non-Muslims? Such, indeed, is the perspective of much Orientalist scholarship. In the 1930s the German Orientalist Paul Wittek propounded the thesis that the Turkish drive westward across Anatolia at the expense of Byzantine Greek civilization had been propelled by an ethos of Islamic holy war, or *jihād*, against infidels. Although this thesis subsequently became established in Middle Eastern historiography, recent scholarship has shown that it suffers from lack of contemporary evidence.[4] Instead, as Rudi Lindner has argued, the association of a holy war ethic with the early rise of Ottoman power was the work of ideologues writing several centuries after the events they described. What they wrote, according to Lindner, amounted to an "*ex post facto* purification of early Ottoman deeds, [speaking] more of later propaganda than of early history."[5]

A similar historiographical pattern is found in Bengal. While it is true

2. Z. A. Desai, "An Early Thirteenth-Century Inscription from West Bengal," *Epigraphia Indica, Arabic and Persian Supplement* (1975): 6–12. The inscription was found in the village of Siwan, in Bolpur Thana of Birbhum District.

3. D. C. Sircar, "New Light on the Reign of Nayapala," *Bangladesh Itihas Parishad: Third History Congress, Proceedings* (Dacca: Bangladesh Itihas Parishad, 1973): 36–43.

4. Lindner, *Nomads and Ottomans*, 1–38; R. C. Jennings, "Some Thoughts on the Gazi Thesis," *Wiener Zeitschrift für die Kunde des Morgenlandes* 76 (1986): 151–61.

5. Lindner, *Nomads and Ottomans*, 7. See also Rudi Paul Lindner, "Stimulus and Justification in Early Ottoman History," in *Greek Orthodox Theological Review* 27, nos. 2–3 (Summer–Fall 1982): 207–24.

that Persian biographies often depict early Sufi holy men of Bengal as pious warriors waging war against the infidel, such biographies were not
contemporary with those Sufis. Take, for example, the case of Shaikh Jalal
al-Din Tabrizi (d. 1244–45), one of the earliest-known Sufis of Bengal. The
earliest notice of him appears in the *Siyar al-ʿārifīn*, a compendium of Sufi
biographies compiled around 1530–36, three centuries after the shaikh's
lifetime. According to this account, after initially studying Sufism in his
native Tabriz (in northwestern Iran), Jalal al-Din Tabrizi left around 1228
for Baghdad, where he studied for seven years with the renowned mystic
Shaikh Shihab al-Din Suhrawardi. When the latter died in 1235, Jalal al-
Din Tabrizi traveled to India and, not finding a warm welcome in the court
of Delhi, eventually moved on to Lakhnauti, then the remote provincial
capital of Bengal. There he remained until his death ten years later.[6]
"When he went to Bengal," the account records,

> all the population there came to him and became his disciples. There he
> built a hospice and a public kitchen, and bought several gardens and
> lands as an endowment for the kitchen. These increased. There was also
> there a (river) port called Deva Mahal, where an infidel had built a tem-
> ple at great cost. The shaikh destroyed that temple and in its place con-
> structed a (Sufi) rest-house [*takya*]. There, he made many infidels into
> Muslims. Today [i.e., 1530–36], his holy tomb is located at the very site
> of that temple, and half the income of that port is dedicated to the up-
> keep of the public kitchen there.[7]

Since no contemporary evidence shows that he or any other Sufi in Bengal
actually indulged in the destruction of temples, it is probable that as with
Turkish Sufis in contemporary Anatolia, later biographers reworked Jalal
al-Din Tabrizi's career for the purpose of expressing their own vision of
how the past ought to have happened. For such biographers, the shaikh's
alleged destruction of a Hindu temple, his conversion of the local population, and his raising a Sufi hospice on the temple site all defined for later
generations his imagined role as one who had made a decisive break between Bengal's Hindu past and its Muslim future.

Much the same hagiographical reconstruction was given the career of
Shah Jalal Mujarrad (d. 1346), Bengal's best-known Muslim saint. His biography was first recorded in the mid sixteenth century by a certain
Shaikh ʿAli (d. ca. 1562), a descendant of one of Shah Jalal's companions.
Once again we note a gap of several centuries between the life of the saint
and that of his earliest biographer. According to this account, Shah Jalal
had been born in Turkestan, where he became a spiritual disciple of Saiyid

6. Maulana Jamali, *Siyar al-ʿārifīn* (Delhi: Matbaʿ Rizvi, 1893), 164–69.
7. Ibid., 171.

Ahmad Yasawi, one of the founders of the Central Asian Sufi tradition.[8]
The account then casts the shaikh's expedition to India in the framework
of holy war, mentioning both his (lesser) war against the infidel and his
(greater) war against the lower self. "One day," the biographer recorded,
Shah Jalal

> represented to his bright-souled *pīr* [i.e., Ahmad Yasawi] that his ambi-
> tion was that just as with the guidance of the master he had achieved a
> certain amount of success in the Higher (spiritual) *jihād*, similarly with
> the help of his object-fulfilling courage he should achieve the desire of
> his heart in the Lesser (material) *jihād*, and wherever there may be a
> Dār-ul-Ḥarb [i.e., Land of non-Islam], in attempting its conquest he
> may attain the rank of a *ghāzī* or a *shahīd* [martyr]. The revered *pīr* ac-
> cepted his request and sent 700 of his senior fortunate disciples . . .
> along with him. Wherever they had a fight with the enemies, they un-
> furled the banner of victory.[9]

It is true that the notion of two "strivings" (*jihād*)—one against the unbe-
liever and the other against one's lower soul—had been current in the
Perso-Islamic world for several centuries before Shah Jalal's lifetime.[10] But
a fuller reading of the text suggests other motives for the shaikh's journey
to Bengal. After reaching the Indian subcontinent, he and his band of followers are said to have drifted to Sylhet, on the easternmost edge of the
Bengal delta. "In these far-flung campaigns," the narrative continued,
"they had no means of subsistence, except the booty, but they lived in
splendour. Whenever any valley or cattle were acquired, they were charged
with the responsibility of propagation and teaching of Islam. In short,
[Shah Jalal] reached Sirhat (Sylhet), one of the areas of the province of
Bengal, with 313 persons. [After defeating the ruler of the area] all the
region fell into the hands of the conquerors of the spiritual and the material worlds. Shaikh [Jalal] Mujarrad, making a portion for everybody, made
it their allowance and permitted them to get married."[11]

Written so long after the events it describes, this account has a certain

8. The account of Shaikh ʿAli was later reproduced in the well-known hagiography
Gulzār-i abrār, compiled ca. 1613, the relevant extracts of which were published
by S. M. Ikram, "An Unnoticed Account of Shaikh Jalal of Sylhet," *Journal of the
Asiatic Society of Pakistan* 2 (1957): 63–68. Since Ahmad Yasawi died in 1166,
Shah Jalal's own spiritual master must have been an unidentified intermediary between Yasawi and Shah Jalal.
9. Ibid., 66. Ikram's translation.
10. The oldest Persian treatise on Sufism, the *Kashf al-mahjūb* by ʿAli Hujwiri (d.
ca. 1072), composed in Lahore, had already elaborated Sufi ideas on the two kinds
of *jihād*. See *The Kashf al-mahjub*, trans. Reynold A. Nicholson, 2d ed. (reprint,
London: Luzac, 1970), 201.
11. Ikram, "Unnoticed Account," 66.

paradigmatic quality. Like Shaikh Jalal al-Din Tabrizi, Shah Jalal is presented as having brought about a break between Bengal's Hindu past and its Muslim future, and to this end a parallel is drawn between the career of the saint and that of the Prophet of Islam, Muhammad. The number of companions said to have accompanied Shah Jalal to Bengal, 313, corresponds precisely to the number of companions who are thought to have accompanied the Prophet Muhammad at the Battle of Badr in A.D. 624, the first major battle in Muhammad's career and a crucial event in launching Islam as a world religion. The story thus has an obvious ideological drive to it.

But other aspects of the narrative are more suggestive of Bengal's social atmosphere at the time of the conquest. References to "far-flung campaigns" where Shah Jalal's warrior-disciples "had no means of subsistence, except the booty" suggest the truly nomadic base of these Turkish freebooters, and, incidentally, refute the claim (made in the same narrative) that Shah Jalal's principal motive for coming to Bengal was religious in nature. In fact, reference to his having made "a portion for everybody" suggests the sort of behavior befitting a tribal chieftain vis-à-vis his pastoral retainers, while the reference to his permitting them to marry suggests a process by which mobile bands of unmarried nomads—Shah Jalal's own title *mujarrad* means "bachelor"—settled down as propertied groups rooted in local society. Moreover, the Persian text records that Shah Jalal had ordered his followers to become *kadkhudā*, a word that can mean either "householder" or "landlord."[12] Not having brought wives and families with them, his companions evidently married local women and, settling on the land, gradually became integrated with local society. All of this paralleled the early Ottoman experience. At the same time that Shah Jalal's nomadic followers were settling down in eastern Bengal, companions of Osman (d. 1326), the founder of the Ottoman dynasty, were also passing from a pastoral to a sedentary life in northwestern Anatolia.[13]

12. The Persian original, compiled in 1613 by Muhammad Ghauthi b. Hasan b. Musa Shattari, reads: "Shaikh Mujarrad hama-rā hiṣṣa sākhta . . . wa har yak-rā dastūrī-yi kadkhuda shudan nīz bar dād." *Gulzār-i abrār* (Asiatic Society of Bengal, Calcutta, Persian MS. 259), fol. 41a. The Persian version published by Ikram mistakenly reads: ". . . wa har yak-rā dastūrī ki khudā shudan nīz bar dād," which would mean, ". . . and he gave an order that each of them also become God"(!) Ikram, "Unnoticed Account," 65.

13. Lindner argues that "the pastoral Ottomans followed their own economic self-interest, that is, they settled because they made a much better and more secure living as landlords or cultivators in Bithynia." Moreover, "a given area used for cultivation, if it is as fertile as Bithynia, can support a much larger population than it can if used as pasture alone. The yield, in calories, of a plot of good land used for crops is much higher than the ultimate yield if that land is merely grazed." Lindner,

Fortunately, we are in a position to compare the later, hagiographic account of Shah Jalal's career with two independent non-hagiographic sources. The first is an inscription from Sylhet town, dated 1512–13, from which we learn that it was a certain Sikandar Khan Ghazi, and not the shaikh, who had actually conquered the town, and that this occurred in the year 1303–4.[14] The second is a contemporary account from the pen of the famous Moroccan traveler Ibn Battuta (d. 1377), who personally met Shah Jalal in 1345. The shaikh was quite an old man by then and sufficiently renowned throughout the Muslim world that the great world traveler made a considerable detour—he had been sailing from South India to China—in order to visit him. Traveling by boat up the Meghna and Surma rivers, Ibn Battuta spent three days as Shah Jalal's guest in his mountain cave near Sylhet town. As the Moroccan later recalled,

> This shaikh was one of the great saints and one of the unique personalities. He had to his credit miracles (*karāmat*) well known to the public as well as great deeds, and he was a man of hoary age. . . . The inhabitants of these mountains had embraced Islam at his hands, and for this reason he stayed amidst them.[15]

One would like to know more about the religious culture of these people prior to their conversion to Islam. The fragmentary evidence of Ibn Battuta's account suggests that they were indigenous peoples who had had little formal contact with literate representatives of Brahmanism or Buddhism, for the Moroccan visitor elsewhere describes the inhabitants of the East Bengal hills as "noted for their devotion to and practice of magic and witchcraft."[16] The remark seems to distinguish these people from the agrarian society of the Surma plains below the hills of Sylhet, a society Ibn Battuta unambiguously identifies as Hindu.[17] It is thus possible that in Shah Jalal these hill people had their first intense exposure to a formal, literate religious tradition.

Nomads and Ottomans, 30. The same arguments would apply to the Bengal delta, where the economic value of a plot of land in rice paddy is considerably greater than if it were used for pasture.

14. Shamsud-Din Ahmed, ed. and trans., *Inscriptions*, 4: 25. Shah Jalal's fame at the time of this inscription is evident from its opening lines, which honor "the exalted Shaikh of Shaikhs, the revered Shaikh Jalal, the ascetic, son of Muhammad." It is not clear to what building in Sylhet the inscription, currently preserved in the Dhaka Museum, was originally affixed.

15. Ibn Battuta, *The Rehla of Ibn Battuta*, trans. Mahdi Husain (Baroda: Oriental Institute, 1953), 238–39.

16. Ibid., 237–38.

17. "The inhabitants of *Habanq* [near Habiganj] are infidels under protection (*dhimma*) from whom half of the crops which they produce is taken." Ibid., 241.

In sum, the more contemporary evidence of Sufis on Bengal's political frontier portrays men who had entered the delta not as holy warriors but as pious mystics or freebooting settlers operating under the authority of charismatic leaders. No contemporary source endows them with the ideology of holy war; nor is there contemporary evidence that they slew non-Muslims or destroyed non-Muslim monuments. No Sufi of Bengal—and for that matter no Bengali sultan, whether in inscriptions or on coins—is known to have styled himself *ghāzī*. Such ideas only appear in hagiographical accounts written several centuries after the conquest. In particular, it seems that biographers and hagiographers of the sixteenth century consciously (or perhaps unconsciously) projected backward in time an ideology of conquest and conversion that had become prevalent in their own day. As part of that process, they refashioned the careers of holy men of the thirteenth and fourteenth centuries so as to fit within the framework of that ideology.

Bengali Sufis and Hindu Thought

From the beginning of the Indo-Turkish encounter with Bengal, one section of Muslims sought to integrate into their religious lives elements of the esoteric practices of local yogis, together with the cosmologies that underpinned those practices. Contemporary Muslims perceived northern Bengal generally, and especially Kamrup, lying between the Brahmaputra River and the hills of Bhutan, as a fabulous and mysterious place inhabited by expert practitioners of the occult, of yoga, and of magic. During his visit to Sylhet, Ibn Battuta noted that "the inhabitants of these mountains . . . are noted for their devotion to and practice of magic and witchcraft."[18] Around 1595 the great Mughal administrative manual *Ā'īn-i Akbarī* described the inhabitants of Kamrup as "addicted to the practice of magic [*jādūgarī*]."[19] Some twenty-five years later a Mughal officer serving in northern Bengal described the Khuntaghat region, in western Kamrup, as "notorious for magic and sorcery."[20] And in 1662–63 another Mughal chronicler, referring to the entire Assam region, of which Kamrup is the western part, remarked that "the people of India have come to look upon

18. Ibid., 237–38.
19. Abu'l-fazl 'Allami, *Ā'īn-i Akbarī* (Lucknow: Nawal Kishor, 1869), 2: 74. Vol. 1 trans. H. Blochmann, ed. D. C. Phillott; vols. 2 and 3 trans. H. S. Jarrett, ed. Jadunath Sarkar, 3d ed. (New Delhi: Oriental Books Reprint Corp., 1978), 2: 130.
20. Mirza Nathan, *Bahāristān-i ghaibī*, Persian MS., Bibliothèque nationale, Paris, Sup. Pers. 252, fol. 146b; trans. M. I. Borah as *Bahāristān-i-ghaybī: A History of the Mughal Wars in Assam, Cooch Behar, Bengal, Bihar and Orissa during the reigns of Jahāngīr and Shāhjahān, by Mīrza Nathan* (Gauhati: Government of Assam, 1936), 1: 273.

the Assamese as sorcerers, and use the word 'Assam' in such formulas as dispel witchcraft."[21]

Since Sufis were especially concerned with apprehending transcendent reality unmediated by priests or other worldly institutions, it is not surprising that they, among Muslims, were most attracted to the yogi traditions of Kamrup. Within the very first decade of the Turkish conquest, there began to circulate in the delta Persian and Arabic translations of a Sanskrit manual on tantric yoga entitled *Amṛtakuṇḍa* ("The Pool of Nectar"). According to the translated versions, the Sanskrit text had been composed by a Brahman yogi of Kamrup who had converted to Islam and presented the work to the chief *qāẓī*, or judge, of Lakhnauti, Rukn al-Din Samarqandi (d. 1218). The latter, in turn, is said to have made the first translations of the work into Arabic and Persian.[22] While this last point is uncertain, there is no doubt that for the following five hundred years the *Amṛtakuṇḍa*, through its repeated translations into Arabic and Persian, circulated widely among Sufis of Bengal, and even throughout India.[23] The North Indian Sufi Shaikh ʿAbd al-Quddus Gangohi (d. 1537) is known to

21. Shihab al-Din Talish, *Fatḥiyah-i ʿibriyah*, in H. Blochmann, "Koch Bihar, Koch Hajo, and Assam in the 16th and 17th Centuries, According to the Akbarnamah, the Padshahnamah, and the Fathiyah i 'Ibriyah," *Journal of the Asiatic Society of Bengal* 41, no. 1 (1872): 79.

22. For notices on Rukn al-Din Samarqandi, see *Encyclopaedia of Islam*, new ed. (Leiden: Brill, 1960), 1: 434–35. For a discussion of the problems of identifying the translators of the *Amṛtakuṇḍa*, see Yusuf Husain, "Haud al-hayat: La Version arabe de l'Amratkund," *Journal asiatique* 113 (October–December 1928): 292–95.

23. Although there are no known copies of the original Sanskrit work, there are many translations in Islamic languages, indicating the enormous influence this work had in and beyond Bengal. *Islamic Culture* 21 (1947): 191–92 refers to a Persian manuscript version of the text, entitled *Baḥr al-ḥayāt*, preserved in the library of Pir Muhammad Shah in Ahmedabad, Gujarat (No. 223). Another Persian copy of this work is in the India Office Library, London (Persian MS. No. 2002). A third manuscript copy is in the Ganj Bakhsh Library, Rawalpindi (MS. No. 6298). A fourth, dating to the late sixteenth or early seventeenth century, and containing twenty-one illustrations of yogic postures, is in the library of A. Chester Beatty in Dublin; see Thomas A. Arnold, *The Library of A. Chester Beatty: A Catalogue of the Indian Miniatures*, revised and ed. J. V. S. Wilkinson (London: Oxford University Press, 1936), 1: 80–81, 3: 98. According to the *Islamic Culture* article cited above (p. 192), an edition of the Persian *Baḥr al-ḥayāt* was published in Madras in 1892–93. Arabic translations of the *Amṛtakuṇḍa* are entitled *Ḥauz al-ḥayāt*, and five of those preserved in European libraries were compared and analyzed by Yusuf Husain in his article "Haud al-hayat: La Version arabe," to which the author appended an Arabic version of the text. Carl Ernst, who is now preparing for publication a critical edition of the Arabic text, together with an annotated translation and monographic introduction, has identified forty manuscript copies of Arabic translations, seventeen of which are in Istanbul. Turkish translations began appearing in the mid eighteenth century, and one was published in 1910–11. A nineteenth-century Urdu translation survives in a manuscript in Hyderabad,

have absorbed the yogic ideas of the *Amṛtakuṇḍa* and to have taught them to his own disciples.[24] In the mid seventeenth century, the Kashmiri author Muhsin Fani recorded that he had seen a Persian translation of the *Amṛtakuṇḍa*,[25] and in the same century the Anatolian Sufi scholar Muhammad al-Misri (d. 1694) cited the *Amṛtakuṇḍa* as an important book for the study of yogic practices, noting that in India such practices had become partly integrated with Sufism.[26]

In both its Persian and Arabic translations, the *Amṛtakuṇḍa* survives as a manual of tantric yoga, with the first of its ten chapters affirming the characteristically tantric correspondence between parts of the human body and parts of the macrocosm, "where all that is large in the world discovers itself in the small." In the mid sixteenth century, there appeared in Gujarat a Persian recension of the *Amṛtakuṇḍa* under the title *Baḥr al-ḥayāṭ*, attributed to the great Shattari shaikh Muhammad Ghauth of Gwalior (d. 1563).[27] A prologue to this version, written by a disciple of the shaikh, records how these yogic ideas were thought to have entered the Bengali Sufi tradition:

> This wonderful and strange book is named *Amṛtakuṇḍa* in the Indian language [i.e., Sanskrit]. This means "Water of Life," and the reason for the appearance of this book among the Muslims is as follows. When Sultan 'Ala al-Din [i.e., 'Ali Mardan] conquered Bengal and Islam became manifest there, news of these events reached the ears of a certain gentleman of the esteemed learned class in Kamrup. His name was Kama, and he was a master of the science of yoga.
>
> In order to debate with the Muslim *'ulamā* [scholars] he arrived in the city of Lakhnauti, and on a Friday he entered the Congregational Mosque. A number of Muslims showed him to a group of *'ulamā*, and they in turn pointed him to the assembly of Qazi Rukn al-Din Samarqandi. So he went to this group and asked: "Whom do you worship?" They replied, "We worship the Faultless God." To his question "Who is your leader?" they replied, "Muhammad, the Messenger of Allah." He said, "What has your leader said about the Spirit [*rūḥ*]?" They replied,

---

India. See Carl W. Ernst, trans., *The Arabic Version of "The Pool of the Water of Life"* (*Amṛtakuṇḍa*), forthcoming.

24. S. A. A. Rizvi, *A History of Sufism in India* (Delhi: Munshiram Manoharlal, 1978), 1: 335.

25. Muhsin Fani, *Dabistān-i maẕāhib*, ed. Nazir Ashraf and W. B. Bayley (Calcutta, 1809), 224.

26. Husain, "Haud al-hayat: La Version arabe," 294.

27. The *Gulzār al-abrār*, compiled around 1613, or just fifty years after the death of Shaikh Muhammad Ghauth, mentions a translation (from the Arabic to Persian) of the *Baḥr al-ḥayāt* as among the written works of the great saint of Gwalior. See Muhammad Ghauthi Shattari Mandawi, *Gulzār-i abrār*, Urdu trans. by Fazl Ahmad Jiwari (Lahore: Islamic Book Foundation, 1975), 300.

"God the All-nourishing has commanded (that there be) the Spirit." He said, "In truth, I too have found this same thing in books that are subtle and committed to memory."

Then that man converted to Islam and busied himself in acquiring religious knowledge, and he soon thereafter became a scholar (*muftī*). After that he wrote and presented this book to Qazi Rukn al-Din Tamami [Samarqandi]. The latter translated it from the Indian language into Arabic in a book of thirty chapters, and somebody else translated it into Persian in a book of ten chapters. . . . And when Hazrat Ghauth al-Din himself went to Kamrup he necessarily spent several years in studying this science. . . . The name of this book is *Baḥr al-ḥayāṭ*.[28]

The exchange between the yogi and the *qāzī* cited here appears to have been modeled on a passage in the Qur'an (17:85), in which God tells the Prophet Muhammad: "They [the Jews] will ask thee concerning the Spirit. Say: the Spirit is by command of my Lord." By putting into the mouth of a yogi words that in the Qur'an were those of the Jews of Muhammad's day, the author of this recension apparently intended to make the yogi's exchange comprehensible to a Muslim audience.

A second prologue to the *Baḥr al-ḥayāṭ* established a framework within which a text on yoga could be accommodated within the rich body of classical Sufi lore. In it, the translator tells of once being in a country whose king summoned him and ordered that he undertake a great journey to a distant but fabulous realm. The king reminded the traveler that they were joined together by a covenant and that they would meet again at the end of the traveler's voyage. Then the translator/traveler describes the hardships he endured while on his journey: the two seas (the soul and nature), the seven mountains, the four passes, the three stations filled with dangers, and the path narrower than the eye of an ant. Ultimately, he reached the promised land, where he found a shaikh who mirrored or echoed each of his own moves and words. Realizing that the man was but his own reflection, the traveler remembered his covenant with his master, to whom he was now led. The story's climax is reached in the traveler's epiphanic self-discovery: "I found the king and minister in myself."[29] The dominant motifs of this second prologue—the traveler, the arduous path with its temptations and dangers, and the ultimate realization that the goal is identified with the seeker—all show the influence of Sufi notions current in the

---

28. *Islamic Culture* 21 (1947), 191–92. The Persian extract published in *Islamic Culture* was taken from a manuscript copy of the *Baḥr al-ḥayāṭ* in the library of Pir Muhammad Shah of Ahmadabad (No. 223). See also the copy in the India Office Library, Persian MS. 2002, fols. 2a–3a, in which the yogi's name is given as Kanama.

29. *Baḥr al-ḥayāṭ* (India Office Library, London, Persian MS. 2002), fols. 3a–6b.

thirteenth-century Perso-Islamic world.[30] The placement of the yogic text immediately after this prologue suggests that the esoteric practices described therein constitute, in effect, the means to achieving the mystical goals stated in the second prologue.

Although some scholars have regarded the *Bahr al-ḥayāt* as a work of religious syncretism, this judgment is difficult to sustain if by syncretism one means the production of a new synthesis out of two or more antithetical elements.[31] Rather, the work consists of two independent and self-contained worldviews placed alongside one another—a technical manual of yoga preceded by a Sufi allegory—with later editors or translators going to some lengths to stress their points of coincidence. Although Islamic terms and superhuman agencies are generously sprinkled through the main text, allusions to Islamic lore serve ultimately to buttress or illustrate thoroughly Indian concepts.[32] Here, at least, yoga and Sufi ideas resisted true fusion.

Nonetheless the book's popularity illustrates the Sufis' considerable fascination with the esoteric practices of Bengal's indigenous culture. The renowned Shattari saint Shaikh Muhammad Ghauth even traveled from

30. In particular, they recall the classic statement of the Sufi path, *The Conference of the Birds*, or *Mantiq al-tayr*, composed by Farid al-Din ʿAttar (d. 1220). In fact, since both ʿAttar and Shaikh Rukn al-Din Samarqandi, perhaps the first translator of the *Amṛtakuṇḍa*, were contemporaries in Khurasan toward the end of the twelfth century, it is possible that the latter was familiar with ʿAttar's mystical philosophy. Certainly, both were steeped in the same Perso-Islamic literary and religious culture. On the other hand, it is possible that this second prologue was written not by Samarqandi but by Muhammad Ghauth three centuries later, since we know that the latter retranslated the work into Persian. Carl Ernst, following the views of Henry Corbin, has argued that the frame story was ultimately derived from the "Hymn of the Pearl," found in the gnostic Acts of Thomas. See Ernst, *Arabic Version* (forthcoming), and Henry Corbin, "Pour une morphologie de la spiritualité Shīʿite," *Eranos-Jahrbuch 1960* (Zurich: Rhein-Verlag, 1961), 29: 102–7.

31. Yusuf Husain, among others, has argued for the work's syncretic nature. See Husain, "Haud al-hayat: La Version arabe," 292.

32. For example, in a passage in which proper breathing technique is compared with the way a foetus breathes in its mother's womb, the foetus is identified with al-Khiẓr, a popular saint in Islamic lore, associated with water and eternal life. Again, where such techniques are compared with the way a fish breathes in water without swallowing it, the fish is identified with the one that swallowed the Prophet Jonah. And the seven Sanskrit mantras associated with the seven spinal nerve centers are all identified with Arabic names of God, so that, for example, *hūm* is translated as *Yā rabb* ("O Lord"), and *aum* is translated *Yā qadīm* ("O Ancient One"). These were not so much "translations" as they were attempts at finding functional equivalents between yogic words of spiritual power and the names of God as used by the Sufis. See Yusuf Husain, "Haud al-hayat: La Version arabe," 300, and Ernst, *Arabic Version* (forthcoming).

Gwalior in Upper India to Kamrup in order to study the esoteric knowledge that Muslims had identified with that region. In doing so he was following a tradition of Sufis of the Shattari order, whose founder, Shah 'Abd Allah Shattari (d. 1485), included Bengal on his journey from Central Asia through India.[33] Although one cannot establish a continuous intellectual tradition between Bengali Muslims of the thirteenth century and the Shattari Sufis of the fifteenth and sixteenth centuries, the association of the *Baḥr al-ḥayāṭ* both with Rukn al-Din Samarqandi in the former century and with Shaikh Muhammad Ghauth in the latter century suggests the likelihood of its continued use in Bengal during the intervening period.

Sufis of the Capital

The principal carriers of the Islamic literary and intellectual tradition in the Bengal sultanate were groups of distinguished and influential Sufis who resided in the successive capital cities of Lakhnauti (from 1204), Pandua (from ca. 1342), and Gaur (from ca. 1432). Most of these men belonged to organized Sufi brotherhoods—especially the Suhrawardi, the Firdausi, and the Chishti orders—and what we know of them can be ascertained mainly from their extant letters and biographical accounts. The urban Sufis about whom we have the most information are clustered in the early sultanate period, from the founding of the independent Ilyas Shahi dynasty at Pandua in 1342 to the end of the Raja Ganesh revolution in 1415.[34]

The political roles played by Sufis in Bengal's capital were shaped by ideas of Sufi authority that had already evolved in the contemporary Persian-speaking world. We have already referred to the central place that Sufi traditions assigned to powerful saints, a sentiment captured in 'Ali

33. While in Bengal, Shah 'Abd Allah made a spiritual disciple of Shaikh Muhammad 'Ala, who enthusiastically propagated the Shattari order in the delta, and whose own spiritual successor, Shaikh Zuhur Baba Haji Hamid (d. 1524), was the spiritual master of Shaikh Muhammad Ghauth. Rizvi, *History of Sufism in India*, 2: 153–55. Muhammad Ghauth's elder brother, Shaikh Bahlul, also resided in Bengal after having arrived with the first Mughal invasion in 1538. Jahangir, *Tūzuk-i Jahāngīrī* 2: 63.

34. Around 1414 the Chishti shaikh Ashraf Jahangir Simnani stated that seventy disciples of Shaikh Shihab al-Din Suhrawardi (d. 1144) had been buried in Devgaon (site not identified), and that other Sufis of the Suhrawardi order, together with followers of Shaikh Jalal al-Din Tabrizi (see above), were buried in Mahisantosh and Deotala, both near Pandua. "In short," he noted, "in the country of Bengal, not to speak of the cities, there is no town and no village where holy saints did not come and settle down." Shaikh Ashraf Jahangir Simnani, *Maktūbāt-i ashrafī*, Aligarh Muslim University History Department, Aligarh, Persian MS. no. 27, letter 45, fols. 139b–140a. See also S. H. Askari, "New Light on Rajah Ganesh and Sultan Ibrahim Sharqi of Jaunpur from Contemporary Correspondence of Two Muslim Saints," *Bengal Past and Present* 57 (1948): 35.

Hujwiri's statement that God had "made the Saints the governors of the universe." Being in theory closer to God than warring princes could ever hope to be, Muslim saints staked a moral claim as God's representatives on earth. In this view, princely rulers possessed no natural right to earthly power, but had only been entrusted with a temporary lease on such power through the grace of some Muslim saint. This perspective perhaps explains why in Indo-Muslim history we so often find Sufis predicting who would attain political office, and for how long they would hold it. For behind the explicit act of "prediction" lay the implicit act of appointment—that is, of a Sufi's entrusting his *wilāyat*, or earthly domain, to a prince. For example, the fourteenth-century historian Shams-i Siraj 'Afif recorded that before his rise to royal stature, the future Sultan Ghiyath al-Din Tughluq, founder of the Tughluq dynasty of Delhi (1321–1398), had been one of many local notables attracted to the spiritual power of the grandson of the famous Chishti Sufi Shaikh Farid al-Din Ganj-i Shakar (d. 1265). The governor made frequent visits to the holy man's lodge in the Punjab, and on one occasion brought along his son and nephew, the future sultans Muhammad bin Tughluq and Firuz Tughluq. All three were given turbans by the saint and told that each was destined to rule India. The length of each turban, moreover, exactly corresponded to the number of years each would reign.[35] In this anecdote one may discern the seeds of the complex pattern of mutual patronage between shaikhs of the Chishti order and one of the mightiest empires in India's history.

Similar traditions circulated in Bengal concerning the foundation of independent Muslim rule there. In 1243–44 the historian Minhaj al-Siraj visited Lakhnauti, where he recorded the following anecdote.[36] Before embarking for India, the future sultan of Bengal Ghiyath al-Din 'Iwaz (1213–27) was once traveling with his laden donkey along a dusty road in Afghanistan. There he came upon two dervishes clothed in ragged cloaks. When the two asked the future ruler whether he had any food, the latter replied that he did and took the load down from the donkey's back. Spreading his garments on the ground, he offered the dervishes whatever victuals he had. After they had eaten, the grateful dervishes remarked to each other that such kindness should not go unrewarded. Turning to their benefactor, they said, "Go thou to Hindustan, for that place, which is the extreme (point) of Muhammadanism, we have given unto thee." At once the future

35. Shams-i Siraj 'Afif, *Tārīkh-i Fīrūz Shāhī*, ed. Maulavi Vilayat Husain. (Calcutta: Asiatic Society of Bengal, 1891), 27–28.
36. Since Sultan Ghiyath al-Din 'Iwaz had died only seventeen years before Minhaj's visit, it is probable that this story had been in circulation in the Bengali capital soon after, and perhaps during, the king's reign.

sultan gathered together his family and set out for India "in accord with
the intimation of those two Darweshes."³⁷ In the Perso-Islamic cultural
universe of the thirteenth and fourteenth centuries, Bengal really did in
some sense "belong" to those two dervishes, that they might "entrust" it
to a kind stranger.

In Bengal as in North India, the connection between political fortune
and spiritual blessing is most evident in the early history of the Chishti
order, the order to which the most ascendant shaikhs of early-fourteenth-
century Delhi belonged. "Anybody who was anyone," as Simon Digby puts
it, visited the lodge of Delhi's most eminent shaikh of the time, Nizam al-
Din Auliya (d. 1325). Indeed, the two principal Persian poets of the early
fourteenth century, Amir Khusrau and Amir Hasan, together with the sultanate's leading contemporary historian, Zia al-Din Barani, were all spiritual disciples of this shaikh. Since Delhi at this time happened to be the
capital of a vital and expanding empire, it is not surprising that the literary,
cultural, and institutional traditions of that city—together with the
shaikhs and institutions of its dominant Sufi order—expanded along with
Khalaji and Tughluq arms to the far corners of India, including Bengal.³⁸

But there was a deeper reason why Indo-Muslim courts patronized
Chishti shaikhs. By the fourteenth century, when other Sufi orders in India
still looked to Central Asia or the Middle East as their spiritual home, the
Chishtis, with their major shrines located within the Indian subcontinent,
had become thoroughly indigenized. Seeking to establish their legitimacy
both as Muslims and as Indians, Indo-Muslim rulers therefore turned to
prominent shaikhs of this order for blessings and support. For the same
reason, leading Chishti shaikhs dispersed from Shaikh Nizam al-Din's
lodge to all parts of the empire and often enjoyed the patronage of
provincial rulers. Conversely, many young Indian-born Muslims journeyed from all over India to live in or near that shaikh's lodge, later to
return to their native lands, where they would establish daughter Chishti
lodges and enjoy the patronage of local rulers (see table 2).

The first Bengal-born Muslim known to have studied with Shaikh
Nizam al-Din was Akhi Siraj al-Din (d. 1357), who journeyed to Delhi as

37. Minhaj-ud-Din 'Usman, *Ṭabakāt-i-Nāṣirī*, 1: 581.
38. Simon Digby, "The Sufi Shaikh as a Source of Authority in Mediaeval India,"
in *Puruṣārtha*, vol. 9: *Islam et société en Asie du sud*, ed. Marc Gaborieau (Paris:
Ecole des Hautes études en sciences sociales, 1986), 68–69. Even when Bengal was
independent of Delhi, prominent shaikhs of this order maintained close institutional links with North India—a circumstance that led A. B. M. Habibullah to describe the Chishtis of Bengal as a sort of "fifth column" for the Delhi sultanate.
A. B. M. Habibullah, review of Abdul Karim, *Social History of the Muslims in
Bengal*, in *Journal of the Asiatic Society of Pakistan* 5 (1960): 216–17.

Table 2. Leading Chishti Sufis of Bengal

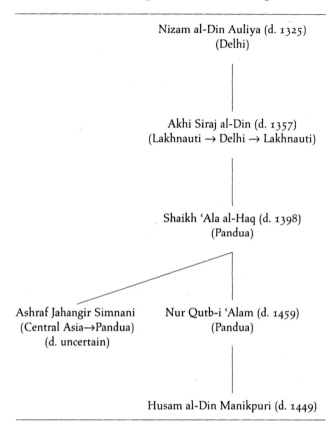

Nizam al-Din Auliya (d. 1325)
(Delhi)

Akhi Siraj al-Din (d. 1357)
(Lakhnauti → Delhi → Lakhnauti)

Shaikh 'Ala al-Haq (d. 1398)
(Pandua)

Ashraf Jahangir Simnani   Nur Qutb-i 'Alam (d. 1459)
(Central Asia→Pandua)   (Pandua)
(d. uncertain)

Husam al-Din Manikpuri (d. 1449)

a young man. Having distinguished himself at the Sufi lodge of the renowned shaikh, Siraj al-Din received a certificate of succession and so thoroughly associated himself with the North Indian Chishti tradition that he
was given the epithet "Āyina-yi Hindūstān," or "Mirror of Hindustan."
Returning to Bengal some time before 1325, when his master died, he
inducted others into the Chishti discipline, his foremost pupil being another Bengal-born Muslim, Shaikh 'Ala al-Haq (d. 1398).[39] But unlike his
own teacher, who had no known dealings with royalty,[40] Shaikh 'Ala al-

39. 'Abd al-Rahman Chishti, *Mirāt al-asrār*, fol. 514a.
40. Indeed, Akhi Siraj endeavored to break his more highborn disciples of their
aristocratic ways. In the case of 'Ala al-Haq, whose father was a prominent migrant
from Lahore and the treasurer of Bengal's provincial government, Siraj taught his
disciple to humble himself by walking with a hot cauldron on his head through
the quarter of Lakhnauti where his family lived. *Akhbār al-akhyār*, comp. 'Abd al-
Haq Muhaddis Dihlavi (Deoband, U.P.: Kitab Khana-yi Rahimia, 1915–16), 149. In

Haq was destined to play a special role in the political history of Muslim Bengal. In fact, the earliest-known monument built by the founder of Bengal's longest-lived dynasty, the Ilyas Shahi line of kings (1342–1486), was dedicated to this shaikh. On a mosque built in 1342 in what is now part of Calcutta, Shams al-Din Ilyas Shah praised the Sufi as "the benevolent and revered saint (Shaikh) whose acts of virtue are attractive and sublime, inspired by Allah, may He illuminate his heart with the light of divine perception and faith, and he is the guide to the religion of the Glorious, 'Alaul-Haqq . . . may his piety last long."[41]

The importance of this inscription derives from its political context. Shams al-Din Ilyas Shah, an ambitious and politically astute newcomer to the delta, was just then launching a bid for independence from Delhi, evidently using southwestern Bengal as his power base. The imperial governor of nearby Satgaon having recently died, Shams al-Din, aware that Delhi was convulsed by the various crises provoked by the eccentric Sultan Muhammad bin Tughluq, seized the moment to attain provincewide power.[42] As his earliest-known coin was minted at Pandua in A.D. 1342–43 (A.H. 743),[43] Shams al-Din's ascendancy exactly synchronizes with the dedication of this mosque and his patronage of Shaikh 'Ala al-Haq. Moreover, the patronage of the two men was mutual, since Shaikh 'Ala al-Haq, attaching himself to this rising political star, adopted Shams al-Din as a recipient of his teachings and blessings. This early connection cemented an alliance between government and prominent Chishti shaikhs that would last for the duration of Muslim rule in Bengal.

Not all alliances between Sufis and sultans were initiated by would-be rulers seeking to broaden their political bases. Some Sufis were drawn to the court out of a fervent desire to advance the cause of Islam as they understood it, and to augment the welfare of Muslims in the realm. We see this in the correspondence between Muzaffar Shams Balkhi (d. 1400) and Sultan Ghiyath al-Din A'zam Shah (r. 1389–1410). An immigrant from Central Asia, Muzaffar had left his native Balkh for Delhi, where he

---

1357 Akhi Siraj died and was buried in a suburb of Lakhnauti. Alexander Cunningham identified his tomb and shrine with a high mound in "Sadullahpur," near the northeast corner of the Sagar Dighi tank. Cunningham, "Report of a Tour in Bihar and Bengal in 1879–80 from Patna to Sunargaon," in *Archaeological Survey of India, Report* 15 (Calcutta, 1882): 70.

41. Shamsud-Din Ahmed, ed. and trans., *Inscriptions*, 4: 31–33. The editor himself found the stone with this inscription "while strolling through the eastern suburb of Calcutta, early in 1939." He was told that around 1900 the stone had been picked up from a ruined mosque in the neighborhood.

42. Ibid., 32.

43. Karim, *Corpus*, 47.

taught at the college of Firuz Shah Tughluq. But the man's restless spirit led him to Bihar city, where, after meeting and becoming the disciple of the great Firdausi shaikh Sharaf al-Din Maneri (d. 1381), he experienced a major change in life-orientation. Abandoning his pride in scholarship, Muzaffar subjected himself to various austerities and distributed all his worldly possessions in charity. He also made several pilgrimages to Mecca, where he once stayed for four years, teaching lessons in *hadīth* scholarship.[44] His extant letters reveal him not as an ecstatic, quiescent, or contemplative sort, but as committed to imposing his understanding of the Prophet's religious vision on the here-and-now world, a man inclined to scrutinize human society by scriptural standards and, finding it wanting, to transform it so as to meet those standards. In the sultan of Bengal, the Sufi found an outlet for these impulses.

Muzaffar Shams first seems to have become concerned about tutoring Sultan Ghiyath al-Din while waiting in Pandua for official permission to embark on a trip from Chittagong to Mecca. "The four months of the ship season are ahead of us," he wrote; "there are eight months still left; during all this while I have spent my life as a guest in the auspicious threshold of your majesty, may not your exaltation lessen."[45] Although the Sufi politely described himself as a mere "guest" of the sultan, it is evident that he felt himself entrusted with a higher calling. "In my opinion," he wrote the king,

> by the gifts of God, the cherisher of mankind, you have developed a capacity of looking at the inside of things of the pure faith and the understanding of things of manifold signification. It appears that my heart would be opened out to you. A pious inspired man, Abdul Malik, has been a recipient of my letters[,] which might form a volume. It may be at Pandua or at Muazzamabad, but I don't remember where it exactly is. Oh, my son, get the permission and go through its contents. Something of my inward part may be opened out to you. You are the second person on whom I have poured out my secret (mystic) thoughts. It behooves you not to disclose these to anyone else.[46]

Who, here, is patronizing whom? The Sufi's reference to the sultan as his "son" signals a clear inversion of the usual relationship between a patrimo-

44. S. H. Askari, *Maktub and Malfuz Literature as a Source of Socio-Political History* (Patna: Khuda Bakhsh Oriental Public Library, 1981), 22.

45. Muzaffar Shams Balkhi, *Maktūbāt-i Muzaffar Shams Balkhī* (Khuda Bakhsh Oriental Public Library, Patna, Persian MS., Acc. no. 1859), letter 148, p. 448. Partially translated by S. H. Askari in *Maktub and Malfuz Literature*, 16. Askari's translation.

46. The Sufi then advised the sultan that whenever he was confronted with an important concern, he should notify the Sufi of it by sending either a letter or a

nial king and his subjects. Nor would the Sufi give the king privileged access to his personal correspondence; to see it the monarch had first to secure permission from a third party. Muzaffar Balkhi also reminded the king that although Sultan Firuz Tughluq of Delhi had repeatedly requested letters and spiritual guidance from Muzaffar's own master, Shaikh Sharaf al-Din Maneri, the latter had refused to oblige him, choosing instead to correspond with Sultan Sikandar of Bengal, Ghiyath al-Din's father. "You," he noted pointedly, "have had the effects and legacy of those blessings on yourself."[47] In short, Muzaffar felt that he and his own master had been doing the Bengal sultans a favor by bestowing their blessings and advice on them instead of on the sultans of Delhi.[48]

In addition to his recommendations concerning Islamic piety—for example, on the need to suppress innovation not prescribed by the Shari'a, or to enforce the payment of alms by Muslims[49]—Muzaffar cautioned the king against placing non-Muslims in positions of authority. "The substance of what has come in the tradition and commentaries," wrote the shaikh, "is this":

> "Oh believers, don't make strangers, that is infidels, your confidential favourites and ministers of state." They say that they don't allow any to approach or come near to them and become favourite courtiers; but it was done evidently and for expedience and worldly exigency of the Sultanate that they are entrusted with some affairs. To this the reply is that according to God it is neither expediency nor exigency but the reverse of it, that is an evil and pernicious thing. . . . Don't entrust a work into the hands of infidels by reason of which they would become a *walī* (Governor-ruler or superior) over the Musalmans, exercise their authority in their affairs, and impose their command over them. As God says in the Quran, "It is not proper for a believer to trust an infidel as his friend and *walī*, and those who do so have no place in the estimation of God." Hear God and be devout and pious; very severe warnings have come in the Kitab (holy book) and traditions against the appointment of infidels as a ruler over the believers.[50]

messenger to Mecca. Balkhi, *Maktūbāt*, letter 163, p. 493. See also Askari, *Maktub and Malfuz Literature*, 19. Askari's translation.

47. Balkhi, *Maktūbāt*, letter 163, p. 503. See also Askari, *Maktub and Malfuz Literature*, 21. Askari's translation.

48. Also at work here was a keen rivalry between two major Sufi orders for royal patronage—the Chishtis, who were dominant in Delhi, and the Firdausis, who under Shaikh Sharaf al-Din Maneri's leadership were dominant in Bihar. In this correspondence, the Firdausis were clearly making a bid for patronage from the kings of Bengal. For the Firdausi-Chishti rivalry, see Digby, "Sufi Shaikh as a Source," 65–67.

49. Balkhi, *Maktūbāt*, letter 165, p. 495. See also Askari, *Maktub and Malfuz Literature*, 20.

50. Balkhi, *Maktūbāt*, letter 165, pp. 508–9. See also Askari, *Maktub and Malfuz Literature*, 22. Askari's translation.

The Sufi thus saw in Islamic Law a clear course of action the sultan should take in order to avert certain disaster. For in Bengal's affairs Muzaffar Shams discerned more than just a political crisis. Referring to Timur's recent sacking of Delhi (A.D. 1398, or A.H. 801), which marked the eclipse of the once-mighty Tughluq empire, he wrote: "The eighth century has passed out, and the signs of the coming Resurrection are increasingly visible. An Empire like that of Delhi with all its expanse and abundance, spiritual and physical comfort, peace and tranquility, has turned upside down (is in a topsy-turvy condition). Infidelity has now come to hold the field; the condition of other countries is no better. Now is the time, and this is the opportunity."[51] His gaze riveted on scripture, Muzaffar saw a palpable link between worldly decay and the Day of Judgment, heralded by that decay. Only by removing infidelity could Muslims forestall an otherwise inevitable cosmic process. And since the sultan had the power to stamp out infidelity by suppressing non-Muslims in a kingdom originally established by Muslims, the Sufi saw the sultan as capable of playing a pivotal role in implementing what he understood as God's will in that process.

It was shaikhs of the Chishti order, however, who by the early fifteenth century had emerged as the principal spokesmen for a Muslim communal perspective in Bengal. If Shaikh 'Ala al-Haq had risen to prominence with the ascending fortunes of the founder of the Ilyas Shahi dynasty, his son and successor, Nur Qutb-i 'Alam (d. 1459), presided over Bengal's Chishti tradition when Ilyas Shahi fortunes had sunk to their lowest point—the period of Raja Ganesh's domination over the Ilyas Shahi throne.[52] According to Sufi sources, Raja Ganesh even persecuted Chishti shaikhs, banishing Nur Qutb-i 'Alam's own son, Shaikh Anwar, to Sonargaon, and plotting the death of the son of another Chishti shaikh, Husain Dhukkar-

---

51. Balkhi, *Maktūbāt*, letter 165, p. 502. See also Askari, *Maktub and Malfuz Literature*, 21. Askari's translation.

52. The traditional date of Shaikh Nur Qutb-i 'Alam's death is 818 A.H. (1415–16 A.D.), as recorded in the *Mirāt al-asrār* (fol. 603b). But this date conflicts with the same work's statement that the shaikh was the spiritual teacher of Sultan Ahmad, who ruled in 1432–33 (ibid., fol. 517b). Moreover, an inscription at the kitchen of Nur Qutb-i 'Alam's shrine in Pandua honors "Our revered master, the Teacher of Imams, the Proof of the congregation, the Sun of the Faith, the Testimony of Islam and of the Muslims, who bestowed advantages upon the poor and the indigent, the Guide of saints and of such as wish to be guided." The inscription gives the death of this unnamed saint, who is evidently Nur Qutb-i 'Alam, as 28 Zi'l-Hajj, 863, or 1459 A.D. (see Dani, "House of Raja Ganesh," 139–40). The shaikh's surviving writings attest to the vitality of Chishti thought and traditions in the capital city at this time. A surviving mystical work of his is the *Mu'nis al-fuqarā'* (Asiatic Society of Bengal, Calcutta, Persian MS. No. 466). We also have his letters, the *Maktūbāt-i Shaikh Nūr Qutb-i 'Ālam* (Indian National Archives, New Delhi, Persian MS., Or. MS. No. 332, and Maulana Azad Library, Aligarh Muslim University, Aligarh, Subhan Allah No. 297671/18).

posh.[53] In these circumstances, as noted in Chapter 2, the shaikh implored Sultan Ibrahim Sharqi of Jaunpur to invade Bengal and remove the "menace" of Raja Ganesh. The following passage shows the extent to which the Chishtis of Bengal had come to identify the fortunes of Islam with the political fortunes of the Ilyas Shahi dynasty. "After a period of three hundred years," wrote the Sufi, "the Islamic land of Bengal—the place of mortals, the kingdom of the end of the seven heavens—has been overwhelmed and put to the run by the darkness of infidels and the power of unbelievers." The shaikh elaborated this point using the Sufi and Qur'anic metaphor of light:

> The lamp of the Islamic religion and of true guidance
>   Which had [formerly] brightened every corner with its light,
> Has been extinguished by the wind of unbelief blown by Raja Ganesh.
>   Splendor from envy of the victorious news,
> The lamp of [the celebrated preacher, Abu'l-Husain] Nuri, and the
>   candle of [the Shi'a martyr] Husain
>   Have all been extinguished by the might of swords and the power
>   of this thing in view.
> What does one call the lamp and candle of men
>   Whose nature is devoid of virility [lit., "has eaten camphor"]?
> When the abode of faith and Islam has fallen into such a fate,
>   Why are you sitting happily on your throne?
> Arise, come and defend the religion,
>   For it is incumbent upon you,
>   O king, possessed of power and capacity.[54]

While publicly clamoring for military intervention, privately, in a letter to his exiled son, Nur Qutb-i 'Alam brooded over the theological implications of Raja Ganesh's appearance in Bengali history. To the anguished Sufi, it seemed that God had not been heeding the supplication of the very people to whom the Qur'an had promised divine favor and protection. "Infidelity," he wrote,

> has gained predominance and the kingdom of Islam has been
> spoiled. . . . Neither the devotion and the worship of the votaries of God
> proved helpful to them nor the unbelief of the infidels fettered their
> steps. Neither worship and devotion does any good to His Holy Divine
> Majesty, nor does infidelity do any harm to Him. Alas! Alas! O, how
> painful! With one gesture and freak of independence he caused the con-

53. 'Abd al-Rahman Chishti, *Mirāt-i asrār,* fol. 517a. See also Askari, "New Light," 37; Abdul Karim, "Nur Qutb Alam's Letter on the Ascendancy of Ganesa," in *Abdul Karim Sahitya-Visarad Commemoration Volume,* ed. Muhammad Enamul Haq (Dacca: Asiatic Society of Bangladesh, 1972), 336–37.
54. Quoted by Shaikh Ashraf Jahangir Simnani in his *Maktūbāt-i ashrafī,* letter no. 45, fol. 139a.

sumption of so many souls, the destruction of so many lives, and shedding of so much of bitter tears. Alas, woe to me, the sun of Islam has become obscured and the moon of religion has become eclipsed.[55]

But the fortunes of Bengali Muslims did not ebb as the shaikh had feared. Once the stormy period of Raja Ganesh had subsided, his converted son resumed the patronage of the Chishti establishment, reconfirming the Chishti-court alliance that had been established between Nur Qutb-i 'Alam's father and the dynasty's founder. Both Sultan Jalal al-Din and his son and successor Ahmad (r. 1432–33) became disciples of Nur Qutb-i 'Alam himself, and twelve succeeding sultans down to the year 1532 enlisted themselves as disciples of the descendants of Shaikh 'Ala al-Haq.[56] By the end of the fifteenth century, the tomb of Shaikh Nur Qutb-i 'Alam in Pandua had become in effect a state shrine to which Sultan 'Ala al-Din Husain Shah (r. 1493–1519) made annual pilgrimages.[57]

Despite the mutual patronage and even dependency between Bengal's Sufis and its rulers, one also detects an undercurrent of friction between the two. Occasionally erupting into open hostility, this friction derived from the radical distinction made in Islam between *dīn* and *dunyā*, "religion" and "the world." Withdrawn from worldly affairs and living in a state of poverty, self-denial, and remembrance of God, the Sufi recluse was in theory dramatically opposed by the ruler-administrator, glittering in his wealth and utterly immersed in worldly affairs. Sufis who rejected the world made much of their refusal to consort with "worldly" people—including above all royalty. Conversely, rulers sometimes suspected their Sufi allies, or even feared having around them such popular, charismatic leaders who might conceivably stir up the mob to riot or rebellion.[58]

55. Shaikh Nur Qutb-i 'Alam, *Maktūbāt-i Shaikh Nūr Qutb-i 'Ālam* (Maulana Azad Library, Aligarh Muslim University, Aligarh, Persian MS., Subhan Allah No. 297671/18), letter no. 9, p. 60. See also Abdul Karim, "Nur Qutb Alam's Letter," 342–43. Karim's translation. These sentiments, like those found in the correspondence of Muzaffar Shams Balkhi, suggest that the words and actions of Pandua's shaikhs were motivated by a genuine concern with advancing the cause of Islamic piety in Bengal, and not, as Jadunath Sarkar has suggested, by a narrow desire to safeguard their own economic and political interests. In referring to a "vast horde of unruly and ambitious disciples of the Shaikhs and Muslim monks, whose wealth and power had lately begun to overshadow the civil power," Sarkar depicts these men as little more than parasites who preyed upon ageing or weak rulers, and compares their position "to that of the Buddhist monks to whom the Emperor Asoka gave away all his State treasure in his dotage." Sarkar, ed., *History of Bengal*, 2: 126, 127.

56. 'Abd al-Rahman Chishti, *Mir'āt al-asrār*, fols. 517a–b.

57. Nizamuddin Ahmad, *Tabaqāt-i Akbarī*, text, 3: 270; trans. B. De, 3, pt. 1, 443.

58. For a discussion of these issues, see Digby, "Sufi Shaikh as a Source of Authority," esp. 63–69.

Here we may consider an inscription of Sultan Sikandar Ilyas Shah, dated 1363, in which the king dedicated a dome he had built for the shrine of a saint named Maulana 'Ata. Although the shaikh may have been the king's contemporary, Maulana 'Ata was more likely an earlier holy man whose shrine had become the focus of an important cult by the time the inscription was recorded.[59] "In this dome," the inscription reads,

> which has been founded by 'Ata, may the sanctuary of both worlds remain. May the angels recite for its durability, till the day of resurrection: *"We have built over you seven solid heavens"* [Qur'an 78:12].
>
> By the grace of (the builder of) the seven wonderful porticos *"who hath created seven heavens, one above another"* [Qur'an 67:3], may His names be glorified; the building of this lofty dome was completed. (Verily it) is the copy of a vault (lit., shell) of the roof of Glory, (referred in this verse) *"And we have adorned the heaven of the world"* (lit., lamps) [Qur'an 67:5]. (This lofty dome) in the sacred shrine of the chief of the saints, the unequaled among enquirers, the lamp of Truth, Law and Faith, Maulana 'Ata, may the High Allah bless him with His favours in both worlds; (was built) by order of the lord of the age and the time, the causer of justice and benevolence, the defender of towns, the pastor of people, the just, learned and great monarch, the shadow of Allah on the world, distinguished by the grace of the Merciful, Abu'l Mujahid Sikandar Shah, son of Ilyas Shah, the Sultan, may Allah perpetuate his kingdom.
>
> The king of the world Sikandar Shah, in whose name the pearls of prayer have been strung; regarding him they have said, "May Allah illuminate his rank," and regarding him they have prayed "May Allah perpetuate his kingdom."[60]

While outwardly acclaiming the greatness of Maulana 'Ata, Sultan Sikandar was also asserting his own claims to closeness to God, styling himself the one in whose name "the pearls of prayer have been strung," and "the Shadow of God on Earth." And by referring to this shrine as a copy

59. The shrine is in the ancient Muslim garrison city of Devikot, located in modern West Dinajpur District some 33 miles northeast of Sikandar's capital at Pandua. From the language of the inscription, it would appear that Sikandar was patronizing the construction only of the dome and not of the shrine itself, which in turn suggests the existence of a cult focused on a long-deceased saint. Three other inscriptions were fixed to the wall of this shrine, one of which, dated 1297, referred to the construction in that year of a mosque by Sultan Rukn al-Din Kaikaus. Another, dated 1493, stated that "the construction of this mosque was made during the time of the renowned saint, the chief of the holy men, Makhdum Maulana 'Ata, may Allah make his ashes fragrant and may He make Paradise his resting place." If the latter inscription refers to the same mosque referred to in the 1297 inscription—and this is not absolutely certain—then Maulana 'Ata would have been alive about sixty years before Sultan Sikandar ascended the throne. Shamsud-Din Ahmed, ed. and trans., *Inscriptions*, 4: 15–18, 143–44.
60. Ibid., 34–35. Italicized words are from the Qur'an.

(*nuskha*) of the heavens, the sultan drew attention to parallels between God's creative activity and his own. For if it had been God's creative act to adorn the seven heavens with lamps (*maṣābīḥ*), that is, stars, it was Sultan Sikandar's creative act to adorn the earth with a tomb for the lamp (*sirāj*) of Truth, Law, and Faith, that is, Maulana 'Ata. Implicitly, then, had it not been for the munificence of Sultan Sikandar, Maulana 'Ata would have remained shrouded in obscurity.

Royal distrust of or aversion to Sufis, even those of the Chishti order, is seen in other ways. Although Shams al-Din Ilyas Shah had patronized a prominent Chishti shaikh while establishing a new dynasty, the king's son and successor, Sultan Sikandar, was suspicious of the disciples of his father's saintly patron. He was especially suspicious of the most eminent of these, Shaikh 'Ala al-Haq, whose shrine complex had become in Sikandar's day a major nexus for economic transactions, redistributing amongst the city's poor large sums of money received in the form of pious donations.[61] Alarmed at the Sufi's substantial expenditure on the urban populace, Sikandar declared: "My treasure is in the hands of your father [the kingdom's Treasurer]; [yet] you are giving away as much as he spends." Evidently jealous of the shaikh's wealth and influence, the king banished the Sufi to Sonargaon.[62]

Bengal's Sufis and sultans, then, were fatefully connected by ties of mutual attraction and repulsion. Generally, when they were first establishing themselves politically, and especially when launching new dynasties, rulers actively sought the legitimacy powerful saints might lend them. Sultan Ghiyath al-Din 'Iwaz's earliest chronicler situated the launching of Bengal's first independent dynasty (1213) in the context of the grace, or *baraka*, of two simple dervishes in Afghanistan. And in 1342, when Sultan Shams al-Din Ilyas Shah launched the longest-lived dynasty in Muslim Bengal, he did so with the blessings of a renowned scion of the prestigious

---

61. Moreover, disciples from throughout the region and beyond came to study at the lodge of Shaikh 'Ala al-Haq, the most prominent being Ashraf Jahangir Simnani, an immigrant from Central Asia whose letters form a major hagiographical source for this period. Although his *Maktūbāt-i ashrāfī* has never been published, manuscript copies are available in the Aligarh Muslim University History Department (MS. No. 27) and the British Library (Or. MS. No. 267).

62. 'Abd al-Rahman Chishti, *Mirāt al-asrār*, fols. 515b–516a. 'Ala al-Haq's exile lasted for only several years, after which he was allowed to return to the capital, where he outlived the sultan by nine years. His experience compares with that of Maulana Ashraf al-Din Tawwama, a scholar and Sufi who had migrated from Bukhara to Delhi in the early fourteenth century, and who was exiled to Sonargaon by the Delhi court after having acquired an immense following among the city's masses. See Shaikh Shu'aib Firdausi, comp., *Manāqib al-asfiyā* (Calcutta: Nur al-Afaq, 1895), 131.

Chishti line. Struck by the awesome spiritual powers people attributed to charismatic shaikhs, or believing that their own lease on power was somehow extended by such forceful men, new Muslim kings sought their favor, built lodges or mausolea for them, or made public pilgrimages to their tombs. Conversely, some Sufis sought royal patronage out of their own reformist impulses to bring "the world" (*dunyā*) into proper alignment with their understanding of the dictates of normative "religion" (*dīn*).

On the other hand, once dynasties were securely entrenched in power, some kings no longer considered it necessary to call upon the charismatic authority of holy men to legitimate their rule. In fact, the wealth and influence of charismatic shaikhs were sometimes seen as potential threats to royal authority. Sikandar Ilyas Shah only begrudgingly patronized a saint on whose mausoleum he heaped more praise on himself than on the saint. And he actually banished the most eminent shaikh of the day from his capital when he felt his authority rivaled. Only after the death of Nur Qutb-i 'Alam in the mid fifteenth century, when Sufism's intellectually vibrant tradition was replaced by a politically innocuous tomb-cult, did the state once again wholeheartedly ally itself with the Chishti tradition.

4 Economy, Society, and Culture

These people [the Bengalis] owe all their tranquility and
prosperity to themselves, for its source lies in their devotion to
agriculture, whereby a land originally covered with jungle has
been reclaimed by their unremitting toil in tilling and planting.

Wang Ta-yüan (1349)

The Political Economy of the Sultanate

The advent of Indo-Turkish rule fundamentally altered Bengal's physical
and social landscape. In the mid fourteenth century, for example, the visiting Chinese merchant Wang Ta-yüan noted that the agrarian frontier
had pushed far into the delta's hinterland, transforming formerly forested
areas into fields of rice paddy (see chapter epigraph above).[1] It was under
Muslim rule, too, that Bengal's economy first became thoroughly monetized. Now it is true that kings of the Chandra dynasty (ca. 825–1035) had
minted silver coins, and that from the ninth or tenth century at least the
delta's southeastern corner had been integrated into a wider Indian Ocean
economy.[2] But in Pala or Sena times, the major part of the delta is not

1. Rockhill, "Notes on the Relations," 436. The pitch of the state's land revenue
demand is not known for certain. In his "Descriptions of the Barbarians of the
Isles," cited by Rockhill, Wang Ta-Yüan noted in 1349 that the government demanded one-fifth of the total produce in taxes. Just four years later, however, Ibn
Battuta wrote that the government claimed one half of the produce of Hindu farmers in the Habiganj region of Sylhet District. It is possible that both observations
were correct, and that the higher rate noted by Ibn Battuta represented the claim
(jamaʿ) demanded by the government, whereas the lower rate noted by the Chinese represented the amount of revenue actually collected (ḥāṣil). In any event, it
would be wrong to see Bengal's Muslim rulers as having driven the peasants into
the forested hinterland by policies of excessive taxation, since any abandonment of
cultivable lands would only have deprived the state of its principal source of wealth.
Rather, the state evidently tolerated, and probably encouraged, a moderate and
controlled movement of peasants into formerly forested areas. See Rockhill,
"Notes on the Relations," 435; Ibn Battuta, Rehla, 241.
2. Silver, which was mined nowhere within the delta itself, had for centuries before
the Turkish conquest been imported from the Burma-Yunnan border region where
the upper Yangtze, Mekong, Salween, and Irrawady rivers nearly converge. From
there it migrated into the delta via overland and river routes leading to the Arakan

known to have used metal coinage at all. By contrast, from the thirteenth century to the seventeenth, the Muslim rulers' silver coin, the *tanka*, circulated uninterrupted throughout the region.

In fact, the sequence of local conquests and bulges in the money supply suggests that Indo-Turkish rulers were driven into Bengal's hinterland, at least in part, by their thirst for uncoined silver. Each new conquest on Bengal's southern, eastern, or northern frontiers was followed by an expansion in the volume of silver coinage in circulation, the victors minting *tankas* from the accumulated silver stocks of defeated Hindu kingdoms. Sultan Rukn al-Din Kaikaus's conquest of southeastern Bengal in 1291 was followed by a substantial inflow of bullion, for example, which was quickly converted to coinage. The conquest of the Sonargaon region in eastern Bengal by Sultan Fakhr al-Din Mubarak Shah (r. 1338–49) was also followed by increases in the silver supply. The same was true of Sultan Sikandar's 1358 conquests in Kamrup, or northern Bengal.[3] The supply of coined silver leveled off during the late fourteenth century, but in 1420, when Sultan Jalal al-Din Muhammad reconquered much of eastern Bengal after an unsuccessful rebellion there, stocks of silver coinage again soared. So did they in 1494 when Sultan 'Ala al-Din Husain Shah reconquered Kamrup in northern Bengal.[4]

In addition to silver coined from the booty of defeated kingdoms in the region, substantial quantities of treasure were imported in exchange for goods locally manufactured for export. As early as 1415 we hear of Chinese trade missions bringing gold and silver into the delta, in addition to satins, silks, and porcelain.[5] A decade later another Chinese visitor remarked that long-distance merchants in Bengal settled their accounts with *tankas*.[6] The pattern continued throughout the next century. "Silver and Gold," wrote the Venetian traveler Cesare Federici in 1569, "from Pegu [Burma] they carrie to Bengala, and no other kind of Merchandize."[7] The monetization of Bengal's economy and its integration with markets throughout the Indian Ocean greatly stimulated the region's export-

---

coast and the upper Brahmaputra Valley. John Deyell, "The China Connection: Problems of Silver Supply in Medieval Bengal," in *Precious Metals in the Later Medieval and Early Modern Worlds*, ed. J. F. Richards (Durham, N.C.: Carolina Academic Press, 1983), 207–24.

3. Ibid., 214–15.
4. See Ibid., chart 2, 227.
5. Rockhill, "Notes on the Relations," 444.
6. Ibid., 437.
7. Cesare Federici, "Extracts of Master Caesar Frederike his Eighteene Yeers Indian Observations," in *Hakluytus Posthumus, or Purchas his Pilgrimes,* by Samuel Purchas (1625; Glasgow: James MacLehose & Sons, 1905), 10: 136.

manufacturing sector. Although textiles were already prominent among locally manufactured goods at the dawn of the Muslim encounter in the tenth century, the volume and variety of textiles produced and exported increased dramatically after the conquest. In the late thirteenth century, Marco Polo noted the commercial importance of Bengali cotton,[8] and in 1345 Ibn Battuta admired the fine muslin cloth he found there.[9] Between 1415 and 1432 Chinese diplomats wrote of Bengal's production of fine cotton cloths (muslins), rugs, veils of various colors, gauzes (Pers., *shāna-bāf*), material for turbans, embroidered silk, and brocaded taffetas.[10] A century later Ludovico di Varthema, who was in Gaur between 1503 and 1508, noted: "Fifty ships are laden every year in this place with cotton and silk stuffs. . . . These same stuffs go through all Turkey, through Syria, through Persia, through Arabia Felix, through Ethiopia, and through all India."[11] A few years later Tome Pires described the export of Bengali textiles to ports in the eastern half of the Indian Ocean.[12] Clearly, Bengal had become a major center of Asian trade and manufacture.

Ashrāf *and Non-*Ashrāf *Society*

Bengal's Muslim society from the thirteenth century through the sixteenth was overwhelmingly urban, concentrated in the sultanate's successive capital cities—Lakhnauti from 1204, Pandua from about 1342, and Gaur from about 1432—and in the provincial towns of Satgaon, Sonargaon, and Chittagong. Although new garrison towns regularly sprang up in the interior, as the numismatic and epigraphic evidence shows (see map 2), the preeminence of the capital cities was assured, since members of the provincial nobility, regardless of where their land assignments were

8. *The Book of Ser Marco Polo*, trans. and ed. Yule and Cordier, 2: 115.
9. Ibn Battuta, *Rehla*, 235.
10. Rockhill, "Notes on the Relations," 439–40, 443–44.
11. Ludovico di Varthema, *The Travels of Ludovico di Varthema . . .* A.D. *1503–1508*, trans. John W. Jones (Hakluyt Society Publications, 1st ser., no. 32, 1863; reprint, New York: Burt Franklin, n.d.), 212.
12. "A junk goes from Bengal to Malacca once a year," Tome Pires wrote, "and sometimes twice. Each of these carries from eighty to ninety thousand *cruzados* worth. They bring fine white cloths, seven kinds of *sinabafos*, three kinds of *chautares, beatilhas, beirames* and other rich materials. They will bring as many as twenty kinds. They bring steel, very rich bed-canopies, with cut-cloth work in all colours and very beautiful; wall hangings like tapestry. . . . These people sail four or five ships to Malacca and to Pase every year, and this is still done to a large extent. Bengali cloth fetches as high price in Malacca, because it is a merchandise all over the East." Pires, *Suma Oriental*, 1: 92. For a discussion of Bengal's external trade in the sixteenth century, see Sanjay Subrahmanyam, "Notes on the Sixteenth-Century Bengal Trade," *Indian Economic and Social History Review* 24, no. 3 (1987): 265–89.

Fig. 14. Dakhil Darwaza (ca. 1433–59), seen from within the citadel of Gaur.

located, had to maintain residences there.[13] Gaur, especially, was by all accounts a splendid city (see figs. 14 and 15). "One of the best that I had
hitherto seen," wrote Ludovico di Varthema[14] in the early sixteenth century, when it had attained a population of forty thousand.[15] In 1521 a visiting Portuguese described the city as

> very big, stretching for four leagues along the river and, it is said, ex-
> tending so far inland that houses are still found beyond six leagues. . . .
> The town is situated on a large plain which is flat like the whole of the
> surrounding area. The streets and lanes are paved with brick like the Lis-
> bon New Street. The market is everywhere and everything—food and
> other goods alike—is in plentiful supply and very cheap. The streets
> and cross-lanes are so full of people that [it] is impossible to move and
> it has reached the point where the high noblemen have taken to being
> preceded along the road to the palace by men carrying bamboo sticks to
> push people out of the way.[16]

Foreigners were much impressed by the wealth of long-distance merchants
residing in the sultanate's capitals. In 1415 a Chinese envoy wrote of men

13. Moreover, on the death of one of these nobles, half of his property reverted to
the crown. This also served to concentrate wealth in the hands of the sultan, and
hence at the royal capital. *Voyage dans les deltas du Gange*, 326.
14. Varthema, *Travels of Ludovico di Varthema*, 211.
15. Pires, *Suma Oriental*, 1: 90. By contrast, Satgaon, a principal seaport located
north of modern Calcutta, had a population of ten thousand at this time. Ibid., 91.
16. *Voyage dans les deltas du Gange*, 323.

Fig. 15. Ruined ramparts of the citadel of Gaur, looking east from the top of the Dakhil Darwaza.

in Pandua who "wear a white cotton turban and a long white cotton shirt. On their feet they wear low sheep-skin shoes with gold thread. The smarter ones think it the correct thing to have designs on them. Everyone of them is engaged in business, the value of which may be ten thousand pieces of gold."[17] Around 1508, Varthema found in Gaur "the richest merchants I have ever met with."[18] Ten years later, Duarte Barbosa also described wealthy Arabs, Iranians, Abyssinians, and "Indians" of Gaur. "The respectable Moors," he wrote,

> walk about clad in white cotton smocks, very thin, which come down to their ankles, and beneath these they have girdles of cloth, and over them silk scarves; they carry in their girdles daggers garnished with silver and gold, according to the rank of the person who carries them. . . . They are luxurious, eat well and spend freely, and have many other extravagancies as well. They bathe often in great tanks which they have in their houses. Every one has three or four wives or as many as he can maintain.[19]

The nobles and traders described above formed part of the Muslim elite, or *ashrāf*, which also included urban Sufis, religious officials (*'ulamā*), and

17. Rockhill, "Notes on the Relations," 442–43.
18. Varthema, *Travels of Ludovico di Varthema*, 212.
19. Duarte Barbosa, *The Book of Duarte Barbosa*, trans. M. L. Dames (1921; reprint, Nendoln/Liechtenstein: Kraus Reprint, 1967), 2: 135–39, 147–48.

foreign-born soldiers and administrators. In fact, foreign origin, even if only of one's ancestors, formed an important, if not defining, element of *ashrāf* identity. Writing around 1495, the poet Vipra Das referred to the Muslim preachers (*mullās*) and judges (*qāzīs*) of Satgaon as "Saiyids," "Mughals," and "Pathans"—that is, men claiming an Arab, Central Asian, or Afghan origin.[20] About a century later the poet Mukundaram (fl. 1590), like Vipra Das a native of the southwestern delta, described urban Muslims as men who had immigrated from points west of Bengal.[21] Religious sentiment also inclined *ashrāf* Muslims to look westward. In 1505 the patron of a mosque in Sonargaon proudly counted himself as one "who has made a pilgrimage to Macca and Madina, and has visited the two foot-prints of the Prophet."[22] Similarly, a 1567 inscription on the congregational mosque in Old Malda compared it with the holy shrine in Mecca, referring to Malda's house of worship as the "second Ka'aba" (*thānī ka'aba*).[23] For the devout, phrases such as these served to mitigate the great distance separating Bengal from Islam's holiest shrines in Arabia, tenuously linked to the delta by a long and dangerous sea voyage.

Prominent among the *ashrāf* were judges, or *qāzīs*, who possessed sufficient expertise in Islamic Law to arbitrate disputes involving fellow Muslims. Below them in status were the *mullās*, the ubiquitous ordinary preachers and the least-educated members of the Muslim establishment. An inscription on the congregational mosque at Satgaon, dated 1529, hints at how these two members of the *ashrāf* interrelated:

> Because the body of *mullās* and landholders (*arbāb*) will be cursed by God if they defraud public endowments, it is binding and necessary that governors and *qāzīs* prevent such frauds, so that on the Day of Judgment they will not be seized for their oppressions.[24]

This suggests that the court relied on the *qāzīs*, together with governors, to curb what it considered the *mullās'* fraudulent ways—in this case, a tendency to defraud public endowments. *Qāzīs* were also the most visible

---

20. Cited in Abdul Karim, *Social History of the Muslims of Bengal (down to A.D. 1538)* (Dacca: Asiatic Society of Pakistan, 1959), 153–54.
21. Mukundaram, *Kavikaṅkaṇa Caṇḍī*, ed. Srikumar Bandyopadhyay and Visvapati Chaudhuri (Calcutta: University of Calcutta, 1974), 343–44. As a sociologist remarked, "nobility was determined by immigration from the west in direct proportion to the nearness in point of time and distance in point of land of origin from Bengal to Arabia." Abdul Majed Khan, "Research about Muslim Aristocracy in East Pakistan," in P. Bessaignet, ed., *Social Research in East Pakistan* 2d ed., (Dacca: Asiatic Society of Pakistan, 1964), 22.
22. Shamsud-Din Ahmed, ed. and trans., *Inscriptions of Bengal*, 4: 170–71.
23. Ibid., 259.
24. Ibid., 225. My translation.

representatives of royal authority vis-à-vis non-Muslims, since they were charged with maintaining public order generally. In the early sixteenth century, for example, when the devotees of a Hindu cult caused a public disturbance with their ecstatic singing in the West Bengal town of Nadia, local Muslims complained to the town's *qāzī*. Although the judge excused that particular violation of public order, he warned that he would punish future infractions by confiscating the property of violators.[25]

Socially distinct from the *ashrāf* were Muslim urban artisans who formed part of Bengal's growing industrial proletariat. Their organization into separate, endogamous communities (*jāti*) with distinctive occupations paralleled the organization of Hindu society in the southwestern delta, and suggests their origins in that society. Mukundaram mentions fifteen Muslim *jātis* in a list of communities inhabiting an idealized Bengali city of his day—weavers (*jolā*), livestock herders (*mukeri*), cake sellers (*piṭhāri*), fishmongers (*kābāri*), converts from the local population (*garasāl*), loom makers (*sānākār*), circumcisers (*hājām*), bow makers (*tirakar*), papermakers (*kāgajī*), wandering holy men (*kalandar*), tailors (*darji*), weavers of thick cord (*benaṭā*), dyers (*rangrej*), users of hoes (*hālān*), and beef sellers (*kasāi*).[26] So thoroughly were these groups integrated with Bengali society that by the late sixteenth century, when Mukundaram was writing, it was impossible to conceive of a city that did not have, alongside a long list of Hindu *jātis*, a full complement of Muslim artisan groups.[27]

Moreover, these groups constituted the earliest-known class of Bengali Muslims. Fully five of them—the weavers, loom makers, tailors, weavers of thick ribbon, and dyers—were linked to the growing textile industry, and were probably recruited from amongst existing Hindu castes already engaged in these trades, or from amongst former agriculturalists or unskilled laborers responding to labor demands created by the expanding industry.[28] Government demand appears to have brought into existence still other groups of Muslim artisans. The bow makers, for example, provided weaponry for the kingdom's armed forces, while papermakers would have

25. Krsnadasa Kaviraja Gosvami, *Śrī Caitanya-Caritāmṛta*, ed. and trans. A. C. Bhaktivedanta Swami (New York: Bhaktivedanta Book Trust, 1974), ch. 17, text, 123–128; 3: 323–26.

26. Mukundaram, *Kavikaṅkaṇa Caṇḍī*, 345–46.

27. The poet's description of the Muslim and Hindu communities of the idealized Bengali city of "Gujarat" is discussed in Edward C. Dimock, Jr., and Ronald B. Inden, "The City in Pre-British Bengal," in Edward C. Dimock, Jr., *The Sound of Silent Guns and Other Essays* (Delhi: Oxford University Press, 1989), 121–25.

28. Duarte Barbosa, writing in 1518, seems to have had these groups in mind when he mentioned the presence of converted Muslim communities in the capital city of Gaur. See *Book of Duarte Barbosa*, 2: 148.

met both the bureaucracy's appetite for files and the Muslim religious elite's demand for books. In fact, nearly half of the Muslim *jātis* listed by Mukundaram bore Perso-Arabic names, suggesting that they had come into being only after the Turkish conquest.[29]

Hindu Society — Responses to the Conquest

The advent of Indo-Turkish rule meant an abrupt end to official patronage for those Brahmans who had served the Sena government as ritual priests, astrologers, ministers, advisors, or financial officers. Doubtless, many of these fled into the eastern hinterland along with the Sena household in 1204, or soon thereafter. In time, however, most Brahmans moved from an initial position of disdain for the new political order to one of uneasy accommodation with it. By the fifteenth and sixteenth centuries, the predominant view was that government employment was perfectly possible as long as one did not engage in marital relations with Mlecchas ("polluted outsiders").[30] For, ultimately, the Brahmans and the higher Muslim officers of the sultanate needed each other: the former were historically conditioned to look to a ruling class for patronage and livelihood, while the latter required the administrative talents that Brahmans had traditionally monopolized. Hence, while the period before 1415 witnessed few instances of Brahmans serving the sultanate, the picture changed dramatically after the Raja Ganesh revolution. That chieftain's own converted son, Sultan Jalal al-Din Muhammad, signaled the change by honoring Brahman poets. By the reign of Sultan 'Ala al-Din Husain Shah, many Brahmans had taken service in the court.

Serving the sultanate proved far less traumatic for the Kayasthas, who had been the dominant landholding caste prior to the conquest and who continued in this role under Muslim rule.[31] Indeed, after the conquest, the Kayasthas absorbed remnants of Bengal's old ruling dynasties—the Sena, Pala, Chandra, Varman, and so on—and in this way became the region's surrogate Kshatriya or "warrior" class.[32] Judging from the correspondence

29. These groups included the *hājām* (from Ar. *ḥajjām*), *tirakar* (from Pers. *tīrgar*), *kāgajī* (from Ar.-Pers. *kāghażī*), *kalandar* (from Pers. *qalandar*), *darji* (from Pers. *darzī*), *rangrej* (from Pers. *rangrīz*), and *kasāi* (from Ar. *qaṣṣāb*).
30. Ronald B. Inden, *Marriage and Rank in Bengali Culture: A History of Caste and Class in Middle-Period Bengal* (Berkeley and Los Angeles: University of California Press, 1976), 75–76.
31. Around 1595 Abu'l-fazl wrote that most of the Bengal *zamīndārs* were Kayasthas, and that they had comprised Bengal's ruling class under the Pala dynasty and even earlier. Abu'l-fazl 'Allami, *Ā'īn-i Akbarī* (Lucknow ed.), 2: 82, 113; trans., 2: 141, 158–59.
32. N. K. Dutt, *Origin and Growth of Caste in India* (Calcutta: Firma K.L.M., 1965), 2: 58–63, 97.

of Maulana Muzaffar Shams Balkhi, who in 1397 complained bitterly of the power enjoyed by Hindus, it seems that Muslim rulers had from a very early time confirmed the Kayasthas in their ancient role as landholders and political intermediaries.

Looking at Bengal's Hindu society as a whole, it seems likely that the caste system—far from being the ancient and unchanging essence of Indian civilization as supposed by generations of Orientalists—emerged into something resembling its modern form only in the period 1200–1500. Central to this process, as Ronald Inden has argued, was the collapse of Hindu kingship. Before the Turkish conquest, the Sena king had maintained order by distributing wealth and by judging between socially high and low in the context of his court and its rituals. With the dissolution of Hindu kingship that followed the Turkish conquest, however, these functions appear to have been displaced onto society at large. Hindu social order was now maintained by the enforcing of group endogamy, the regulation of marriage by "caste" councils, and the keeping of genealogies by specialists.[33] In the western delta, one sees the result of these processes in the detailed list of Hindu communities mentioned by the poet Mukundaram, who describes a hierarchy of four tiers of occupationally differentiated endogamous groups (*jāti*). The first tier included Brahmans, Kayasthas, and Baidyas, or traditional healers. The second included productive classes such as cultivators, herders, iron smiths, potters, weavers, gardeners, barbers, candy makers, spice merchants, brass smiths, gold merchants, and so on. These were followed by a third tier composed of the ritually less pure castes: fishermen, oil pressers, woodcutters, launderers, tailors, molasses makers, carpenters, ferrymen, and beggars. At the very end of the list, compelled to live outside the poet's imaginary city, were the grass cutters, leatherworkers, prostitutes, and Dom tribals, who were scavengers and sweepers.[34]

Hindu Religion—the Śiva-Śākta Complex

As elsewhere in India, there arose in Bengal a need to harmonize Vedic religion, which focused on male deities, with indigenous Indian cults, in which female deities dominated. One way this was accomplished was in the context of the orthodox Śaiva cult, which before the Turkish conquest had been presided over by Brahmans and lavishly patronized by Hindu kings such as the early Senas, for whom Śiva was the kingdom's cosmic overlord. The cosmic reunion of Śiva and Śakti—that is, pure conscious-

---

33. Ronald B. Inden, *Marriage and Rank*, 71–77; id., *Imagining India* (Cambridge, Mass.: Basil Blackwell, 1990), 49–84.
34. Mukundaram, *Kavikaṅkaṇa Caṇḍī*, 355–61.

ness, corresponding to the male principle; and pure energy, corresponding to the female principle—was typically concretized in aniconic symbols placed in temples, access to which was controlled by Brahman
priests. However, this state-supported cult declined when Indo-Turkish
conquerors withdrew the royal patronage on which such public cults depended.

Both before and after the conquest, numerous popular cults dedicated
to various manifestations of the Goddess also flourished. Celebrated in a
literary genre called *mangala-kāvya*, these cults thrived among those
groups least touched by Indo-Aryan culture and least integrated into the
hierarchic scheme of social organization as promoted by Brahmans. They
were also among the oldest, the most vibrant, and the most authentically
Bengali religious traditions in the delta. In their earliest form, Goddess
cults seem to have sprung from ancient female domestic rites not presided
over by Brahman priests, as in the cult of the snake goddess Manasa, whose
core story was anciently recited by women and for women as a component
of their domestic rites.[35] But throughout the period 1200–1600 and doubtless for some time earlier, Brahman ideologues sought to appropriate such
cults by identifying female divine power in all its manifestations with the
Śakti, or pure energy, which is the counterpart of the Brahmanical god
Śiva. Thus Śiva was understood as son to Dharma; husband to Chandi/
Durga, Kali/Ganga, and Śitala; father to Manasa and Neto; guru/father to
various Nath saints; master/father to Daksin Ray; and father-in-law to
Sasthi. Noting these relationships, W. L. Smith aptly describes Śiva as "the
hub around which the Bengali divine hierarchy revolves."[36] But these
folk deities experienced varying degrees of accommodation with Brahmanical orthodoxy, ranging from a rather complete incorporation into
the Hindu pantheon, with full benefits of Brahmanical patronage, to a
more marginal place within that pantheon, with only hesitant acceptance
by Brahmans.

Extending at least to A.D. 1000, with its core myths and rituals dating
from the period 500–1000, if not earlier, the cult of the snake goddess
Manasa was well established by the time of the Turkish conquest.[37] Yet
this cult, having first emerged among low-ranked tribals of Burdwan, failed
to achieve full acceptance in Brahmanic literature, and it was to some extent resisted by orthodox Śaivas. Nor did Manasa enjoy a satisfactory connection with Śiva. Like other folk deities, she had a kin tie with the great

35. William L. Smith, *The One-eyed Goddess: A Study of the Manasā-Mangal.*
Oriental Studies, No. 12 (Stockholm: Almquist & Wiksell, 1980), 134.
36. Ibid., 51.
37. Ibid., 132–33.

god—in her case as a daughter—but she could never compete with deities identified as Śiva's wife, such as her principal rival, the goddess Chandi. The cult's struggle to gain full acceptance is evident in its central myth. Having already gained a following among ritually low-ranking communities like fishermen and cowherds, Manasa was convinced that she could win universal human devotion only through gaining the submission of Chando, an upper-caste merchant and fervent devotee of Śiva. Although Chando initially despised Manasa and viewed her as one of inferior status, he ultimately (though reluctantly) recognized Manasa's popularity and submitted to her cult.[38] The story thus suggests a steadily widening circle of the cult's social basis: from cowherds to fishermen, to farmers, to upper-class women, to upper-class men, and finally to Brahman priests.[39]

If the Manasa cult enjoyed only a limited or reluctant acceptance among Bengal's upper castes in our period, it fared much better among the masses, especially in the delta's less-Aryanized east. In 1540 the poet Vrindavan Das, though himself not devoted to any of the Goddess cults, affirmed their popularity when he wrote:

> All "religious" people know this only:
> They sing the song of Maṅgal Caṇḍī at the *jāgaran* [the last night of
> the festival for the goddess Chandi],
> With pomp some give *pūjā* to Viṣahari [Manasa],
> And another puts on a puppet show at great expense.[40]

Relief images of stone preserved in the Chittagong University Museum can be confidently identified with the goddess Manasa. Two of these stand several feet in height and depict the deity with a hood of seven snakes over her head, her left hand holding another snake, and her principal iconographic symbol, a sacred pot, at her feet (figs. 16 and 17).[41] The appearance of such votive images, evidently intended for installation in simple, thatched shrines dedicated to her worship, marked an important step in the progression of the Manasa cult from a domestic rite to an established

38. As W. L. Smith notes, Chando's initial objection to the goddess and the nature of his ultimate acceptance of her cult "reflects that of the upper castes—it was qualified, reluctant and done without enthusiasm." Smith, *One-eyed Goddess*, 182.
39. P. K. Maity, *Historical Studies in the Cult of the Goddess Manasā* (Calcutta: Punthi Pustak, 1966), 169–82. T. W. Clark, "Evolution of Hinduism in Medieval Bengali Literature: Śiva, Caṇḍī, Manasā," *Bulletin of the School of Oriental and African Studies* 17, no. 3 (1955): 507–15.
40. Vrindavan Das, *Śrī-śrī Caitanya-Bhāgavat* (4th ed., Calcutta, n.d.), 11. Cited in Smith, *One-eyed Goddess*, 30. Smith's translation.
41. These iconographic features compare with those characterizing a Manasa relief from Birbhum in West Bengal. See Jitendra Nath Banerjea, *The Development of Hindu Iconography* (Calcutta: University of Calcutta, 1956), 350.

Fig. 16. Stone sculpture of the goddess Manasa. Chittagong University
Museum, no. 657.

Fig. 17. Stone sculpture of the goddess Manasa. Chittagong University Museum, no. 659.

cult, complete with officiating priests, even though these may not have been Brahmans.

Enjoying far more support among Brahmans, and at the mass level perhaps the widest support of any cult in the premodern Bengali pantheon, was the cult of the goddess Chandi. Like her rival Manasa, Chandi was a forest goddess whose cult had sprung up from the delta's aboriginal society. But Chandi's identification as the wife of the great god Śiva rendered her more mild and generous than the nasty, manipulative Manasa.[42] Moreover, though Chandi's cultic literature is also very ancient, it appeared in written form only in the late sultanate period, the best-known text being Mukundaram's *Caṇḍī-Maṅgala* (ca. 1590).[43] Perhaps because the written versions of the myth appeared so late in the cult's evolution, Chandi emerges in Mukundaram's work as rather well integrated into the Indo-Aryan pantheon and with Brahmanic values. She is portrayed, for example, as having put an end to the primordial chaos prevailing at a time before gods and Brahmans imposed order on earth. Furthermore, she not only protects all the animals of the woods, but presides over their hierarchic ranking in a scheme exactly mirroring the ideal human society as seen from the Brahmanical perspective. And finally, her protection of the animals is conditioned on their renunciation of mutual violence, for society is to accord with the norms of *dharma*, or righteous law.

The myth's story line also illustrates the post-eighth-century Hindu conception of the interrelationship of religion and politics. In a world where both deities and kings seek to enlarge their circles of authority, a deity "entrusts" earthly sovereignty to an appointed king on condition that he propagate and promote that deity's cult in human society. Craving human devotion like most Indian deities, Chandi embarks on a project designed to establish a royal kingdom on earth. Here the narrative focuses on a low-caste hunter named Kalaketu, to whom the goddess assigns the sovereignty of her forest kingdom. In return for this, the hunter must renounce the hunt, build and populate a city in the forest, and construct a glorious temple dedicated to her, in this way propagating Chandi's cult among humans. All this underscores the goddess's fundamentally political role, seen in the dual sovereignty that she and her human protégé exercise

42. Mild characteristics were generally typical of those female deities who have been more comfortably accommodated in the Brahman-controlled Hindu pantheon. See Lawrence A. Babb, *The Divine Hierarchy: Popular Hinduism in Central India* (New York: Columbia University Press, 1975), 221–26.

43. An excellent analysis of the *Caṇḍī-Maṅgala* is found in Bhattacharya, "La Déesse." See esp. 22–33.

over the forest kingdom. As Chandi's earthly representative, Kalaketu rules on behalf of that goddess, behind whom stands the kingdom's cosmic overlord—her spouse, Śiva.[44] Yet, for all her dharmic trappings and her trucking with the highest gods of the Indo-Aryan pantheon, Chandi remains of the forest—that dark domain of jungle beasts and non-Aryan tribes—and not of the city, the proper domain of Brahmans and their ritual performances.[45] Moreover, Chandi's protégé Kalaketu is a hunter who pursues a violent and unclean livelihood typical of Bengal's indigenous tribes, amongst whom the myth had originally evolved. No amount of Brahmanical revision could disguise the underlying association of both goddess and king with non-Aryan, indigenous Bengali culture.[46]

It is worth recalling that the only known nativist rebellion mounted against the sultanate was waged in the name of Chandi, this thoroughly Bengali goddess and protectress of the forest. Dated A.D. 1417–18 and minted in Chittagong, Sonargaon, and Chhota Pandua—that is, the delta's forested southern and eastern hinterland—the coins of Danuja Marddana Deva and his son Mahendra Deva bore the Sanskrit legend *Śrī Caṇḍī Caraṇa Parāyaṇa,* "devoted to the feet of Goddess Chandi." Inasmuch as armed insurrection against established political authority is always serious business, we may be sure that rebel leaders would have invoked only such supernatural assistance as was judged most powerful and most likely to respond to human entreaties. Chandi's appearance on the Deva kings' coins during this rebellion clearly attests to her widespread popularity, and to belief in her protective power.

Hindu Religion — the Vaishnava Complex

From epigraphic, artistic, and literary evidence—notably the Sanskrit poem *Gīta Govinda*, composed by the thirteenth-century poet Jayadeva— we know that the Vishnu cult had been gaining royal favor immediately prior to the Turkish conquest. During the first several centuries of Turkish rule, however, this public cult, like that of Śiva, suffered from the with-

---

44. At one point Kalaketu states, "The king of my kingdom is Mahes Thakur [Śiva]; I am its chief minister [*mahāpatra*], and Chandi its proprietress [*adhikārī*]." Mukundaram, *Kavikaṅkaṇa Caṇḍī,* 413.

45. Charles Malamoud, "Village et forêt dans l'idéologie de l'Inde brahmanique," *Archives européennes de sociologie* 17, no. 1 (1976), 3–14.

46. Once he took possession of the kingdom, Kalaketu was to renounce violence against the very animals he had formerly killed, becoming now their protector. In this way the written form of the myth, clearly influenced by Brahmanical revision, attempts to resolve a classical problem of Indian kingship, namely, the king's ritual impurity arising from his professional obligation to kill.

drawal of state patronage.[47] It next appeared in deltaic Bengal as a popular devotional movement unmediated by priestly rituals or court patronage, and marked by the appearance of vernacular literature glorifying the various incarnations of Vishnu. Sometime in the fifteenth century, Kirtivas Pundit made a Bengali translation of the *Rāmāyaṇa*, the famous epic of Rama.[48] Yet what ultimately won over the mainstream of Bengali Vaishnavas was Vishnu's incarnation, not as Rama, but as Krishna—the naughty child-god, the slayer of the snake king Kaliya, the seducer of the pastoral Gopi women, and especially, the lover of Radha. The popularization of a new Krishna literature can be attributed, in part, to patronage by the Muslim court at Gaur. Between 1473 and 1480, the Kayastha poet Maladhara Basu composed his *Śrī Kṛṣṇa-Vijaya,* "The Triumph of Lord Krishna," under the patronage of Sultan Rukn al-Din Barbak (r. 1459–74). Somewhat later, Sultan 'Ala al-Din Husain Shah (r. 1493–1519) patronized composition by Yasoraj Khan of the *Kṛṣṇa-Maṅgala,* now lost.[49] The most famous early poem of the Krishna story was the *Śrī Kṛṣṇa-Kīrtan.* Composed by Chandi Das, probably in the fifteenth century,[50] this work explores the devious tactics deployed by the lusty young Krishna in winning the love of the cowherdess Radha. Once won, Radha's passionate love for the divine Krishna became the central motif of Bengali devotionalism, or *bhakti.*

The movement crystallized around a single, charismatic personality who appeared in West Bengal early in the sixteenth century—the saint and mystic Chaitanya (d. 1533). Born a Brahman in 1486, Chaitanya began his career studying and teaching at Nadia, then a bastion of Brahmanical learning, but in 1508 he met a devotee of Krishna while on a trip in Bihar, and his life took a decisive turn. Once initiated into the cult, Chaitanya renounced his former life for that of an ecstatic worshiper of Vishnu manifested as Krishna. Upon returning to Bengal he became the center of a group of devotees who established a tradition of devotional worship through enraptured dance and songs (*kīrtan*) praising Krishna. The practice soon became a public one, as Chaitanya and his followers took to parading through the streets of Nadia shouting the name of God in moods of raptured devotion. Although officers of the sultanate placed curbs on

47. Some Vaishnava literature and art nonetheless continued to be locally produced, as in late fifteenth century Vishnupur. See Jeremiah P. Losty, *The Art of the Book in India* (London: British Library, 1982), 62.
48. Sukumar Sen, *History of Bengali Literature,* 3d ed. (New Delhi: Sahitya Akademi, 1979), 63–64.
49. Ibid., 66.
50. Dusan Zbavitel, *Bengali Literature,* vol. 9, fasc. 3 of *A History of Indian Literature,* ed. Jan Gonda (Wiesbaden: Otto Harrassowitz, 1976), 149.

the cult's ecstatic excesses when they disturbed the public peace,[51] the true adversaries of the growing neo-Vaishnava movement were neither local Muslims nor the court at Gaur—which actually patronized Vaishnava literature—but Brahman supporters of the cults of Chandi and Manasa. First, in their view, the Vaishnava custom of communal song, the *kīrtan*, not only disturbed the peace but lacked scriptural authority. Second, Chaitanya had identified himself with God ("Gaurhari"). Third, he had usurped from Brahmans their monopoly over the use of mantras, or sacred oral formulae. And finally, his cult was charged with having attracted followers from amongst the lower classes, a point hinting at the social basis of the leading Hindu sects in this period.[52] Since Goddess cults enjoyed broad popular support, the Śākta Brahmans, as patrons of those cults, viewed the lower classes as their own natural constituency, even though they were sometimes ambivalent about extending their support to such cults. Chaitanya's movement thus threatened to cut into their pool of religious clients.

Despite initial Brahman attempts to resist the movement, and later to control it by incorporating it into a broader Brahmanical framework, Vaishnavism managed to carve out and maintain for itself an autonomous identity in the delta's religious landscape. By emphasizing non-Brahman inclusiveness as opposed to high-caste exclusiveness, the practice of devotion rather than ritual, and the use of Bengali rather than Sanskrit, the movement posed a real alternative to the Brahman-supported Śaiva movement, with its ties to various Goddess cults. Devotional and hagiographical literature composed in the sixteenth century dramatized the assurance of salvation through love of Krishna and fixed the historical Chaitanya as one who was at least divinely inspired, if not identified with both Krishna and his lover Radha.[53] Even during his lifetime, Chaitanya had been deified by enthusiastic devotees, and by the end of the century, when his name was included among those of the gods praised in the introductory lines of contemporary poems, his divinity seems to have been widely accepted.[54]

Vaishnava piety spread dramatically across Bengali Hindu society. In

51. Krsnadasa, *Śrī Caitanya-Caritāmṛta*, trans. Bhaktivedanta, ch. 17, text, 124–28; 3: 324–26.
52. Ibid., text, 204–12; 3: 363–66.
53. The chief such works are the *Caitanya-Bhāgavat* by Vrindavan Das, composed ca. 1540; the *Caitanya-Maṅgala* by Jayananda, composed in the sixteenth century; the *Caitanya Maṅgala* by Locan Das, composed in the mid sixteenth century; the *Gaurāṅga-Vijaya* by Curamani Das, composed before 1560, and the *Caitanya-Caritāmṛta* by Krishna Das, composed ca. 1575–95. Of these, that of Krishna Das is generally considered the most authoritative. See Zbavitel, *Bengali Literature*, 172–75; Sen, *History of Bengali Literature*, ch. 8.
54. Sen, *History of Bengali Literature*, 94.

his idealized image of a Bengali kingdom the poet Mukundaram included Vaishnavas among the city's Brahmans, referring to them as homesteaders who engaged in devotional singing, or as prosperous city-dwellers living amidst beautiful Vishnu temples adorned with golden spires and fluttering flags.[55] This suggests that by the late sixteenth century, while the ecstatic spirit of Chaitanya's devotional movement was still vibrant, the upper castes had already begun to ally themselves with the movement, in the process redefining it along orthodox lines. In subsequent centuries, Vaishnava piety, though originating in cities, would make deep inroads among Bengal's Hindu artisan and cultivating castes. By 1893 James Wise could write, "It may be said with perfect truth that Vaishnavism, in one or another of its diverse forms, to the exclusion of Saivism and all other [Hindu] creeds, is the faith professed by the agricultural, artizan, and fisher tribes of Bengal."[56]

In sum, Hindu society in the sultanate period was dominated by two principal religious orientations—the various Goddess cults and Vaishnava devotionalism—with Brahmans endeavoring to appropriate both. In terms of geographical reach, the Vaishnava movement appears to have been centered in western Bengal, whereas the cults dedicated to the Goddess prevailed throughout the delta, especially in the south and the east, where rebellious Hindu political movements rose up in the name of Chandi. Although the public Śiva cult never recovered from the withdrawal of court patronage that followed the Turkish conquest, its Śākta Brahman patrons eventually succeeded in grafting the high god to indigenous cults, and especially to that focusing on the goddess Chandi. Similarly, Vaishnava Brahmans in time managed to check the unrestrained emotionalism of Chaitanya's movement.

It was in the context of these religious currents that Islamic devotionalism became a force in its own right in the Bengal delta. Thus far we have seen Muslims as rulers, soldiers, Sufis, merchants, administrators, or judges. But we have not yet seen them in the role of the ordinary cultivators who came to pervade the modern Bengali countryside. Indeed, Bengali Muslim cultivators would eventually form the basis of one of the largest Muslim communities on earth. This raises the question of Islamization, and the contested issue of conversion to Islam.

55. Mukundaram, *Kavikaṅkaṇa Caṇḍī*, 348, 350.
56. James Wise, "The Hindus of Eastern Bengal," *Journal of the Asiatic Society of Bengal* 62, no. 3 (1893), 8. For the diffusion of Vaishnava piety in post-Chaitanya Bengal, see Ramakanta Chakrabarty, *Vaisnavism in Bengal, 1486–1900* (Calcutta: Sanskrit Pustak Bhandar, 1985), 275–304.

5 Mass Conversion to Islam: Theories and Protagonists

The most interesting fact revealed by the census of 1872 was the enormous host of Muhammadans resident in Lower Bengal—not massed around the old capitals, but in the alluvial plains of the Delta.

James Wise (1894)

Four Conventional Theories of Islamization in India

Theories purporting to explain the growth of Islam in India may be reduced to four basic modes of reasoning. Each is inadequate. The first of these, which I shall call the Immigration theory, is not really a theory of conversion at all since it views Islamization in terms of the diffusion not of belief but of peoples. In this view, the bulk of India's Muslims are descended from other Muslims who had either migrated overland from the Iranian plateau or sailed across the Arabian Sea. Although some such process no doubt contributed to the Islamization of those areas of South Asia that are geographically contiguous with the Iranian plateau or the Arabian Sea, this argument cannot, for reasons to be discussed below, be used to explain mass Islamization in Bengal.

The oldest theory of Islamization in India, which I shall call the Religion of the Sword thesis, stresses the role of military force in the diffusion of Islam in India and elsewhere. Dating at least from the time of the Crusades, this idea received big boosts during the nineteenth century, the high tide of European imperial domination over Muslim peoples, and subsequently in the context of the worldwide Islamic reform movements of the late twentieth century. Its general tone is captured in the way many nineteenth- and twentieth-century Orientalists explained the rise of Islam in seventh-century Arabia, as illustrated in these lurid lines penned in 1898 by Sir William Muir:

> It was the scent of war that now turned the sullen temper of the Arab tribes into eager loyalty. . . . Warrior after warrior, column after column, whole tribes in endless succession with their women and children, issued forth to fight. And ever, at the marvelous tale of cities conquered; of rapine rich beyond compute; of maidens parted on the very field of

battle "to every man a damsel or two". . . . fresh tribes arose and went. Onward and still onward, like swarms from the hive, or flights of locusts darkening the land, tribe after tribe issued forth and hastening northward, spread in great masses to the East and to the West.[1]

In the end, though, after the thundering hooves have passed and the dust has settled, in attempting to explain the Arab conquests, Muir leaves us with little of substance. Rather, he simply asserts the Arabs' fondness for the "scent of war," their love of "rapine," and the promise of "a damsel or two." Muir's vision of a militant, resurgent Islam gone berserk reflected, in addition to old European associations of Islam with war and sex, colonial fears that Europe's own Muslim subjects might, in just such a locustlike manner, rise up in revolt and drive the Europeans back to Europe. Sir William, after all, was himself a senior British official in colonial India, as well as an aggressive activist for the Christian missionary movement there.[2]

If colonial officials could imagine that the reason for the rise of Islam was its inherently militant nature, they had little difficulty explaining its extension in India in similar terms. Yet as Peter Hardy has observed, those who argued that Indian Muslims were forcibly converted have generally failed to define either *force* or *conversion*,[3] leaving one to presume that a society can and will alter its religious identity simply because it has a sword at its neck. Precisely how this mechanism worked, either in theoretical or in practical terms, has never, however, been satisfactorily explained. Moreover, proponents of this theory seem to have confused conversion to the Islamic religion with the extension of Turko-Iranian rule in North India between 1200 and 1760, a confusion probably originating in too literal a translation of primary Persian accounts narrating the "Islamic" conquest of India. As Yohanan Friedmann has observed, in these accounts one frequently meets with such ambiguous phrases as "they submitted to Islam" ("iṭā'at-i Islām numūdand"), or "they came under submission to Islam" ("dar iṭā'at-i Islām āmadand"), in which "Islam" might mean either the religion, the Muslim state, or the "army of Islam." But a contextual reading of such passages usually favors one of the latter two interpretations, especially as these same sources often refer to Indo-Turkish armies as the *lashkar-i Islām*, or "army of Islam," and not the *lashkar-i Turkān*, or "army

1. William Muir, *The Caliphate: Its Rise, Decline, and Fall* (London, 1898; reprint, Beirut: Khayats, 1963), 45.
2. Richard M. Eaton, *Islamic History as Global History* (Washington, D.C.: American Historical Association, 1990), 13.
3. Peter Hardy, "Modern European and Muslim Explanations of Conversion to Islam in South Asia: A Preliminary Survey of the Literature," in *Conversion to Islam*, ed. Nehemia Levtzion (New York: Holmes & Meier, 1979), 78.

of Turks."[4] In other words, it was the Indo-Muslim state, and, more explicitly, its military arm, to which people were said to have submitted, and not
the Islamic faith.

Nor does the theory fit the religious geography of South Asia. If Islamization had ever been a function of military or political force, one would
expect that those areas exposed most intensively and over the longest period to rule by Muslim dynasties—that is, those that were most fully exposed to the "sword"—would today contain the greatest number of Muslims. Yet the opposite is the case, as those regions where the most dramatic
Islamization occurred, such as eastern Bengal or western Punjab, lay on
the fringes of Indo-Muslim rule, where the "sword" was weakest, and
where brute force could have exerted the least influence. In such regions
the first accurate census reports put the Muslim population at between 70
and 90 percent of the total, whereas in the heartland of Muslim rule in the
upper Gangetic Plain—the domain of the Delhi Fort and the Taj Mahal,
where Muslim regimes had ruled the most intensively and for the longest
period of time—the Muslim population ranged from only 10 to 15 percent.
In other words, in the subcontinent as a whole there is an *inverse* relationship between the degree of Muslim political penetration and the degree of
Islamization. Even within Bengal this principle holds true. As the 1901
Census of India put it:

> None of these [eastern] districts contains any of the places famous as
> the head-quarters of Muhammadan rulers. Dacca was the residence of
> the Nawab for about a hundred years, but it contains a smaller propor-
> tion of Muslims than any of the surrounding districts, except Faridpur.
> Malda and Murshidabad contain the old capitals, which were the center
> of Musalman rule for nearly four and a half centuries, and yet the Mus-
> lims form a smaller proportion of the population than they do in the ad-
> jacent districts of Dinajpur, Rajshahi, and Nadia.[5]

Indeed, it has even been proposed that, far from promoting the cause of
Islamization, the proximity of Muslim political power in some cases actually hindered it. According to S. L. Sharma and R. N. Srivastava, Mughal
persecution of the nominally converted Meo community of Rajasthan had
the effect, not of strengthening the Meos' Islamic identity, but of reinforcing their resistance to Islam.[6]

---

4. See Yohanan Friedmann, "A Contribution to the Early History of Islam in India,"
in *Studies in Memory of Gaston Wiet*, ed. Myrian Rosen-Ayalon (Jerusalem: Institute of Asian and African Studies, 1977), 322.
5. *Census of India, 1901*, vol. 6, *The Lower Provinces of Bengal and Their Feudatories* (Calcutta: Bengal Secretariat Press, 1902), 156.
6. See S. R. Sharma and R. N. Srivastava, "Institutional Resistance to Induced Islamization in a Convert Community—an Empiric Study in Sociology of Religion,"
Sociological Bulletin 16, no. 1 (March 1967): 77.

A third theory commonly advanced to explain Islamization in India is what I call the Religion of Patronage theory. This is the view that Indians of the premodern period converted to Islam in order to receive some non-religious favor from the ruling class—relief from taxes, promotion in the bureaucracy, and so forth. This theory has always found favor with Western-trained secular social scientists who see any religion as a dependent variable of some non-religious agency, in particular an assumed desire for social improvement or prestige. Many instances in Indian history would appear to support this theory. In the early fourteenth century, Ibn Battuta reported that Indians presented themselves as new converts to the Khalaji sultans, who in turn rewarded them with robes of honor according to their rank.[7] According to nineteenth-century censuses, many landholding families of Upper India had declared themselves Muslims in order to escape imprisonment for nonpayment of revenue, or to keep ancestral lands in the family.[8] The theory might even be stretched to include groups employed by Muslim rulers that assimilated much Islamic culture even if they did not formally convert. The Kayasthas and Khatris of the Gangetic Plain, the Parasnis of Maharashtra, and the Amils of Sind all cultivated Islamic culture while meeting the government's need for clerks and administrative servants, a process that Aziz Ahmad once compared with nineteenth- and twentieth-century "Westernization."[9] The acculturation of captured soldiers or slaves perhaps formed another dimension of this process. Severed from their families, and with no permanent sociocultural ties to their native homes, these men not surprisingly fell into the cultural orbit of their patrons.[10]

Although this thesis might help explain the relatively low incidence of Islamization in India's political heartland, it cannot explain the massive conversions that took place along the political fringe—as in Punjab or Bengal. Political patronage, like the influence of the sword, would have decreased rather than increased as one moved away from the centers of that patronage. What we need is some theory that can explain the phenomenon of mass Islamization on the periphery of Muslim power and not just in the heartland, and among millions of peasant cultivators and not just among urban elites.

To this end a fourth theory, which I call the Religion of Social Liberation

7. Ibn Battuta, *Rehla*, trans Mahdi Hussain, 46.
8. Hardy, "Modern European and Muslim Explanations," 80–81.
9. Aziz Ahmad, *Studies in Islamic Culture in the Indian Environment* (Oxford: Clarendon Press, 1964), 105.
10. Beyond India, one thinks of the janissaries of the contemporary Ottoman Empire, who had been Christian youths conscripted in the Balkans before they were Turkified and Islamized by their imperial patrons.

thesis, is generally pressed into service. Created by British ethnographers and historians, elaborated by many Pakistani and Bangladeshi nationals, and subscribed to by countless journalists and historians of South Asia, especially Muslims, this theory has for long been the most widely accepted explanation of Islamization in the subcontinent. The theory postulates a Hindu caste system that is unchanging through time and rigidly discriminatory against its own lower orders. For centuries, it is said, the latter suffered under the crushing burden of oppressive and tyrannical high-caste Hindus, especially Brahmans. Then, when Islam "arrived" in the Indian subcontinent, carrying its liberating message of social equality as preached (in most versions of the theory) by Sufi shaikhs, these same oppressed castes, seeking to escape the yoke of Brahmanic oppression and aware of a social equality hitherto denied them, "converted" to Islam en masse.

It can be seen that by juxtaposing what it perceives as the inherent justice of Islam and the inherent wickedness of Hindu society, the Religion of Social Liberation theory identifies motives for conversion that are, from a Muslim perspective, eminently praiseworthy. The problem, however, is that no evidence can be found in support of the theory. Moreover, it is profoundly illogical. First, by attributing present-day values to peoples of the past, it reads history backward. Before their contact with Muslims, India's lower castes are thought to have possessed, almost as though familiar with the writings of Jean-Jacques Rousseau or Thomas Jefferson, some innate notion of the fundamental equality of all humankind denied them by an oppressive Brahmanic tyranny. In fact, however, in thinking about Islam in relation to Indian religions, premodern Muslim intellectuals did not stress their religion's ideal of social equality as opposed to Hindu inequality, but rather Islamic monotheism as opposed to Hindu polytheism.[11] That is, their frame of reference for comparing these two civilizations was theological, not social. In fact, the idea that Islam fosters social equality (as opposed to religious equality) seems to be a recent notion, dating only from the period of the Enlightenment, and more particularly from the legacy of the French Revolution among nineteenth-century Muslim reformers.[12]

Second, even if Indians *did* believe in the fundamental equality of mankind, and even if Islam *had* been presented to them as an ideology of social

11. See Yohanan Friedmann, "Medieval Muslim Views of Indian Religions," *Journal of the American Oriental Society* 95 (1975): 214–21.
12. See Albert Hourani, *Arabic Thought in the Liberal Age, 1798–1939* (London: Oxford University Press, 1962), 75–79, 99, 138, 155–56, 162, 164–70, 173, 182, 238; Bernard Lewis, "The Impact of the French Revolution on Turkey: Some Notes on the Transmission of Ideas," *Journal of World History* 1, no. 1 (July 1953): 105–25.

equality—though both propositions appear to be false—there is abundant evidence that Indian communities failed, upon Islamization, to improve their status in the social hierarchy. On the contrary, most simply carried into Muslim society the same birth-ascribed rank that they had formerly known in Hindu society.[13] This is especially true of Bengal. As James Wise observed in 1883: "In other parts of India menial work is performed by outcast Hindus; but in Bengal any repulsive or offensive occupation devolves on the Muhammadan. The Beldar [scavenger, and remover of carcasses] is to the Muhammadan village what the Bhuinmali is to the Hindu, and it is not improbable that his ancestors belonged to this vile caste."[14]

Finally, as with the Sword and Patronage theories, the Religion of Social Liberation theory is refuted by the facts of geography. In 1872, when the earliest reliable census was taken, the highest concentrations of Muslims were found in eastern Bengal, western Punjab, the Northwest Frontier region, and Baluchistan. What is striking about those areas is not only that they lay far from the center of Muslim political power but that their indigenous populations had not yet, at the time of their contact with Islam, been fully integrated into either the Hindu or the Buddhist social system. In Bengal, Muslim converts were drawn mainly from Rajbansi, Pod, Chandal, Kuch, and other indigenous groups that had been only lightly exposed to Brahmanic culture, and in Punjab the same was true of the various Jat clans that eventually formed the bulk of the Muslim community.[15]

But this is hardly surprising. The *Baudhāyana-Dharmasūtra*, a late Vedic text (fifth–sixth centuries B.C.) reflecting the values of self-styled "clean" castes, divided the subcontinent into three concentric circles, each one containing distinct sociocultural communities. The first of these, Aryavarta, or the Aryan homeland, corresponded to the Upper Ganges–Jumna region of north-central India; there lived the "purest" heirs to Brahmanic tradition, people styling themselves highborn and ritually clean. The second circle contained an outer belt (Avanti, Anga-Magadha, Saurastra, Daksinapatha, Upavrt, and Sindhu-Sauvira) corresponding to Malwa, East and Central Bihar, Gujarat, the Deccan, and Sind. These regions lay within the pale of Indo-Aryan settlement, but they were inhabited by people "of mixed origin" who did not enjoy the same degree of ritual purity as those

13. See, e.g., *Caste and Social Stratification among the Muslims*, ed. Imtiaz Ahmed (Delhi: Manohar Book Service, 1973).

14. James Wise, *Notes on the Races, Castes and Traders of Eastern Bengal*, 2 vols. (London: Harrison & Sons, 1883), 1: 40.

15. See Richard M. Eaton, "The Political and Religious Authority of the Shrine of Baba Farid," in *Moral Conduct and Authority: The Place of Adab in South Asian Islam*, ed. Barbara D. Metcalf (Berkeley and Los Angeles: University of California Press, 1984), 333–56.

of the first region. And the third concentric circle contained those outer regions inhabited by "unclean" tribes considered so far beyond the pale that penances were prescribed for those who visited such places. Peoples living in this third circle included the Arattas of Punjab, the Sauviras of southern Punjab and Sind, the Pundras of North Bengal, and the Vangas of central and East Bengal.[16]

Now, the theory of Social Liberation assumes the prior existence of a highly stratified Hindu social order presided over by an entrenched and oppressive Brahman community. If the theory were valid, then, the greatest incidence of conversion to Islam should logically have occurred in those areas where Brahmanic social order was most deeply entrenched—namely, in the core region of Aryavarta. Conversely, Islam should have found its fewest adherents in those areas having the least exposure to Brahmanic civilization, that is, along the periphery or beyond the pale of that civilization, in the outermost of the three concentric circles cited in the *Baudhāyana-Dharmasūtra*. But it is precisely in that outer circle—the area roughly coinciding with the areas included in the original (1947) state of Pakistan, with its eastern and western wings—that the vast majority of South Asian Muslims reside. The modern, pre-Partition distribution of South Asian Muslims thus indicates an outcome precisely opposite to the one predicted by the theory—namely, the less the prior exposure to Brahmanic civilization, the greater the incidence of subsequent Islamization. If the aboriginal peoples inhabiting India's "periphery" had never been fully absorbed in a Brahman-ordered society in the first place, the matter of their escaping an oppressive Hindu social order cannot arise logically, just as it did not arise empirically.

Theories of Islamization in Bengal

It was relatively late in their experience in Bengal that Englishmen became aware of the full extent of the province's Muslim population. With British activity centered on Calcutta, in the predominantly Hindu southwest, colonial officials through most of the nineteenth century perceived Bengal's eastern districts as a vast and rather remote hinterland, with whose cultural profile they were largely unfamiliar. They were consequently astonished when the first official census of the province, that of 1872, showed Muslims totaling 70 percent and more in the Chittagong, Noakhali, Pabna,

16. *Baudhāyana-Dharmasūtra* I.1.9–14, in Georg Bühler, trans., *Sacred Laws of the Aryas as Taught in the Schools of Apastamba, Gautama, Vasishtha, and Baudhayana*, part 2, *Vasishtha and Baudhayana*, vol. 14 of Sacred Books of the East, ed. F. Max Müller (Oxford: Clarendon Press, 1882), 147–48. See also *History of Bengal*, ed. R. C. Majumdar, 2d ed. (Dacca: University of Dacca, 1963), 8, 290.

and Rajshahi districts, and over 80 percent in Bogra (see map 3).[17] Writing in 1894, James Wise, a government official with considerable experience in the province, wrote that "the most interesting fact revealed by the census of 1872 was the enormous host of Muhammadans resident in Lower Bengal—not massed around the old capitals, but in the alluvial plains of the Delta." He went on to observe that "the history of the spread of the Muhammadan faith in Lower and Eastern Bengal is a subject of such vast importance at the present day as to merit a careful and minute examination."[18]

The subject certainly was examined. The census of 1872 touched off a heated debate that lasted the rest of the nineteenth century and well into the twentieth. Its opening salvo was fired by the compiler of the census report itself, Henry Beverley. Noting the apparent incongruity of masses of Muslims turning up in regions far from the ancient centers of Muslim domination, Beverley concluded that "the existence of Muhammadans in Bengal is not due so much to the introduction of Mughul blood into the country as to the conversion of the former inhabitants for whom a rigid system of caste discipline rendered Hinduism intolerable."[19] In short, he rejected the Immigration theory and instead sketched out an early version of the Social Liberation theory. Henceforth this theory would dominate British thinking about Islamization in the province, and eventually most Muslims would subscribe to it as well.

But Beverley's interpretation did not go unchallenged. Soon after the publication of the 1872 census findings, a respectable Muslim gentleman of Mymensingh District, Abu A. Ghuznavi, submitted a report to the Collector of his district strenuously opposing Beverley's argument that mass conversion had taken place. Ghuznavi proposed instead that "the majority of the modern Mahomedans are not the descendants of Chandals and Kaibartas but are of foreign extraction, though in many cases it may be of more or less remote degree."[20] In favor of his argument, Ghuznavi cited Arab migration before the Turkish conquest, land grants made by Sultan Husain Shah to foreigners, the dispersion of Afghans "in every hamlet" after the Mughal conquest, the greater fertility of Muslims owing to their

17. H. Beverley, *Report on the Census of Bengal, 1872* (Calcutta: Secretariat Press, 1872), 12–15.
18. James Wise, "The Muhammadans of Eastern Bengal," *Journal of the Asiatic Society of Bengal* 63 (1894): 28.
19. Beverley, *Report*, 132.
20. Abu A. Ghuznavi, "Notes on the Origin, Social and Religious Divisions and Other Matters Touching on the Mahomedans of Bengal and Having Special Reference to the District of Maimensing" (India Office Library, London, European MSS., E 295., vol. 17 [n.d.]), 3.

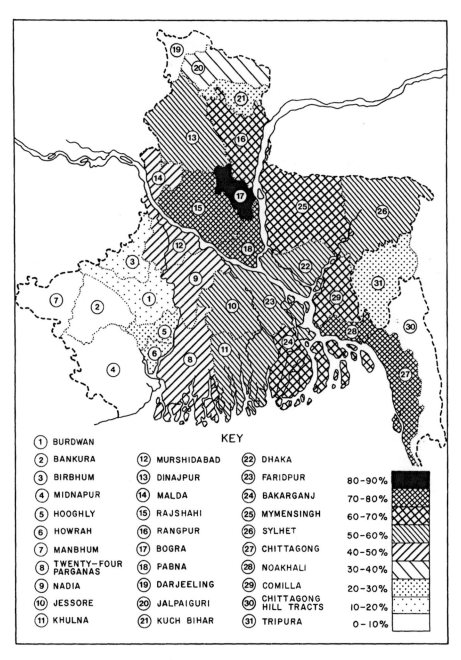

KEY

(1) BURDWAN	(12) MURSHIDABAD	(22) DHAKA
(2) BANKURA	(13) DINAJPUR	(23) FARIDPUR
(3) BIRBHUM	(14) MALDA	(24) BAKARGANJ
(4) MIDNAPUR	(15) RAJSHAHI	(25) MYMENSINGH
(5) HOOGHLY	(16) RANGPUR	(26) SYLHET
(6) HOWRAH	(17) BOGRA	(27) CHITTAGONG
(7) MANBHUM	(18) PABNA	(28) NOAKHALI
(8) TWENTY-FOUR PARGANAS	(19) DARJEELING	(29) COMILLA
(9) NADIA	(20) JALPAIGURI	(30) CHITTAGONG HILL TRACTS
(10) JESSORE	(21) KUCH BIHAR	(31) TRIPURA
(11) KHULNA		

▓	80–90%
▨	70–80%
▨	60–70%
▨	50–60%
▨	40–50%
▨	30–40%
⣿	20–30%
⡀	10–20%
☐	0–10%

Map 3. Distribution of Muslim population in Bengal, 1872

practices of polygamy and widow remarriage, their greater longevity, and the absence among Muslims of a caste system or institutionalized celibacy.[21] Although he conceded that there had been "some" conversions, Ghuznavi insisted that they had not been among low-caste Hindus. "Why should we speak of conversion of low-caste Hindus only?" he asked, "Why should we forget the Musalman Rajput diwans of different districts and notably of Maimensing. . . . Similarly, there are Mozumdars of Sylhet, Raja Sahebs of Faridpore, Gangulies of Bikrampore, and a host of others."[22]

Ghuznavi was here outlining the Immigration theory of Islamization, the view favored by *ashrāf* classes throughout India. To the extent that local conversions took place at all, Ghuznavi argued, they came not from the despised low castes, but from the upper orders of Hindu society. At the turn of the twentieth century, claims were indeed made that in the Mughal period some members of Bengal's landed elite and even of the priestly caste had converted to Islam. The rajas of Kharagpur (in Monghyr District), defeated by one of Akbar's generals, were said to have accepted Islam as the condition for retaining their family estates; Raja Purdil Singh of Parsouni in Darbhanga, in northern Bihar, became a Muslim by way of expiation after having rebelled against the Mughal emperor; the Muslim *dīwān* families of *pargana* Sarail in Tippera, and of Haibatnagar and Jungalbari in Mymensingh, had formerly been Brahmans; and the Pathans of Majhouli in Darbhanga sprang from the family of the raja of Narhan.[23] These instances, however, could have accounted for only a tiny fraction of the total Muslim population and cannot explain the appearance of the millions of Muslim peasant cultivators recorded in the census figures.

Meanwhile, in the final decades of the nineteenth century, a consensus on the Islamization issue began to emerge in British official circles. Here we may examine the work of James Wise, a veteran official who had served ten years as civil surgeon in Dhaka, and who elaborated his views in an important article entitled "The Muhammadans of Eastern Bengal" (1894).[24] Wise opened by dismissing the Immigration theory favored by *ashrāf* spokesmen like Ghuznavi. "In Muhammadan histories," he noted, "no mention is made of any large Muhammadan immigration from Upper India, and we know that in the reign of Akbar the climate of Bengal was considered so uncongenial to the Mughal invaders, that an order to proceed

---

21. Ibid., 4–12.
22. Ibid., 14.
23. E. A. Gait, "The Muhammadans of Bengal," in *Census of India, 1901*, vol. 6, *The Lower Provinces of Bengal and Their Feudatories*, pt. 1, "Report" (Calcutta: Bengal Secretariat Press, 1902), 170.
24. Wise, "Muhammadans of Eastern Bengal," 28–63.

thither was regarded as a sentence of banishment."[25] Wise then offered a number of arguments to explain how and why ethnic Bengalis became Muslims. First, he invoked the Religion of the Sword thesis, citing without evidence the "enthusiastic soldiers who, in the thirteenth and fourteenth centuries, spread the faith of Islam among the timid races of Bengal, made forcible conversions by the sword, and, penetrating the dense forests of the Eastern frontier, planted the crescent in the villages of Silhet." He also accepted the view that the Chittagong region had been colonized by Arab merchants. The latter, he argued, again without citing evidence, carried on an extensive trade along the Chittagong coast, where they "disseminated their religious ideas among the people." Furthermore, he suggested, captured slaves from the villages of eastern Bengal might have swelled the ranks of the Muslim population, since desperate and impoverished families would have been driven to sell their children to Muslims as slaves. He also suggested that Hindus might have converted "as the only means of escaping punishment for murder, or adultery, as this step was considered full atonement for either crime."[26] All of this was conjecture.

Wise's central argument, however, was the one that would achieve widest currency in government circles. "When the Muhammadan armies poured into Bengal," he wrote,

> it is hard to believe that they were not welcomed by the hewers of wood and drawers of water, and that many a despairing Chandal and Kaibartta joyfully embraced a religion that proclaimed the equality of all men, and which was the religion of the race keeping in subjection their former oppressors. Hinduism had prohibited the outcast from residing in the same village as the twice-born Brahman, had forced him to perform the most menial and repulsive occupations, and had virtually treated him as an animal undeserving of any pity; but Islam announced that the poor, as well as the rich, the slave and his master, the peasant and the prince, were of equal value in the eyes of God. Above all, the Brahman held out no hopes of a future world to the most virtuous helot, while the Mulla not only proffered assurances of felicity in this world, but of an indefeasible inheritance in the next.[27]

This is as vigorous a statement of the Social Liberation thesis as can be found anywhere, and contains all the essential elements of that theory: the a priori presence of a highly stratified Hindu social order, an exploited class

---

25. Ibid., 29. Moreover, he added, viceroys and nobles governing Bengal generally left the inhospitable province after having amassed as much wealth as they could, "while only a few officers and private soldiers, having married into native families, remained and settled in their new homes."

26. Ibid., 28–30.

27. Ibid., 32.

of menial outcasts, an oppressive class of Brahmans, and an understanding of Islam as an ideology of social egalitarianism that would be "joyfully" embraced by the masses.

But Bengal's *ashrāf* Muslims did not accept such reasoning. Even if inclined to agree with Wise's characterization of Brahmans as cruel oppressors, they would not agree that the majority of the Muslims of Bengal were indigenous to the delta. So in 1895, the year after the publication of Wise's essay, Khondkar Fuzli Rubbee published his *The Origin of the Musalmans of Bengal*. Like his predecessor Abu Ghuznavi, Rubbee denied "that the natives of this country, either from compulsion or free will, were converted to Islam, in any appreciable number at a time."[28] Rather, he asserted, "the ancestors of the present Musalmans of this country were certainly those Musalmans who came here from foreign parts during the rule of the former sovereigns."[29] In fact, Rubbee viewed the delta's geographic isolation as evidence for this process, arguing that the region "always enjoyed immunity from foreign invasions, and consequently it formed a great asylum for the Musulmans."[30] Rubbee did not explain why the same natural frontiers that had protected Muslims from foreign invaders failed to protect Bengalis from Muslim invaders. Presumably he did not consider Muslims to have been invaders, but merely immigrant settlers.

Rubbee also cited numerous charitable grants (*aima*) to "venerable Muslims" in Bengal, suggesting that these became the bases of foreign settlement. "With regard to the three ancient divisions of Bengal," he wrote, "namely Rarh [the southwest], Barind [the north], and Bang [the east], *Aimas* are to be found mostly in Rarh, less in Barind, and rarely in Bang."[31] But the difficulty with this reasoning is that the majority of the Muslims were found in the very areas where, according to Rubbee, there were the fewest charitable grants. The author also had difficulty explaining how one of the largest peasant populations in the world could have been descended from high-born immigrants who refused to cultivate the soil. They took to agriculture, he speculated, when "their resources failed them," or when those among them who were soldiers failed to obtain military employment. Subsequently, when agricultural productivity improved and internal peace and security prevailed in Bengal, these classes of Muslim cultivators naturally multiplied.[32]

The publication of Rubbee's book was soon followed by the controver-

28. Khondkar Fuzli Rubbee, *The Origin of the Musalmans of Bengal* (1895; 2d ed., Dacca: Society for Pakistan Studies, 1970), 40–41.
29. Ibid., 43.
30. Ibid., 17.
31. Ibid., 59.
32. Ibid., 87–94.

sial 1901 *Census of India,* which restated the position to which Ghuznavi and Rubbee had reacted. In his report in this census, E. A. Gait concluded that probably nine-tenths of those returning themselves as "Shekhs"— the typical response of Muslim Bengali cultivators when asked their caste—were of local origin.[33] Gait doubted that any significant migration of Muslim settlers had taken place even within Bengal, much less from beyond the delta. Observing that Muslim settlers generally sought the higher levels of land near the old capitals, he reasoned that "they would never willingly have taken up their residence in the rice swamps of Noakhali, Bogra and Backergunge."[34]

Gait's most important contribution to the ongoing debate was his observation that in Bengal high Muslim populations correlated with the simplest social organization—that is, with the least elaboration of castes. Noting the affinities of the Muslims of the east with indigenous Pod and Chandal communities, and those of the north with indigenous Rajbansi and Kuch communities, Gait remarked that "the proportion of Hindus of other castes in these parts of the country is, and always has been, very small. The main castes are the Rajbansis (including Koches) in North Bengal, and the Chandals and other castes of non-Aryan origin in East Bengal."[35] This observation might have led to a breakthrough in the fuzzy and tendentious thinking that had theretofore characterized the debate. For it follows that where there was little caste elaboration, there was little Brahmanic dominance, and hence little oppression of outcasts. And without such oppression, the Social Liberation theory collapses, since the "lower orders" would not have had an entrenched, Brahman-ordered society against which to rebel.

But Gait did not follow up on the implications of his own observation; indeed, he offered no coherent theory of Islamization at all, apart from stating that the vast majority of Muslims were of local origin. But since they were published in the authoritative *Census of India,* even these views carried weight. Soon they were replicated in the Settlement Reports and the widely influential *Bengal District Gazetteers* that began appearing in the early twentieth century. For example, the gazetteer for Noakhali District (1911) stated that the "vast majority of the Shekhs [i.e., Muslim cultivators] and lower sections of the community are descended from the aboriginal races of the district," meaning, primarily, the Chandals.[36] Similarly, the Settlement Report of Bogra and Pabna districts (1930)

33. Gait, "Muhammadans," in *Census of India, 1901,* 6: 169.
34. Ibid., 166.
35. Ibid., 169.
36. J. E. Webster, *East Bengal and Assam District Gazetteers: Noakhali* (Allahabad: Pioneer Press, 1911), 39.

traced the Muslim communities of those districts to "Hindus converted at a comparatively recent date," and stated that the majority of the population were "descendants of the aboriginals of North Bengal, the Koches."[37]

In the decade before 1947, three anthropological studies produced data corroborating the consensus view in official circles. Although differing in methodology, sampling techniques, and regions studied within the delta, they all agreed that the masses of Bengali Muslims were descended from indigenous communities and not from outsiders. In the first of them, conducted in the Twenty-four Parganas District in 1938, Eileen Macfarlane concluded that "the blood-group data of the Muhammadans of Budge Budge show clearly that these peoples are descended from lower caste Hindu converts, as held by local traditions, and the proportion remains almost the same as among their present-day Hindu neighbors."[38] Three years later, B. K. Chatterji and A. K. Mitra made another study of blood-group distributions comparing not only low-caste Bengali Hindus with rural Muslims, again in the Twenty-four Parganas District, but also the latter with both urban Muslims and non-Bengali Muslims. This study found an affinity between rural Muslims and their low-caste Hindu neighbors, the Mahisyas and Bagdis, and further concluded that urban Bengali Muslims were serologically closer to the distant Pathans of India's Northwest Frontier than they were to rural Bengali Muslims, lending substance to the urban Muslims' claims of their own descent from foreign immigrants to Bengal.[39]

Finally, in 1960, D. N. Majumdar and C. R. Rao published a study based on data collected in both East and West Bengal in 1945, just prior to the massive population shifts that followed partition of the province in 1947. Using stature, frontal breadth, and nasal height in defining group divergences, these investigators concluded that "we should look among the tribal and scheduled caste Non-Muslim groups of Bengal for a possible origin of the Muslim population in Bengal. . . . The serological data obtained from the Muslim population of Bengal (pre-Partition) tends to the same view, viz., the dissociation of the Bengali Muslims from those outside India, and even from the Shias and Sunnis of Uttar Pradesh. This indicates

37. D. MacPherson, *Final Report on the Survey and Settlement Operations in the Districts of Pabna and Bogra, 1920–29* (Calcutta: Bengal Secretariat Book Depot, 1930), 31, 32.
38. Eileen W. E. Macfarlane, "Blood-Group Distribution in India with Special Reference to Bengal," *Journal of Genetics* 36, no. 2 (July 1938): 230, 232.
39. B. K. Chatterji and A. K. Mitra, "Blood Group Distributions of the Bengalis and Their Comparison with Other Indian Races and Castes," *Indian Culture* 8 (1941–42): 197, 201, 202.

the local origin of the Muslims, if blood group evidence has any meaning at all."[40] The authors also found that in terms of the more important anthropometric indicators (head length and breadth, nasal length and breadth), East Bengal groups, both Muslim and non-Muslim, differed fundamentally from West Bengalis.[41] This last finding would diminish the historical significance even of internal migration from western to eastern Bengal.

In the early twentieth century, as the Indian nationalist movement gathered momentum, and especially after the founding of the Muslim League in 1906, when the drive for a separate Muslim "homeland" in British India began to gather strength, arguments for or against the various theories of Islamization became more heated. Indian nationalists tended to sidestep the issue altogether, since any recognition of foreign origin of a large segment of the Indian community, or of past Islamization among that community, would have weakened the nationalist position concerning the fundamental unity and homogeneity of all Indian peoples. Nor was it easy for Hindus to embrace the thesis favored by Muslim intellectuals, the Religion of Social Liberation argument, since it placed high-caste Hindus in the unsavory role of oppressors.[42]

For many Muslims, on the other hand, the issue of a separate Muslim community on the Indian subcontinent was fundamental, since it formed the historical justification for the future state of Pakistan. This made it difficult to relinquish the Immigration thesis entirely, even though, so far as Bengal is concerned, considerable ethnographic data had shown that the ancestors of the Muslim masses had been indigenous to the delta long before the thirteenth century. This led some to embrace a hybrid theory that combined elements of both the Immigration theory and the Religion of Social Liberation thesis. In this view, *ashrāf* immigrants had settled the land and become naturalized Bengalis, while at the same time masses of ethnic Bengalis were attracted to the egalitarian ethic of Islam. As this mutual accommodation was said to have obliterated social differences between the *ashrāf* and the masses, the theory became ideologically conve-

40. D. N. Majumdar and C. R. Rao, *Race Elements in Bengal* (Calcutta: Asia Publishing House, 1960), 96, 98, 114.
41. Ibid., 96.
42. An exception to this was Niharranjan Ray, who wrote in 1945: "To some of the lower grades of Hindus, Islam with its more democratic appeal in the social plane and a simpler code of tenets on the religious, along with the easy temptation of favours at the dispersal of the ruling class and their proselytising zeal, opened up an inviting vista, while to a limited number at least it proved to be a haven from religious and social persecution by the upper classes." Ray, "Medieval Bengali Culture," 49.

nient for post-1947 Muslim governments, which naturally sought to stress the unity of all Muslims residing within their borders.[43]

Historiographically, the legacies of the colonial era and the independence movement were to polarize Hindus and Muslims into exclusive and even hostile categories, to project these categories into the past, and to read premodern Bengali history in terms of a struggle between them. Here is a lurid portrayal of the Turkish conquest penned in 1963 by the reputed linguist and historian of Bengali language S. K. Chatterji:

> The conquest of Bengal by these ruthless foreigners was like a terrible hurricane which swept over the country, when a peace-loving people were subjected to all imaginable terrors and torments—wholesale massacres, pillages, abduction and enslavement of men and women, destruction of temples, palaces, images and libraries, and forcible conversion. The Muslim Turks, like the Spanish Catholic *conquistadores* in Mexico and Peru and elsewhere in America, sought to destroy the culture and religion of the land as the handiwork of Satan.[44]

And here is how the well-known Indian Bengali historian R. C. Majumdar, writing in 1973, described the growth of Islam in premodern Bengal:

> The Hindu and Muslim communities resembled two strong walled forts, standing side by side, each of which had only one gate,—that of exit in the case of the Hindus, and that for entrance in the case of the Muslims. Even for the slightest deviation from the rules of touch and purity the Hindus were cast out of society, with no chance of re-entry, and once they entered the fort of Islam the door of exit for the newcomer was forever barred. This, together with forcible conversion, and voluntary acceptance of Islam by temptation of material gain or benefit,

43. This thesis was articulated by one of the most influential Bengali historians of the post-independence period, Abdul Karim, who wrote: "The facts that the Muslims settled in this country, learnt the local language, lived in harmony with the local people, accepted local wives, adopted various professions suited to their genius, and that in their dietary system and dwelling houses they depended on materials locally available, bear out that they considered Bengal as their homeland. Side by side they adhered to the Islamic religious principles and built religious institutions of their own. There is, therefore, good ground to suggest that a Bengali Muslim society already passed its formative stage, took a definite shape, and breathed a new spirit of tolerance, equality and universal love in the country so much so that large masses accepted Islam and even the then Hinduism was deeply affected as traceable in some of the elements of the Chaitanya movement." Karim, *Social History*, 210–11. For a recent restatement of the Immigration theory, combined with a measure of the Social Liberation thesis, see Muhammad Mohar Ali, *History of the Muslims in Bengal* (Riyadh: Imam Muhammad Ibn Sa'ud Islamic University, 1985), 1B: 750–88.
44. Suniti Kumar Chatterji, *Languages and Literatures of Modern India* (Calcutta: Bengal Publishers, 1963), 160–61.

rarely by conviction, resulted in the steady flow of the Hindus to the
fold of Islam, which constitutes the most important change in the
Hindu society during the middle age.[45]

Implicit in Chatterji's overheated rhetoric, and explicit in Majumdar's
military imagery of forts and gates, is the presumption that religions
themselves are timeless essences—closed, self-contained, and mutually
exclusive. Although such an ahistorical and normative conception is not
confined to the modern age, it has become especially widespread in the
twentieth century. From the Partition of Bengal (1905) down to the razing
of the Babri Masjid at Ayodhya in nearby Uttar Pradesh (1992), colonial
and post-colonial politicians have encouraged and effectively exploited the
idea. Nor have historians been immune to this essentialist conception of
religion, which Chatterji and Majumdar simply projected backward in time
and displaced onto Bengal's premodern history.[46]

The Appearance of a Bengali Muslim Peasantry

What is striking about the historiography of Islamization in Bengal is that
so few advocates of any of the theories discussed above—Immigration,
Sword, Patronage, Social Liberation—grounded their theories on original
evidence. Nor did they attempt to establish exactly when and where Islam
first became a mass religion. Inasmuch as any coherent historical reconstruction must be based on established facts of geography and chronology,
before we can explain mass conversion to Islam, we must first establish, in
as precise terms as possible, exactly when and where the Bengali Muslim
peasant community first emerged.

As to the direction from which Islamic influence first reached the delta,
a glance at a map of the Indian Ocean might suggest a maritime connection with the Middle East. It is true that Arab geographers such as Sulaiman Tajir (d. 851), Ibn Khurdadbhih (d. ca. 850), Mas'udi (d. 956), and
Idrisi (d. ca. 1150), were familiar with Bengal, and that one of these,
Mas'udi, actually mentions Muslims—evidently long-distance maritime

---

45. R. C. Majumdar, *History of Medieval Bengal* (Calcutta: G. Bharadwaj & Co.,
1973), 196–97.
46. Actually, Majumdar saw himself as only correcting what he felt to be an unwar-
ranted view of communal unity put forward by Indian nationalists caught up in
the independence movement. "Since the beginning of the struggle for freedom of
India," he wrote, "the complete Hindu-Muslim unity was regarded as an indis-
pensable factor for its success. As a result of this view, there has been a deliberate
attempt to re-write the history of India by considerably toning down, if not altogether effacing from pages of history, the whole episode of the bigotry and intoler-
ance shown by the Muslim rulers towards Hindu religion." Ibid., vi.

merchants—living there in the tenth century.[47] The tradition of local coinage in southeastern Bengal during the Chandra dynasty (ca. 825–1035), and the discovery of Abbasid coins in the Lalmai region, further point to this region's economic integration with the wider world of the Indian Ocean at a time when Arab Muslims dominated that ocean's trade.[48] However, study of the global distribution of the four legal traditions in Sunni Islam—Hanafi, Shafi'i, Maliki, and Hanbali—suggests that Islamization did not occur by way of the seas. In the Islamic world generally, converted populations have tended to adopt the school of law adhered to by the carriers of Islam in their region. From the tenth century on, the Shafi'i school was dominant in southern and western Arabia, the region of the peninsula most firmly tied into Indian Ocean trade. In the succeeding centuries, coastal East Africa, India's Malabar coast, and island Southeast Asia all underwent Islamization through commercial contact with Shafi'i Arabs. And by 1500 all these regions adhered to the Shafi'i legal tradition. Had Bengal, too, been Islamized by the predominantly Shafi'i seafaring Arabs, or by other maritime Muslims in touch with such Arabs, one might expect the Muslims of Bengal also to have followed the Shafi'i school. But by 1500 and thereafter, Bengali Muslims were mainly Hanafi, then as now the dominant legal tradition among inland Muslims living further up the Gangetic Plain and throughout Central Asia.[49] This clearly points to a northwestern, overland origin of Bengal's Islamization.

But when and how did this happen? Despite claims that the masses of Bengali Muslims originated in the very distant past, such a proposition finds no support in the primary source materials, not, at least, so far as concerns the peasantry, who comprise the great bulk of the population. With but one exception, pre-sixteenth-century foreign references to Muslims in Bengal mention only immigrant or urban Muslims—that is, *ashrāf* society. The exception is the account of Ibn Battuta, who traveled to Sylhet to meet the renowned saint Shah Jalal in 1345. The famed Arab traveler later recorded that "the inhabitants of these mountains had embraced Islam at his [Shah Jalal's] hands, and for this reason he stayed amidst them."[50] But it is not at all clear that Ibn Battuta was referring here to a peasant population. It was, as he said, the inhabitants of the mountains,

47. *The History of India as Told by Its Own Historians,* trans. and ed. H. M. Elliot and John Dowson (Allahabad: Kitab Mahal, 1964), 1: 5, 13–14, 25, 90. Mas'udi, *Prairies d'or,* 1: 155.

48. F. A. Khan, *Mainamati* (Karachi, 1963), 25–27. Cited in Tarafdar, "Trade and Society," 277.

49. See Francis Robinson, *Atlas of the Islamic World since 1500* (Oxford: Phaidon Press, 1982), 29.

50. Ibn Battuta, *Rehla,* 239.

not those of the plains, that accepted Islam through the agency of Shah Jalal. These hill folk probably practiced shifting cultivation, for he seems to have distinguished this population from the peasants of the lowlands who practiced wet rice cultivation, whom he clearly identified as Hindus.[51]

The next foreigner who noticed Muslims in Bengal was the Chinese official Ma Huan, who reached the delta in 1433, some ninety years after Ibn Battuta. At this time Raja Ganesh's turbulent political intrusion had just subsided, and Sultan Jalal al-Din Muhammad had begun patronizing an Islamic culture heavily influenced by its Bengali environment. The Chinese traveler saw a dense and prosperous population during his travels from Chittagong to Sonargaon to Pandua. But his only comments as to the people's ethnic or religious identity were written in the context of Pandua, where he observed that "the king's palace and the large and small palaces of the nobility and temples, are all in the city. They are Musalmans."[52] The only Muslims the foreigner mentioned were city-dwellers, not peasants.

In the early sixteenth century, following Vasco da Gama's maritime voyage to India in 1498, we get the first European accounts of Bengal and its peoples. But again, so far as concerns the delta's Muslims, these writers appear to have been aware only of an urban, and not a rural population. Referring to Gaur, which he claimed to have visited sometime between 1503 and 1508, Ludovico di Varthema wrote that "this city was one of the best that I had hitherto seen, and has a very great realm," adding that the sultan's entire army, two hundred thousand men, were Muslims.[53] Writing between 1512 and 1515, evidently on the basis of reports from merchants or ship captains who had visited Bengal, Tome Pires remarked that the king "is a very faithful Mohammedan" and that "the kings of this kingdom turned Mohammedan three hundred years ago."[54] But Pires makes no reference to the religion of the population at large.

Pires's contemporary Duarte Barbosa, whose writings on Bengal were also based on travelers' accounts and not direct observation, has much to

51. Ibid., 241.
52. Ma Huan in P. C. Bagchi, "Political Relations," 117.
53. Ludovico di Varthema, *Travels*, 211.
54. Tome Pires, *Suma Oriental*, 89. Pires does, however, speak of tributary "heathen" kings such as the raja of Tripura. His remark that the kings of Bengal had "turned Mohammedan" in the early thirteenth century is curious, for it suggests that he understood kingship in Bengal as an unbroken succession from the Sena, or pre-Turkish, days to his own. Could it be that Pires was unaware of the foreign origin of Bengal's Turkish, Afghan, and Arab kings? Evidently the Husain Shahi court had so thoroughly assimilated Bengali culture that the Portuguese official detected no trace of foreignness in either the court or its monarch, seeing instead an unbroken Bengali dynasty that had converted to Islam three hundred years earlier.

say about the "respectable Moors" of Gaur, whom he describes as walking about "clad in white cotton smocks with their cloth girdles, silk scarves, and daggers garnished with silver and gold." His references to their eating well, their free-wheeling spending, and to their "many other extravagances" clearly point to wealthy urban merchants and not to rural society. Indeed, Barbosa speaks of Gaur as a city inhabited by white men, with its "strangers from many lands such as Arabs, Persians, Abexis and Indians."[55] Yet he also makes the important remark that "the Heathen of these parts daily become Moors to gain the favour of their rulers"—the only contemporary evidence that would appear to support the Political Patronage theory of Islamization.[56] But since he never mentions Muslims except in the context of the capital city, Barbosa appears to have been referring to the Islamization not of peasants but of those Hindu artisan castes that other sources associated with the sultanate's urban proletariat.

So far as concerns the countryside, it is only from the late sixteenth century, and in particular after the Mughal conquest (1574), that we have solid evidence of a Muslim peasant population anywhere in Bengal. The earliest reference is that of the Venetian traveler Cesare Federici, who in 1567 noted that the entire population of Sondwip, a large island in Bengal's southeastern corner opposite Chittagong, was Muslim, and that it had its own Muslim "king." Federici was also struck by the agricultural development of Sondwip, which he judged "the fertilest Iland in all the world."[57] In April 1599, not long after Federici's visit, a Jesuit missionary named Francis Fernandez traveled up the channel of East Bengal's Meghna River on an evangelizing tour, carefully noting the customs of the local people and evaluating the prospects of converting them to Christianity. Reaching the rural districts near Narayanganj in southeastern Dhaka District, Fernandez recorded that "I started examining whether there were any chances of propagating the Christian religion, but I found that the people are nearly all Mahometans." This is the earliest unambiguous reference to a Muslim peasantry in the heart of the delta proper.[58]

Several seventeenth-century European travelers made similar observations respecting the appearance of Muslims in the Bengali countryside, and noted that Islam was a very recent movement, dating only from the Mughal conquest. Writing in 1629, by which time Mughal power had become firmly established in the delta, the Augustinian friar Sebastião Man-

55. Duarte Barbosa, *Book of Duarte Barbosa*, 135–39, 147.
56. Ibid., 148.
57. Federici, "Extracts," 137.
58. H. Hosten, "Jesuit Letters from Bengal, Arakan and Burma (1599–1600)," *Bengal Past and Present* 30 (1925): 59.

rique says: "In the early days, all the kingdoms of Bengala followed heathen cults, as the greater part and even now most of them do to this day.
*Except some, however, who since this region became subject to the Mogol
Empire, have abandoned the heathen faith,* and the more difficult road to
hell to follow the wider and easier road which is that of the Alcoran
[Qur'an]."[59] In 1666 the French traveler Jean de Thevenot made much the
same point—as well as exhibiting the same anti-Muslim bias, typical
among seventeenth-century Europeans:

> The Country [i.e., Bengal] was kept in far better order under the *Patan*
> Kings, (I mean) before the Mahometans and *Moguls* were Masters of it,
> because then they had Uniformity in Religion. It has been found by ex-
> perience, that disorder came into it with *Mahometanism*, and that diver-
> sity of Religions hath there caused corruption in Manners.[60]

Like Manrique, Thevenot understood Bengal's pre-Mughal period as pre-
Muslim, and believed that Islam had become dominant in Bengal only
after the Mughal conquest, which had occurred somewhat less than a century before he was writing. It is significant, too, that Europeans observed
concentrations of Muslim peasants only in the eastern half of the delta,
and not in the older, already Hinduized western sector. For in 1699, exactly
a century after Fernandez encountered Muslims in the rural Dhaka region,
another Jesuit, Father Martin, S.J., who so far as we know traveled only in
the Hooghly region of west Bengal, noted that "nearly the whole country
is given to idolatry."[61]

Other contemporary data confirm Manrique's and Thevenot's general
point that Islamization did not appear among the masses until after the
Mughal conquest. The earliest Persian source touching on this matter
dates from 1638, when the Mughal governor of Bengal, Islam Khan Mashhadi, complained to the raja of Arakan about Portuguese raiding of the
Noakhali coast. There, the governor wrote, the Portuguese had been com-
mitting "depredations on the Muslim masses."[62] In the 1660s another
Mughal source, the *'Ālamgīr-nāma* by Kazim b. Muhammad Amin, stated

59. Manrique, *Travels* 1: 67. Emphasis mine.
60. Surendranath Sen, ed., *Indian Travels of Thevenot and Careri* (New Delhi:
National Archives, 1949), 96.
61. M. L. Aimé-Martin, ed., *Lettres édifiantes et curieuses concernant l'Asie,
l'Afrique et l'Amérique* (Paris: Société du Panthéon littéraire, 1843), 2: 258. H.
Hosten, "The Earliest Recorded Episcopal Visitation of Bengal, 1712–1715,"
Bengal Past and Present 6 (1910): 217.
62. S. H. Askari, "The Mughal-Magh Relations Down to the Time of Islam Khan
Mashhadi," in *Indian History Congress, Proceedings,* 22d session, Gauhati, 1959
(Bombay: Indian History Congress, 1960), 210.

that most of the peasants of Ghoraghat, or what is now the Rangpur region of northern Bengal, were Muslims.[63]

Summary

If large numbers of rural Muslims were not observed until as late as the end of the sixteenth century or afterward, we face a paradox—namely, that mass Islamization occurred under a regime, the Mughals, that as a matter of policy showed no interest in proselytizing on behalf of the Islamic faith. Ruling over a vast empire built upon a bottom-heavy agrarian base, Mughal officials were primarily interested in enhancing agricultural productivity by extracting as much of the surplus wealth of the land as they could, and in using that wealth to the political end of creating loyal clients at every level of administration. Although there were always conservative 'ulamā who insisted on the emperors' "duty" to convert the Hindu "infidels" to Islam, such a policy was not in fact implemented in Bengal, even during the reign of the conservative emperor Aurangzeb (1658–1707).

Our attention must therefore turn to the Mughal period in Bengal. Was it merely coincidence that the bulk of the delta's peasant Muslim population emerged after the advent of Mughal rule, or did deeper forces link these two phenomena?

63. "Jam'ī kathīr az saghīr o kabīr-i ra'āyā-yi ānjā ki akthar Musalmān būdand." Munshi Amin Kazim b. Muhammad Amin, *'Ālamgīr-nāma*, ed. Khadim Husain and 'Abd al-Hai (Calcutta: Asiatic Society of Bengal, 1868), 677.

PART 2

BENGAL UNDER THE MUGHALS

6   The Rise of Mughal Power

The country of Bengal is a land where, owing to the climate's
favouring the base, the dust of dissension is always rising.

Abu'l-fazl 'Allami (1579)

In the late sixteenth century, a dynasty of Chaghatai Turks commonly
known as the Mughals annexed Bengal to their vast Indian empire, thereby
ending the delta's long isolation from North India.[1] As just one among
twelve provinces, Bengal was now administered by a class of imperial officials who, regularly rotated through the realm, shared a larger, pan-Indian
view of their political mission. Unlike the later rulers of the sultanate, the
new ruling class lacked attachments to Bengal and its culture. This served
to widen the gulf between *ashrāf* Muslims, identified with the new wave
of outsiders who swept into the delta after the conquest, and non-*ashrāf*
Muslims, increasingly identified as native Bengali Muslims. Economically,
the advent of Mughal rule greatly stimulated the production of manufactured goods in Bengal, especially of exports to the imperial court in North
India. The conquest also furthered the exploitation and settlement of Bengal's forested hinterlands, a process that greatly altered the delta's social
landscape. All of these forces, and especially the last, were to have enduring
significance for the evolution of Islam and Muslim society in Bengal.

The Afghan Age, 1537–1612

The Mughal conquest of Bengal did not occur at once. Although the entry
of imperial forces into the Bengali capital on September 25, 1574, would
appear to have been decisive, the conquest actually took three-quarters of
a century to accomplish, commencing as far back as 1537 and continuing

---

1. The dynasty called itself Timuri, owing to its descent from Timur-i Lang ("Ti-
mur the Lame," or Tamerlane, d. 1405). Since the Mughals were the branch of the
Timurids that rose to power in India, they should properly be called Indo-Timurids.
See Marshall G. S. Hodgson, *The Venture of Islam* (Chicago: University of Chicago
Press, 1974), 3: 62–63, n. 2.

until 1612. The intervening period may be called the Afghan Age, a period when migrants hailing ultimately from Afghanistan, but more immediately from Upper India, held de facto control over much or most of the countryside. In the mid fifteenth century, Afghans had replaced Turks as the Delhi sultanate's ruling class. But in 1526 another Turk from Central Asia, Babur, dislodged the last Afghan ruling house from Delhi and established his own house—the Indo-Timurids, or Mughals. As a result, thousands of refugee Afghans flocked down the Gangetic Plain into Bihar and Bengal, where they established themselves as warrior chieftains (see map 4).

Bengal's Sultan Nasir al-Din Nusrat Shah (1519–32), who seems to have understood the long-term significance of Babur's conquest of Delhi, encouraged the buildup of Afghans in Bihar in order that it might serve as a buffer region between himself and the new Mughal dynasty. But the king's younger brother and successor, Mahmud Shah (1532–38), proved less wise. In 1533 the new sultan sent an army into Bihar to punish one of his governors for having meddled in the succession dispute that had broken out upon his brother's death. This governor, however, was allied with one of the most brilliant warriors of the age, the Afghan chieftain Sher Khan Sur (d. 1545). Seeking revenge against Sultan Mahmud, Sher Khan in 1535 skirted the sultan's defenses in the northwestern delta and dashed straight to the capital of Gaur. There he boldly confronted Mahmud, forcing the sultan to concede all territories west of Rajmahal and to pay an annual tribute of 900,000 *tanka*s.[2] Two years later, when the sultan refused to pay his annual tribute, and even had the Afghan's collector brutally killed, Sher Khan, who by now styled himself Sher Shah, sent his generals into the delta and toppled Mahmud's tottering throne.[3]

About this time, in 1538, Babur's son Humayun, the successor to the Mughal throne, had marched a large army down the Gangetic Plain with a view to halting the ascendancy of the Afghans in eastern India. But Sher Shah merely melted into the Bihar interior, allowing Humayun an easy occupation of the Bengal capital.[4] The next year when news reached Humayun that rebellions threatened his own capital, the emperor, notwithstanding that the monsoon rains had already submerged much of the delta,

2. Iqtidar Husain Siddiqui, *Mughal Relations with the Indian Ruling Elite* (New Delhi: Munshiram Manoharlal, 1983), 78–86.
3. Ibid., 88–89. Numismatic evidence indicates that Sher Khan first styled himself Sher Shah in 1535. Ibid., 83–84.
4. Abu'l-fazl 'Allami, *Akbar-nāma*, ed. Abdur Rahim (Calcutta: Asiatic Society of Bengal, 1873–87), 1: 151–53. Translated by Henry Beveridge under the title *The Akbar Nama of Abu-l-Fazl* (Calcutta: Asiatic Society of Bengal, 1897–1921; reprint, New Delhi: Ess Ess Publications, 1979), 1: 332–35.

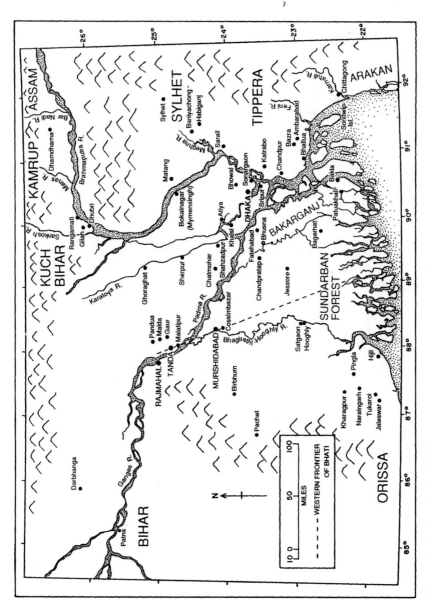

Map 4. Bengal in the Mughal age

entrusted the newly won province to subordinate officers and hastily set off for North India. Sher Shah seized this moment to pounce on Humayun, soundly defeating the emperor at the battle of Chausa in western Bihar (June 7, 1539). From there the Afghan leader went on to dislodge the Mughals not only from Bengal but from Delhi as well, in the process driving the hapless Humayun out of India altogether. For the next sixteen years the whole of northern and eastern India, including Bengal, fell to Afghan domination.

In 1556, however, Humayun managed to reconquer Delhi from Sher Shah's successors. Once again, large numbers of Afghans from North India sought refuge in Bengal, then ruled by remnants of the house of Sher Shah, and after 1564 by the house of another Afghan leader, Taj Khan Karrani (1564–65).[5] The situation became acute in the 1560s, when Mughal power under the brilliant leadership of Akbar (1565–1605), the dynasty's greatest empire builder, began expanding all over North India. Aware of the threat the Mughals would inevitably pose for Bengal, Taj Karrani's successor, Sultan Sulaiman Karrani (1565–72), adopted a posture of outward submissiveness vis-à-vis the powerful emperor, arranging that Akbar's name be included both on his coins and in the sermons of his mosques.[6] Meanwhile, his pragmatic prime minister, Lodi Khan, took care to placate the Mughals with gifts and banqueting.

Yet all the while, Sultan Sulaiman continued to gather more Afghans around him and to acquire treasure and elephants. In 1568 he launched an expedition to Orissa, ruled then by the last independent Hindu house in North India, and sacked the largest and wealthiest Hindu temple in eastern India, that of Jagannath in Puri.[7] This outbreak of royally sponsored temple desecration would appear to have departed from the de facto policy, honored by centuries of Muslim rulers in Bengal, of respect for non-Muslim monuments. But Sultan Sulaiman's motives were clearly political in nature, not religious. Just before the expedition was launched, the raja of Orissa, Mukunda Deva (1557–68), had entered into a pact with Akbar,

5. An Afghan chieftain belonging to the Kakar clan made the following plea to Sultan Taj Khan Karrani: "At our backs are Mughal armies that capture and enslave members of the Afghan race. You also are an Afghan. Therefore it is necessary that we come under your protection." Khwajah Ni'mat Allah, *Tārīkh-i-Khān Jahānī wa makhzan-i-Afghānī*, ed. S. M. Imam al-Din (Dacca: Asiatic Society of Pakistan Publication No. 4, 1960), 1: 411.

6. Ibid., 413. Abu'l-fazl 'Allami, *Akbar-nāma*, trans., 2: 338; text, 2: 219.

7. According to the historian Ni'mat Allah, who wrote some forty years after the event, Sulaiman ordered that an elaborately decorated image of the god Krishna made of gold and rubies be smashed and pitched into a cesspool. His soldiers also carried away with them seven hundred other images dedicated to various deities. Ni'mat Allah, *Tārīkh*, 413–15.

Sulaiman's nominal overlord but actually his ultimate enemy. What is more, the raja had given refuge to Sulaiman's bitter rival for the Bengal throne, Ibrahim Sur, and had suggested to Akbar's envoy that he would gladly assist Ibrahim in his ambitions to conquer Bengal.[8] As Sulaiman could hardly have tolerated threats to the stability of his regime emanating from such a nearby quarter, his expedition to Orissa with a view to punishing Mukunda Deva appears understandable. Moreover, the Jagannath temple was no ordinary temple. As the focus of a state cult lavishly supported by the kings of Orissa's Gajapati dynasty, this monument was the architectural representation of the continuity and integrity of that dynasty.[9] Its destruction was thus a calculated act of realpolitik. Like Muslim and Hindu sovereigns in India generally, the Karranis understood that a state temple—usually a single, well-endowed monument in a raja's principal capital—was the visible manifestation of dynastic kingship, and that its destruction or looting was a logical and necessary aspect of extirpating a Hindu dynasty.[10]

But the Orissa campaign would be the last foreign adventure undertaken by an independent sovereign of Bengal. In October 1572, Sulaiman died, and Akbar, with almost unseemly haste, began preparations for an invasion. The emperor's official historian, Abu'l-fazl, who generally viewed the expansion of Mughal power as a sign of his patron's benevolence to mankind, wrote that the decision was taken "because the [Bengali] peasantry were suffering from the dominion of the evil Afghans."[11] But a more likely reason is found in the vicious and self-destructive fratricide that broke out immediately upon Sulaiman's death, creating a political void that the Mughals could not resist exploiting. Moreover, continued Abu'l-fazl, whereas Sulaiman had at least possessed the tact to wear "an outer garment of submission" to Akbar, his son Daud, who soon emerged in effective control of the government, had rent even this "scarf of hypocrisy."[12] That is to say Daud, unlike his father, had begun striking coins and having the *khutba* read in his own name, either of which was tantamount to a formal declaration of independence.

In response, Akbar in 1574 personally led a large army down the Ganges plain to Patna, whose Afghan defenders he completely routed. He then entrusted the Bengal operation to an army of 20,000 led by his veteran

8. Abu'l-fazl 'Allami, *Akbar-nāma*, trans., 2: 381–82, 480; text, 2: 254–55, 327.

9. A. Eschmann, H. Kulke, and G. C. Tripathi, eds., *The Cult of Jagannath and the Regional Tradition of Orissa* (New Delhi: Manohar, 1978), 200–208.

10. See Richard H. Davis, "Indian Art Objects as Loot," *Journal of Asian Studies* 52, no. 1 (February, 1993): 22–48.

11. Abu'l-fazl 'Allami, *Akbar-nāma*, trans., 3: 5–6, 57; text, 3: 4, 40.

12. Ibid., trans., 3: 96; text, 3: 70.

commander, Munʿim Khan, who advanced rapidly down the Ganges as the Afghans, dispirited and unwilling to resist, fled clear to their capital of Tanda.[13] This too they yielded without a struggle. In September 1574, when Munʿim Khan triumphantly entered Tanda, the Mughal era in Bengal can be said to have begun. As Abuʾl-fazl proudly wrote, "the words of the world-cherishing prince came into operation. The Divine graciousness increased daily."[14]

The Early Mughal Experience in Bengal, 1574–1610

But seizing the capital and possessing the land were two different matters. While Munʿim Khan and Raja Todar Mal, Akbar's finance minister, were in Tanda reorganizing the revenue administration of the newly conquered province, thousands of Afghans melted into the forested Bengali hinterland, where for the next forty years they continued to hold out against the new regime. There they attracted a host of dissidents, including Muslim and Hindu *zamīndārs*, Portuguese renegades, and tribal chieftains, all of whom perceived the Chaghatai Turks from Upper India as foreigners and usurpers.[15]

From Abuʾl-fazl's imperial perspective, however, the years after 1574 were devoted to clearing the delta of "the weeds and rubbish of opposition" (*khas-o-khāshāk-i mukhālif*).[16] Having seized Tanda, the Mughal victors pursued the Afghans in four directions: north to Ghoraghat, south to Satgaon, east to Sonargaon, and southeast into Fatehabad (present-day Faridpur town).[17] These initial campaigns witnessed several pitched battles of great scope and bloodshed, in particular the battle of Tukaroi in southern Midnapur District (March 3, 1575), in which Todar Mal and Munʿim Khan achieved a stunning victory over Sultan Daud Khan. On this occasion the Mughals resorted to terror tactics, filling eight lofty minarets with the skulls of their slain enemies "as a warning to spectators."[18] Actually, though, the use of such violence was exceptional. With their cavalry bogged down in unfamiliar jungle terrain and their troops close to de-

13. Recognizing that Gaur's unhealthy climate had rendered that ancient city unsuitable for large populations, Sulaiman Karrani had transferred the seat of government to nearby Tanda. Ghulam Hussain Salim, *Riyāzu-s-Salātīn*, 152.
14. Abuʾl-fazl ʿAllami, *Akbar-nāma*, trans., 3: 153; text, 3: 109.
15. Soon after the Mughal victory at Tukaroi (March 1575), wrote Abuʾl-fazl, "vagabonds of the country" gathered round Jahan Khan Lodi, who was Daud Khan's governor of Orissa and leading confederate. These were probably Bengali landholders who, familiar with the former order of things under the sultans and apprehensive of what might happen to them under Mughal dominion, initially threw in their lot with the Afghans. Ibid., trans., 183; text, 129.
16. Ibid., trans., 143, 169, 376; text, 102, 118, 259.
17. Ibid., trans., 169; text, 118–19.
18. Ibid., trans., 180; text, 127.

serting from lack of interest in fighting so far from home, the Mughals relied more on bribery, cajolery, diplomacy, impressive displays of military power, and sowing the seeds of dissension within enemy ranks than upon the application of brute force.[19]

Such a policy was not only expedient. It also accorded with Akbar's theory of imperial sovereignty, which, as in traditional Indian political thought, aimed not at annihilating adversaries but at humbling them into recognizing the single, overarching sovereignty of the victorious monarch. Hence on April 12, 1575, there was great celebration in the Mughal camp when Sultan Daud Khan, finally perceiving the futility of continued resistance, appeared before Mun'im Khan and partook of a formal "banquet of reconciliation." Here was a political rite, a ritual of incorporation, in which symbolism was everything. Displaying warm affection, the Mughal general advanced to the edge of the carpet laid out in a ceremonial tent specially arranged for the occasion. There he greeted the defeated king. Daud ungirded his sword and set it aside. Mun'im Khan then presented the Afghan with a Mughal sword, an embroidered belt, and a cloak. Whether or not the cloak had actually been worn by Akbar, by donning it Daud Khan became ritually "incorporated" into the body of the emperor—a political rite the Bengali ruler would well have understood, since his predecessors on the throne of Gaur had followed the same practice.[20] Adorned with Mughal regalia, Daud then turned his face in the direction of Akbar's capital in Fatehpur Sikri and solemnly prostrated himself.[21] His independence formally ended, Daud and his kingdom were now bound to the emperor.

Several events, however, prevented the new province's smooth integration into the Mughal domain. Soon after returning to northern Bengal from Tukaroi, Mun'im Khan transferred the seat of government from Tanda, capital of Bengal since the time of Sulaiman Karrani (1565), back

19. "By the daily-increasing favour of God," wrote Abu'l-fazl concerning Todar Mal's campaign in central Bengal, "the dust of disturbance was laid" ("gubār-i fitna firo-nishast"). In dealing with one group of Afghans, Todar Mal recommended to Mun'im Khan that "the method to restrain the faction was to send money by one who was loyal and smooth-tongued." The author was pleased to observe that this policy had successfully "quieted the slaves to gold." Ibid., trans., 170, 173; text, 120, 121. André Wink has argued that the policy of sowing and then exploiting internal dissensions (*fitna*) among the enemy constituted a key dynamic in the expansion of Mughal power in India. See André Wink, *Land and Sovereignty: Agrarian Society and Politics under the Eighteenth-Century Maratha Svarājya* (Cambridge: Cambridge University Press, 1986).

20. When a Portuguese diplomat was presented to the court of Sultan Nasir al-Din Nusrat Shah in 1521, the sultan, in the words of the foreigner, "turned to me and ordered that I be given a robe that he had worn." *Voyage dans les deltas du Gange*, 333.

21. Abu'l-fazl 'Allami, *Akbar-nāma*, trans., 3: 185; text, 3: 130–31.

to the ancient city of Gaur.[22] The decision proved catastrophic, for a shift in the main course of the Ganges River had turned the river's formerly swift channels into stagnant backwaters, making them breeding grounds for easily communicable diseases. As a result, in the months after April 1575 a devastating plague carried away thousands of Mughal officers and soldiers, not to mention untold thousands of civilians. "The thought of death took hold of everyone," wrote Abu'l-fazl, as the plague's devastation swiftly cut into the morale of officers and troops. Many of these became altogether disgusted with Bengal and began thinking only of gathering their belongings and leaving.[23] We have no figures on how many died during the plague of 1575, or how many left the country. But coming as it did at the very dawn of the Mughal encounter with Bengal, a critical moment in the formation of Mughal perceptions of the delta, this catastrophe surely contributed to the stereotype, soon accepted throughout the imperial service, that Bengal was a hostile and foreign land—a place in which perhaps to endure temporary duty but certainly not somewhere to reside permanently. In the minds of Mughal officers from North India this view persisted for centuries, adding to the profound sense of alienation from the delta province that subsequent generations of *ashrāf* Muslims would nurture down to modern times.[24]

It was in this melancholy atmosphere, in October 1575, that Mun'im Khan died. The infighting among Mughal officers that followed the governor's death encouraged Daud Khan, the last independent sultan of Bengal, to reconsider his submission to Akbar and regroup his scattered Afghan forces for a second try at dislodging the Mughals from the delta. In these circumstances, Akbar appointed another decorated Mughal commander, Khan Jahan, to take charge of the newly won province. Accompanied by the veteran Raja Todar Mal, the new governor reached the restored capital of Tanda in November, and in the following July met Daud's forces along the banks of the Padma River in central Bengal. Again the Afghans suf-

22. According to Abu'l-fazl the change was made because it put the seat of Mughal power somewhat closer to Ghoraghat, where turbulent Afghans were still active, and because Mun'im Khan admired Gaur's noble fort and magnificent buildings. It is also likely, however, that the new Mughal regime wished to associate itself with a city having much older associations with legitimate authority than the upstart Tanda. Gaur had been associated, not only with centuries of Indo-Turkish rule, but before that, as ancient Lakhnauti, with Sena rule as well. Ibid., trans., 226; text, 160.
23. Ibid., trans., 227–28; text, 160–61. So thorough was the devastation that just sixty-five years later a foreign visitor would describe what had become by then the ruins of a totally abandoned metropolis. Manrique, *Travels* 2: 124–28.
24. See Rafiuddin Ahmed, *Bengal Muslims, 1871–1906: A Quest for Identity* (Delhi: Oxford University Press, 1981), 8–17, 22–24, 124, 184.

fered a crushing military reversal. Their finest field commander was killed in action, and Daud himself, his horse stuck in the monsoon's muddy quagmire, was taken alive. This time the Mughals were ruthless with their quarry. Having determined that Daud should be "relieved of the burden of his head," Khan Jahan had the ex-king decapitated and his body fixed to a gibbet in Tanda; the head he sent to Akbar as a trophy.[25] A smooth transition to imperial domination now seemed more certain than ever.

This was just the time, however, when a serious rebellion broke out within Akbar's imperial service. A year before the conquest of Bengal, the emperor had required his *manṣabdārs*—the Mughal corps of military officials—to brand and present for imperial review the precise number of horses, with cavalrymen, that they were paid to maintain. He also centralized the empire's fiscal basis by ordering that land revenues be placed under the direct control of the central government instead of at the disposal of the *manṣabdārs*.[26] Such exertions of central authority naturally provoked resentment among many officials. Worse, the emperor's policy of shipping disaffected *manṣabdārs* to Bengal had the effect of concentrating potential rebels in a region distant from Delhi and legendary for its tradition of resisting central authority. In 1579, rebellion duly broke out. Led by Baba Khan Qaqshal and Ma'sum Khan Kabuli, a *manṣabdār* who had come from Bihar to join the Bengal revolt, the rebels seized and plundered the official fortress in Tanda, executed Akbar's hapless governor, and set up a "revolutionary government" amongst themselves.[27] Hindu *zamīndārs* in both the southeastern and the southwestern delta swiftly threw off their allegiance to the Mughals, while other disaffected *manṣabdārs* in Bihar joined the movement in Bengal.[28] For two years the delta passed completely beyond imperial authority, until 1582–83, when Akbar's application of overwhelming force eventually quashed the revolt.[29] Only one high-ranking Mughal officer would remain at large, the unrepentant Ma'sum Khan Kabuli, who led a bitter fight against Mughal authority down to his death seventeen years later.

In 1583, when the turmoil within the imperial corps had subsided, the imperialists once again turned their attention to suppressing various indigenous resistance movements. These, however, were no longer concentrated in the northwest, the site of Muslim power since 1204, but in East Bengal generally, the vast region known to the Mughals as "Bhati." Wrote Abu'l-

---

25. Abu'l-fazl 'Allami, *Akbar-nāma*, trans., 3: 252–56; text, 3: 180–83.
26. Ibid., trans., 95; text, 69.
27. Ibid., trans., 442–51; text, 299–305.
28. Ibid., trans., 469, 475; text, 320, 324.
29. Ibid., trans., 567, 589–93; text, 384, 398–401.

fazl, "The tract of country on the east called Bhati is reckoned a part of this province."[30] Yet in another passage he treated "Bangala" and "Bhati" as mutually exclusive regions, the distinctive feature of the latter being its topography: the word *bhāti* simply means "downstream direction." "Bhati," wrote Abu'l-fazl, "is a low country and has received this name because Bengal is higher. It is nearly 400 kos in length from east to west and about 300 kos from north to south. East of this country are the ocean and the country of Habsha. West is the hill country where are the houses of the Kahin tribe. South is Tanda. North also the ocean and the terminations of the hill country of Tibet."[31] As used by the Mughals in the sixteenth and early seventeenth centuries, "Bhati" included the entire delta east of the Bhagirathi-Hooghly corridor. In fact, since its western boundary extended from Tanda down to present-day southwestern Khulna District,[32] the frontier between Mughal "Bhati" and "Bangala" approximated the present frontier between Bangladesh and West Bengal. Hence the modern distinction between East and West Bengal dates at least from early Mughal times.

Anti-Mughal resistance now coalesced around a remarkable Bengali Muslim chieftain, 'Isa Khan, whose seat of government lay deep within the delta's eastern riverine tracts in the town of Katrabo near the ancient city of Sonargaon. In 1586 Ralph Fitch, a merchant then exploring the possibilities of opening up trade between England and India, traveled

---

30. More precisely, Bhati was called a *wilāyat* ("region"), and Bengal a *mulk* ("kingdom"). "Āftāb bar āyad wilāyatīst Bhātī nām, az īn mulk shumāra kunand." Abu'l-fazl 'Allami, *Ā'īn-i Akbarī* (Lucknow ed.), 2: 73; trans., 2: 130.
31. Abu'l-fazl 'Allami, *Akbar-nāma*, trans., 3: 645–47; text, 3: 432. Here Abu'l-fazl mistakenly reckons Bengal's cardinal directions 90 degrees clockwise; if one rotates his cardinal directions 90 degrees counterclockwise, all the reference points fall into proper place: the Bay of Bengal and the "Habsha" country would border Bhati to the south, Tanda would lie to the west, the hill country to the north, and the termination of the Himalayan range to the east. This correction of Abu'l-fazl's geography is suggested by Irfan Habib in his *An Atlas of the Mughal Empire* (Delhi: Oxford University Press, 1982), 104.
32. A problem arises with identifying Abu'l-fazl's "Habsha," a place name that means Ethiopia and is therefore quite impossible. However, although both the Calcutta and the Lucknow editions of the text give this place as "Habsha," at least one manuscript—India Office Library, Persian MS. 236—renders it "Jasor," which in the sixteenth century referred, not to modern Jessore town, but to a settlement further south, identified with present-day Iśwaripur in southwestern Khulna District. See Abu'l-fazl 'Allami, *Akbar-nāma*, trans., 3: 646, n. 2; Habib, *Atlas*, 104 and 45. James Westland observes that the name Jessore was applied to successive seats of the Jessore *zamīndārī*, and that in the sixteenth century the seat was located in southwestern Khulna. See Westland, *Report on the District of Jessore* (Calcutta: Bengal Secretariat, 1871), 24; *List of Ancient Monuments in Bengal* (Calcutta: Government of Bengal, 1896), 148.

through Bengal's eastern districts and wrote, "They be all hereabout Rebels against the King Zebaldin Echebar [Jalal al-Din Akbar]: for here are so many Rivers and Ilands, that they flee from one to another, whereby his Horsemen cannot prevaile against them. . . . The chiefe King of all these Countries is called Isacan ['Isa Khan], and he is chiefe of all the other Kings, and is a great friend to all Christians."[33] Fitch's "other Kings" were the "twelve chieftains" (Beng., *bāra bhūyān*) recorded in other European accounts and celebrated in Bengali lore. In December 1600 the annual letter of the Jesuit Mission in Goa, commenting on the Mughal drive against Bengal's former Afghan rulers, stated:

> Twelve princes, however, called Boyones [*bhūyān*] who governed twelve provinces in the late King's name, escaped from this massacre. These united against the Mongols [*sic*], and hitherto, thanks to their alliance, each maintains himself in his dominions. Very rich and disposing of strong forces, they bear themselves as Kings, chiefly he of Siripur [Sripur], also called Cadaray [Kedar Rai], and he of Chandecan [Raja Pratapaditya of Jessore], but most of all the Mansondolin ["Masnad-i ʿĀlī," title of 'Isa Khan]. The Patanes [Afghans], being scattered above, are subject to the Boyones.[34]

All twelve chieftains, now subordinate to 'Isa Khan, had been former governors of the Bengal sultanate.[35]

In September 1584, 'Isa Khan delivered a crushing naval defeat to the Mughal governor,[36] and for the next fifteen years, though always careful to accord Akbar his theoretical overlordship whenever it seemed prudent

33. Federici, "Extracts," 184.
34. Hosten, "Jesuit Letters," 53–54. The date of this report, December 1, 1600, indicates a lag in communications between Jesuit missions in Bengal and Goa; for 'Isa Khan, who appears to have been alive when this report was written, had already died in September 1599.
35. The Jesuit mission report did not, however, specify the identity of the twelve chieftains, beyond noting that three were Hindus—i.e., those of Bakla (Bakarganj), Sripur (southeastern Dhaka), and Chandecan (Jessore)—and the rest Muslims. Some years ago N. K. Bhattasali attempted to identify the "twelve chieftains" and the territories they controlled, among them: 'Uthman Khan, of Bokainagar (Mymensingh town); Maʿsum Khan Kabuli of Chatmohar in Pabna; Madhu Ray, of Khalsi, near Jafarganj in western Dhaka; Raja Ray, of Shahzadpur, in eastern Pabna; Nabud (or "Madan") Ray, of Chandpratap in Manikganj subdivision of Dhaka; Bahadur Ghazi, Sona Ghazi, and Anwar Ghazi of Bhowal, Dhaka; Pahlawan of Matang in southwestern Sylhet; Ram Chandra, of Bakla in southeastern Bakarganj; and Majlis Kutab, of Fatehabad, modern Faridpur. 'Isa Khan himself controlled present-day Comilla, half of Dhaka, western Mymensingh, and perhaps portions of Rangpur, Bogra, and Pabna. See N. K. Bhattasali, "Bengal Chiefs' Struggle for Independence in the Reigns of Akbar and Jahangir," *Bengal Past and Present* 35 (January–June 1928): 30–36.
36. Abu'l-fazl ʿAllami, *Akbar-nāma*, trans., 3: 659; text, 3: 439.

to do so, this "little king" ruled the eastern delta virtually unchecked.[37] His prudence was dictated by the Mughals' gradual mastery of the sort of naval tactics long used by chieftains of the eastern delta. In February 1586, in fact, imperial commanders pushed all the way through the jungle and riverine tracts to the port of Chittagong, on which occasion the city's Arakanese ruler sent gifts of elephants to the Mughals. 'Isa Khan also acted in a conciliatory manner.[38] Yet strikes such as this were essentially raids; throughout this period the Mughals, forced to acknowledge 'Isa Khan's status as tributary "*zamīndār* of Bhati,"[39] were quite unable to consolidate the east under anything like regular administration.

To remedy this situation, Akbar in early 1594 dispatched as governor of Bengal one of his most illustrious generals, the Rajput chieftain Raja Man Singh. After founding Rajmahal as his provincial capital in the delta's northwestern corner, the new governor led a vast army into Bhati in late 1595.[40] Powerful Hindu chieftains like Kedar Rai, *zamīndār* of Bhusna in Faridpur District, and Patkunwar Narain, the cousin of the raja of Kuch Bihar, chose refuge with 'Isa Khan rather than submit to the Mughals.[41] In August 1597, 'Isa Khan joined forces with Ma'sum Khan Kabuli, the die-hard Mughal turncoat, and together they engaged Mughal naval forces with their own Bengali war boats in a battle that resulted in another Mughal defeat, in which Raja Man Singh's own son was killed.[42] But this was the high tide of 'Isa Khan's fortunes; two years later he died, apparently of natural causes.[43] Sporadic resistance to Mughal authority nonetheless continued as 'Isa Khan's Afghan followers flocked to one of his sons,

37. In 1585 'Isa Khan even promised the Mughals that he would dispatch Ma'sum Khan Kabuli, the renegade Mughal, on a compulsory pilgrimage to Mecca—a typical form of political banishment in Indo-Muslim history—and although he did not carry out the promise, he did manage to restrain the rebel. Ibid., trans., 696–97; text, 461.
38. Ibid., trans., 721–22; text, 479.
39. Ibid., trans., 1031; text, 672.
40. Ibid., trans., 1042–43; text, 696.
41. Ibid., trans., 1059, 1068; text, 711, 716.
42. Ibid., trans., 1093; text, 733.
43. 'Isa Khan's career has been variously interpreted. Observing that he was neither a tribal head nor the descendant of any ancient family, the historian Jadunath Sarkar dismissed him as a "bloated *zamīndār*" and a "standing menace to the peace of the province." But such an assessment capitulates to the Mughal imperial perspective and adopts the Mughal definition of "peace." In fact, by Sarkar's standards, any great king of humble origins—for example, Sher Shah or 'Ala al-Din Husain Shah—should have to be similarly dismissed. Even the contemporary observer Abu'l-fazl would have disagreed with Sarkar's judgment. In calling 'Isa Khan "a great landholder" and in declaring that with his death "the thornbush of commotion was extirpated," the official Mughal chonicler was paying a backhanded com-

Daud, while Kedar Rai joined with bands of maritime Arakanese, known as Maghs, who had been plundering Bengali communities far up the Meghna estuary.

In 1602, with a view to thwarting the rebellious ambitions of all these elements, Raja Man Singh established Dhaka as the center of his military operations in the east.[44] Soon it would be Bengal's premier city. To be sure, the Mughals did not create the city ex nihilo. Since at least the mid fifteenth century, it had been an outpost of Muslim settlers,[45] and one Mughal officer remarked that Dhaka, together with Gaur, Rajmahal, and Ghoraghat, had been among Bengal's "ancient forts."[46] Hence it was probably for strategic reasons that, shortly after Mun'im Khan took charge of the province in 1574, Dhaka was made the headquarters of a *thāna* (Beng., *thānā*), or military district, on the Mughals' far eastern frontier. Yet imperial authority there was still precarious, for in 1584 Dhaka's *thānadār*, or military administrator, had been captured and imprisoned by 'Isa Khan.[47]

By the time Raja Man Singh established himself in Dhaka, however, the balance of power had tipped in the Mughals' favor. From his new headquarters the governor, exploiting the disarray that followed 'Isa Khan's death in 1599, mounted a vigorous campaign against the remaining "twelve chieftains." First, he worked on the Afghans loyal to 'Isa Khan's son Daud, and then, in 1603, on Kedar Rai and the Arakanese. In all these campaigns the governor met with consummate success: he pushed back Daud to Sonargaon, defeated and killed Kedar Rai, expelled the Arakanese from the lower delta, and drove 'Uthman Khan, the most powerful of the remaining Afghans, into the jungles of Mymensingh. Alluding to the ascendancy of Mughal power in eastern Bengal between 1599 and 1603,

pliment to this stalwart adversary of imperial expansion, acknowledging his de facto authority in eastern Bengal. This suggests that 'Isa Khan was perceived even in his own day in rather the same light in which subsequent folklore came to see him: as a symbol of native Bengali resistance to Mughal power. See Jadunath Sarkar, ed., *History of Bengal*, 213, 226. Abu'l-fazl 'Allami, *Akbar-nāma*, trans., 3: 1140; text, 3: 763. Dinesh Chandra Sen, ed. and trans., *Eastern Bengal Ballads, Mymensing* (Calcutta: University of Calcutta, 1923–28), 2: 301–75.
44. Abu'l-fazl 'Allami, *Akbar-nāma*, trans., 3: 1214–15; text, 3: 809.
45. In 1456–57, during the reign of Sultan Nasir al-Din Mahmud Shah I (1433–59), a certain "Musammāt Bakht Bīnat, daughter of Marhamat" patronized the construction of a mosque in what is now the city's oldest quarter. Several years later, in 1459, the sultan himself renovated a gate, possibly to another mosque. Although nothing now remains of this gate, the statement that it was *repaired* in 1459 points to the sultanate's presence in Dhaka before that date. Shamsud-Din Ahmed, ed. and trans., *Inscriptions*, 4: 57–58, 62–63.
46. Nathan, *Bahāristān*, text, fol. 19b; trans., 1: 57.
47. Abu'l-fazl 'Allami, *Akbar-nāma*, trans., 3: 659; text, 3: 439.

Abu'l-fazl wrote that "the Rajah's mind being now at ease and having committed the *thanahs* to the charge of able men, he went to Dhaka."[48] But the governor would not remain in the city for long; in early 1605, he left for Agra to attend to the ailing emperor, whose death was approaching. In that same year, Akbar died and was succeeded by his son, Jahangir.

It was in Jahangir's reign (1605–27) that the Mughal enterprise in Bengal passed from an ad hoc pursuit of rebels to the establishment of a regular administration. Initially, the new emperor's efforts to subdue Afghan chieftains proved ineffectual, especially with respect to the redoubtable 'Uthman Khan, who remained firmly entrenched in Bengal's easternmost districts. But in May 1608, aiming to crush such elements once and for all, Jahangir appointed as governor 'Ala al-Din Islam Khan, an extraordinarily able and determined commander.[49] A man about thirty-seven years of age at this time, Islam Khan enjoyed close ties with the emperor—the two had grown up together since childhood as foster-brothers—and possessed remarkable powers of self-discipline.[50] Taking leave of the emperor, he moved down the Gangetic Plain at the head of an immense army of cavalry, artillery, and elephants, and a huge flotilla of war boats. After entering Bengal and pausing in Rajmahal, the army made its way through the jungles of the central delta, subdued rebellious chieftains on both sides of the Ganges-Padma river system, and finally reached Dhaka in 1610.

The Consolidation of Mughal Authority, 1610–1704

With Islam Khan's arrival, the Mughal era of Bengal's history effectively began. Upon reaching the delta, the new governor first moved the imperial provincial capital from Rajmahal, in the far northwest, where all previous Muslim capitals had been located, to Dhaka, deep in the Bengal hinterland. In this way, regions that had hitherto remained beyond the reach of North Indian rulers, and had been only lightly touched by the sultans of Gaur, were directly exposed to the epicenter of Mughal culture and authority. From 1610 to 1715, the Mughals would use Dhaka as a base for integrating diverse peoples into their social and bureaucratic system and for transforming into arable land the vast stretches of forest that still covered most of "Bhati," or the eastern delta. Moreover, as Dhaka was connected to the Padma-Ganges river system at a point midway between the Bay of Bengal

48. Ibid., trans., 1215, 1235–36; text, 809, 824.
49. Jahangir, *Tūzuk*, 1: 142–43, 208.
50. "Islam Khan," wrote the emperor in his memoirs, "is a brave and well-dispositioned youth, and is distinguished in every way above his family. Till now he has never drunk intoxicating drinks, and his sincerity towards me is such that I have honoured him with the title of son." Ibid., 32.

and older seats of Muslim power in the Gaur-Tanda region, the city would serve as an ideal entrepôt for riverine trade between East and West Bengal, between Bengal and Upper India, and between Bengal and the wider world beyond the bay. Since the overland ascendancy of Mughal influence in Bengal's eastern hinterland occurred just as Portuguese, Dutch, and English commercial interests entered the region from overseas, this formerly isolated backwater was now simultaneously integrated into two cosmopolitan and expanding political economies, the Mughal and the European.

Islam Khan could not have foreseen the long-term implications of his planting the provincial capital in the heart of East Bengal. His immediate concern, after all, was to subdue refractory elements that had long eluded imperial authority. An iron-willed man, who demanded of his subordinates an unquestioning submission both to himself and to the Mughal cause, with which he fiercely identified,[51] Islam Khan governed only briefly, dying in office in 1613. Yet it was he who, in a bloody battle in the hills of Sylhet in 1612, defeated and killed 'Uthman Khan, thereby extirpating the last credible remnant of Afghan resistance to Mughal power in the delta. And it was he, too, who established the political ties that would bind local potentates to the Mughal cause. Three factors helped the Mughals consolidate their power in the delta: their more effective use of military force, the diplomacy of Islam Khan, and the financial backing of Hindu merchant-bankers.

Some historians have argued that gunpowder technology played a decisive role in the expansion and consolidation, not only of the Mughal empire, but of those of their Safavid and Ottoman contemporaries, and have even labeled these three polities "gunpowder empires."[52] But how critical was the use of gunpowder in the Mughal conquest of Bengal? Mirza Nathan, a junior Mughal officer who accompanied numerous campaigns dur-

51. He ordered, for example, that no one should enter or leave Bengal without his personal permission. His vigor in enforcing regulations of this type is seen in an incident involving a certain Shaikh Husain, who was in Rajmahal and wished to proceed directly to Delhi. The shaikh, who had grown up with the governor from childhood "in close intimacy and brotherly love," became extremely irritated when informed that the governor intended to apply this regulation even to him. In order to elicit obedience from the shaikh, the governor on the occasion of their interview in Dhaka instructed his aides with the words, "When the Shaykh would proceed to embrace me, you force him to bend his neck and throw him down on my feet." Islam Khan then grabbed the man's beard and, forcefully pulling him to his feet, gave him severe blows to his shoulder. In perhaps the most humiliating gesture of all, the governor ordered his men to place the shaikh's beard under his feet; in this fashion he was beaten again. Nathan, *Bahāristān*, text, fol. 53a–b; trans., 1: 132–33.
52. Hodgson, *Venture of Islam*, 3: 17–18. William H. McNeill, *The Pursuit of Power: Technology, Armed Force, and Society since A.D. 1000* (Chicago: University of Chicago Press, 1982), 95–98.

ing the governorship of Islam Khan and his successors, remarked that "cannon, cross-bows, rockets and other fire-arms of this type . . . are the aggressive firearms of India."[53] This officer evidently associated gunpowder weapons with "India," that is, Mughal Hindustan, as opposed to Bengal's extreme northeastern frontier (in which context the remark was made), whose peoples lacked such firepower. These weapons included not only the type of heavy cannon that the Mughals brought with them to Bengal as early as Mun'im Khan's invasion of 1574,[54] but smoothbore muskets and, by the early 1600s, lightweight cannon that could be transported on the shoulders of foot soldiers and fired by cannoneers from horseback.[55]

There are problems, however, with characterizing the Mughal state as a "gunpowder empire." First, the Mughals did not introduce cannon or the musket to India; both had been found in North India and the Deccan since the second half of the fifteenth century, nearly a century before the Mughal age.[56] Second, the Mughals' use of firepower did not immediately spell the end of mounted archers. Used in combination with musketeers and artillery, archers continued to play a decisive role in Mughal warfare.[57] In the ten major imperial campaigns waged between 1608 and 1618—the most important decade for the consolidation of Mughal power in the delta—the Mughals always deployed a mixed force structure, averaging for each campaign 4,000 musketeers, 2,100 mounted archers, and 300 war boats.[58] On the other hand, the Bengal rulers, like the sultans of Delhi, relied on war elephants as the principal arm of their military.[59] A European visitor once noted that Sultan Nasir al-Din Nusrat Shah maintained a stable of 914 war elephants "trained to fight with swords fixed to their tusks and to throw javelins from their trunks; they can kill and wound many

53. Nathan, *Bahāristān*, text, fol. 230a; trans., 2: 508; "az 'adāwat-i ātishbāzī-yi Hindūstān ast."

54. Abu'l-fazl 'Allami, *Akbar-nāma*, trans., 3: 97; text, 3: 70.

55. Nathan, *Bahāristān*, text, fol. 216b; trans., 2: 468.

56. Iqtidar Alam Khan, "Early Use of Cannon and Musket in India: A.D. 1442–1526," *Journal of the Economic and Social History of the Orient* 24, no. 2 (1981), 146–64.

57. The seventeenth-century French traveler François Bernier noted that Mughal mounted archers could deliver six arrows before a musketeer could fire twice. See Douglas Streusand, *The Formation of the Mughal Empire* (New Delhi: Oxford University Press, 1989), 53.

58. Nathan, *Bahāristān*, text, fols. 20b, 40b, 49b, 53a, 64a, 162b, 163b, 192b, 231a; trans., 1: 60, 97, 121, 131, 163, 316, 319, 405; 2: 510.

59. Simon Digby has argued that the key to the Delhi sultanate's power lay in its monopoly of reliable supplies of elephants and war-horses. The elephants comprised the key arm of the military, with the size of the state reflected in that of its elephant stables. Digby, *War Horse and Elephant in the Delhi Sultanate* (Oxford: Oxford University Monographs, 1971), 23–82.

people in this way."[60] At the battle of Tukaroi (1575), during the Mughals' first serious drive into the Bengal hinterland, Sultan Daud's elephants did indeed produce havoc among the imperial cavalry.[61] But the imperial armies eventually won that battle, and they owed their triumph not to gunpowder but to their superior use of mounted archers.

Moreover, whatever advantage the Mughals may have enjoyed with their superior firepower was at least partially neutralized by the diffusion of gunpowder technology among their adversaries. In 1584 'Isa Khan deployed artillery and muskets in naval battles with the Mughals, and 'Uthman Khan regularly used artillery (*tūp o tufang*) in naval and land battles.[62] When Raja Pratapaditya of Jessore capitulated to Islam Khan in 1609, he agreed to surrender twenty thousand infantry, five hundred war boats, and a thousand "maunds" (41 tons) of gunpowder.[63] Possession of supplies in such quantities implies a rather thorough integration of gunpowder technology in armies opposing the Mughals.[64] By contrast, tribal or semi-tribal peoples living along the fringes of the delta, especially in the extreme north, seem initially to have lacked gunpowder technology. Warriors of Kamrup were described simply as archers, while those of Kuch Bihar used poisoned arrows.[65] Yet by about 1612 even these outlying peoples were reported firing cannon and crossbows (*tūp o ṣandūq o tīr-hāyi takhsh*) from stockades in rebellions against Mughal rule.[66]

Perhaps of greater significance for consolidating Mughal rule were Islam Khan's adroit policies vis-à-vis the "twelve chieftains" and other locally entrenched *zamīndārs*. For in many engagements the actual use of guns, as opposed to their ostentatious display, was obviated by a diplomacy carefully calculated to win over local leaders. Typical was Islam Khan's policy toward Raja Satrajit, the raja of Bhusna, located about twenty miles southwest of Faridpur on the border of modern Jessore. Mirza Nathan

60. *Voyage dans les deltas du Gange*, 326.
61. Abu'l-fazl 'Allami, *Akbar-nāma*, trans., 3: 176; text, 3: 123.
62. Ibid., trans., 3: 659, 1214; text, 438, 809. Nathan, *Bahāristān*, text, fols. 67a, 72b; trans., 1: 174, 189.
63. Nathan, *Bahāristān*, text, fol. 9a; trans., 1: 28.
64. 'Isa Khan and his allies sometimes plundered Mughal supplies for firearms, or employed Portuguese mercenaries, who hired out their services to Mughal and anti-Mughal forces alike. In 1583 some three thousand artillerymen, apparently renegade Portuguese, were in the employ of anti-Mughal forces in East Bengal. See Abu'l-fazl 'Allami, *Akbar-nāma*, trans., 3: 228, 620; text, 3: 161, 417; Nathan, *Bahāristān*, text, fol. 280b; trans., 2: 656. See also Maria Augusta Lima Cruz, "Exiles and Renegades in Early-Sixteenth-Century Portuguese India," *Indian Economic and Social History Review* 23, no. 3 (July 1986), 259.
65. Nathan, *Bahāristān*, text, fol. 152a; 163a; trans., 1: 289, 317.
66. Ibid., text, fol. 177a; trans., 1: 359.

notes that the governor sent one of his generals to negotiate with this powerful chieftain, instructing him that "if luckily Satrajit submitted, then he should be given the hope of the grant of his territory as Jagir and should be brought before Islam Khan in accordance with this covenant; otherwise he should have only himself to thank for the consequences of his acts, and his country should be left as a prey to the horse of the imperial Karoris (revenue-collectors)."[67]

Here was a judicious combination of carrot and stick. From the raja's perspective, the inducement to submit was his integration into a far wider field of activity than the territory of Bhusna could ever offer, even while he retained his former domains in the form of a *jāgīr*, or revenue assignment. As an imperial *jāgīrdār* ("holder of a *jāgīr*"), he would continue to collect land revenues from his former subjects, except that those revenues would now be used to maintain troops available for state service, and in numbers fixed by imperial officers in Dhaka. Vis-à-vis his former subjects, the imperial *jāgīrdār* would still preside over the ritual ceremonies befitting a raja, though he would have to present himself and his troops to the governor at any time the latter wished. If the raja agreed to this new political role, the "covenant" between him and the government would be solemnly ratified by his personal appearance before the governor. But if he resisted and were defeated, imperial revenue officers would assess and collect the land revenue in his territory, while he himself, if he survived the conflict, would face imprisonment.[68]

In general, the more important the chieftain, and the sooner he capitulated, the more inducements Islam Khan was prepared to offer in exchange for submission to Mughal rule. This is well illustrated in the governor's dealings with Raja Pratapaditya of Jessore, one of the most powerful of Bengal's "twelve chieftains." "Islam Khan," wrote Mirza Nathan, "for the sake of drawing the attention of other Zamindars, and also in consideration of the high position held by the aforesaid Raja among the Zamindars of Bengal, bestowed honours upon him beyond measure, and consoled and encouraged him."[69] Aware that lesser chiefs were looking to bigger chiefs such as Pratapaditya for leadership, or at least for direction, the governor promised this chieftain not only his own former possessions as *jāgīr* but other lands far to the east. To seal the covenant, the governor conferred on

---

67. Ibid., text, fol. 6a; trans., 1: 18.
68. After initially resisting Mughal pressure, Raja Satrajit made peace with Islam Khan and joined numerous Mughal expeditions against other chieftains of eastern Bengal.
69. Ibid., text, fol. 9a; trans., 1: 27.

him a stunning array of Mughal regalia: a sword, a bejeweled swordbelt, a camphor-stand, five high-bred horses, three elephants, and an imperial kettledrum.[70]

On the other hand, the Mughal regime tolerated no sign of perfidy on the part of a newly created *jāgīrdār*. Despite his formal submission, Pratapaditya failed to provide Islam Khan with his armies as promised, and to punish him, the governor sent a substantial army and navy into Jessore. After defeating Pratapaditya's forces, the governor imprisoned the raja and annexed his territories.[71] The province's chief fiscal officer was then sent to the raja's former domains in order "to make due assessment of revenue of Jessore and to bring the rent-roll (*nuskha*) to the government record-office" in Dhaka.[72] Clearly, by resisting imperial rule the raja forfeited his chance of keeping his former domains as *jāgīr*, while the fields of his former subjects were reassessed by Mughal revenue officers.[73] Had Pratapaditya not resisted, he would have continued levying and collecting taxes through his own agents.

An even bigger prize was the submission of Musa Khan, a son of 'Isa Khan. Known by the regal title of Masnad-i 'Ālī, "Exalted Throne," Musa Khan had inherited his father's position as the principal ruler of Bhati. Although the Bengali ruler possessed a huge fleet of 700 war boats, many of them armed with cannon, the Mughals met him with their own fleet of 295 war boats, manned by twelve thousand sailors, and compelled him to submit.[74] When Musa Khan rebelled and was again forced to submit, the governor placed him under detention in Dhaka.[75] In 1613, however, when Qasim Khan succeeded to the governorship, the Bengali chieftain was granted his freedom and allowed to participate in major expeditions along the northern and eastern frontiers.[76] Against the raja of Tippera, in fact, he was entrusted with the co-command of an army of five thousand mus-

---

70. Ibid., text, fol. 9a; trans., 1: 28.
71. Ibid., text, fols. 49b, 54b, 57b; trans., 1: 121, 134–38, 143.
72. Ibid., text, fol. 57b; trans., 1: 144.
73. "Khwaja Muhammad Tahir, who was sent to Jessore to assess its revenues," wrote Mirza Nathan, "returned to Islam Khan with the register of revenues of that territory which was prepared to the satisfaction of the ryots [i.e., cultivators] *and to the advantage of the imperial treasury*. It was presented to Islam Khan with the signatures of the Chowdhuries and Qanungus [i.e., intermediate landholders and their clerks]; it was then handed over to the accountants of [the province's chief financial officer] Mu'taqid Khan in order to enforce these regulations on the ryots and the Jagirdars." Ibid., text, fol. 61b; trans., 1: 156. Emphasis mine.
74. Ibid., text, fols. 5a, 19b, 21a; trans., 1: 15, 56–57, 62.
75. Ibid., text, fol. 41b; trans., 1: 100.
76. Ibid., text, fols. 228b–229a; trans., 2: 503–4.

keteers and fifty elephants, and participated in the capture of the raja, personally bringing the captive king to Dhaka.[77] By the time of Ibrahim Khan's governorship (1617–24), Mirza Nathan spoke of "Musa Khan and the Twelve Bhuyans of Bhati" being engaged in Mughal expeditions throughout eastern Bengal, indicating that by this time all the formerly independent chieftains had become integrated into imperial service.[78]

At the center of all this political activity was Dhaka, or "Jahangirnagar," as it was officially known, which in the seventeenth century attained a peak of power and influence. Fray Sebastião Manrique, who was there in 1640, described the place as a "Gangetic emporium," with a population of over two hundred thousand.[79] Recalling that the population of Gaur had been estimated at only forty thousand at the height of the sultanate's power around 1515, one sees how rapidly the Mughal capital must have grown in the thirty years since Islam Khan's arrival. Manrique was especially impressed with the city's wealth. "Many strange nations," he wrote,

> resort to this city on account of its vast trade and commerce in a great variety of commodities, which are produced in profusion in the rich and fertile lands of this region. These have raised the city to an eminence of wealth which is actually stupefying, especially when one sees and considers the large quantities of money which lie principally in the houses of the Cataris [Khatri], in such quantities indeed that, being difficult to count, it is usual commonly to be weighed.[80]

Manrique's reference to wealthy Khatris (known today as Marwaris, because they came from Marwar in Rajasthan)[81] points to the prominence of this caste of Hindu merchants, bankers, and moneylenders, who had accompanied their Mughal patrons to wealth and success.

In fact, the Marwaris and Mughals collaborated in the conquest of Bengal. Where the Mughals provided the Marwaris with the political security essential for transacting business, the latter provided the Mughals with financial capital obtained through their networks of fellow caste-members residing all over northern India.[82] In theory, imperial officeholders spent only the cash raised from their assigned *jāgīr*s, or territorially defined reve-

77. Ibid., text, fols. 231a, 271a; trans., 2: 511, 628.
78. Ibid., text, fol. 273b; trans., 2: 636.
79. Manrique, *Travels*, 1: 45.
80. Ibid., 44.
81. Abdul Karim, *Dacca, the Mughal Capital* (Dacca: Asiatic Society of Pakistan, 1964), 70.
82. Dhaka's attraction of both military men and merchants did not escape Manrique's notice. Some of its population, he wrote, "came on mercantile business in order to take advantage of the great facilities offered by the place; others, followers of Mars [i.e., soldiers], attracted by the high mainas, that is monthly pay and allowance which are given on those frontiers." Manrique, *Travels*, 1: 45.

nue units, to finance their military operations. In fact, though, officers often needed more money than could be derived from their revenue assignments, and in such cases turned to moneylenders. For example, around 1621 Mirza Nathan, whose *jāgīr* provided him with revenue sufficient to support around one thousand cavalrymen, obtained from the "merchant-princes [*mullak-i tujārān*] of Jahangirnagar" the substantial loan of Rs. 100,000 for the purpose of purchasing or hiring boats to transport troops and supplies in northern Bengal.[83] Somewhat earlier, and for a similar purpose, he had borrowed Rs. 30,000 from Hindu lenders in Gilah, a Mughal outpost in the Kuch country far to the north. This indicates that such banking houses followed Mughal arms even to the remotest frontiers of imperial expansion.[84] Moreover, Nathan's casual air in relating these transactions suggests their routine nature. It also indicates that the close collaboration between Hindu merchant bankers and Mughal officers so characteristic of the first half of the eighteenth century extended back to the earliest days of the Mughal connection with Bengal.[85]

Summary

Soon after Islam Khan's arrival in Bengal, the Mughals succeeded in annihilating or winning over all the major chiefs entrenched in the countryside since the time of the sultans. Yet it is fair to ask how far the new rulers were able to extend their political reach beneath the level of important chieftains, or *zamīndārs*, after these had submitted to imperial rule. The Augustinian missionary Fray Sebastião Manrique, who was in Bengal in 1629–30 and again in 1640, remarked on the ability of the *shiqdār*—a Mughal officer responsible for executive matters in the *pargana*, the smallest territorial unit of imperial administration—to collect the revenue demand, by force if necessary, and even to enslave peasants should they default in their payments.[86] Yet internal evidence suggests that the government was also responsive to peasant grievances, so long as they were voiced through legitimate channels. In 1664 the senior revenue officer (*amīn*) in Rangamati, Kuch Bihar, dismissed one of his collectors

83. Nathan, *Bahāristān*, text, fol. 276a–b; trans., 2: 644. We do not know what Nathan's revenue assignment was at the time of the loan, but both before and after the loan, Jahangir raised his assignment by an additional 150 horse, and early in Shah Jahan's reign it was further raised to 1,500 horse. Ibid., text, fols. 272b, 284a, 305a; trans., 2: 632, 666, 723.
84. Ibid., text, fol. 264a–b; trans., 2: 607.
85. For a discussion of the ties between Hindu bankers and government officials in late Mughal Bengal, see Sushil Chaudhury, "Merchants, Companies and Rulers in Bengal in the Eighteenth Century," *Journal of the Economic and Social History of the Orient* 31 (February 1988): 90–109.
86. Manrique, *Travels*, 1: 53.

(*chaudhurī*) when peasants complained of oppression by him. Moreover, before appointing a new collector this senior officer secured the peasants' written approval of his nominee.[87] Nine days later, the new collector was made to sign a written agreement affirming that "I, Balchand, . . . recognize and promise that I will perform the assigned duties diligently in such a manner that the cultivable land should increase, and that I will not oppress anyone."[88]

In sum, by the mid seventeenth century, as both foreign observers and contemporary revenue documents attest, the Mughals had established both power and credibility throughout the delta. They achieved this by means of a military machine that effectively combined gunpowder weaponry with mounted archers and naval forces, a determined diplomacy that rewarded loyalty while punishing perfidy, and the financial services of mobile and wealthy Marwari bankers. Both militarily and diplomatically, success begat success. Bengali chieftains who witnessed these successes increasingly understood that the advantages of joining the new order outweighed those of resisting it. Above all, the advent of the Mughal age, unlike previous changes of the guard at Gaur, did not represent a mere military occupation in which one ruling class simply replaced another. Nor were the changes accompanying Mughal rule merely ones of scale—that is, bigger cannons, a more dazzling court, or taller monuments. Rather, as will be seen in the following chapters, the conquest was accompanied by fundamental changes in the region's economic structure, its sociopolitical system, and its cultural complexion, both at court and in the countryside.

87. "We the peasants of *pargana* Khorla," read their petition, "state that we were being ruined due to the oppressions of Pashupati. Therefore, quite willingly and totally on our own accord we accept (the appointment of) Bulchand for which Suraj Chand *qanungo* has furnished surety (*hazir-zamini*) on his behalf. We undertake that when he obtains the *sanad* of *chaudhurī*, we will pay the revenues as before." S. Z. H. Jafri, "Rural Bureaucracy in Cooch Behar and Assam under the Mughals: Archival Evidence," *Indian History Congress, Proceedings*, 49th session, Karnataka University, 1988 (Delhi, 1989), 280.
88. Ibid.

7 Mughal Culture and Its Diffusion

There is no heavier burden on the neck of a Muslim than the
burden of being true to the salt.

Mirza Nathan (1612)

The Political Basis of Mughal Culture in Bengal

Miniature paintings of the seventeenth-century Mughal court typically
depict rows of nobles neatly arranged and ranked by status, their eyes riveted on the raised figure of the seated emperor, while the latter, his head
enveloped in a luminous halo, gazes benevolently over the gathered flock
(see fig. 18). In our efforts to reconstruct the content of Mughal culture, it
is well to consider the model of order and hierarchy evoked in such paintings. For Mughal culture as it evolved over the course of the sixteenth
century was above all a courtly and imperial culture, one that, in the manner of those miniature paintings, focused on the person and charisma of
the emperor.

Whereas the early Delhi sultans tended to rule as foreigners over a
subjugated Indian population, the Mughals, beginning with Akbar (1556–
1605), sought to knit North India's many religious and ethnic communities
into a single political system. This policy, which crystallized around 1580
in the wake of the emperor's abortive experiment in posing as "king of
Islam,"[1] inclined the court to an extraordinarily accommodative, even syncretic style of politics.[2] Elaborated by Akbar's principal ideologue, Abu'l-

1. For the development of Akbar's religious and political policies, see Iqtidar Alam
Khan, "The Nobility under Akbar and the Development of His Religious Policy,
1560–80," *Journal of the Royal Asiatic Society of Great Britain and Ireland*, pts.
1 and 2 (1968): 29–36.
2. As is well known, Akbar banned activities offensive to Hindus, such as cow-
slaughter. He also abolished discriminatory taxes such as those levied on Hindu
pilgrims, admitted Hindu sages into his private audience and Rajput chieftains into
his ruling class, ordered the translation of Hindu sacred texts into Persian, and
celebrated Hindu festivals. Sri Ram Sharma, *The Religious Policy of the Mughal
Emperors*, 2d ed. (London: Asia Publishing House, 1962), 19–24.

fazl, the model of imperial authority projected from the Mughal court drew on both Indian and Perso-Islamic notions of kingship. It also drew on a Sasanian Persian model of imperial authority, according to which virtue and order radiated outward and downward from an all-benevolent and semi-divine emperor, supported politically and ideologically by a hierarchically graded corps of soldiers-administrators, the *manṣabdārs*.[3] While patronizing Islamic institutions as was expected of any premodern Muslim sovereign, Akbar presented himself to his subjects in the radiant glow of an Indian maharaja, appearing in public audience (*darbār*) seated on a raised platform (*jharokhā*) in the manner in which traditional Indian kings or images of Hindu deities were presented for public viewing (*darśan*). As a result, when Indian courtiers gazed upon the seated emperor, they could share a certain double vision, seeing either a pious Muslim sultan or a traditional maharaja tinged with divine power, or both simultaneously.

Splendidly articulated at imperial courts in Delhi, Agra, or Lahore, this hybrid model of political authority was duplicated in miniaturized form in Mughal provinces. In Dhaka, Islam Khan built a scaled-down replica of Jahangir's imperial court, complete with a *jharokhā*. Located in the inner garden adjoining the governor's palace, his *jharokhā* consisted of a window and enclosed space built on a platform elevated some twelve feet above the ground. Behind the window and raised above those in the garden below, the seated governor received those admitted for private or public audience, or *darbār*.[4] As a stage for enacting political rituals, the *jharokhā* thus expressed themes central to Mughal political culture: the subordination of all state servants (i.e., both imperial appointees and Bengali *zamīndārs* assimilated as imperial *jāgīrdārs*) to the governor, the corporate solidarity of the ruling class, and the precise position of each member relative to others in the graded hierarchy of state service. Mimicking the court of Jahangir, during formal review, officers would stand before the governor's *jharokhā* according to rank, the highest officers situated closest to the *jharokhā* and the lowest officers furthest from it.[5]

3. For a useful summary of the factors that helped shape Akbar's political ideology, see Douglas E. Streusand, *The Formation of the Mughal Empire* (Delhi: Oxford University Press, 1989), esp. 123–81.
4. Nathan, *Bahāristān*, text, fols. 49a, 60b; trans., 1: 120, 153.
5. Ibid., text, fol. 78b; trans., 1: 205. These political rites also carried the danger of encouraging loyalty to provincial governors at the expense of the larger loyalty due the emperor. This possibility was not lost on Jahangir himself, who at one point issued an edict forbidding governors to compel others to salute or make obeisance to them, to hold reviews with a *jharokhā*, or even to sit on places higher than half a human height above the ground. In a political universe in which the substance and symbolism of power overlapped, if not coincided, such niceties of elevation above ground level were far from trivial. Ibid., text, fol. 103a; trans., 1: 213.

Fig. 18. "Shah Jahan Honors Religious Assembly." From Stuart Cary Welch,
Imperial Mughal Painting (New York: George Braziller, 1978), 102, pl. 31. Reprinted by permission of George Braziller, Inc.

Mughal political culture was also expressed in pervasive categories of thought. From the emperor down to the lowest servant, parties were bound together by mutual obligations articulated through the ideology of "salt" (*namak*), a semantically rich term expressing notions of protection and dependency that operated simultaneously at social, political, and superhuman levels. Deeply embedded in the culture of the Middle East, this ideology can be traced to the ancient Mesopotamian world, where the Akkadian phrase meaning "to eat the salt of (a person)" expressed the act of making a covenant with a person or of permitting a reconciliation with another individual.[6] The ancient Hebrews considered that they were tied to God by a "covenant of salt,"[7] and that such a covenant legitimized and underwrote earthly kingship.[8] The ancient Persians, too, used the symbolism of salt in the sense of concretizing political covenants—in their case between the emperor and his corps of servants. Officials serving Artaxerxes I (465–425 B.C.) felt obliged to warn their sovereign of possible threats to the collection of imperial revenues, noting that "we eat the salt of the palace and it is not fitting for us to witness the king's dishonor."[9] Given these deep historical roots, it is hardly surprising that salt appeared as a metaphor for sociopolitical loyalty and dependence in high Perso-Islamic culture. We find the term used in this sense in the poetry of the Khurasani epic poet Firdausi (d. 1020).[10] From Khurasan, Persianized Turks brought the ideology of salt with them to North India, where in the early fourteenth century it appeared in the poetry of Amir Khusrau (d. 1325).[11]

In Mughal Bengal, the behavior of officers and their subordinates illustrates how thoroughly the ideology of salt had penetrated the ruling class. On one occasion in the early seventeenth century, two rival officers conducted a quarrel through messengers who were dependents of one of these

6. Daniel Potts, "On Salt and Salt Gathering in Ancient Mesopotamia," *Journal of the Economic and Social History of the Orient* 27, no. 3 (October 1984): 228.

7. The Lord commanded both Moses and Aaron to include salt in holy offerings made by the people of Israel: "you shall not let the salt of the covenant with your God be lacking from your cereal offering" (Lev. 2:13). See also Num. 18:19.

8. "The Lord God of Israel gave the kingship over Israel forever to David and his sons by a covenant of salt" (2 Chron. 13:4–5).

9. Ezra 4:14. The *Bahman Yast*, composed most probably in the Achaemenid period (553–330 B.C.), stated that men at the Zoroastrian End of Time "have no gratitude and respect for bread and salt, and they have no affection for their country" (*Pahlavi Texts*, trans. E. W. West, vol. 5 of *The Sacred Books of the East*, ed. Max Müller [Oxford: Clarendon Press, 1880], pt. 1, p. 204). I am indebted to Said A. Arjomand for this reference.

10. Ali Akbar Dihkhuda, *Lughat-nāma* (Teheran: University of Tehran, 1341 Solar [1962]), 30: 790.

11. Ibid.

two men. When the messengers were in the company of the other officer, the latter pointed out that their patron had already lost his honor and asked the two why they continued to ally themselves with him. Replied these lowly servants, "We know that our honour has also been lost and will (continue to) be lost; but what can we do? We are under the obligation of his salt."[12] Here *salt* is used to convey its most ordinary, metaphorical sense: patrons gave protection to clients, who in turn gave loyalty to patrons.[13]

Within the corps of Mughal officers, salt was understood as a substance either ceremonially or metaphorically accepted and eaten at the hands of the emperor, exactly as in the case of the court of the Persian emperor Artaxerxes I in the fifth century B.C. Binding members of the imperial corps horizontally to one another and vertically to the emperor, the ideology of salt gave expression to corporate solidarity, especially at times when the group felt itself mortally endangered. In 1615, during an imperial invasion of Assam, for example, Mughal troops once found themselves totally surrounded by the army of the Ahom raja. On this occasion the commanding officer and his comrades wrapped their heads in shrouds and, preparing for death rather than surrender, cried out to the Assamese: "As we have taken the salt of Jahangir, we consider martyrdom to be our blessings for both the worlds."[14]

This usage of the salt metaphor recalls F. W. Buckler's discussion, in a 1926 essay, of the importance of "rituals of incorporation" in the running of the Mughal political system. The emperor, he wrote,

> stands for a system of rule of which he is the incarnation, incorporating into his own body, by means of certain symbolical acts, the persons of those who share his rule. They are regarded as being parts of his body, *membra corporis regis*, and in their district or sphere of activity, they

12. Nathan, *Bahāristān*, text, fol. 213b; trans., 2: 460. "Mā ham mīdānīm ābrū ba bād rafta wa mīravad, valī chi-kunam? Ḥuqūq-i namak khūrdagī dāmangīr shuda."
13. In the modern Persian language, as in Mughal Bengal, the metaphor of "salt" still expresses pervasive ideas of patronage, clientage, loyalty, and betrayal. It reflects a society deeply concerned with the fragility of human relationships—especially across different strata—and with how such relationships can be established, maintained, or broken. Thus *namak khūrdan*, "to eat salt [of someone]," means to accept, acknowledge, and enjoy the benefits of a patron. Conversely, *namak-dān shikastan*, "to break [someone's] salt vessel," means to betray a patron. Similarly, *namak shinās*, "acknowledging [someone's] salt," refers to one who is loyal to a patron; whereas *namak nā-shinās*, "not acknowledging [someone's] salt," refers to one who is disloyal to, or even betrays, a patron.
14. Ibid., text, fol. 260b; trans., 2: 596–97. "Chūn namak-i Jahāngīrī khūrda shahādat-rā saʿādat-i dārain-i khūdimān mīdānīm."

are the King himself—not servants of the King but "friends" or *members* of the King, just as the eye is the *man* in the function of sight, and the ear is the realm of hearing.[15]

Within this conceptual framework, ingesting the salt of the emperor communicates the symbolic sharing in the body of the emperor, analogous to the Christian ritual of Communion, in which the believer ritually partakes of and thus shares in the body of Christ.

Finally, Muslims in the imperial corps regarded salt as a substance binding them both to their emperor and to their religion, thereby combining the ancient Persian sense of the "salt of the palace" with the ancient Hebrew sense of God's "covenant of salt." In 1612, after defeating the last Afghan chieftain in Bengal to resist Mughal authority, Islam Khan's men faced the question of how to deal with their defeated Muslim foes. "It was decided," wrote Mirza Nathan, "to extend hospitality to all the Afghans in the first halting place and to distribute to them the salt of the emperor according to their status: because there was no heavier burden on the neck of a Muslim than the burden of being true to the salt."[16] Here again clients were bound to their patron—now the emperor himself—by receiving his "salt" in what appears to have been a formal political ritual in which actual salt was distributed and consumed. But in the statement that there was "no heavier burden on the neck of a Muslim than the burden of being true to the salt," the ideology of salt is transposed to a religious context in which the patron may be understood as God, imposing obligations of loyalty on his community of believers just as the emperor imposed such obligations on his subjects, or as lesser Mughal officers did on their own clients.

Another Mughal ritual of incorporation was the conferral of the imperial cloak (*khil'at*) upon a subject or former enemy. Authority, Buckler observes, "was exercised in virtue of this incorporation into the royal person by means of succession established by physical contact through royal clothing. Refusal to acknowledge this transmission of authority, by refus-

---

15. F. W. Buckler, "The Oriental Despot," *Oberlin Alumni Magazine* 22, no. 5 (February 1926): 15; and 22, no. 6 (March 1926): 14. Reprinted in *Legitimacy and Symbols: The South Asian Writings of F. W. Buckler*, ed. M. N. Pearson (Ann Arbor: Center for South and Southeast Asian Studies, No. 26, 1985), 177. The idea that imperial servants were "the eyes and the ears of the king" extends far back in the political tradition of the ancient Near East; it was introduced into Perso-Islamic notions of statecraft via Iran's Sasanian dynasty.

16. Nathan, *Bahāristān*, text, fols. 75b–76a; trans., 1: 197. The phrase "according to their status" given in Borah's translation does not appear in the Persian text. "Ṣubḥ-ash kūchīda qarār dād tā ham dar manzil-i avalīn hamagī Afghānān-rā mihmān sākhta, namak-i Bādshāh-i dīn-panāh ba khūrd-ashān badahad, ki az ḥaqq-i namak bārī zīāda-tar dar gardan-i Musalmān namībāshad."

ing the *robe of honour* was an act of independence, that is of treason to the King."[17] This sort of ritual was dramatically enacted at the dawn of Mughal rule in Bengal, when Daud Karrani submitted to imperial forces in April 1575. Before prostrating himself in the direction of Akbar's capital at Fatehpur Sikri, the defeated Bengali sultan donned a Mughal sword and an embroidered belt in addition to a cloak of Akbar. All of this symbolized Daud's incorporation into Akbar's person as well as Akbar's empire.

To be sure, as political symbols the *jharokhā*, salt, and the *khil'at* were already present in pre-Mughal Bengal. Both Chinese and Portuguese travelers to the Bengal capital had described raised platforms on which the sultan sat and reviewed his officials in a manner not unlike Governor Islam Khan Chishti in his Dhaka *darbār*. And we have noted the political usage of salt in the poetry of Firdausi and Amir Khusrau. Presumably, the early governors and sultans of Bengal carried into the delta the same notions of statecraft and political legitimacy that had informed their Persianized Turkish forebears in Khurasan and North India, including the ideology of salt. Finally, the political use of the royal cloak, or *khil'at*, was also known to the Bengal sultans. In the course of an interview with a Portuguese mission in 1521, Sultan Nasir al-Din Nusrat Shah embraced the European captain, laughed, and promised him favors. "Then," narrated the European interpreter, "he turned to me and ordered that I be given a robe that he had worn."[18]

But in other respects Mughal political culture in Bengal can be sharply distinguished from that of the sultanate. Down to the end of the sixteenth century, the Mughal ruling class had been predominantly non-Indian. In 1595, 61 percent of Akbar's nobility were ethnic Iranians or Turks, of whom the vast majority had migrated directly from Iran or Central Asia. During the seventeenth century, however, the empire's foreign character steadily diminished. By the end of that century, just over a third of the nobility were of known Iranian or Turkish ancestry, and fewer than a quar-

17. Buckler in *Legitimacy and Symbols*, ed. Pearson, 181
18. *Voyage dans les deltas du Gange*, 333. Just as the ideology of salt, although of foreign origin, harmonized with Indian ideas of reciprocal obligations between people of different occupation or social rank (e.g., *jājmān* and *kamīn*), so also the donning of clothing already worn by the ruler/donor paralleled indigenous conceptions of religious authority. In the context of the ordinary Indian *pūjā* ceremony, the religious devotee accepts and eats *prasād*, or the leftovers of a meal offered a deity by the devotee. As these leftovers are considered ritually touched, discarded, and hence "polluted" by the divinity, ingesting them, like wearing the robe worn by a donor, expresses subordination to the divinity. Therefore, even though the terms *namak* and *khil'at* were foreign to India—one is Persian, the other Arabic—both found ready reception in the broader context of Indian culture.

ter of these were foreign-born immigrants.[19] Already by Jahangir's reign there had emerged in the imperial corps an important and growing section of Muslims who, while claiming a paternal ancestry beyond the Khyber, had been born in India of Indian mothers. These persons not only spoke a form of vernacular Hindi-Urdu as their "mother tongue"; they also carried with them deeply held assumptions about life and death that for several centuries had been nurtured in North India within the matrix of Rajput culture.

Thus, for example, when the Mughal governor Qasim Khan faced imminent defeat in a bitterly fought battle near Dhaka in 1617, he personally beheaded his chief wives, after which many of his comrades similarly performed the rites of murdering their own families in one another's presence.[20] The practice of *jūhar*, or the destruction of women and children as an alternative to suffering them to be captured by enemy forces, was a Rajput rite assimilated into imperial culture through Akbar's policy of incorporating Rajputs into the Mughal corps and the inclusion of Rajput women in the Mughal harem. Now it was carried into Bengal. Similarly, too, Mughal officials in Bengal preferred Ayurvedic, or native Indian, medical theory over the Yunani, or Greek ("Yunani" is a corruption of "Ionian"), medical system inherited by classical Islamic civilization. The ailing Islam Khan, himself an Indian Muslim, requested an Indian physician when he neared death. There not being one available, the governor only reluctantly accepted a Muslim *ḥakīm*, who was later blamed for having administered the wrong treatment and unnecessarily killing him.[21] When the governor of Bihar suffered from an illness that paralyzed half his body, the Emperor Jahangir sent him two Indian physicians from amongst his personal staff.[22] And when illness seized Mirza Nathan, the officer's advisors sent for a practitioner of Ayurvedic medicine (*kabirāj*) who successfully treated him by consulting the appropriate astrological signs and having him drink a poisonous drug mixed with lemon juice and ginger.[23] Such reliance on Indian systems of medical therapy in the face of fatal illness

19. M. Athar Ali, *The Apparatus of Empire* (Delhi: Oxford University Press, 1985), xx; and id., *The Mughal Nobility under Aurangzeb* (Bombay: Asia Publishing House, 1966), 16–17, 34–35.
20. Nathan, *Bahāristān*, text, fols. 203b–204a; trans., 1: 440.
21. Ibid., text, fol. 140b; trans., 1: 256.
22. Ibid., text, fol. 143a; trans., 1: 262.
23. Ibid., text, fol. 165a; trans., 1: 323–24. Earlier, when Mirza Nathan's father had been ill, a *kabirāj* from Alapsingh, in Mymensingh District, was similarly called upon. Again the patient's astrological signs were studied, his pulse taken, and a poisonous brew dissolved in ginger and lemon juice administered. Ibid., text, fol. 14a–b; trans., 1: 39.

and on Rajput customs when faced with imminent annihilation in battle—both of them life-threatening situations—suggests how thoroughly Indian values had penetrated Mughal culture by the early seventeenth century.

The Place of Bengal in Mughal Culture

Despite the extraordinary ways in which imperial culture had accommodated itself to North India, with respect to distant Bengal, isolated for centuries from the north, the Mughals saw themselves as distinctly alien. In part, this was because of the delta's wet monsoon climate, of which North Indian officers posted in Bengal frequently complained.[24] Too, the Mughal policy of frequently transferring officials around the empire inclined imperial servants to regard the delta more as a temporary assignment to be endured than as a permanent, adopted home. Most important, perhaps, were the sheer numbers of new immigrants who inundated the delta as a result of Bengal's political reintegration with North India. These included soldiers recruited from the north, Marwari merchants who accompanied and helped finance their Mughal patrons, swarms of petty clerks attached to Mughal officers, and the many artisans who supplied and equipped the Mughal military establishment. In effect, Bengal had become a colony for outsiders, effectively reversing the long-term pre-Mughal trend whereby a Muslim ruling class had progressively accommodated itself to the Bengali environment owing to generations of intermarriage with Bengali women and centuries of isolation from the north.

Both the literature and the architecture of the period reveal the new ruling class's profoundly foreign—that is, non-Bengali—character. In 1626 an Afghan, Mahmud Balkhi, journeyed to Rajmahal and wrote of encountering people whose family origins lay in Balkh, Bukhara, Khurasan, Iraq, Baghdad, Anatolia, Syria, and North India.[25] These would have been remnants of the predominantly Sunni *ashrāf* of Akbar's day, when Rajmahal was the provincial capital. Some years later the poet-official Muhammad Sadiq Isfahani, who lived in Dhaka from 1629 to his death in

24. In 1583 Mirza 'Aziz Koka, one of Akbar's early governors, grew so disgusted with the delta's soggy weather that he pleaded for and won a transfer. Abu'l-fazl 'Allami, *Akbar-nāma*, trans., 3: 594; text, 3: 401. Military men, particularly cavalry officers, faced special difficulties moving men and equipment in a terrain utterly unlike the plains of North India. Mirza Nathan describes becoming hopelessly lost in a "swamp which appears in the whole country of Bengal during the rainy season. He found no way out of it and wandered about in that deep water in the whirlpool of perplexity." Nathan, *Bahāristān*, text, fol. 15b–16a; trans., 1: 43.
25. Mahmud b. Amir Wali Balkhi, *The Bahr ul-Asrar: Travelogue of South Asia*, ed. Riazul Islam (Karachi: University of Karachi, 1980), 48.

1650, kept a diary, the Ṣubḥ-i Ṣādiq, in which he mentions the dozens of artists, poets, generals, and administrators he had come to know in that city. Most of these men were Shi'as whose ancestors had migrated from distant centers of Persian culture—for example, Mashhad, Teheran, Ardistan, Isfahan, Mazandaran, Qazvin, Taliqan, Shiraz, Tabriz, Herat, Bukhara, or Gilan.[26] This suggests that between the reign of Akbar (1556–1605), when Rajmahal was capital, and that of Shah Jahan (1628–58), when Dhaka was capital, an increasing proportion of Bengal's urban *ashrāf*, although born in North India, claimed Iranian ancestry.[27]

The most striking statement of the imperial attitude toward Bengal was made by Akbar's chief advisor, Abu'l-fazl. "The country of Bengal," he wrote in 1579, shortly after imperial armies had routed the capital's Afghan occupants, "is a land where, owing to the climate's favouring the base, the dust of dissension is always rising. From the wickedness of men families have decayed, and dominions [have been] ruined. Hence in old writings it was called Bulghākkhāna (house of turbulence)."[28] Here, in this "Mughal colonial discourse," we find a remarkable theory of political devolution: an enervating climate corrupts men, and corrupted men ruin sovereign domains, thereby implicitly preparing the way for conquest by stronger, uncorrupted outsiders. In linking Bengal's climate with the debased behavior of people exposed to it, Abu'l-fazl's theory of sociopolitical decay anticipated by several centuries the similar views adopted by British colonial officials.[29]

26. See A. Halim, "An Account of the Celebrities of Bengal of the Early Years of Shahjahan's Reign Given by Muhammad Sadiq," *Journal of the Pakistan Historical Society* 1 (1953): 355; Nazir Ahmad, "Muhammad Sadiq Isfahani, an Official of Bengal of Shah Jahan's Time," *Indo-Iranica* 24 (1972): 103–25; S. N. H. Rizvi, "Literary Extracts from Kitab Subh Sadiq," *Journal of the Asiatic Society of Pakistan* 16, no. 1 (April 1971), 1–61.
27. Moreover, Dhaka's Muslim elite was overwhelmingly Shi'a, whereas the older *ashrāf* of Rajmahal had been generally Sunni. The predominance of Shi'as in Bengal became even more evident during the 21-year governorship of Prince Shujā' (1639–60), who according to later traditions brought three hundred Shi'a nobles to Bengal and even turned Shi'a himself. Halim, "Account," 355–56. See also Jadunath Sarkar, ed., *History of Bengal*, 334–35.
28. Abu'l-fazl 'Allami, *Akbar-nāma*, trans. Beveridge, 3: 427; text, 3: 290.
29. Typical were those of Robert Orme, written in 1763: "The abundance of advantages peculiar to this country," he wrote, "through a long course of generations, have concurred with the languor peculiar to the unelastic atmosphere of the climate, to debase all the essential qualities of the human race, and notwithstanding the general effeminacy of character which is visible in all the Indians throughout the [Mughal] empire, the natives of Bengal are still of weaker frame and more enervated disposition than those of any other province." Orme, *History of the Military Transactions of the British Nation in Indostan* (reprint, Madras: Pharoah, 1861), 2: 4–5. Passages like this are often cited as representative of Orientalism, or

Even immigrant holy men harbored negative attitudes about the delta. Shah Ni'mat Allah Firuzpuri (d. 1669), an *ashrāf* shaikh from the Punjab who settled down in Malatipur near Malda early in the reign of Shah Jahan, quickly grew tired (*malūl*) of the region. Mincing no words, he revealed his thoughts in the following clumsy but blunt quatrain:

> Bengal is a ruined and doleful land;
> Go offer the prayers to the dead, do not delay.
> Neither on land nor water is there rest;
> It is either the tiger's jaws, or the crocodile's gullet.[30]

While harboring such attitudes toward his adopted home, the shaikh nonetheless curried favor with the province's ruling class, whose life-style he and his descendants adopted, and from whom he accepted substantial lands in personal endowments (*madad-i ma'āsh*).[31]

The Mughals' feeling of alienation from the land was accompanied by a sense of superiority to or condescension toward its people. In matters of language, dress, and diet, newly arrived officials experienced great differences between Bengal and the culture of North India. The delta's diet of fish and rice, for example, disagreed with many immigrants brought up on wheat and meat, basic to the diet in Punjab. Written in 1786, the *Riyāẓ*

---

of a British "colonial discourse." Whether located in the modern imposition of European rule over the peoples of Asia or traced to the writings of Dante or even Homer, this discourse has been identified as peculiarly European in origin and character. However, passages like this one from Abu'l-fazl suggest that at least some of its elements were rooted not in Europe but in India itself, and specifically in Mughal culture as articulated in or with reference to Bengal. Rather than bringing to Bengal ideas that were "inherently" European, men like Orme appear to have appropriated and assimilated values and attitudes that were already present in India, and that were associated in particular with Bengal's former ruling class. For a useful discussion of the Orientalism debate, see Aijaz Ahmad, "Between Orientalism and Historicism: Anthropological Knowledge of India," *Studies in History* 7, no. 1 (1991): 135–63.

30. Imam al-Din Rajgiri, *Manāhij al-shaṭṭār* (Khuda Bakhsh Library, Patna, Pers. MSS. Nos. 1848, 1848-A), 2: fol. 383b:

> Bangāla zamīn kharāb va dil-tang;
> Rū fātḥa khwān va manumā'ī dirang.
> Andar bar-o baḥr jā-yi āsāyish nīst,
> Yā hast dahan-i shīr, yā kām-i nahang.

31. The shaikh was connected with the highest levels of power in the province. Having met the governor when the latter was once hunting in the Malda region, Shah Ni'mat Allah requested and received a grant of four hundred *bighas* of land. Later, Prince Muhammad Shuja', son of Emperor Shah Jahan and governor of Bengal from 1639 to 1660, became a disciple of the shaikh's, while his servants and descendants amassed such fortunes from the ancestral grant that they were able to acquire horses, elephants, camels, and hunting animals. Ibid., fols. 384b–385a.

al-Salāṭīn faithfully reflects the *ashrāf* perspective regarding Bengali culture, and reads almost like a colonial British manual on how to survive
"amongst the natives":

> And the food of the natives of that kingdom, from the high to the low,
> are fish, rice, mustard oil and curd and fruits and sweetmeats. They also
> eat plenty of red chilly and salt. In some parts of this country, salt is
> scarce. The natives of this country are of shabby tastes, shabby habits
> and shabby modes of dress. They do not eat breads of wheat and barley
> at all. Meat of goats and fowls and clarified butter do not agree with
> their system[s].[32]

Mughal officers also associated Bengalis with fishermen, whom they
openly despised. Around 1620 two imperial commanders, aiming to belit-
tle the martial accomplishments of one of their colleagues, taunted the
latter with the words: "Which of the rebels have *you* defeated except a
band of fishermen who raised a stockade at Ghalwapara?" In reply, the
other observed that even the Mughals' most formidable adversaries in
Bengal, 'Isa Khan and Musa Khan, had been fishermen. "Where shall I
find a Dawud son of Sulayman Karrani to fight with, in order to please
you?" he asked rhetorically, and with some annoyance, adding that it was
his duty as a Mughal officer to subdue all imperial enemies in Bengal,
"whether they are *Machwas* [fishermen] or Mughals or Afghans."[33] In this
view the only truly worthy opponents of the Mughal army were state
rebels or Afghans like the Karranis; Bengalis, stereotyped as fishermen,
were categorized as less worthy adversaries.

Mughal officials thus distinguished themselves from Bengalis not only
as tax-receivers as opposed to taxpayers but as North Indian fighting men
as opposed to docile fishermen. On one occasion Islam Khan's chief naval
officer, Ihtimam Khan, expressed resentment that the governor had once
treated him and his son like "natives."[34] Since the Persian term used here,
ahl-i Hind, means simply "Indian," one might expect to find it used only
by nobles who had immigrated from beyond India. But Ihtimam Khan was
himself an India-born Muslim from the Punjab;[35] hence his use of the term
in a pejorative sense suggests he had acquired *ashrāf* attitudes through his
service with the Mughals. That *ashrāf* Muslims occupied a social category
distinct from the "natives" was also noted by the Portuguese friar Sebas-

32. Salim, *Riyāzu-s-Salātīn*, trans. Abdus Salam, 21.
33. Nathan, *Bahāristān*, text, fol. 278b; trans., 2: 650–51. Emphasis mine.
34. Ibid., text, fol. 18a; trans., 1: 51.
35. M. Athar Ali, *The Apparatus of Empire: Awards of Ranks, Officers and Titles
to the Mughal Nobility, 1574–1658* (Delhi: Oxford University Press, 1985), 32.
Abu-l-Qadir Ibn-i Muluk Shah al-Badaoni, *Muntakhabu't-Tawarikh*, trans. and
ed. T. Wolseley Haig (1899; reprint, Delhi: Idarah-i Adabiyat-i Delli, 1973), 2: 300.

tião Manrique, who in 1629 described Bengal's population as composed of three groups—"the Portuguese, the Moors, and the natives of the country."[36] In this social classification Muslims were, by definition, foreigners to the land. From the perspective of the *ashrāf* Muslims whom Manrique met, it was conceptually impossible for "natives" also to be "Moors"— that is, that there could be Bengali Muslims.

The Mughals' foreign character is also seen in their monuments. The earliest surviving architectural record of the new order is the Kherua mosque, built in 1582 by members of the Qaqshal clan in Sherpur, southern Bogra. Although the Qaqshals had participated in the Mughal conquest of 1574, six years later they spearheaded the *mansabdārs'* revolt against Akbar's authority, in the midst of which they patronized the construction of this monument. But the Qaqshals' alienation from North India was political, not cultural. Unlike the Afghans before them, they had not been in the province long enough to absorb the local culture fully, which perhaps explains the mosque's somewhat hybrid nature. Its brick exterior, engaged corner turrets, and curved cornice were all staple indices of the native Bengali mosque as it had evolved for over a century under the patronage of Bengal sultans. On the other hand its ground plan—a single-aisled rectangle divided into three bays—had been popular in the Delhi region since the fifteenth century; beginning with this mosque, it would become a characteristic feature of the Mughal style in Bengal. The building's inscription, moreover, was in Persian, the official language of the Mughals, whereas most pre-Mughal Muslim inscriptions in Bengal had been in Arabic. Thus the mosque aptly reflects the culturally ambiguous position of its patrons, with one foot in Bengal, the other still in Delhi.

More emphatically North Indian, and hence from a Bengali perspective more foreign, is the congregational mosque of Rajmahal. Built during the governorship of Raja Man Singh (1594–1605) as the principal mosque of Akbar's provincial capital, this imposing structure (252 × 212 feet) was an architectural assertion of the Mughals' claim to the province. In no other provincial capital during this period was such a large mosque built.[37] In it we find Akbar's characteristic architectural signatures as already articulated in the imperial capital at Fatehpur Sikri (c. 1570): a high monumental gateway, a single-aisle plan, ornamentation on the façade, battlements around the exterior, and a division of the bays into two stories, each containing chambers.[38]

It was in Dhaka, however, that the imperial style was most lavishly

36. Manrique, *Travels* 1: 40.
37. Asher, "Inventory," in *Islamic Heritage of Bengal*, ed. Mitchell, 120.
38. Ibid., 120–21.

Fig. 19. Satgumbad Mosque, Dhaka (ca. 1664–76).

indulged in. Overturning a Bengali architectural tradition patronized by centuries of Muslim rulers, Mughal rulers raised buildings here that were virtual transplants from the North Indian heartland. Typical was the Bara Katra (1644), a huge hostelry that once contained chambers, shops, and an imposing multistoried southern gate with an octagonal central chamber.[39] Although the Bara Katra is now ruined, a number of splendid mosques from the period have survived, in particular the Satgumbad mosque (ca. 1664–76) and the mosques of Haji Khwaja Shahbaz (1679) and Khan Muhammad Mirza (1704). With their battlements, cusped entrance arches, increased articulation of exterior and interior surfaces, and, especially in the Satgumbad mosque, projecting corner turrets with pavilions, these monuments firmly established in Bengal the aesthetic vision of Mughal imperialism (see fig. 19).[40] That vision reached its acme in the handsome ensemble of garden and monuments in Dhaka's Lalbagh Fort (fig. 20). Included in this complex are a mosque, a tomb, an audience hall (Diwan-i

39. Ibid., 55.
40. Catherine B. Asher, "The Mughal and Post-Mughal Periods," in *The Islamic Heritage of Bengal*, ed. George Michell (Paris: UNESCO, 1984), 203–4.

Fig. 20. Lalbagh Fort, Dhaka. Foreground: Fountains and tomb of Bibi Pari (late seventeenth century). Background: Two domes of the Lalbagh Fort Mosque (1649).

Khas), a bath, a tank, and a walled enclosure with gates.[41] Standing within Lalbagh one readily recalls the great palace-garden complexes of the imperial heartland—at Lahore, Delhi, and Agra—and realizes that this, too, could only have been conceived and built by outsiders to Bengal. No element of the complex is indigenous to the delta.

The concentration of Mughal power in Dhaka also had the effect of driving remnants of Bengal's pre-Mughal Muslim political tradition into the hinterland. One sees this most clearly in the Atiya mosque in Mymensingh District (fig. 21). Built in 1609 by Afghan patrons, this mosque, with its complex terra-cotta façade, its ringed corner towers, and its curved cornice, is a highly evolved elaboration of the sultanate style, now rusticated to the interior. Architecturally, it would appear to have been the last gasp of the old order, soon to be submerged under the Mughal tide. Yet one should not exaggerate the notion of a monolithic Mughal architectural style expanding inexorably from its North Indian heartland as new provinces were annexed. Even as the old, Bengali style of mosque was rusticated into the hinterland after the Mughal intrusion into the delta, certain

41. All but the mosque, dated 1649, were built between 1678 and 1684. Ibid., 200–201.

Fig. 21. Atiya Mosque, Mymensingh District (1609).

elements of the indigenous style—especially the sharply curved cornice—
were absorbed into the Mughal tradition and subsequently surfaced in the
imperial capitals of Delhi and Lahore. Thus the evolution of the Mughal
architectural tradition shows a certain double movement. Reflecting the
imposition of central authority on the periphery, a new style moved outward from the center to the provinces; yet features associated with the
provinces were simultaneously appropriated by the imperial center and
absorbed into a new, composite style, reflecting the assimilation of the
periphery into the center.[42] This model of cultural expansion, assimilation, and feedback—here reflected in architecture—closely paralleled the
growth of Islam as a religious system in Bengal, a theme to which we shall
return in later chapters.

The Place of Islam in Mughal Culture

As regards their religious culture, Bengal's Mughal *ashrāf* were distinctive
in at least three respects—their special link with the pan-Indian Chishti
order, their conceptual separation of religion and state, and, as a corollary

42. See Catherine B. Asher, "The Architecture of Raja Man Singh: A Study of Sub-
Imperial Patronage," in *The Powers of Art: Patronage in Indian Culture*, ed. Barbara S. Miller (New Delhi: Oxford University Press of India, 1992), 191–96.

to this, their disinclination to convert Bengalis to Islam. Since the Tughluq period, the Chishti order of Sufism had enjoyed a special status among Delhi's rulers, who lavishly patronized the descendants of the great Chishti shaikhs with magnificent tombs and considerable tax-free land. Mirza Nathan counted himself a "faithful disciple" (*murīd-i bandagī*) of Shaikh Farid al-Din Ganj-i Shakar (d. 1265), perhaps because his ancestors had come from the Punjab, where the cult of that saint enjoyed special prominence.[43] And Governor Islam Khan, the man most responsible for consolidating Mughal rule in Bengal, was the grandson of Akbar's chief spiritual guide, Shaikh Salim Chishti,[44] which explains why the governor once referred to Sufism as "our ancestral profession."[45]

The extent to which Sufi piety was integrated with the imperial vocation is aptly illustrated in vignettes from the career of Mirza Nathan. In early 1612, Islam Khan, having earlier promised Nathan a month's leave of absence, subsequently ordered the junior officer to assist in repelling an Arakanese invasion of southern Bengal. The Mirza vigorously protested this order by shaving his head and donning the ragged garb of the *faqīr*, that is, one who abandons the world by embracing a life of poverty (*fuqr*). What is more, 4,700 of his fighting men, plus a large number of camp followers (*bāzārīān*), did the same. Some, the officer wrote, acted from fear of losing their rations if they did not mimic their patron's behavior, and others did so "out of their simple and pure devotion for him."[46] The governor's response to all of this is equally revealing. "Alright," he replied through messengers,

> No body has to say anything about any mode of life one selects to lead. But in taking to the life of a Faqir, which is the profession of our ancestors, it will be graceful of you to come to us to receive our benediction and then to engage yourself in that profession.[47]

On another occasion, exasperated over political intrigues during one of his military campaigns in northern Bengal, Nathan again referred to the Sufi model of renunciation, writing that he "derived consolation in his trouble by recounting what happened to Mansur Hallaj," a reference to the classic

43. Nathan, *Bahāristān*, text, fol. 302b; trans., 2: 716.
44. Akbar's patronage of the Chishti order was most visibly expressed in his pilgrimages to the shrine of Shaikh Muʿin al-Din Chishti at Ajmer, which the emperor performed nearly every year between 1568 and 1579. Iqtidar Alam Khan, "Nobility under Akbar," 34, n. 28.
45. "Faqīrī ki kasb-i buzurgān-i māst." Nathan, *Bahāristān*, text, fol. 60a; trans., 1: 152.
46. Ibid., text, fol. 60a; trans., 1: 150.
47. Ibid., text, fol. 60a; trans., 1: 152.

martyr in the Islamic mystical tradition.[48] And in 1624, when his loyalties were irreconcilably divided between Emperor Jahangir and his rebel son, the future Shah Jahan, and having betrayed both, Nathan ultimately chose the drastic step of deserting imperial service altogether. Feeling as though he were "thrown into the well of calamity," he repaired on foot, and nearly alone, directly to the shrine of Mir Saiyid Ahmad al-Husaini in Malatipur, where in confusion and despair he fell before the successor to that saint, kissing his feet.[49]

It would seem, then, that Sufism, or more precisely the style of piety informed by institutionalized world-rejection and the cult of saints, was very much built into the ethos of Mughal service in Bengal. Just as a Mandarin official in contemporary Ming China could be a Confucian at his desk but a Taoist when at home or retired, in Mughal Bengal the activities of the soldier-administrator and the world-renouncing mystic/ascetic were similarly integrated. Tamed through routinized saint cults and the close historical ties between the Chishti order and the Mughal ruling house (and before that the sultans of Pandua and Gaur), Sufism's world-renouncing vision formed, not an antithesis to the worldly business of running an empire, but a complement to it.

Secondly, the ruling class in Bengal maintained a clear separation between matters of religion and matters of state. We see this in the functional specialization of Mughal cities. As the provincial capital and administrative center, Dhaka was devoted to the secular concerns of revenue collection, politics, and military reviews. Even its most imposing mosques, such as the Satgumbad mosque (ca. 1664–76), bear the stuccoed stamp of their North Indian patrons and seem intended at least as much to display imperial power as to inspire piety. The city was also devoted to trade and money-making. Fray Manrique noted that Dhaka's merchants had raised the city "to an eminence of wealth which is actually stupefying."[50]

By contrast, the ancient capitals of Pandua and Gaur were denied any political significance under the Mughals and emerged instead as Islamic sacred centers. One-third of all extant Mughal inscriptions down to 1760

---

48. Ibid., text, fol. 161b; trans., 1: 313. In A.D. 922, Mansur Hallaj was publicly executed in Baghdad on the grounds that his theologically unorthodox ideas threatened the stability of Abbasid society and government. However, throughout his execution his love of God never faltered, providing subsequent generations of Muslims with a model of steadfast devotion to God despite social or political persecution.

49. Ibid., text, fol. 328a; trans., 2: 786.

50. Manrique, *Travels*, 1: 44.

are found on sacred sites in these two cities alone.[51] Gaur's sanctity rested primarily on the Qadam Rasul, a reliquary established by Sultan 'Ala al-Din Husain Shah in 1503, containing a dais and black marble stone purporting to bear the impression of the Prophet's footprint.[52] But the institutions most lavishly patronized by the Mughals were the older and more important tomb complexes in nearby Pandua—the shrines of Shaikh 'Ala al-Haq (d. 1398) and Shaikh Nur Qutb-i 'Alam (d. 1459), Bengal's most prominent Chishti saints. The latter had been the object of state patronage ever since the saint's death in the mid fifteenth century, and by the end of that century it had become the focus of annual pilgrimages by Sultan 'Ala al-Din Husain Shah (r. 1493–1519).[53] A century later, in 1609, Mirza Nathan made a three-day pilgrimage to the shrine, having vowed to do so should his father recover from an illness.[54] And on the occasion of his own marriage, he made a pilgrimage to Gaur's Qadam Rasul and the shrine of Shaikh 'Ala al-Haq in Pandua.[55]

A third feature of *ashrāf* religious sentiment was a hands-off policy toward non-Muslim religions. Unlike the contemporary Ottoman Empire, where Christian military recruits were converted to Islam as part of their assimilation into the ruling class, in Bengal, as in Mughal India generally, it was imperial symbols such as salt, not Islam, that conferred corporate identity on the officer corps. Moreover, bonds of loyalty among Mughal officers not only ran across community lines but persisted over several generations. When Mirza Nathan donned the garb of the Sufi by way of lodging a personal protest against Governor Islam Khan, several Hindu officers obstinately stood by Nathan and even suffered imprisonment and flogging for showing their loyalty to him. When brought before the governor to explain their behavior, one of the Hindus, Baikuntha Das, was interrogated with the words, "'You are a Hindu; why did you join this rebellion?' He replied, 'God forbid! No rebellion will ever be raised either by Ihtimam Khan or his son [Mirza Nathan]. But as from my childhood, my

---

51. Shamsud-Din Ahmed, ed. and trans., *Inscriptions*, 4: 256–305.

52. Ibid., 163. In 1609 Mirza Nathan, while in the midst of military operations in northwestern Bengal, paid his respects to this shrine, noting that the marble footprint had been purchased and brought from Arabia by one of the sultans "so that the people of Bengal and everybody else, who were destined to come there, might attain eternal blessing by kissing the holy footprint." Nathan, *Bahāristān*, text, fol. 58a; trans., 1: 146.

53. 'Abd al-Rahman Chishti, *Mirāt al-asrār*, fol. 517b; Nizamuddin Ahmad, *Tabaqāt-i Akbarī*, text, 3:270; trans., 3, pt. 1: 443.

54. Nathan, *Bahāristān*, text, fol. 15a–b; trans., 1: 42–43.

55. Ibid., text, fol. 299b; trans., 2: 707.

father, at the request of his father, has given me to serve him and as I have been equally sharing his prosperity and adversity from my early life, so I can not leave his company.'"[56]

When making vows or swearing oaths, moreover, members of the imperial corps appealed to different deities according to the officers' particular religious identities. On one occasion, a copy of the Qur'an and a black geode representing a form of Vishnu (*sālagrām*) were brought to a mixed group of Mughal officers who had resolved to swear an oath among themselves. Placing their hand on the Qur'an, the Muslim officers took solemn oaths in the name of Allah, while the Hindu officers, placing their hands on the geode, did the same in the name of Vishnu.[57] Clearly, unlike the early sultans of Bengal, Mughal officials did not perceive Islam as the state religion. Except for a brief episode of anti-Hindu persecution in the early 1680s—which in any event had been initiated in Delhi and not Dhaka[58]— Bengal's rulers, despite pressure from local *mullās* and Sufis to support Islam against other religions, maintained a strictly non-interventionist position in religious matters.[59]

A corollary of this policy was the refusal to promote the conversion of Bengalis to Islam. Indeed, given the Mughals' negative sentiments toward Bengal's "natives," one should hardly expect otherwise. For Muslims in the

56. Ibid., text, fol. 60b; trans., 1: 153. "Tā tū Hindū būda, chūn mushtamal bar fasād kamarbast-ī?"
57. Ibid., text, fol. 219b; trans., 2: 476–77.
58. In 1679 Aurangzeb (r. 1658–1707), the most controversial of Mughal emperors, imposed the religion-sanctioned *jizya* tax on all non-Muslims of the empire. Theoretically required of non-Muslims in return for state protection, the *jizya* had never previously been imposed or collected in Bengal. But in early 1681 Dutch observers noted that imperial officials had begun collecting the *jizya* from the Hindus of Dhaka "ever so strictly." *Dagh-Register gehouden int Casteel Batavia vant passerende daer ter plaetse als over geheel Nederlandts-India* (Batavia: C. Kolff, 1928), A.D. 1680: 121. And in Cossimbazar, at that time the center of Bengal's flourishing textile industry, officials forcibly demanded the *jizya* from Hindu silk workers, which disrupted the local textile production business and drove the city's "little people" into the interior. Bengal's *dīwān*, or chief revenue officer, demanded that even resident European officials of the Dutch East India Company, as non-Muslims, pay the tax. *Generale missiven van gouverneurs-generaal en raden aan Heren XVII der Verenigde Oostindische Compagnie* (The Hague: Martinus Nijhoff, 1960), 4: 391, 445, 564.
59. Fray Manrique, who was in Dhaka in 1640, wrote that both *mullās* and Sufis had urged the Mughal government in Dhaka to prosecute European Christian missionaries on grounds that they had been encouraging Muslims to break Islamic injunctions against taking pork and wine. But both Shah Jahan and the governor rejected these appeals. "These attempts at persecution," the friar observed, "would have succeeded had the [Christian] Brethren not obtained the support of the Emperor and consequently of the Nababo [governor]." Manrique, *Travels*, 1: 46–47.

imperial elite, their religion and their family and political contacts with North India served, in their own minds at least, to distinguish them from the delta's indigenous peoples. Islam Khan is known to have discouraged the conversion of Bengalis, and on one occasion he actually punished one of his officers for bringing about the conversion of a Bengali Hindu. In 1609, when the governor's army was moving across the present Bogra region subduing hostile chieftains, one of his officers, Tuqmaq Khan, defeated the *zamīndār* of Shahzadpur. Soon after this the officer employed the son of the defeated raja as his personal servant and at the same time converted him to Islam. This news so annoyed the governor that he had Tuqmaq Khan transferred from his *jāgīr*.[60] Clearly, the governor did not view government service as a reward for conversion to Islam. Moreover, it was not only Islam Khan who opposed the conversion, but also "the other officers of the State," suggesting that this non-interventionist policy was a general one.

The Administration of Mughal Law — the Villagers' View

The Mughals' policy of not interfering with Hindu society was also noted by outsiders, in particular Fray Sebastião Manrique, the Augustinian friar who traveled through Bengal in 1629–30 and 1640.[61] Manrique's narrative richly illustrates how a Mughal court of law actually adjudicated, at the village level, a dispute involving Bengali Muslims and Hindus.

It was August 1640, and Manrique, having just been shipwrecked in a violent monsoon storm off the coast of Orissa, had elected to return to Europe overland. Riding a horse and accompanied by a party of Muslim attendants, the missionary was making his way up Bengal's western corridor from Orissa toward the Ganges River, which he intended to take through Upper India. He had adopted the dress of a Muslim merchant, apparently in the hope of not drawing undue attention to his true vocation. As the monsoon rains were then drenching lower Bengal with full force, Manrique and his party became bogged down in muddy swamps about ten miles north of Jaleswar, near the present border between Orissa and West Bengal. Unable to make further progress that day, the travelers were obliged to pass an uncomfortable night, tormented by swarms of mosquitoes, in the cowshed of a Hindu village. There they spent the next day, too, for heavy rains prevented immediate resumption of their journey.

While Manrique was dozing through the gray afternoon, one of his Muslim attendants, with an eye to a good meal, seized and killed a couple

60. Nathan, *Bahāristān*, text, fol. 10b; trans., 1: 32.
61. The following narrative is drawn from Manrique, *Travels* 2: 95–115.

of peacocks that had wandered into the cowshed.[62] Awakened to what had
happened, Manrique suddenly became agitated lest the Hindu villagers
learn of the killing, which he knew would be seen as a grave transgression.
So he ordered his attendants to conceal the birds until nightfall. Then,
under the cover of darkness, they cooked and ate their quarry, promptly
burying the birds' feathers so as to hide the crime. The next day, however,
a few uncovered feathers betrayed the deed to the villagers who, armed
with bows and arrows, pursued the travelers out of the village and along
the road with great fury. Manrique fired a musket shot over the heads of
the villagers, but the gun blast so terrified his Hindu guide that the latter
fell down in panic, causing the villagers to believe they had mistakenly
killed one of their own with an arrow. In the confusion, Manrique revived
his guide and got him to lead the party to the nearby town of Naraingarh,
in present-day Midnapur District, where there was a caravansarai intended
for travelers such as himself.[63]

Once in the safety of Naraingarh, Manrique tried with a gift of pepper
to persuade his Hindu guide to forget about the unfortunate peacocks,
while he and his party made themselves comfortable in the caravansarai.
But the attempted bribe failed in its purpose, and the guide, together with
another aggrieved villager, hastened to the house of the local *shiqdār*
where they filed a formal complaint against the entire party. The *shiqdār*,
appointed by Mughal authorities to supervise the collection of revenue,
also maintained law and order at the *pargana* level, and it was in this capacity that he was approached by the aggrieved Hindus. Throwing themselves
on their knees before the *shiqdār* in the middle of the night, the two loudly
remonstrated that although they and the other villagers had received the
foreigners with great kindness, these "robbers" and "men of violence" had
nonetheless violated their religion by killing the peacocks. Evidently aware
that to Hindus the peacock was a sacred bird, the *shiqdār* promptly ordered
Manrique and his party arrested, bound, and brought to a dungeon beneath his house, where they spent the night and all the next day in a state
of misery and fright.

After a detention of twenty-four hours, around midnight the next day

62. Manrique wrote that the birds had been strangled to death. But for Muslims,
the taking of life in this manner is unlawful; the bird would have to have been
properly decapitated with a knife. Either Manrique's Muslim assistant was not
aware of the unlawfulness of his action, or, as is more likely, Manrique recalled this
detail of his account incorrectly, substituting strangulation for a proper killing.
63. This is the town listed in the *Ā'īn-i Akbarī* as Narainpur. It was a *pargana*
headquarters of some considerable size and importance, for Abu'l-fazl mentions
that it had a strong fort on a hill, and that it maintained one hundred imperial
cavalry and four thousand imperial infantry. *Ā'īn-i Akbarī*, trans., 2: 156.

the prisoners were brought before the *shiqdār*, who, seated in his tribunal, prepared to adjudicate the dispute. Summoned before the official, Manrique presented a document he had received from the Mughal governor of Orissa, affirming that he was a Portuguese from Hooghly (Manrique here dropped his Muslim guise) and permitting him to travel through Mughal territories. After hearing the document read out loud, the *shiqdār* salaamed and asked Manrique to approach nearer. "He told me of the Heathens' complaint," Manrique related,

> in reply to which I gave him the true story of the occurrence. He then asked which of my attendants had committed the outrage on the peacocks; and while I hesitated in my reply, pretending not to understand, so as not to condemn the offender, one of his companions, with greater assiduity, at once named him. The Siguidar [*shiqdār*] then turned to the offender and said, "Art thou not, as it seems, a Bengali and a Musalman . . . ? How then didst thou dare in a Hindu district to kill a living thing?"
>
> As the wretched man was more dead than alive with fear, and unable to reply, I was obliged to take his hand and, after the usual salaam, exclaim, "Sahib! as a good Musalman and follower of your Prophet Maomet's [Muhammad's] tenets he pays no heed to the ridiculous precepts of the Hindus; as you yourself would not. This, principally because God in His final, sacred, and true faith has nowhere prohibited the slaying of such animals; for His Divine Majesty created all of them for man's use. And, if we accept this dictum, this man has committed no fault against God or against His precepts or those of your Alcoran [Qur'an]."[64]

The *shiqdār* and several other venerable Muslim officials on hand leaned forward in rapt attention to Manrique's speech, an impromptu homily on Islamic teachings respecting animal life. When it was finished they stared at one another in surprise and approval, while the *shiqdār* commented to his colleagues that "Allah, the sacred, has bestowed much wisdom on the Franguis [European]."

But the friar's appeals to Islam and Islamic sentiment were to no avail. The *shiqdār* turned to Manrique and replied that notwithstanding the religious truths he had just uttered, when Akbar had conquered Bengal—sixty-five years previous to this time—he had given his word "that he and his successors would let [Bengalis] live under their own laws and customs: he [the *shiqdār*] therefore allowed no breach of them." With that the Muslim offender was led off to prison, while the others were given leave to return to their caravansarai, it now being 3:00 A.M. The punishment would be severe. By local custom, Manrique tells us, this particular offense re-

64. Manrique, *Travels*, 2: 111–12.

quired a whipping and the amputation of the right hand. Feeling compassion for the prisoner, Manrique tried the next day to intervene on his behalf by plying the *shiqdār's* wife with a piece of silken Chinese taffeta, worked with white, pink, and yellow flowers. This time his gift yielded its intended effect. "She, by importuning her husband, cajoling him, and pretending to be annoyed with him," he wrote,

> at length accomplished what we so ardently desired, that no mutilation
> of any of the prisoner's members should take place; for although the
> Governor had decided to forgo the punishment of the amputation of a
> hand, it did not follow that they would not cut off the fingers from it.
> But such is the power of a lovely face, strengthened by the seal of matrimony, that even the remission of the fingers was acceded to, and in the
> end it resolved itself into no more than the carrying out of the
> whipping.[65]

What is remarkable in this narrative is not that the culprit was released with only a whipping. Given that the accused was a Bengali Muslim being tried and sentenced by a Muslim judge, and that the offense was understood as one that violated specifically Hindu sensibilities, it may seem remarkable to modern readers that the man was punished at all. Yet we hear the words the *shiqdār* used when interrogating the accused: "How then didst thou dare in a Hindu district to kill a living thing?"[66] The *shiqdār* clearly ruled on the principle that the district's predominantly Hindu population must be judged according to its own customs and not by Islamic or any other law. Nor were Muslims to be judged differently from Hindus when it came to breaching local custom, informed in this case by Hindu sentiment. Notwithstanding Manrique's appeals to the official's own religious beliefs, the *shiqdār*, though duly impressed by the friar's knowledge of Islam, at once invoked the pledge made by Akbar to allow non-Muslims to live under their own laws and customs.

The incident compares with Islam Khan's refusal to encourage or reward religious conversion while subduing Bengali rebels some thirty years earlier. The Mughal government was simply not interested in imposing or

65. Ibid., 115.
66. Manrique's own words are "in a Hindu *pargana*" (*em pragana de Indus*). As the translator remarks, the friar "must be recording the actual Hindi [i.e., Bengali] words as he remembered them, since the expression *pargana* is not one he would have used in giving a mere paraphrase" (*Travels*, 2: 112n). This is all the more likely given that Manrique referred to his prosecutors not as "Heathens" or "Unbelievers," as was his usual practice when referring to non-Muslims of India, but by the Bengali word "Indu." Hence the phrase *em pragana de Indus* is probably a nearly verbatim representation of the *shiqdār's* own words as recalled by Manrique, *Hindu parganae*, "in a Hindu *pargana*."

advancing religious causes, either in its official pronouncements or, what is more important, in the way provincial commanders or local district officials implemented official policy. Ultimately, the Mughals had conquered Bengal in order to augment the wealth of the empire, and not for the glory of Islam. And they understood that the application of social justice was a more practical means to achieving this end than was religious bigotry. This, in any case, was the policy that a lowly *shiqdār* of Naraingarh professed on that rainy night in August 1640. Neither a foreigner's appeal to the common Islamic faith binding the judge and the judged nor bribes slipped to the *shiqdār's* wife prevented the execution of that policy.

In sum, the vignette of Fray Manrique and the several peacocks illustrates the functional compartmentalization of religion and politics in Mughal Bengal. Legally, such compartmentalization was expressed in the strict protection of Hindu custom in local courts. Spatially, it was expressed in the emergence of two functionally discrete cities—Dhaka, the administrative center, and Gaur-Pandua, the sacred center. It was also expressed in the lack of congruence between the Mughal heritage and the Islamic religion in the imperial service, since non-Muslims were not obliged to convert to Islam on entering the Mughal ruling class. This de facto separation of religion and state permitted a distinctively Mughal style of political authority, etiquette, patronage, and architecture to survive and flourish throughout the seventeenth and eighteenth centuries.

Yet the functional compartmentalization of religion and politics also encouraged an autonomous Muslim *ashrāf* class to view itself as a self-contained community encapsulated within the larger Mughal ruling class. Seeing Islam as the proud emblem of their cultural heritage, *ashrāf* Muslims did not regard their religion as something that should properly be assimilated by the indigenous classes of non-Muslim "natives," whether those were the more Sanskritized Hindus of West Bengal or the less Sanskritized semi-tribals of the east. Hence the Mughals did not officially encourage conversion to Islam among the general population. Nonetheless, Bengalis in various parts of the delta responded quite differently to the imposition of Mughal rule and the influx of Mughal culture, including Islam. Politically, responses ranged from placid acceptance to outright rebellion; religiously, they ranged from indifference to an exceptional degree of Islamization. Let us look closer at these responses.

West Bengal: The Integration of Imperial Authority

Despite Abu'l-fazl's frequent pronouncements that Mughal forces had finally dispersed the "weeds and rubbish" of rebellion and brought peace to all of Bengal, it is clear that at the time of his writing (in 1595) Mughal authority remained confined to the western delta, represented today by India's state of West Bengal. Both Raja Man Singh in 1594 and Islam Khan in 1608 had been ordered into the province to quell refractory chieftains of the east, not the west. Hence, when Islam Khan marched through western Bengal en route to Dhaka, the three chieftains controlling the cultivated tracts to the west of the Bhagirathi-Hooghly River—Birbhum, Pachet, and Hijli—all submitted without resistance.[67] The same was true of Jessore, the large, densely populated tract just east of that river. When Raja Prataspaditya failed to abide by the terms of his submission to Islam Khan, the chief provincial revenue officer had no difficulty securing the written agreements of local landholders and clerks to remit the land revenue on new, more stringent terms.[68]

We should not be surprised at the ease with which Islam Khan consolidated Mughal authority over the lands on either side of the Bhagirathi-Hooghly. Local officials of the west had long served as mediators between cultivators and the region's entrenched *zamīndārs* and had for long been integrated into the revenue system of the sultans of Gaur and Pandua. Thus in West Bengal the shift of administration from the sultans to the Mughals passed with minimal social or political disruption. Substantive changes occurred only at the uppermost levels, while in the rural districts old and familiar local officials worked side by side with the Mughal officers through whose hands the cash revenue was sent up to Dhaka, and thence to Delhi. Fray Manrique's experience with a local official in southwestern Bengal shows the extent to which Mughal authority had been accepted by rural society there.

The west was also the region of Bengal where, at the advent of Mughal rule, Hindu civilization was most deeply established. This is seen in the appearance of dated brick temples patronized by Hindu *zamīndārs* and dedicated to Brahmanical deities (see table 3). Such temples began appearing concurrently with the rise of Mughal power and proliferated throughout the seventeenth and eighteenth centuries. Most were dedicated to one of the incarnations of Vishnu, especially Krishna, until the

---

67. Bir-Hamir, the *zamīndār* of Birbhum, which lay to the immediate west and southwest of Gaur, readily submitted to a Mughal army of two thousand cavalry and four thousand infantry. So did Shams Khan, the *zamīndār* of Pachet, located in the Damodar valley, in the present Bankura District. Salim Khan, the *zamīndār* of Hijli, which roughly corresponded to the present-day Midnapur District, ignored the advice of Afghans who counseled resistance; instead, he presented a tribute payment (*pīshkash*) to Mughal officers, who "conferred upon him the right of administration of his whole territory." Nathan, *Bahāristān*, text, fol. 6b; trans., 1: 19–20.

68. Ibid., text, fol. 61b; trans., 1: 156–57.

Table 3. Construction of Dated Brick Temples, by Sect, 1570–1760

	Vaishnava	Śaiva	Goddess	Total
1570–1580	1	—	—	1
1580–1600	3	3	—	6
1600–1620	3	—	2	5
1620–1640	5	1	—	6
1640–1660	15	3	2	20
1660–1680	16	2	2	20
1680–1700	17	2	4	23
1700–1720	12	4	2	18
1720–1740	24	22	6	52
1740–1760	18	40	10	68

Source: Brick Temples of Bengal: From the Archives of David McCutchion, ed. George Michell (Princeton: Princeton University Press, 1983), 195–254.

Note: The temples listed by Michell are limited to monuments "in reasonable state of preservation."

eighteenth century, when temples dedicated to Śiva or the Goddess began to predominate.[69] The geographical distribution of these temples, moreover, shows a clear concentration in the delta's western and especially southwestern sections. Of the total 230 surviving temples built between 1570 and 1760, over half (127) are located in Hooghly, Burdwan, and Bankura districts, and over a quarter (62) in Jessore, Howrah, Midnapur, and Birbhum districts. By contrast, in East Bengal only one temple of this period has survived in each of Bogra, Dhaka, and Bakarganj districts, and none at all in Chittagong, Noakhali, Comilla, Faridpur, Rajshahi, Mymensingh, and Sylhet districts.[70] As measured by temple construction, then, in

69. The architecture of these brick temples also points to Vaishnava influence: whereas classical Hindu temples in Bengal had been small, single-doored structures intended for little more than housing the deity's image, those built from the late sixteenth century on featured larger rooms, multiple doorways, porches, and additional chambers intended to accommodate the sort of convivial religious gatherings typical of Vaishnava devotionalism. Hitesranjan Sanyal, "Temple-building in Bengal from the Fifteenth to the Nineteenth Century," in *Perspectives in Social Sciences,* ed. Barun De, vol. 1, *Historical Dimensions* (Calcutta: Centre for Studies in Social Sciences, 1977), 131–32.

70. The distribution is as follows: Hooghly, 49; Burdwan, 43; Bankura, 35; Jessore, 18; Howrah, 16; Midnapur, 17; Birbhum, 12; Twenty-four Parganas, 8; Murshidabad, 5; Nadia, 6; Pabna, 4; Khulna, 4; Dinajpur, 4; Rangpur, 3; Purulia, 2; Kushtia, 1; Bakarganj, 1; Bogra, 1; Dhaka, 1. George Michell, ed., *Brick Temples of Bengal: From the Archives of David McCutchion* (Princeton: Princeton University Press, 1983), 195–254.

the Mughal period, patronage of Hindu institutions decidedly weakened as one moved from west to east.

The greater extent to which Brahmanical culture had penetrated the west is also seen in the elaborated caste system there. Toward the end of the sixteenth century, the poet Mukundaram, a native of Burdwan, described a stratified society dominated at its upper end by Brahmans and Kayasthas who controlled the region's ritual and landholding functions respectively, followed by a large class of cultivators and artisan castes, each endogamous, and each ranked according to a graded hierarchy. These were followed by the lower castes of fishermen and boatmen, and, finally, by unclean untouchables (tanners, sweepers, scavengers, etc.).[71] The latter were mainly devotees of the Goddess in her various manifestations, folk deities whose wrath and volatility required appeasement by blood sacrifice.[72] In the Mughal period, West Bengal's middle castes of cultivators and artisans were mainly Vaishnava, devotees of Krishna,[73] and it was owing mainly to their support and the patronage of Vaishnava *zamīndārs* that the region's Vaishnava temples proliferated in the seventeenth century. For their part, West Bengal's higher-caste Brahmans and Kayasthas were primarily devoted to Śiva, though many had become Vaishnava with the growth in popularity of the Krishna cult among their cultivating and artisan clients.[74] In short, West Bengal presented a stable agrarian society whose constituent strata were, relative to other parts of the delta, well advanced in their religious and social integration with the hierarchical values of Brahmanical Hinduism.

There is also evidence of pockets of North Indian Muslims settling in the west, but their social impact appears to have been negligible. As this area already possessed a monetized economy based on surplus rice cultivation and a revenue system designed to extract that surplus, the introduction of Mughal rule had little sociopolitical impact beyond making changes of personnel at the apex of a densely populated and highly stratified agrarian order. In these circumstances the local population neither resisted Mughal authority nor adopted the religious ideology of the dominant section of the new ruling class, Islam.

The Northern Frontier: Resistance to Imperial Authority

To the north, following the Brahmaputra River upstream, where it makes its great bend eastward toward the plains of Assam, Mughal officers en-

71. Mukundaram, *Kavikaṅkaṇa Caṇḍī*, 347–61.
72. Smith, *One-eyed Goddess*, 56, 73, 133, 173.
73. Bhattacharya, "La Déesse," 40, 41; Wise, "Hindus of Eastern Bengal," 8.
74. Ray, "Medieval Bengali Culture," 90.

countered peoples who responded very differently to the imposition of imperial rule. In their efforts to dominate this region, the Mughals followed in the footsteps of earlier Muslim governors and sultans, who had made repeated invasions of the region, with results ranging from temporary success to utter catastrophe.[75] Bordering Mughal Bengal to the north was Kuch Bihar, which stretched from the Karatoya River to the Brahmaputra and Sankosh rivers. East of Kuch Bihar lay Kamrup, which extended along the banks of the Brahmaputra to the Bar Nadi River, the frontier of the kingdom of Assam.[76]

Kuch Bihar was more than a political frontier. The "Pani Kuch" peoples had for long lived along the fringes of Indo-Aryan civilization: they dwelt in forests, cultivated by hoe, drank rice beer, were matrilineal and matrilocal, and spoke a language distinct from Bengali. From at least the sixteenth century on, however, Brahmanical culture had been making inroads into their society.[77] In the early decades of that century there appeared a dynasty of Kuch kings descended from Haria Mandal, a village headman whose son, Bisu, had put together a powerful confederation of Kuch tribes. Having established supremacy from the Karatoya to the Bar Nadi, Bisu adopted the title of "raja" and proclaimed himself king of the region. On his death around 1555, Bisu's son Nara Narayan (d. 1586) succeeded to the throne, and he, like his father, avidly patronized Sanskritic culture.

The emergence of a Kuch kingdom was accompanied by the adoption of fictive genealogies appropriate for an upwardly mobile tribal dynasty. Thus the humble headman Haria Mandal and his twelve Kuch family heads were said to have been sons of twelve fugitive Kshatriya princes who had settled in the hills of Kamrup and intermarried with women belonging to the Mech tribe. Linked thereby with the uppermost rungs of the Hindu social hierarchy, the dynasty now sought linkage with the Hindu divine

75. Muslim commanders had invaded Kuch Bihar, Kamrup, or Assam in ca. 1206, ca. 1238, 1257, 1321–22, 1332–33, 1457, 1493–94, and 1567–68. The longest period of the sultanate's domination of this region followed 'Ala al-Din Husain Shah's 1494 invasion and conquest of Kuch Bihar and Kamrup. Coins minted by the Husain Shahi government continued to mention "Kamru" until 1518, and from evidence in Ahom chronicles it appears the sultans remained in control over these frontier regions until 1533, when they were decisively defeated by the Ahom kings and forced to withdraw from Kuch Bihar and Kamrup altogether. See Sudhindra Nath Bhattacharyya, *A History of Mughal North-east Frontier Policy* (Calcutta: Chuckervertty, Chatterjee & Co., 1929), 52–80; and Momtazur Rahman Tarafdar, *Husain Shahi Bengal, 1494–1538 A.D.: A Socio-Political Study* (Dacca: Asiatic Society of Pakistan, 1965), 40–80.

76. Bhattacharyya, *Mughal North-east Frontier*, 6–9.

77. Buchanan-Hamilton MSS., "List of Papers Respecting the District of Ronggopur" (India Office Library, London, Eur. MSS. D 74, vol. 1), bk. 2, 127–31.

188 / Bengal under the Mughals

hierarchy, accomplished by the myth that Bisu's mother had been miraculously impregnated by Śiva. These legends thus established Bisu as the son of a major Hindu god and the grandson of a Kshatriya warrior. Not surprisingly, Bisu lavishly patronized the North Indian Brahman priests who were evidently responsible for furnishing the king with his illustrious genealogies.[78] Here, then, was a familiar process: tribes aspiring to access to economic power and political domination employed Puranic mythology to link themselves with the ritually clean gods and castes of Brahmanical culture. For millennia this had been a route of upward mobility for India's indigenous tribes living on the fringes of Brahmanical society, and the vehicle for their integration into caste society.

From the sixteenth century on, the Kuch religious system also absorbed considerable Brahmanical content. Formerly, native priests called "kolitas" had officiated at ritual sacrifices to the sun, the moon, the stars, and to various gods associated with local forests, hills, and rivers. They employed no images in worshiping their pantheon of deities, headed by a supreme god named Rishi, married to a goddess named Jogo. By the sixteenth century, however, neighboring Brahmans had begun informing the Kuch people that the deities they called Rishi and Jogo were in fact identical with Śiva and his wife Parvati. This identification of local divinities with Hindu divinities validated by Sanskrit lore and supported by Brahman priests proved crucial in the Kuch adoption of a Brahmanic worldview and social system. At the same time, the Kuch priests, whose status had initially been threatened by the Brahmans introduced by Bisu, reestablished themselves by adopting Brahmanical ritual functions. Under their direction the entire society gradually became "Sanskritized," and by 1810 Kuch peasants would be calling themselves "pure Sudras."[79]

Kuch society consisted of a number of clan-based tribes loosely organized around a king to whom local landholders owed fealty, and to whom their subordinate clansmen owed tribute. This tribute was paid not in cash or crops but in corvée labor, a system apparently modeled after the practice of the Ahom kings in neighboring Assam. Peasants known as *pāīks* belonged to units of four cultivators and owed service to the king in turn by rotation within these units. A peasant would render his services to the king for a period of one year while the other three members of his unit looked after the land, so that every peasant served the king one year in

78. K. L. Barua, *Early History of Kamarupa from the Earliest Times to the End of the Sixteenth Century* (Shillong: n.p., 1933), 284–88.
79. Buchanan-Hamilton MSS., "List of Papers," bk. 2, 133–38.

four.[80] Unlike that of Bengal proper, then, the Kuch political economy was not monetized. Never lastingly integrated into the Bengal sultanate, its population had never evolved the institutional mechanisms of land-revenue extraction long prevalent in western deltaic Bengal. Nor was its peasantry organized into endogamous and hierarchically arranged castes like West Bengal's stratified social order. In fact, it was only in the sixteenth century that Kuch society had moved from hoe to plow, adopting with it the sedentary life associated with the cultivation of wet rice.[81]

Thus the Mughal army sent to conquer Kuch Bihar and Kamrup confronted a society very different from that of the Bengal delta. Satisfied that he had subdued the "twelve chieftains" of Bengal proper, Islam Khan in early 1613 sent into Kuch Bihar an army of five thousand musketeers, over a thousand cavalrymen, four hundred war boats equipped with large cannon, and three hundred state elephants, with Rs. 700,000 for expenses. This was the first important expedition in which the recently defeated chieftains of Bhati participated, fighting now on the side of their new masters and patrons.[82] Reaching Dhubri, an important Kuch fortress on the western banks of the Brahmaputra, the Mughal forces settled into a three-month siege against a hostile population.[83] Mughal forces eventually prevailed, pursuing the Kuch to their capital of Gilah, and driving the Kuch raja, Parikshit Narayan, out of the country altogether. Having entered the capital city, which they triumphantly renamed "Jahangirabad," the imperialists annexed Kuch Bihar to Mughal Bengal and pursued the former king across the Sankosh and Manas rivers into Kamrup. There the fugitive raja at last submitted to Mughal authority and was sent off to Dhaka in order, as Mirza Nathan put it, "to learn the court etiquettes."[84]

By July 1613 both Kuch Bihar and Kamrup had been annexed and brought under Mughal fiscal administration. The land was divided into twenty revenue circles, taxes were levied on the peasantry, and imperial agents (*kurūrī*) were sent out to collect the newly imposed land revenue.

80. See Amalendu Guha, "The Medieval Economy of Assam," in *The Cambridge Economic History of India*, ed. Tapan Raychaudhuri and Irfan Habib (Cambridge: Cambridge University Press, 1982), 1: 483–85.

81. Buchanan-Hamilton MSS., "List of Papers," bk. 2, 128, 137–38.

82. These included the Afghans formerly loyal to 'Uthman Khan of Sylhet, Raja Satrajit, Bahadur Ghazi, Suna Ghazi, and the forces of Musa Khan. Nathan, *Bahāristān*, text, fol. 105b; trans., 1: 222–23.

83. An exasperated Mirza Nathan, who played a leading role in this expedition, complained of Mughal forces during this siege "wallowing perpetually in mud like buffaloes." Ibid., text, fol. 112b; trans., 1: 236.

84. Ibid., text, fols. 116b–118b, 153a–b; trans., 1: 248–53, 292.

Some revenue circles were given to revenue farmers (mustājir) with whom the government contracted for stipulated amounts of revenue to be remitted to Dhaka.[85] Soon the Mughals sent a new revenue officer to Jahangirabad, Mir Safi, who introduced further changes in the revenue assessment and demanded that the local militia, or pāīks, be paid salaries out of the general land tax. In this way a corvée militia intended for the service of a local king was transformed into a salaried army under the authority of a distant governor. Moreover, the army was supported by additional revenue burdens placed on a peasantry unfamiliar with a monetized economy. To make matters worse, Mughal revenue farmers, having contracted to pay the government at agreed levels of revenue, further squeezed the peasantry for their own profit by raising taxes within their revenue circles.[86]

The entire Kuch political economy now fundamentally shaken, and with no king to articulate the considerable resentment caused by these changes, a series of violent peasant rebellions erupted throughout Kuch Bihar and Kamrup. In 1614 peasant rebels overpowered the Mughal garrison at Rangamati and besieged the regional headquarters at Gilah. Mughal forces responded by relieving Gilah, recovering Rangamati, and establishing garrisons in eastern Kamrup, between the Manas and Bar Nadi rivers. Around August–September 1615 they launched a full-scale invasion of Assam, at which point insurgents in eastern Kamrup seized the Mughal garrison of Dhamdhama. There, Kuch rebels made a bold bid for independence under the leadership of a peasant named Sanatan, probably the hereditary leader of a number of pāīks.[87] Sanatan communicated four demands to the besieging Mughal forces: that the revenue collector sent to Kamrup be punished for his oppression, that all Mughal taxes be remitted for a full year, that the imperial army withdraw from Kamrup, and that "the allowance of the pāīks should be given to them direct and not made an addition to revenue due to government." In response, the Mughals expressed willingness to appease the rebels by dismissing Mir Safi, the oppressive collector. But they were not willing to rescind the new system of taxation they had introduced; nor were they willing to restore the former status of the pāīks.[88] At this impasse Sanatan, seizing the symbols of Hindu political authority, proclaimed himself "raja" of the area.[89] Mughal commanders, deploying their overwhelming superiority in manpower and

85. Ibid., text, fol. 147a; trans., 1: 272–73.
86. Ibid., text, fol. 152a; trans., 1: 288–89.
87. Gautam Bhadra, "Two Frontier Uprisings in Mughal India," in Subaltern Studies II: Writings on South Asian History and Society, ed. Ranajit Guha (Delhi: Oxford University Press, 1983), 55n.
88. Nathan, Bahāristān, text, fol. 181a; trans., 1: 370.
89. Ibid., text, fol. 183b; trans., 1: 378.

firepower, now doggedly mowed down Sanatan's fortified stockades, killed a thousand rebels, and ultimately compelled Sanatan to flee for his life.[90]

In this way, Bengal's northern frontier region was forcibly subjugated to imperial authority. Accompanied as it was by a drastic break in the region's former political economy, the conquest sharply contrasted with the orderly transition to Mughal power in western Bengal. In Kuch Bihar and Kamrup a monetized economy replaced a non-monetized one; a distant governor replaced a local king; and an armed militia paid from a general tax levied on the whole peasantry replaced a corvée militia paid by a system of customary service to a king. These disruptions explain the widespread and popular resistance to the imposition of Mughal authority, reflected in the support given Sanatan's warriors by several thousand villagers, who brought rations for their besieged comrades in the garrison.[91]

Finally, the advance of the plow over the hoe in Kuch society, a change already in progress before the Mughals' arrival, seems to have been identified with the advance of Hindu culture and the Bengali language from the plains, and not with Islamic culture or the Mughal administration. "At this time," wrote Buchanan-Hamilton with reference to this period, "the nation had in general betaken themselves to the plough, and the Kolitas [traditional priests] could read the Bengalese language, and that seems at least to have been in frequent use."[92] In short, by the early seventeenth century the Sanskritization of Kuch society had progressed to such an extent that the Mughal conquest, by posing a broadside threat to that society, not only ensured the survival of Brahmanic culture on Bengal's northern frontier, but evidently strengthened it.

East Bengal: Conquest and Culture Change

The instruments of Mughal conquests in Bhati, or eastern Bengal—the threat or the use of brute force and the use of sizable rewards for enticing enemy defections—did not differ from those used in the west or the north. Typical was Islam Khan's annexation of the *zamīndārī* of Bhallua, in what is now the Comilla-Noakhali region of the southeastern delta. Around 1611 a force of four thousand cavalry, three thousand musketeers, and fifty elephants entered the territory of Raja Ananta Manik with orders to extend to the king the hope of imperial favors should he submit; and if he resisted, to bring to Dhaka either the king's person or his severed head.[93] Advancing into the Comilla region, the army easily reduced one of the

90. Ibid., text, fol. 184b; trans., 1: 381.
91. Ibid.
92. Buchanan-Hamilton MSS., "List of Papers," bk. 2, 138.
93. Nathan, *Bahāristān*, text, fol. 40b; trans., 1: 97.

king's forts near modern-day Chandpur, while groups of Mughal soldiers pillaged the countryside and terrorized the peasants by killing or imprisoning those who refused submission.[94] Here as elsewhere military sticks were accompanied by political carrots. After making overtures to Mughal officers, the raja's chief minister was offered and accepted a middle-level imperial rank.[95] His military and political positions thus undermined, Ananta Manik eventually abandoned his territories, which were forthwith annexed to Mughal Bengal.

About the same time, Raja Ram Chandra of Bakla in eastern Bakarganj, one of the "twelve chieftains" of eastern Bengal, was similarly overwhelmed. Although placed under detention in Dhaka, the ex-king was allowed to retain enough of his former territory to maintain a naval fleet, while his remaining lands were handed over to Mughal collectors and assigned to other *jāgīrdārs*.[96] As we have seen, in the delta's central and northeastern sectors—today's Dhaka, Mymensingh, and Sylhet districts—'Isa Khan's son Musa had already been defeated and integrated into Mughal service, and in 1612 'Uthman Khan, the last major holdout against Mughal authority in the province, was killed and his Afghan troops were absorbed into Mughal service.

Unlike the population of the northern frontier region, however, and despite the pillaging of village communities as had occurred in the campaign against Ananta Manik, the people of eastern Bengal did not mount a prolonged resistance to the imposition of Mughal authority. On the contrary, for much of this region's population, political submission was gradually followed by the adoption of a distinctly Islamic identity. In the Dhaka region, Muslim peasant communities were reported as early as 1599, even as the balance of power in the region was shifting from 'Isa Khan to Raja Man Singh. Such communities were also reported in the Noakhali region in the 1630s, and in the Rangpur region in the 1660s (see pp. 132–34 above). Map 3 indicates that by 1872, when the earliest reliable census data come to hand, Muslims predominated in Bengal's eastern districts in proportions ranging from 60 to 90 percent, in contrast to western districts, where they shaded off from less than 40 percent of the total to virtually zero along the delta's western edge.

Clearly, given its extraordinary incidence of Islamization, the cultural evolution of the east departed radically from that of the rest of the delta— or, for that matter, the rest of India. Yet Mughal policy, which in any case

---

94. "Ba tākht-i nawāḥī rafta, ra'āyā-rā ba khūd īl mīgardānīd wa har ki rujū' namī-numūd mīkushtand wa asīr mīsākhtand." Ibid., text, fol. 40b; trans., 1: 97.
95. Ibid., text, fol. 41a; trans., 1: 98.
96. Ibid., text, fol. 53a, trans., 1: 131–32.

was not directed at converting the "natives," does not appear to have been applied any differently in the east than in the west. Nor is there any evidence that Sufis were any more pious, preachers any more zealous, or warriors any more courageous in East Bengal than were those in the west. For so different an outcome to have occurred, there must have been other factors or forces operating in the east that were altogether unique to the region. In the next few chapters we shall explore this question in detail.

8 Islam and the Agrarian Order in the East

Niranjan [God] has commanded that agriculture will be your destiny.

> The angel Gabriel to Adam, in Saiyid Sultan,
> *Nabī-Baṃśa* (ca. 1584)

Riverine Changes and Economic Growth

A distinguishing feature of East Bengal during the Mughal period—that is, in "Bhati"—was its far greater agricultural productivity and population growth relative to contemporary West Bengal. Ultimately, this arose from the long-term eastward movement of Bengal's major river systems, which deposited the rich silt that made the cultivation of wet rice possible. Geographers have generally explained the movement of Bengal's rivers in terms of the natural process of riverine sedimentation. In this view, in prehistoric times the entire delta was once under the ocean, and the Ganges met the sea in what is now the region's northwestern corner (modern Murshidabad District), while the Brahmaputra did the same in the extreme north (modern Rangpur District). As sediment and debris accumulated at the rivers' confluence with the ocean, a small delta began to form, through which the present-day Bhagirathi River carried the bulk of the Ganges to the Bay. The continued buildup of sediment from both the Ganges and the Brahmaputra steadily pushed the delta further southward into the Bay.

But the great rivers, flowing over the flat floodplain, could not move fast enough to flush out to sea the sediment they carried, and instead deposited much of it in their own beds. When such sedimentation caused riverbeds to attain levels higher than the surrounding countryside, waters spilled out of their former beds and moved into adjoining channels.[1] In this

1. See R. K. Mukerjee, *The Changing Face of Bengal: A Study of Riverine Economy* (Calcutta: University of Calcutta, 1938), 3–10; S. C. Majumdar, *Rivers of the Bengal Delta* (Calcutta: University of Calcutta, 1942), 65–72; W. H. Arden Wood, "Rivers and Man in the Indus-Ganges Alluvial Plain," *Scottish Geographical Magazine* 40, no. 1 (1924): 9–10; C. Strickland, *Deltaic Formation, with Special Reference to the Hydrographic Processes of the Ganges and the Brahmaputra* (Calcutta:

way the main course of the Ganges, which had formerly flowed down what
is now the Bhagirathi-Hooghly channel in West Bengal, was replaced in
turn by the Bhairab, the Mathabhanga, the Garai-Madhumati, the Arial-
khan, and finally the present-day Padma-Meghna system. "When the dis-
tributaries in the west were active," writes Kanangopal Bagchi, "those in
the east were perhaps in their infancy, and as the rivers to the east were
adolescing, those in the west became senile. The active stage of delta formation thus migrated southeastwards in time and space, leaving the rivers
in the old delta, now represented by Murshidabad, Nadia and Jessore with
the Goalundo Sub-Division of Faridpur, to languish or decay."[2] As the delta's active portion gravitated eastward, the regions in the west, which received diminishing levels of fresh water and silt, gradually become moribund. Cities and habitations along the banks of abandoned channels
declined as diseases associated with stagnant waters took hold of local communities. Thus the delta as a whole experienced a gradual eastward movement of civilization as pioneers in the more ecologically active regions cut
virgin forests, thereby throwing open a widening zone for field agriculture.
From the fifteenth century on, writes the geographer R. K. Mukerjee,
"man has carried on the work of reclamation here, fighting with the jungle,
the tiger, the wild buffalo, the pig, and the crocodile, until at the present
day nearly half of what was formerly an impenetrable forest has been converted into gardens of graceful palm and fields of waving rice."[3]

Although the process described by Mukerjee had actually begun long
before the fifteenth century, it dramatically intensified after the late sixteenth century. As contemporary European maps show, this was when the
great Ganges river system, abandoning its former channels in western and

---

Longmans, Green, 1940), 104; Kanangopal Bagchi, *The Ganges Delta* (Calcutta:
University of Calcutta, 1944), 33. Geographers and geologists have not agreed on
the fundamental cause of Bengal's riverine dynamics. Whereas geographers generally see sedimentation as the driving force behind riverine movement, geologists
have pointed to tectonic activity that has produced a torsion in the crust of East
Bengal. According to this view, torsion caused the uplift of the Barind in northern
Bengal and the subsidence of the Sylhet Basin, which in turn produced a major
fault line passing south by southeast from eastern Rangpur to eastern Barisal, into
which Bengal's major rivers have tended to gravitate. See J. Fergusson, "Delta of
the Ganges," *Journal of the Geological Society of London* 19 (1863): 321–54; F. C.
Hirst, *Report on the Nadia Rivers, 1915* (Calcutta, 1916); and James P. Morgan and
William G. McIntire, "Quaternary Geology of the Bengal Basin, East Pakistan and
India," *Bulletin of the Geological Society of America* 70 (March 1959): 319–42.
2. Bagchi, *Ganges Delta*, 58. See also N. D. Bhattacharya, "Changing Course of the
Padma and Human Settlements," *National Geographic Journal of India* 24, nos. 1
and 2 (March–June 1978): 63–65.
3. Mukerjee, *Changing Face*, 137.

Map 5. Changing courses of Bengal rivers, 1548–1779

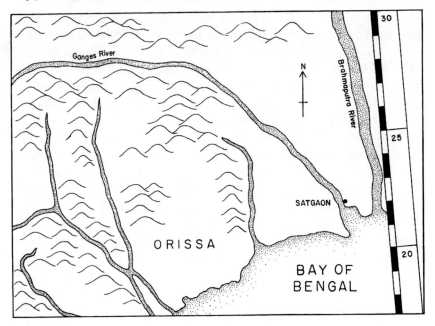

(a) 1548 (Gastaldi)

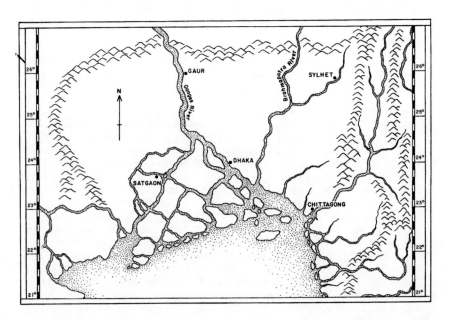

(b) 1615 (de Barros)

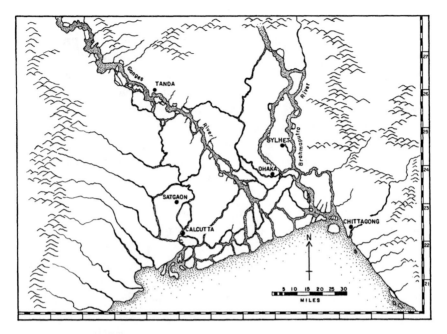

(c) 1660 (van den Broecke)

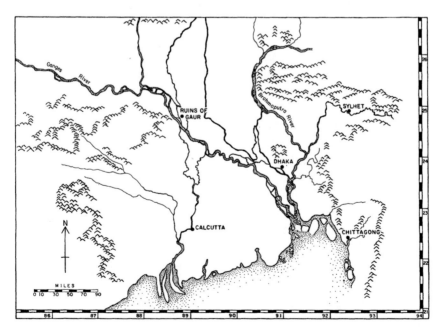

(d) 1779 (Rennell)

southern Bengal, linked up with the Padma, enabling its main course to flow directly into the heart of the east (see maps 5b and c). Already in 1567 the Venetian traveler Cesare Federici observed that ships were unable to sail north of Satgaon on the old Ganges—that is, today's Bhagirathi-Hooghly in West Bengal.[4] About the same time the Ganges silted up and abandoned its channels above Gaur, as a result of which that venerable capital of the sultanate, only recently occupied by Akbar's forces, suffered a devastating epidemic and had to be abandoned. In 1574 Abu'l-fazl remarked that the Ganges River had divided into two branches at the Afghan capital of Tanda: one branch flowing south to Satgaon and the other flowing east toward Sonargaon and Chittagong.[5] In the seventeenth century the former branch continued to decay as progressively more of its water was captured by the channels flowing to the east, to the point where by 1666 this branch had become altogether unnavigable.[6]

To the east, however, these changes had the opposite effect. With the main waters of the Ganges now pouring through the channel of the Padma River, the combined Ganges-Padma system linked eastern Bengal with North India at the very moment of Bengal's political integration with the Mughal Empire. Geographic and political integration was swiftly followed by economic integration, for direct river communication between East Bengal and North India would have dramatically reduced costs for the transport of East Bengali products, especially textiles and foodstuffs, from the frontier to the imperial metropolis. At the same time, the main body of Ganges silt, now carried directly into the east, was deposited over an ever greater area of the eastern delta during annual flooding. This permitted an intensification of cultivation along the larger rivers where rice culture had already been established, and an extension of cultivation into those parts of the interior not yet brought under the plow. As a result, East Bengal attained agricultural and demographic growth at levels no longer possible in the western delta. These changes are reflected above all in the statistics of the Mughal government's share (*khālisa*) of the land revenue demand (*jamaʿ*). Since the revenue demand represents the government's estimate of the land's income-generating capacity, and since Bengal's major income-producing activity was the cultivation of wet rice, a labor-intensive crop, these statistics also suggest changes in the relative population density of different sectors within the delta.

4. Federici, "Extracts," 113. As he wrote, "the River is very shallow, and little water."
5. Abu'l-fazl ʿAllami, *Akbar-nāma*, trans., 3: 153; text, 3: 109.
6. Jean Baptice Tavernier, *Travels in India*, ed. V. Ball (London: Macmillan, 1889; reprint, Lahore: Al-Biruni, 1976), 1: 125.

Table 4. Changes in Revenue Demand in Bengal, 1595–1659

	Revenue Demand (in rupees)		Percentage Change
Quadrant	1595	1659	
Northwest	1,374,859	1,190,064	−13%
Southwest	2,258,138	3,482,127	+54%
Northeast	1,379,529	2,720,115	+97%
Southeast	1,346,730	2,921,314	+117%
Total	6,359,256	10,313,620	+62%

Sources: For 1595: Abu'l-fazl 'Allami, *Ā'īn-i Akbarī*, as given in Shireen Moosvi, *The Economy of the Mughal Empire, c. 1595: A Statistical Study* (Delhi: Oxford University Press, 1987), 26–27. For 1659: *Dastūr al-'amal-i 'Ālamgīrī* (British Library MS., Add. 6599), fols. 120a–121a.

Note: Totals stated for *sarkār*s are given in *dām*s, which must be divided by 40 to give the rupee equivalent. Areas included in the northwest quadrant are the Mughal *sarkār*s of Purnea, Tajpur, Gaur (Lakhnauti), Panjra, and Barbakabad; for the southwest quadrant, *sarkār*s Tanda (Udambar), Sharifabad, Satgaon, Sulaimanabad, and Mandaran; for the northeast quadrant, *sarkār*s Ghoraghat, Bazuha, and Sylhet; for the southeast quadrant, *sarkār*s Mahmudabad, Khilafatabad, Fatehabad, Bakla, Sonargaon, and Chatgaon. As most of the eastern *sarkār*s lay beyond Mughal administration in 1595, imperial revenue officials evidently based their figures for those districts on records, known to them but lost today, of the independent sultans of Bengal. By 1659 all of Bengal had come under Mughal administration with the exception of Chittagong (Chatgaon), then still under Arakanese overlordship and not annexed until 1666. Provincial revenue officers nonetheless obtained current revenue figures for Chittagong and included them in the revenue demand for the entire province.

Table 4 divides the delta into four quadrants and shows changes in revenue demand for each quadrant during the first century of Mughal rule. It can be seen that between 1595 and 1659 the revenue demand for the northeastern portion of the delta increased by 97 percent, while that of the southeastern quadrant, the most ecologically active part of Bengal, increased by 117 percent. On the other hand, the revenue demand for southwestern Bengal, an ecologically older sector, increased by only 54 percent in this period, while that for northwestern Bengal, the most moribund part of the delta, actually declined by 13 percent. These earlier trends in Bengal's changing regional fertility compare with demographic data drawn from the modern period. During the century between 1872 and 1981, as is shown in table 5, population density increased much more in the eastern

Table 5. Increase in Population Density in Bengal, 1872–1981

| Quadrant | Population per sq. mi. | | Percentage Increase |
	1872	*1981*	
Northwest	503	1,544	207%
Southwest	598	1,701	184%
Northeast	406	1,933	376%
Southeast	526	1,941	269%

Sources: H. Beverley, *Report on the Census of Bengal, 1872* (Calcutta: Secretariat Press, 1872), 6–9; *Census of India, 1981* (New Delhi, 1985), pt. II-A [i], "General Population Tables," section 2, 182–85; *The Preliminary Report on Bangladesh Population Census, 1981* (Dacca: Bangladesh Secretariat, 1981), 2–3. The districts included in the northwest quadrant are the 1872 districts of Rangpur, Bogra, Pabna, Dinajpur, Malda, Rajshahi, and Murshidabad. Those included in the southwest quadrant are Burdwan, Bankura, Birbhum, Midnapur, Hooghly and Howrah, Twenty-four Parganas, and Nadia. Those included in the northeast quadrant are Mymensingh, Sylhet, and Dhaka. And those included in the southeast quadrant are Jessore (including Khulna), Tippera (Comilla), Faridpur, Bakarganj, Noakhali, and Chittagong.

half of Bengal, averaging 323 percent, than it did in the western half, where it averaged 196 percent.[7] Thus both seventeenth-century revenue data and nineteenth- and twentieth-century demographic data point to a moving demographic frontier, the product of a long-term process whereby land fertility, rice cultivation, and population density all grew at a faster rate in the east than in the west.

As a result, already by the late sixteenth century, southern and eastern Bengal were producing so much surplus grain that for the first time rice emerged as an important export crop. From two principal seaports, Chitta-

7. In the British period the movement of prosperity and population from northwest to southeast was observed to occur even *within* districts. Thus between 1881 and 1911 the population of northern Faridpur increased by 7 percent while that of southeastern Faridpur increased by 50 percent. "The stagnation of the north," it was noted in the Faridpur settlement report, "is clearly due to the drying up of the rivers and streams which has made the soil less fertile, the transport of produce more difficult and the climate more unhealthy. . . . During the cold weather the rivers become a chain of dirty pools; there are few tanks and no good drinking water. Epidemics of cholera are very frequent and other diseases take toll of the population; malaria is constant everywhere and the people generally have a very low degree of vitality." J. C. Jack, *Final Report on the Survey and Settlement Operations in the Faridpur District, 1904 to 1914* (Calcutta: Bengal Secretariat Book Depot, 1916), 7.

gong in the east and Satgaon in the west, rice was exported throughout the Indian Ocean to points as far west as Goa and as far east as the Moluccas in Southeast Asia.[8] In this respect rice now joined cotton textiles, Bengal's principal export commodity since at least the late fifteenth century, and a major one since at least the tenth. In 1567 Cesare Federici judged Sondwip to be "the fertilest Iland in all the world," and recorded that one could obtain there "a sacke of fine Rice for a thing of nothing."[9] Twenty years later, when 'Isa Khan still held sway over Sonargaon, Ralph Fitch wrote: "Great store of Cotton doth goeth from hence, and much Rice, wherewith they serve all India, Ceilon, Pegu, Malacca, Sumatra, and many other places."[10] The most impressive evidence in this regard comes from François Pyrard. After spending the spring of 1607 in Chittagong, still under independent rulers beyond the Mughals' grasp, the Frenchman wrote:

> There is such a quantity of rice, that, besides supplying the whole country, it is exported to all parts of India, as well to Goa and Malabar, as to Sumatra, the Moluccas, and all the islands of Sunda, to all of which lands Bengal is a very nursing mother, who supplies them and their entire subsistence and food. Thus, one sees arrive there [i.e., Chittagong] every day an infinite number of vessels from all parts of India for these provisions.[11]

Under the Mughals the export of surplus rice continued unabated, and indeed grew.[12] In 1629 Fray Manrique noted that every year over a hundred vessels laden with rice and other foodstuffs left Bengali ports for overseas export.[13] And in common with earlier observers, Manrique was impressed by the low prices of local foodstuffs.[14] Although the eastward export of rice declined from about 1670 on,[15] in lower Bengal it remained

8. Subrahmanyam, "Notes," 268.
9. Federici, "Extracts," 137.
10. Ibid., 185.
11. François Pyrard, *The Voyage of François Pyrard of Laval to the East Indies, the Maldives, the Moluccas and Brazil*, ed. and trans. Albert Gray (Hakluyt Society, 1st ser., nos. 76, 77, 80, 1887–90; reprint, New York: Burt Franklin, n.d.), 2: 327.
12. S. Arasaratnam, "The Rice Trade in Eastern India, 1650–1740," *Modern Asian Studies* 22, no. 3 (1988): 531–49.
13. Manrique, *Travels*, 1: 56. In 1665 François Bernier noted that Bengal "produces rice in such abundance that it supplies not only the neighboring but remote states. It is carried up the *Ganges* as far as *Patna*, and exported by sea to *Maslipatam* and many other ports on the coast of *Koromandel*. It is also sent to foreign kingdoms, principally to the island of *Ceylon* and the *Maldives*." Bernier, *Travels in the Mogul Empire, A.D. 1656–68*, trans. Archibald Constable, 2d ed. (New Delhi: S. Chand & Co., 1968), 437.
14. Manrique, *Travels*, 1: 54.
15. Om Prakash, *The Dutch East India Company and the Economy of Bengal, 1630–1720* (Princeton: Princeton University Press, 1985), 224–29.

cheap and abundant throughout the seventeenth century and well into the eighteenth, for in 1763 an English observer wrote that rice, "which makes the greater part of their food, is produced in such plenty in the lower parts of the province, that it is often sold on the spot at the rate of two pounds for a farthing."[16]

If the most productive area of rice production gradually shifted eastward together with the locus of the active delta, the production of cash crops, especially cotton and silk, flourished throughout the delta in the Mughal period. The most important centers of cotton production were located around Dhaka and along a corridor in western Bengal extending from Malda in the north through Cossimbazar to Hooghly and Midnapur in the south.[17] In 1586 Ralph Fitch remarked that in Sonargaon, just fifteen miles east of Dhaka, "there is the best and finest cloth made of Cotton that is in all India."[18] Even in distant Central Asia fine muslin cloth was called *Dāka*,[19] a consequence of Bengal's political integration with North India, and of its access to markets both there and beyond.[20] The Mughal connection also made Bengal a major producer for the imperial court's voracious appetite for luxury goods. This was especially so in the case of raw silk, whose major center of production was located in and around Cossimbazar in modern Murshidabad District.[21]

Bengal's agricultural and manufacturing boom coincided not only with the consolidation of Mughal power in the province but also with the growth in overland and maritime trade that linked Bengal ever more

16. Orme, *Military Transactions*, 2: 4.
17. For the geographical distribution of Bengal's textile indutry, see the maps in K. N. Chaudhuri, *The Trading World of Asia and the English East India Company, 1660–1760* (Cambridge: Cambridge University Press, 1978), 248; and Irfan Habib, *An Atlas of the Mughal Empire* (Delhi: Oxford University Press, 1982), map 11B.
18. Ralph Fitch, "The Voyage of Master Ralph Fitch Merchant of London to Ormus, and so to Goa in the East India, to Cambaia, Ganges, Bengala . . . ," in Samuel Purchas, *Hakluytus Posthumus, or Purchas his Pilgrimes* (1625; Glasgow: James MacLehose and Sons, 1905), 10: 184.
19. Henry Yule and A. C. Burnell, *Hobson-Jobson: A Glossary of Colloquial Anglo-Indian Words and Phrases*, 2d ed., ed. William Crooke (Delhi: Munshiram Manoharlal, 1968), 290.
20. As Manrique noted in 1640, "Most of the cloth is made of cotton and manufactured with a delicacy and propriety not met with elsewhere. The finest and richest muslins are produced in this country, from 50 to 60 yards long and 7 to 8 handbreadths wide, with borders of gold and silver or coloured silks. So fine, indeed, are these muslins that merchants place them in hollow bamboos, about two spans long, and thus secured, carry them throughout Carazane [Khurasan], Persia, Turkey, and many other countries." Manrique, *Travels*, 1: 56–57.
21. In 1655, for example, Indian merchants from Agra bought up six thousand bales at Cossimbazar for export to the imperial court, a quantity twice the size of the Dutch purchase two years later. *Generale missiven*, 2: 795; 3:101.

tightly to the world economy. We have already noted that the thirteenth-century Muslim conquest of the delta had been followed by increased exports of Bengali textiles to Indian Ocean markets.[22] Later, during the twilight years of the sultanate, Portuguese merchants intruded themselves into the Bay of Bengal, establishing trading stations in both Chittagong and Satgaon in the mid 1530s. In the last two decades of the sixteenth century, during the Mughal push into the heart of the delta, the Portuguese established the major port of Hooghly (downstream from Satgaon), built up their community in Chittagong, and established mercantile colonies in and around Dhaka. Although the Portuguese never replaced Asian merchants in Bengal's maritime trade, as is often supposed,[23] the appearance of European merchants in the sixteenth century certainly stimulated demand for Bengali manufactures, which served to accelerate local production of those goods.

In the early seventeenth century, the Dutch and English trading companies gradually replaced the overextended Portuguese as the dominant European merchants in Bengal's port cities. Granted permission by Shah Jahan in 1635 to trade in Bengal, the Dutch East India Company opened a trading station at Hooghly the following year. In 1650 it ordered 50,000 lbs. of raw silk from Bengali suppliers, and four years later this figure grew to 200,000 lbs.[24] By the end of the seventeenth century, the export of raw silk and cotton textiles had grown so rapidly that Bengal emerged as Europe's single most important supplier of goods in all of Asia.[25] But this manufacturing boom did not result from European stimulus alone. Clear down to the 1760s Asian merchants—especially Gujaratis, Armenians, and Punjabis—bought even more Bengali textiles than did Europeans, and exported them throughout South Asia and the Indian Ocean region.[26]

22. See pp. 96–97.
23. See Subrahmanyam, "Notes," 265–89.
24. Sushil Chaudhury, *Trade and Commercial Organization in Bengal, 1650–1720* (Calcutta: Firma K.L.M., 1975), 178–79. In 1652 Dutch East India Company officials wrote that raw silk was so abundant in Bengal that in Cossimbazar alone they could invest ten tons of gold in that commodity, noting that local merchants would accept only silver or gold for such purchases. *Generale missiven*, 2: 622.
25. Prakash, *Dutch East India Company*, 75. Raw silk and cotton textiles, followed by saltpetre and opium, were the principal commodities exported from Bengal by the Dutch. Silk comprised nearly 40 percent of Dutch exports in 1675–76, and 29 percent between 1701 and 1703. In the same periods Bengali textiles comprised 22 and 54 percent respectively. Ibid., 72.
26. Sushil Chaudhury, "The Asian Merchants and Companies in Bengal's Export Trade, circa mid-Eighteenth Century" (paper presented at the International Conference on "Merchants, Companies, and Trade" held at the Maison des Sciences de l'homme, Paris, May 30–June 2, 1990). See also Sushil Chaudhury, *Pre-Modern*

One consequence of this manufacturing boom was that substantial quantities of silver were attracted from outside the province, whether carried by European or Asian merchants. In 1516 Bengali ships carrying local textiles to Burma brought mainly silver back to the delta.[27] And in the 1550s the Portuguese found themselves shipping so much treasure to Bengal that the value of silver currency in Goa actually fluctuated with their sailing seasons to Bengal and Malacca.[28] From the second half of the seventeenth century on, we have precise figures in this matter. The Dutch alone imported an annual average of 1.28 million florins in treasure during the 1660s, and 2.87 million florins in the 1710s.[29] To this must be added the imports of the English East India Company, which in 1651 had also established a trading factory in Hooghly. Between 1709 and 1717 the two companies together shipped cargoes averaging Rs. 4.15 million in value into Bengal annually, 85 percent of which was silver.[30] Advanced to Bengali agents, merchants, or weavers, this treasure was absorbed into the regional economy, adding considerably to the existing stocks of rupee coinage already in circulation.[31] All the while, the overland import of silver by Asian merchants continued until the very end of Mughal rule in the delta.[32]

Economists have long understood the inflationary effects that any increase in money supply can have on regional economies. In the sixteenth

Industries and Maritime Trade in South Asia: Bengal in the First Half of the Eighteenth Century, chs. 7 and 8 (forthcoming).

27. Subrahmanyam, "Notes," 269.

28. Ibid., 279. Between 1626 and 1635 imperial mints in Bengal (including Patna) turned out an estimated annual average of 85.76 metric tons of silver coinage, a figure surpassing the output of the imperial mints of Gujarat, of the Northwest (Lahore, Multan, Thatta, Kabul, Qandahar), and of the central provinces. Shireen Moosvi, *The Economy of the Mughal Empire, c. 1595: A Statistical Study* (Delhi: Oxford University Press, 1987), 357–61. As this was a period after the decline of Portuguese commerce in Bengal, and before the advent of the Dutch or English there, a good part of this silver probably accompanied the influx of Mughal men and arms into the new frontier province.

29. Prakash, *Dutch East India Company,* 249.

30. Om Prakash, "Bullion for Goods: International Trade and the Economy of Early Eighteenth Century Bengal," *Indian Economic and Social History Review* 13, no. 2 (April–June 1976): 162–63.

31. Chaudhury, *Trade and Commercial Organization,* 100–125.

32. "Till of late years," wrote the Englishman Luke Scrafton in 1760, "inconceivable numbers of merchants from all parts of Asia in general, as well as from the rest of Hindostan in particular, sometimes in bodies of many thousands at a time, were used annually to resort to Bengal with little else than ready money or bills to purchase the produce of these provinces." Scrafton, *Reflections on the Government of Indostan* (London, 1760), 20. Cited in Sushil Chaudhury, "The Asian Merchants and Companies in Bengal's Export Trade," 18.

century, for example, the massive import of treasure from Mexico to Spain is thought to have contributed to price inflation in the latter country.[33] In the late sixteenth and seventeenth centuries Mughal India experienced a similar expansion in money supply, but ten or twenty years after Spain, suggesting that much of the silver mined in America and hauled to Europe was then re-exported to India.[34] Moreover, there is evidence that in Mughal India, as in Spain, the influx of silver caused consumer price inflation, at least in the western and northern domains of the empire.[35]

But in Bengal during the seventeenth and eighteenth centuries, the well-documented influx of silver had no such inflationary effect on consumer prices, which remained stable throughout this period.[36] Such an outcome might be explained if, during these centuries, the influx of outside coinage or bullion had been offset by a proportionate outflow of precious metal from Bengal to North India in the form of enhanced revenues. It is true that provincial authorities gradually increased land revenue demand between 1659 and 1722.[37] But the amount of revenue actually sent to Delhi remained about the same throughout this period, while the additional

33. See Earl J. Hamilton, *American Treasure and Price Revolution in Spain, 1501–1652* (Cambridge, Mass.: Harvard University Press, 1934; reprint, New York: Octagon Books, 1965), 283–306.

34. Aziza Hasan, "The Silver Currency Output of the Mughal Empire and Prices in India during the 16th and 17th Centuries," *Indian Economic and Social History Review* 6, no. 1 (March 1969): 85–116.

35. In Gujarat during the first third of the seventeenth century, the price of both indigo and sugar rose with the money supply, as did that of grain in North India between 1595 and 1669. Ibid., 104–10.

36. According to Dutch records, between 1657 and 1713, a period that saw a dramatic influx of silver in Bengal, the prices of basic commodities such as rice, wheat, clarified butter, and sugar did show fluctuations, but no consistent pattern of inflation. For example, in 1658, the earliest date for which there are data, a hundred maunds of rice cost Rs. 49, whereas in 1717 the same amount cost Rs. 48. Prakash, *Dutch East India Company*, 251–53.

37. In 1659, provincial land revenue demand (*jama'*) in round figures stood at Rs. 10.3 million, but from 1700 on this figure was gradually increased each year, reaching Rs. 14.2 million in 1722. Of this, Rs. 10.9 million was intended for the central treasury in Delhi (*khāliṣa*), and Rs. 3.3 million for maintenance of local officials in the province (*jāgīr*). See *Dastūr-i 'amal-i 'Ālamgīrī* (British Library MS., Add. 6599), fols. 120a–121a; *Fifth Report from the Select Committee of the House of Commons on the Affairs of the East India Company, dated 28 July, 1812*, ed. Walter K. Firminger (Calcutta: R. Cambray & Co., 1917), 2: 189–91. The annual enhancements made between 1700 and 1721 were the work of the provincial governor Murshid Quli Khan and are found in Appendix No. 6 to John Shore's "Minute on the Rights and Privileges of Zamindars" (West Bengal Government Archives, Calcutta, Board of Revenue Proceedings for April 2, 1788, vol. 127), 539–40. Cited in Philip B. Calkins, "Revenue Administration and the Formation of a Regionally Oriented Ruling Group in Bengal, 1700–1740" (Ph.D. diss., University of Chicago, 1972), 146.

taxes imposed on the peasantry and collected seem to have stayed in Bengal.[38] Some silver doubtless left the delta when high-ranking officers or governors like Shaista Khan (1664–78), Khan Jahan Bahadur Khan (1688–89), or 'Azim al-Din (1697–1712) embezzled large sums of provincial revenue, some of which they took with them when they were transferred out of the province.[39] But such practices by self-serving officers were probably commonplace throughout the Mughal period, and they cannot alone explain the absence of price inflation from the mid seventeenth century on.

One can, on the other hand, relate Bengal's known price stability between ca. 1650 and 1725 to the economic boom then taking place in the province. Put simply, consumer prices remained stable because the production of agricultural and manufactured goods, together with the population base, grew at levels high enough to absorb the expanding money supply caused by the influx of outside silver. Moreover, since additional increments to the money supply did not flow out of the province, newly minted silver percolated freely throughout Bengali society, penetrating ever lower levels and facilitating the kinds of land transfers and cash advances that necessarily accompanied an expanding agrarian frontier. The importance of ready cash in this process is suggested in Mukundaram's *Caṇḍī-Maṅgala*, composed around 1590. In it, the goddess Chandi gives the poem's hero, Kalaketu, a valuable ring and tells him to exchange it for cash. With the money thus obtained—seventy million *tankas*—Kalaketu is to clear the forest and establish a city and temple in honor of the goddess. Once the land is ready for agricultural operations, Kalaketu promises to advance Kayastha landlords as much cash as they need for their own thousands of laborers (*prajā*, lit., "subjects") to come and settle on the newly

38. The central government evidently failed to receive even the Rs. 10.3 million demanded in the 1659 land revenue revision. Around 1687 the collected land revenue (*ḥāṣil*) sent to Delhi amounted to Rs. 8.6 million. Between 1712 and 1727, Delhi received from Bengal an annual average of Rs. 8.9 million in land revenue, which between 1728 and 1739 rose somewhat to Rs. 9.4 million. These figures were calculated by Philip Calkins on the basis of raw data in "Comparative Tables of the Revenue of Bengal," British Library, London, Add. MS. 6586, ff. 46b–48a. See Calkins, "Revenue Administration," 162. The reason for the gap between the *khā-liṣa* demand and the figure actually sent to Delhi was hinted at by M. de Thevenot, a Frenchman who traveled through India in 1666 and meticulously recorded what he heard. "My *Indian*," he wrote in that year, "reckons the yearly Revenue of the Mogul [in Bengal] to amount to Ten millions; but I learnt from other hands, that it hardly makes Nine, though it be far richer than other Provinces that yield him more: The reason given for that, is, that it lies in the extremity of his Empire, and is Inhabited by a capricious sort of People, who must be gently used, because of the Neighbourhood of Kings that are enemies." Surendranath Sen, ed., *Indian Travels of Thevenot and Careri* (New Delhi: National Archives of India, 1949), 97.
39. See Jadunath Sarkar, ed., *History of Bengal*, 413.

claimed lands.[40] Such contemporary literary evidence points, not only to the high level of monetization in the late sixteenth century, but to the role that cash played in transforming virgin jungle into settled agrarian communities.

In sum, a number of factors—natural, political, and economic—combined to create the seventeenth century's booming rice frontier in the east: the eastward movement of Bengal's rivers and hence of the active delta, the region's political and commercial integration with Mughal India, and the growth in the money supply with the influx of outside silver in payment for locally manufactured textiles. We shall see that the high volume of cash circulating in Bengal during the Mughal period not only contributed to the movement of men and resources to and within the frontier. It also depersonalized economic transactions by permitting land to change hands across communal or cultural lines. Finally, Bengal's rice boom coincided both in time and place—the eastern delta between the late sixteenth and early eighteenth centuries—with the emergence of a Muslim peasantry. Such a correlation between economic change and religious change invites inquiry into their possible connections.

Charismatic Pioneers on the Agrarian Frontier

The advance of wet rice agriculture into formerly forested regions is one of the oldest themes of Bengali history. Wang Ta-yüan, the Chinese merchant who visited the delta in 1349–50, observed that the Bengalis "owe all their tranquility and prosperity to themselves, for its source lies in their devotion to agriculture, whereby a land originally covered with jungle has been reclaimed by their unremitting toil in tilling and planting. . . . The riches and integrity of its people surpass, perhaps, those of Ch'iu-chiang (Palembang) and equal those of Chao-wa (Java)."[41]

Although peoples of the delta had been transforming forested lands to rice fields long before the coming of Muslims, what was new from at least the sixteenth century on was the association of Muslim holy men (*pīr*), or charismatic persons popularly identified as such, with forest clearing and land reclamation. In popular memory, some of these men swelled into vivid mythico-historical figures, saints whose lives served as metaphors for the expansion of both religion and agriculture. They have endured precisely because, in the collective folk memory, their careers captured and

40. Mukundaram, *Kavikaṅkaṇa Caṇḍī*, 290, 295–96, 354–55. See also Bhattacharya, "La Déesse," 33.
41. Wang Ta-yüan, *Tao i chih lio* ("Description of the Barbarians of the Isles"), in W. W. Rockhill, "Notes on the Relations," *T'oung Pao* 16, pt. 2, section 4 (1915): 436.

telescoped a complex historical socioreligious process whereby a land originally forested and non-Muslim became arable and predominantly Muslim.
Let us begin by examining twentieth-century narratives and work our way
back through the nineteenth, eighteenth, and seventeenth centuries to the
sixteenth century, the earliest period to which traditions of pioneering
holy men in Bengal can confidently be dated.

According to oral narratives collected in the 1980s, a certain Mehr 'Ali
is said to have come to the jungles of Jessore from the Deccan in the early
Mughal period, accompanied by his sister and another companion. Having
arrived in a settlement now named after him, Mehrpur, this holy man
assisted the local population in clearing the jungle and in making possible
the cultivation of wet rice.[42] In Murarbond, in the Habiganj region of Sylhet District, Shah Saiyid Nasir al-Din is said to have come from the Middle
East in the Mughal period and instructed the local population in clearing
the land and planting rice; before him, the land had been jungle. He also
taught them the rudiments of Islam. In Pail, several miles from Habiganj,
stands the shrine of another pioneer holy man who is said to have come
from the Middle East and taught the local people the techniques of rice
farming and the fundamentals of Islam. Later, his sons settled in what are
now the Comilla and Sylhet districts, where they did the same.[43] In Pingla,
Midnapur District, a Muslim holy man named Khondkar Shah 'Ala is said
to have founded a settlement on land donated by Sultan Taj Khan Karrani
(r. 1564–65), who instructed the *pīr* to let a horse roam from dawn to noon,
with the understanding that the enclosed area would be his spiritual and
terrestrial domain for life. Arriving and settling in the area with his family,
Khondkar Shah cleared the area of its forests with the help of the local
people, whom he converted to Islam. Both during and after his lifetime the
community honored him as their *pīr*.[44]

The gazetteer for Khulna District, compiled in 1908, reports that in the
early twentieth century parts of the Sundarban forests were still identified
with the charismatic authority of Muslim holy men.[45] In 1898 James Wise

42. Interview with Muhammad Sharif Hussain, secretary, Jessore Public Library,
Kharki Post, District Jessore, May 19, 1982.
43. Interview with Muhammad Badrur Huda, additional subdivisional officer, Revenue, Noakhali District Collectorate, June 17, 1982.
44. Mohendra Nath Karan, *Hijli Masnad-i Ala*, 621, cited in Sultan Jahan Ahmad,
"Muslim Society in Midnapur—a Social Study of a Bengal District (1800 A.D.–
1919 A.D.)" (Ph.D. diss., Jadavpur University, Calcutta, 1982), 58. The story contains elements of a classical Indian rite of Hindu kingship, the "horse sacrifice"
(*asvamedha*), according to which a raja asserted his claims to territorial sovereignty
over lands traversed by a horse set loose to roam at will.
45. L. S. S. O'Malley, *Eastern Bengal District Gazetteers, Khulna* (Calcutta: Bengal
Secretariat Book Depot, 1908), 193–94. A class of professional woodcutters "proceed in boats to certain localities in the forests called *gais*, each of which is presided

wrote of Zindah Ghazi, a legendary protector of woodcutters and boatmen all over the eastern delta, who was "believed to reside deep in the jungle, to ride about on tigers, and to keep them so subservient to his will that they dare not touch a human being without his express commands."[46] In 1833 another British officer, Francis Buchanan, noted that *pīrs* and tigers of Dinajpur District usually inhabited the same tracts of the woods:

> As these animals seldom attack man in this district, the Pir is generally allowed by persons of both religions to have restrained the natural ferocity of the beast, or, as it is more usually said, has given the tiger no order to kill man. The tiger and Faquirs [holy men] are therefore on a very good footing, and the latter . . . assures the people that he [the tiger] is perfectly harmless toward all such as respect the saint, and make him offerings.[47]

The earliest European notice of the symbiotic relationship between the delta's tigers and its Muslim holy men, or their tombs, dates to 1670.[48]

Based on traditions collected in 1857, Wise also wrote of Mubarra Ghazi, a legendary *pīr* identified with clearing the Sundarban forests of Twenty-four Parganas. This saint, he wrote, "is said to have been a faqir, who reclaimed the jungle tracts along the left bank of the river Hooghly, and each villager has an altar dedicated to him. No one will enter the forest, and no crew will sail through the district, without first of all making offerings to one of the shrines. The faqirs residing in these pestilential forests, claiming to be lineally descended from the Ghazi, indicate with pieces of wood, called *Sang*, the exact limits within which the forest is to be cut."[49] By appealing to the saint's authority for delimiting the areas in the forest to be cut, men claiming descent from Mubarra Ghazi continued to acknowledge the saint's religious sovereignty in this part of the delta.

Another nineteenth-century narrative concerns the career of Khan Jahan (d. 1459), the patron saint of Bagerhat in Khulna, near the edge of the

---

over by a *faqīr*, who is supposed to possess the occult power of charming away tigers and who has undoubtedly some knowledge of woodcraft. Here the woodcutters work six days in each week, for one day of the week (but no particular day) is set apart for the worship of the sylvan deity presiding over that particular forest."
46. Wise, "Muhammadans of Eastern Bengal," 40.
47. Francis Buchanan, *A Geographical, Statistical, and Historical Description of the Districts, or Zila, of Dinajpur* (Calcutta: Baptist Mission Press, 1833), 93.
48. The Englishman John Marshall, traveling from Orissa to Hooghly, recorded the following on February 14, 1670: "Tis reported That every Thursday at night a Tyger comes out and Salams to a Fuckeers [*faqīr's*] Tomb there [in Ramchandpur, near Balasore], and when I was there on thursday at night, it was both heard and seene." Shafaat Ahmad Khan, ed., *John Marshall in India: Notes and Observations in Bengal, 1668–1672* (London: Oxford University Press, 1927), 62.
49. Wise, "Muhammadans of Eastern Bengal," 40.

Sundarban forests. The inscription on his tomb identifies this man as "Ulugh Khan-i 'Azam Khan Jahan," suggesting he was an ethnic Turk ("Ulugh") and a high-ranking officer ("Khan-i 'Azam") in the Bengal sultanate.[50] His remembered accomplishments include clearing the local jungle preparatory to rice cultivation, converting the local population to Islam, and constructing many roads and mosques in the area.[51] According to local traditions collected in 1870, he had come to the region

> to reclaim and cultivate the lands in the Sundarbans, which were at that time waste and covered with forest. He obtained from the emperor, or from the king of Gaur, a jaghir [revenue assignment] of these lands, and in accordance with it established himself on them. The tradition of his cutcherry site [court] in both places corresponds with this view of his position, and the fact of his undertaking such large works—works which involve the necessity of supporting quite an army of laborers— also points to his position as receiver of the rents, or chief of the cultivation of the soil. . . . After he had lived a long time as a great zamindar, he withdrew himself from worldly affairs and dwelt as a faqir.[52]

Khan Jahan was clearly an effective leader, since superior organizational skills and abundant manpower were necessary for transforming the region's formerly thick jungle into rice fields: the land had to be embanked along streams in order to keep the salt water out, the forest had to be cleared, tanks had to be dug for water supply and storage, and huts had to be built for the workers. When these tasks were accomplished, rice had to be planted immediately, lest a reed jungle soon return. These were all arduous operations, made more difficult by the ever-present dangers of tigers and fevers.[53] Khan Jahan also turned his men to stupendous works of architecture. Surveys have credited him with having built over fifty monuments around Bagerhat, while oral traditions claim for him 360 mosques and as many large tanks.[54] Some 126 tanks in Bara Bazar, ten miles north of Jessore town, are also attributed to him, as is the construction of numerous roads in the Bagerhat region.[55] The unparalleled masterpiece of the Bager-

50. Shamsud-Din Ahmed, ed. and trans., *Inscriptions*, 4: 66.
51. Syed Murtaza Ali, *Saints of East Pakistan* (Dacca: Oxford University Press, 1971), 41.
52. Westland, *Report*, 20–21.
53. O'Malley, *Khulna District Gazetteer*, 194.
54. Westland, *Report*, 15; Johana E. van Lohuizen de Leeuw, "The Early Muslim Monuments at Bagerhat," in *The Islamic Heritage of Bengal*, ed. George Michell (Paris: UNESCO, 1984), 169.
55. Some of these roads were said to have been so well engineered that they never required repair. The best of these, a road running along the Bhairab River at Bagerhat, was made of bricks about five or six inches square and less than two inches thick, laid on edge to form a road about ten feet across, raised on a slightly elevated embankment. Westland, *Report*, 11–12, 19.

hat complex is the Saithgumbad mosque, which, with its sixty-seven domes and measurements of 157 by 106 feet, is even today the largest mosque in Bangladesh.[56] In short, Khan Jahan is remembered, not just as a forest pioneer, but as a civilization builder in the widest sense.

From eighteenth-century British revenue accounts, we learn of Pir 'Umar Shah, the patron saint of Ambarabad in Noakhali District. This man, after whom the region was named, is said to have come to the jungles of Noakhali from Iran in the early 1700s and to have "lived there in his boat working miracles and making multitudes of converts by whom the wastes were gradually reclaimed."[57] The area cleared by Pir 'Umar Shah and his local followers covered about 175 square miles of land, which Mughal authorities in 1734 declared a separate *pargana*, their basic territorial unit of administration. Some thirty years later, control over revenue collection in Bengal passed to the British, who described the area as virgin forest recently cleared and brought into cultivation for the first time by a number of small landholders called *jangal-burī ta'alluqdārs*, or "jungle-cutting landholders." These landholders claimed that they had originally been independent of any governmental authority, and only later had "requested" Mughal authorities to appoint collectors, or *zamīndārs*, to manage the collection of their revenue due to the state. The first two collectors were the sons of Pir 'Umar Shah, the man who had converted the local people to Islam and organized them for the purpose of clearing the jungle. The *ta'alluqdārs* allowed both sons a share of the revenue of several of their villages, and in 1734 one of them, Aman Allah, built a mosque in the town of Bazra, five miles north of Begamgunj.[58] Mughal authority and Islamic institutions thus reached the Noakhali interior at roughly the same time.

Pir 'Umar Shah must have established contact with the people of Noakhali before 1734, for that was when Mughal authorities organized the region he settled into a *pargana*, by definition a district capable of producing revenue. Although the men who cleared the forests claimed to have "requested" government-appointed revenue collectors, it is more likely that by 1734 they were forced to come to terms with Mughal power in

56. The mosque's tapering walls, not found in any other monument in Bengal, are reminiscent of the Tughluq style of architecture and point to North India as Khan Jahan's likely place of origin. Van Lohuizen de Leeuw, "Early Muslim Monuments," 177.
57. Webster, *Eastern Bengal and Assam District Gazetteers: Noakhali*, 100–101.
58. The information on Pir 'Umar and his sons is found in British revenue records of the late eighteenth century, cited in W. H. Thompson, *Final Report on the Survey and Settlement Operations in the District of Noakhali, 1914–1919* (Calcutta: Bengal Secretariat Book Depot, 1919), 24, 60–61.

that part of Noakhali, and that the provincial government, recognizing the sons of Pir 'Umar Shah as persons of local influence on their southeastern frontier, found it expedient to rely on them for purposes of revenue collection. Thus, as the state incorporated these forest-dwelling peoples within its political orbit, the charismatic authority of the *pīr* became routinized into the bureaucratic authority of the *pīr's* two sons, now transformed into government collectors.

Legends of pioneering *pīrs* can be found in Bengali literature of the seventeenth century. The epic poem *Rāy-Maṅgala*, composed by Krishnaram Das in 1686, concerns a conflict between a tiger god named Daksin Ray and a Muslim named Badi' Ghazi Khan. As the former name means "King of the South," or Lower Bengal, the tiger god was evidently understood as a sovereign deity of the Sundarban forest generally, whereas Badi' Ghazi Khan likely represents a personified memory of the penetration of these same forests by Muslim pioneers. Although the encounter between these two was initially hostile, the conflict was ultimately resolved in compromise: the tiger god would continue to exercise authority over the whole of Lower Bengal, yet people would show respect to Badi' Ghazi Khan by worshiping his burial spot, marked by a symbol of the tiger god's head.[59] In this way Badi' Ghazi Khan, probably the legendary residue of some sanctified pioneer like Khan Jahan or Pir 'Umar Shah, was remembered as having established the cult of Islam in the Sundarban forests.

It was also in the seventeenth century that traditions concerning Bengal's most famous Muslim saint, Shah Jalal Mujarrad (d. 1346) of Sylhet, became transformed in ways approximating present-day oral accounts. We have seen in Chapter 3 that the earliest written record of Shah Jalal's life, composed in the mid 1500s, identified the saint as a Turk sent to India by a Central Asian *pīr* for the purpose of waging war against the infidel. Later hagiographical traditions, however, substantially reinterpreted his career. The *Suhail-i Yaman*, a biography compiled in the mid nineteenth century, but based on manuscripts dating to the seventeenth century,[60] identifies the saint not as a Turk from Turkestan sent to India by a Central Asian Sufi but as an Arab from Yemen sent to India by a Sufi master in Mecca.[61] Giving him a clump of soil, the master instructed Shah Jalal to wander

59. Asutosh Bhattacharyya, "The Tiger-Cult and Its Literature in Lower Bengal," *Man in India* 27, no. 1 (March 1947): 49–50.
60. The work is based on two manuscripts now lost: the *Rauẓat al-Ṣāliḥīn*, said to have been composed in the reign of Aurangzeb (1658–1707), and an account by Mu'in al-Din, a servant of Shah Jalal's shrine, written during the governorship of Murshid Quli Khan (1713–27).
61. The relocation of Shah Jalal's original home from Central Asia to Arabia seems to reflect the efforts of later Muslim reformers to Arabize the identity of the Ben-

through the world until he found a place whose soil exactly corresponded to it. Only after he had reached Bengal and assisted in the defeat of the raja of Sylhet did he discover that the soil there exactly matched his clump. He therefore selected the mound of earth he had tested as the site of his *khānaqāh,* or Sufi hospice.[62] An almost identical version of this story is found in oral traditions recounted in the 1970s by villagers of Pabna District, nearly two hundred miles west of Sylhet in the central delta. When asked about the Islamization of Bengal, they responded with the story of Shah Jalal and his clump of soil, maintaining that one of the reasons Islam had flourished in the delta was that the soil had been right for Shah Jalal's message.[63] Thus, if sixteenth-century biographers depicted Shah Jalal as a holy warrior, and used his career as a vehicle for explaining the political transition from Hindu Bengal to Muslim Bengal, traditions dating from the seventeenth century saw Shah Jalal through the prism of agrarian piety, and viewed the saint as representing Bengal's transition not only from pre-Islam to Islam, but from a pre-agrarian to an agrarian economy.

The sixteenth century is the earliest firm horizon for the appearance of pioneering shaikhs in either Persian or Bengali sources. Composed in the Burdwan region around 1590, at the dawn of Mughal rule in Bengal, Mukundaram's *Caṇḍī-Maṅgala* celebrates the goddess Chandi and her human agent, the hunter Kalaketu.[64] As noted above, the goddess entrusted Kalaketu with temporal sovereignty over her forest kingdom on the condition that he, as king, renounce the violent career of hunting and bring peace on earth by promoting her cult. To this end Kalaketu was enjoined to oversee the clearing of the jungle and to establish there an ideal city whose population would cultivate the land and worship the king's divine benefac-

---

gali Muslim population generally, and especially the delta's Muslim saints and heroes. See Rafiuddin Ahmed, *Bengal Muslims,* 106–13.

62. Maulvi Muhammad Nasir al-Din Haidar, *Suhail-i Yaman,* or *Tārīkh-i Jalālī* (Persian MS., comp. 1277 A.H. [1860–61 A.D.], Muslim Sahitya Samsad, Sylhet), 4–27. An English summary of this is found in J. Wise, "Note on Shah Jalal, the Patron Saint of Silhat," *Journal of the Asiatic Society of Bengal* 42, no. 3 (1873), 278–80.

63. John P. Thorp, "Masters of Earth: Conceptions of 'Power' among Muslims of Rural Bangaldesh" (Ph.D. diss., University of Chicago, 1978), 63–64. The difference between the oral tradition and the account of the *Suhail-i Yaman* is that the villagers of Pabna identified Shah Jalal's teacher as the Prophet Muhammad, and not as a Sufi master. The villagers also omitted any reference to Shah Jalal having defeated a Hindu raja in combat.

64. The poem and the Chandi cult have been analyzed by Bhattacharya, "La Déesse," 17–53. For the text, see Mukundaram, *Kavikaṅkaṇa Caṇḍī,* 271–361. See also Somnath Mukhopadhyay, *Candi in Art and Iconography* (Delhi: Agam Kala Prakashan, 1984).

tor, Chandi. Just as the goddess extended her protection to the king, so also Kalaketu extended his protection to the peasants, to whose chiefs he gave golden earrings, symbolizing his intermediary role between them and the goddess. To assist the beginnings of agriculture, Kalaketu promised not to collect any revenue for six years. Moreover, he gave each cultivator a document (*pāṭṭā*) recognizing his tenure, and specified that payment of taxes, when collected, would be based on the number of plows. Attracted by such favorable terms and promises, peasants and other rural castes representing the full complement of Bengali society as Mukundaram saw it, emerged in the new forest kingdom and took an oath of loyalty to the king by accepting a piece of betel from his mouth.

Mukundaram's poem can thus be read as a grand epic dramatizing the process of civilization-building in the Bengal delta, and specifically, the push of agrarian civilization into formerly forested lands. It is true that the model of royal authority that informed Mukundaram's work is unambiguously Hindu. The king, Kalaketu, was both a devotee of the forest goddess Chandi and a Hindu raja in the medieval (i.e., post-eighth-century) sense, while the peasant cultivators in the poem showed their allegiance to the king by accepting betel nut from his mouth, an act drawing directly on the common Hindu ritual expressing devotion to a deity, the *pūjā* ceremony. Yet it was Muslims who were the principal pioneers responsible for clearing the forest, making it possible for both the city and its rice fields to flourish. "The Great Hero [Kalaketu] is clearing the forest," wrote the poet,

> Hearing the news, outsiders came from various lands.
> The Hero then bought and distributed among them
> > Heavy knives [*kāṭh-dā*], axes [*kuṭhār*], battle-axes [*ṭāngī*], and
> > > pikes [*bān*].
> From the north came the Das (people),
> > One hundred of them advanced.
> They were struck with wonder on seeing the Hero,
> > Who distributed betel nut to each of them.
> From the south came the harvesters
> > Five hundred of them under one organizer.
> From the west came Zafar Mian,
> > Together with twenty-two thousand men.
> Sulaimani beads in their hands,
> > They chanted the names of their *pīr* and the Prophet [*pegambar*].
> Having cleared the forest
> > They established markets.
> Hundreds and hundreds of foreigners
> > Ate and entered the forest.

> Hearing the sound of the ax,
>> Tigers became apprehensive and ran away, roaring.[65]

Muslim pioneers are here unambiguously associated with important processes taking place in the poet's time—the clearing of forests and the establishment of local markets. Moreover, the Muslims involved in forest-
clearing operations are said to have come from the west, suggesting origins
in Upper India or beyond, in contrast to the aboriginals ("the Das people")
who came from the north and the harvesters who came from the south—
that is, from within the delta. Far surpassing the other pioneers in point
of numbers, the twenty-two thousand Muslims were led by one "Zafar
Mian," evidently the chieftain or the organizer of the Muslim work force.
It is also significant that members of that force of laborers chanted the
name of a *pīr*, quite possibly that of Zafar Mian himself.[66] In sum, while
the poem cannot be read as an eyewitness historical narrative, we know
that its author drew the themes of his poem from the culture of his own
day. Even if there had been no historical "Zafar Mian," the poet was clearly
familiar with the theme of thousands of Muslims attacking the forest under the leadership of charismatic *pīrs*.

As a final literary illustration of Islamization and agrarian expansion,
we may examine the legendary career of Shaikh Jalal al-Din Tabrizi, the
patron saint of Pandua in the northwestern delta. In Chapter 3, we saw
that early Persian hagiographies identify this saint as a holy warrior and
a destroyer of temples. But a quite different view of Shaikh Tabrizi is found
in an extraordinary Sanskrit text, *Sekaśubhodayā*. Although the events
described in this work are set in the period immediately prior to the Turkish conquest, and although its author purports to have been the minister
of Lakshmana Sena, the Hindu king defeated by the Turks in 1204, the
composition of the text as we have it dates from the sixteenth century.[67]
This means that the composition of the *Sekaśubhodayā*, like that of Mukundaram's *Caṇḍī-Maṅgala*, was contemporary with the early consolidation of Mughal power in the delta. Like Mukundaram's and Krishnaram
Das's poems, this too belongs to the *maṅgala-kāvya* genre of premodern

65. Mukundaram, *Kavikaṅkaṇa Caṇḍī*, 299–300.
66. It is possible that this Zafar Mian represents a hazy memory of Zafar Khan,
the historical pioneer who in 1298 patronized the construction of a mosque and
madrasa at Tribeni, not distant from Mukundaram's home in Burdwan. See
Shamsud-Din Ahmed, ed. and trans., *Inscriptions*, 18–21.
67. Sukumar Sen, ed. and trans., *Sekasubhodaya of Halayudha Misra* (Calcutta:
Asiatic Society, 1963), ix–xi. A manuscript of this text was discovered in the late
nineteenth century at the Bais Hazari mosque in Pandua. There it served a magical
function, being taken out from time to time and read in order to avert public evil.

Bengali literature, a genre that typically glorified a particular deity and promised the deity's followers bountiful auspiciousness in return for their devotion. The hero of the *Sekaśubhodayā* is not a traditional Bengali deity, however, but Shaikh Jalal al-Din Tabrizi himself.[68]

The account makes Shaikh Tabrizi a native not of Tabriz in Iran but of the kingdom of "Aṭṭāva"[69]—perhaps identifiable with ancient Āṭavya, in present-day Mandia District, Madhya Pradesh—and relates that the holy man had been ordered by the "Great Person" (*pradhānpuruṣa*, i.e., God) to go to "the eastern country," where he would meet Raja Lakshmana Sena, known for his hostility to Muslims.[70] The account thus fixes Shaikh Tabrizi's career in Bengal at a time *before* the Turkish conquest.[71] Giving him an amulet, a pot of water, a staff (Ar., *'aṣā*), a pair of shoes with which to walk on fire or water, and the necklaces of two celestial nymphs, the "Great Person" charged Shaikh Tabrizi with the task of building a "house of God" (*devasadana*), or mosque, in Lakshmana Sena's kingdom.[72] After traveling to "the eastern country" the shaikh, wearing his magical shoes, reached the banks of the Ganges in the Sena capital city.

> Bowing low his head to the (river) goddess after muttering "Ganga, Ganga," the king saw him in the west, (walking) over water. He, wearing black clothes, stalwart, engaged in putting on a turban and looking about, was approaching the king quicker and quicker. . . . The king said: "I have indeed seen a wondrous act: (a man) rising up from the stream and walking on water. His person appears shining with the glow of penance."[73]

The two having met, the shaikh questioned the validity of the king's title "ruler of the earth" and challenged the Hindu monarch to cause a nearby heron to release a fish caught in its bill. When the king declined, the shaikh merely glanced at the bird, which at once dropped the fish. Seeing this, the astonished Lakshmana Sena asked for the shaikh's grace (*prasād*),[74] and from then on remained a steadfast devotee of Shaikh Tabrizi, who assured him, "As long as I am (here) you have nothing to fear."[75] Meanwhile the shaikh proceeded to win over the city's populace by performing a variety

68. Ibid., iii. As the text proclaims, "Whoever hears the narrative of the sheikh or makes (others) hear his auspicious advent, no harm comes to him and his prosperity increases." Ibid., 160.
69. Ibid., 160.
70. Ibid., 179.
71. But the text gives A.H. 604, or A.D. 1207–8, as the date of his arrival, which makes it four years after the Turkish conquest. Ibid., 255.
72. Ibid., 179.
73. Ibid., 135.
74. Ibid., 136–37.
75. Ibid., 194.

of miracles, such as subduing three tigers that had threatened the son of a washerman, reviving a dead man, and rescuing a ship caught in a gale.[76]

It is when Shaikh Tabrizi sets out to build a mosque, to be located in the ancient Hindu political center of Pandua, that the story takes on special interest. Having first cleared the selected mosque site of demons, the shaikh consecrates the area by offering handfuls of holy water in turn to the "Great Person," to Sunrise Mount in the east, to the Himalayas to the north, to his parents, to the people of the world, to any king who will honor him, to anyone in the village who will honor him, and to those who desire money and children.[77] For his part, Lakshmana Sena donates forest land for the site of the mosque and orders masons to contribute their labor toward building it. This done, Shaikh Tabrizi "invited people from the country and had them settled in that land."[78] Thus we see a division of labor between the Muslim holy man and the Hindu monarch: the former performs magical and ritual feats appropriate for establishing the mosque, while the latter discharges the kingly functions of donating forest land and mobilizing a labor force. It is significant that the shaikh is made to play the central role in the land's transition from forest to paddy; it is he, and not the monarch, who invites people to settle the formerly forested land.

The text also tells us how the mosque, once built, was managed. The shaikh informed Lakshmana Sena that the institution should be endowed so that it could make a charitable donation of fifty coins a day to all persons, whether kings or beggars. When asked for money for this purpose, the king replied that he did not have the cash, but would donate villages and lands instead. This done, Shaikh Tabrizi acquired a list of settled villages, ordered them surveyed, and had documents prepared fixing their combined revenue at 22,000 (coins).[79] "Then," continued the text, "the sheikh brought (all men) together and issued documents of settlement." When this was done, he arranged for the daily distribution of the revenues in charity to indebted persons, travelers, the lowborn, and the poor.[80]

We are not concerned here with recovering the "historical" Shaikh Jalal al-Din Tabrizi. We should rather see the *Sekaśubhodayā* as revealing the folk process at work: the shaikh's career is made a metaphor for historical changes experienced by people all over the delta. Above all, the story seeks

76. Ibid., 142–43, 151.
77. Ibid., 217.
78. Ibid., 218, 220.
79. Ibid., 220, 222–24. The estate of Jalal al-Din Tabrizi is still known as "Bais Hazari," or "Twenty-two Thousand," and is still held by a *mutawallī*, or caretaker, for the benefit of *faqīrs* and the poor. 'Abid 'Ali Khan, *Memoirs of Gaur and Pandua*, ed. H. E. Stapleton (Calcutta: Bengal Secretariat, 1931), 99.
80. Sen, *Sekasubhodaya*, 224, 225.

to make sense of the gradual cultural shift, well under way by the sixteenth century, when the text achieved its present form, from a Bengali Hindu world to a Bengali Muslim world. This was accomplished in part by presenting the new in the guise of the familiar. Even as Shaikh Tabrizi established what was initially an alien cult, he did so within a Hindu conceptual framework: his person shone with "the glow of penance," or *tapah-prabhāb*, which in classical Indian thought refers to the power acquired through the practice of ascetic austerities; the "grace" he gave to the king was *prasād*, the food that a Hindu deity gives a devotee; the shaikh's consecration of the mosque followed a ritual program consistent with the consecration of a Hindu temple; and the shaikh's patron deity, "Allah," although not identified with a Hindu deity, was given the generic and hence portable name *pradhānpuruṣa*, "Great Person."

Shorn of the fabulous qualities characteristic of all *maṅgala-kāvya* literature, the *Sekaśubhodayā* suggests something of how the Islamic frontier and the agrarian frontier converged in the premodern period. Instead of presenting the shaikh as a holy warrior—at no point in the narrative does he engage the Hindus of Pandua in armed combat—the text seeks to connect the diffusion of Islam with the diffusion of agrarian society. In this respect, several elements in the story are crucial: (1) the shaikh's charismatic authority and organizational ability, (2) the construction of the mosque, (3) state support of the institution, (4) the shaikh's initiative in settling forested lands transferred to the institution, and (5) the transformation of formerly forested lands into wealth-producing agrarian communities that would continue to support the mosque. In this way, the poem sketches a model of patronage—a mosque linked economically with the hinterland and politically with the state—that was fundamental to the expansion of Muslim agrarian civilization throughout the delta.

In sum, from the sixteenth to the twentieth centuries, Bengalis have kept alive memories of charismatic *pīrs* whose authority rested on three overlapping bases: their connection with the forest, a wild and dangerous domain that they were believed to have subdued; their connection with the supernatural world, a marvelous, powerful realm, with which they were believed to wield continuing influence; and their connection with mosques, which they were believed to have built, thereby institutionalizing the cult of Islam. Whereas the first two bases may or may not have been present in any one *pīr*, the third was present in nearly all cases, with Shaikh Tabrizi's mosque at Pandua having established the paradigmatic model.

Moreover, as happened in the case of the sons of Pir 'Umar Shah of Naokhali, some of these men or their descendants became petty landholders. In cases where religious charisma became transformed into landholding rights, or supplemented such rights, a new class of men emerged—Bengal's "religious gentry." Combining piety with land tenure, this class played a decisive role in establishing Islamic institutions in Bengal's countryside during the Mughal period. Two sorts of data at our disposal reveal the evolution of this class: contemporary Persian records pertaining to land transfers and village surveys of the early twentieth century. The remainder of this chapter will be devoted to examining the latter type of data so far as concerns two districts in the heart of Bengal's active delta: Bakarganj and Dhaka.

The Religious Gentry in Bakarganj and Dhaka, 1650–1760

Known in Mughal times as *sarkār* Bakla, and in British times as Bakarganj District, the lower Bengali coastal region consisting of the present-day Barisal and Patuakhali districts had long been an economic frontier zone. Lying in the heart of the active portion of the delta, Bakarganj is one of Bengal's geologically youngest districts. The entire area is composed of an amalgamation of marshlands formed by the merging of islands brought into existence and built up by alluvial soils washed down the great channels of the combined Brahmaputra-Ganges-Meghna river systems. In the early thirteenth century, this forested region became a refuge area for Hindu chieftains dislodged from power in northwestern Bengal. Here they reestablished themselves along the banks of the great rivers and forest islands, far from the reach of Turkish cavalry. But, as J. C. Jack observed in his Settlement Report for the district, "the great rivers which put a limit upon the pursuit of their persecutors put a limit equally upon the size of their kingdoms, which clustered round the banks of the fresh water rivers and were surrounded by impenetrable forests."[81] At the time of the Mughal conquest, the centers of Hindu civilization were confined to northern and western Bakarganj, while the district's southern portions remained covered by forests and laced with lagoons, which in time consolidated into marsh. The northwest was also the only part of Bakarganj where the Hindu population exceeded Muslims in early British census records, for as Hindu immigrants pushed into this area, those native groups already inhabiting the region—mainly Chandal fishing tribes—were absorbed into Hindu society as peasant cultivators.[82] Today they constitute the Namasudras, the largest Hindu peasant community in eastern Bengal.

81. J. C. Jack, *Final Report on the Survey and Settlement Operations in the Bakarganj District, 1900–1908* (Calcutta: Bengal Secretariat Book Depot, 1915), 45.
82. Ibid., 17; H. Beveridge, *The District of Bakarganj: Its History and Statistics* (London: Trubner, 1876), 229–30, 242. Hindu colonizers continued to settle north-

A second great period of economic and social expansion in the Bakarganj forests and marshes occurred in the late seventeenth and early eighteenth centuries. Now it was Muslim pioneers who assumed the leading
role. The emergence of Dhaka as the provincial Mughal capital in the early
seventeenth century made the Bakarganj region more accessible to entrepreneurs and developers than at any previous time. But rampant piracy
along the coasts and rivers of southeastern Bengal by Arakanese and renegade Portuguese seamen inhibited any sustained attempts by Mughal governors to push into the Bakarganj forests.[83] After 1666, when Mughal naval forces cleared the Meghna estuary of such external threats, the
Bakarganj interior lay ripe for colonization. Land developers acquired
grants of plots of land, *ta'alluq*, from provincial authorities in Dhaka or,
after 1704, in Murshidabad.[84] Abundant and easily obtainable by purchase
from the late seventeenth century on, these grants tended to be regarded
by their possessors, *ta'alluqdārs*, as deeds conferring permanent land
tenure rights on them.[85] Having brought their *ta'alluqs* into agricultural

---

ern Bakarganj in Mughal times. "The Pals, Dasses and the Chandras are the own-
ers," we read in a 1906 survey of a village in Swarupkata Thana. "They came down
to settle here on receiving farming leases from the then zamindars of Nayerkaleri
some 220 years ago [i.e., ca. 1686]." "Mauza Notes," Barisal District Collectorate
Record Room, Swarupkati Thana, vol. 2, R.S. 2984.
83. François Bernier, who was in Bengal in 1665, wrote that renegade Portuguese
under the protection of the Arakanese king "pursued no other trade than that of
rapine and piracy. They scoured the neighboring seas in light galleys, called *galle-
asses*, entered the numerous arms and branches of the lower *Ganges*, ravaged the
islands of *Lower Bengal*, and, often penetrated forty or fifty leagues up this country, surprised and carried away the entire population of villages on market days. . . .
The marauders made slaves of their unhappy captives, and burnt whatever could
not be removed. It is owing to these repeated depredations that we see so many
fine islands at the mouth of the *Ganges*, formerly thickly peopled, now entirely
deserted by human beings, and become the desolate lairs of tigers and other wild
beasts." Bernier, *Travels in the Mogul Empire*, 175.
84. Bengal's revenue administration shifted from Dhaka to Makhsusabad (later
Murshidabad) when the chief provincial revenue officer (*dīwān*), the future Murshid Quli Khan, moved his residence there in 1704. The royal mint was also established there in that year. When Murshid Quli Khan was formally made governor
in 1715–16 (he had been de facto governor since 1713), the provincial seat was
officially transferred to Murshidabad. See Abdul Karim, *Murshid Quli Khan and
His Times* (Dacca: Asiatic Society of Pakistan, 1963), 21–24, 63.
85. "The extensive sale transactions of the 17th and 18th centuries," writes B. R.
Grover, "established a large class of petty *taaluqdars*. A person who did not hold
any *Zamindari* from the state but purchased *Zamindari* rights of a few villages or
a village from the original *Zamindar* was known as a *taaluqdar*. Ordinarily, the
sale or mortgage of the petty *Zamindari* shares would take place without the prior
sanction of the Government[,] but in the case of transactions involving large *Za-*

production, these men passed up the land revenue through a class of non-cultivating intermediaries, or *zamīndārs*. These latter, or their agents, typically resided in the provincial capital, where they had ready access to the chief provincial revenue officer (*dīwān*) or his staff.

The process of forest clearing and land reclamation in Bakarganj produced complex tenure chains extending from the *zamīndār* at the upper end down to the actual cultivator at the lower end, with numerous *ta'alluq-dārs* and sub-*ta'alluqdārs* in between. "These talukdars," wrote Jack, "had usually no intention of undertaking personally the reclamation of their taluks, and pursued in their turn the same system of subletting, but they generally selected as their sub-lesses men who were prepared to take colonies of cultivators to the land." In other words, the agricultural development boom in Bakarganj afforded wide scope for countless intermediaries who were, in effect, capitalist speculators, or classical revenue farmers. Together, they created a complex subinfeudation structure described by Jack as "the most amazing caricature of an ordered system of land tenure in the world."[86] In fact, an expandable tenure chain proved an appropriate form of land tenure for an economic frontier that was itself expanding. As Jack himself observed:

> Reclamation of forest was no easy task. It took three or four years to clear the land for regular cultivation during which cultivators and labourers had to be maintained in a country where communications were difficult, rivers dangerous and markets few. Such work was in any case easier when responsibility was divided and it happened that reclamation was taken up when Dacca teemed with men whose occupations were gone. Such men were eager to get rich and unable by caste scruples to cultivate; but their attraction was drawn to colonisation and to Bakarganj by the example of Raja Raj Ballabh and many lesser men who lived in their neighborhood. The owners of the estates who had neither the energy nor the resources to reclaim their forests unaided turned naturally to such men, often their friends or relatives, for assistance.[87]

This passage hints at the origins of the distinctive land tenure system that emerged in Mughal East Bengal. In order to maintain their claims to social dominance in a region chronically short of resident Brahmans, high-caste Hindus already established in the southern delta encouraged and prob-

mindari shares formal sanction of the Government was generally solicited and always granted by the state." B. R. Grover, "Evolution of the Zamindari and Ta-luqdari System in Bengal (1576–1765 A.D.)," in *Bangladesh Itihas Parishad: Third History Congress, Proceedings* (Dacca: Bangladesh Itihas Parishad, 1973), 110.
86. Jack, *Final Report . . . Bakarganj District*, 58.
87. Ibid., 59.

ably financed the settlement of other high-caste *zamīndārs* in the region.[88] But such Hindus predominated only at the upper reaches of the tenure chain, for, as Jack noted, social taboos prevented them from undertaking cultivation themselves. On the other hand, those same classes—typically Brahman or Baidya traders and moneylenders—had accumulated sufficient capital to advance loans to sublessees; and these, in turn, hired sublessees below them, and so on, until one reached the mass of cultivators at the bottom of the tenure chain. Whether recruited from amongst indigenous peoples or brought in from the outside, these latter worked as ordinary cultivators on lands newly reclaimed from the jungle.

Crucial in this tenure chain were the Muslim religious gentry who typically occupied its middle ranks as *ta'alluqdārs*, situated between the *zamīndārs* and the cultivators. Described in early British sources as *qāzīs*, *pīrs*, or simply as "Shaikhs," these men comprised a good part of that class of "Muhammadan adventurers" who, in addition to high-caste Hindu "capitalists," spearheaded the colonization movement, according to Jack.[89] Men of this class were often credited with the original founding of agricultural settlements in Mughal times. For example, rural surveys made between 1902 and 1913 record that in Barahanuddin Thana of Bakarganj, "This mouza [settlement] has got its name [Kazi Abad] from one Kazi [*qāzī*, "judge"] who settled here first.... The population is chiefly Mussalmans."[90] In Gaurnadi Thana, "the Mahomedans owe their origin directly or indirectly to one Kazi who was one of the original settlers of this village."[91] Or again: "There are a few families of Mohamedan Kazis who are the original settlers of this village. They were once prosperous. The population is 715, mostly Muslim."[92] Similarly, in Narayanganj Thana of Dhaka District, the all-Muslim village of Kutubpur derived its name from a saint named Pir Qutb, who, we are told, settled in this area "when there was no *basti*," or crude homesteads, in the area.[93]

88. A village survey conducted in 1904 recorded that in Barisal Thana "the Chakravartys of Rahamatpur previously resided in the North Rahamatpur, laterly they came and settled in this mouza [village]. The Chakravartys of Rahamatpur are staunch Brahmans and in order to keep their social position high they brought several good kulin [i.e., pure] Brahmans from different parts and made them settle here." "Mauza Notes," Barisal District Collectorate Record Room, Barisal Thana, vol. 2, R.S. 2120.
89. Jack, *Final Report . . . Bakarganj District*, 46.
90. "Mauza Notes," Barisal District Collectorate Record Room, Barahanuddin Thana, R.S. 1846.
91. Ibid., Gaurnadi Thana, vol. 1, R.S. 696.
92. Ibid., vol. 2, R.S. 717.
93. "Mauza Notes," Dhaka District Collectorate Record Room, Narayanganj Thana, vol. 3, No. 4534.

There were two patterns by which such men became established as members of the rural landscape's religious gentry. Most often, they acquired *ta'alluqs* from some higher authority, either a local chieftain or a revenue contractor in the provincial capital, and then went out into the forest or marshlands to organize the clearing and settling of the land. Speculators who agreed to pay the Mughal revenue demand hoped to make a profit by subcontracting the work of reclamation to sublessees. These latter established themselves as de facto landlords over whole regions, which eventually coalesced into settled communities. We see this happening in the following record concerning the establishment of a Muslim settlement named Mithapur in Patuakhali, deep in the Sundarbans forest. In the eighteenth century a certain Shaikh Ghazi

> befriended himself with Janaki Ballav Roy immediately after he [Roy] got the Zamindari of Arangapur from the Nawab [i.e., governor]. Janaki Ballav also got material assistance from this man in the work of reclamation of lands from Sundarbans [i.e., forest]. Shekh Gazi subsequently settled in Mithapur.[94]

Here was the classic pattern of subinfeudation in the forests of eighteenth-century Bakarganj: an absentee Hindu acquired *zamīndārī* rights from the Mughal governor, permitting him to extract as much wealth as he could from a given *ta'alluq* so long as he remitted a stipulated amount to the government as land revenue. The *zamīndār* then contracted with some enterprising middleman, typically a member of the Muslim petty religious establishment, to undertake the arduous tasks of organizing the clearing of the jungles and preparing the land for rice cultivation. In such cases the reclamation process often bridged communal lines. In the instance cited above, it was the Hindu Janaki Ballav Roy who had the contacts with the governor and who settled with the latter's revenue officials on a tax payment. At that point Roy withdrew from the work of reclamation, getting "material assistance" from a Muslim whose name, Shaikh Ghazi, suggests religious charisma and who actually settled in Mithapur to organize forest-clearing operations.

Thus, contrary to J. C. Jack's picture of two distinct classes of developers—Hindu "capitalists" and Muslim "adventurers"—moving separately into the forests of Bakarganj, it appears that the two types moved in tandem with each other, although at different ends of the land tenure chain. Influential urban Hindus supplied the cash, or at least the commitment to pay the revenue to the government; and enterprising Muslims supplied

94. "Mauza Notes," Barisal District Collectorate Record Room, Patuakhali Thana, vol. 2, R.S. 2855.

the organizational ability and charisma to mobilize labor forces on the ground. This pattern of collaboration contributed to the characteristic configuration of land tenure in much of pre-1947 East Bengal, where high-caste Hindus, typically absentee *zamīndārs*, emerged at the upper end of the tenure chain, and Muslim cultivators at the lower end.

In a second pattern of land development, Muslim *pīrs* or *qāzīs* went directly into uncultivated regions, organized the local population for clearing the jungles, and only later, after having established themselves as local men of influence, entered into relations with the Mughal authorities. In such instances the government endeavored to appropriate men of local influence by designating them petty collectors. In southern Dhaka District, the settlement of Panam Dulalpur emerged in the early eighteenth century around a *pīr* named Hazrat Daner Mau. Early in the history of this settlement, the inhabitants had given this *pīr* regular donations of *nazr*, or charitable gifts of money, "out of reverence for the good and popular religious man." Later, this charitable gift crystallized into fixed amounts from each tenant in the village. Some inhabitants—we do not know who—refused payment and took the matter to the authorities in Murshidabad, but the latter declined to consider the case.

> The people of Panam were thus obliged to come to an agreement with the Pir who agreed to receive a fixed amount annually from the inhabitants of the entire mauza. This amount was 118 *siccas* [rupees]. . . . This became the fixed rent of the entire mauza of Panam Dulalpur, and the Pir whose name was Hazrat Daner Mau, became the landowner of the Mouzah and thus obtained the sanction of the Nawab of Murshidabad.[95]

Hazrat Daner Mau's transition from holy man to landholder was thus linked to the intervention of state power. With its hearty appetite for land revenue, the government sought to capture and transform into revenue-paying officials whatever local notables appeared on the horizon. In the above-cited case, the government exploited the refusal by some villagers to pay a charitable fee by establishing a fixed villagewide figure to be owed the *pīr;* it then redefined that fee as land tax, and the *pīr* as the revenue-paying landholder.

Where *pīrs* themselves did not become defined as *zamīndārs*, their sons and descendants often did, as was the case with the sons of Pir 'Umar Shah of Noakhali, discussed above.[96] But the relationship between the religious

95. "Mauza Notes," Dhaka District Collectorate Record Room, Narayanganj Thana, vol. 9, No. 4269.
96. Village records compiled in 1912 refer to a "renowned Moslem saint" named Shah Fateh Allah, described as "one of twelve Derwishes who came from the west and landed at Chittagong to spread the light of Islam" during the reign of Jahan-

gentry and Mughal authorities was not always happy, since a *pīr's* natural ties of authority and patronage generally lay with the masses of peasants beneath him and not with the governors and bureaucrats in distant Dhaka or, after 1704, Murshidabad. For example, in remote Jhalakati Thana in the Bakarganj Sundarbans, an eighteenth-century *pīr* named Saiyid Faqir wielded enormous influence with the cultivators of the all-Muslim village of Saiyidpur, named after the *pīr*. But a difficulty arose, noted a 1906 village survey, because "the people of this part looked upon the Fakir as their guide and did not pay rent to the Nawab." In this situation, one Lala Chet Singh, a captain in the employ of the governor, "succeeded in persuading the Fakir to leave the country." Though we do not know how the officer managed to dislodge the *pīr* from the village, he was evidently successful, since the authorities in Murshidabad rewarded him for his efforts by giving him the right to collect the *pargana's* revenue.[97] This suggests that on the politically fluid Bengal frontier, the peasants' loyalty did not necessarily extend beyond their local holy man. From the government's perspective, while it was always preferable when possible to coopt influential holy men, the Mughals did not hesitate, when necessary, to impose their own revenue machinery on rural settlements.

In the early twentieth century, the Muslim cultivators of eastern Bengal were described as an industrious, unruly, and socially unstratified population, with few loyalties beyond those given their *pīrs*. The population of one settlement in Bakarganj's Swarupkati Thana, we read, consisted entirely of Muslims, who were "rather fierce. They played a conspicuous role in the history of the pargana. . . . They were the first men who rallied around . . . [illegible] . . . when he created the taluk after the transfer of his zamindari."[98] Concerning a settlement in Bakarganj's Jhalakati Thana, we find the following account, recorded in 1906:

> The village is now inhabited by Mohammedans. Formerly there were
> several families of Nama Sudras in the village, but for the oppression of
> the Mahommedans they were compelled to leave the village. Their
> lands and homesteads are now in possession of the Mahommedans. The
> people of the village are all very refractory and riotous. On slight provo-

---

gir. From there he traveled to southern Dhaka District, where he and his son 'Abd Allah, also a *pīr*, established themselves as renowned saints. Later—when and how we are not told—their descendants became the landlords (*chaudhurī*) of a village named "Fatulla" after its founder, and their descendants remained landlords there down to the twentieth century. Ibid., vol. 4, No. 1286.
97. "Mauza Notes," Barisal District Collectorate Record Room, Jhalakati Thana, vol. 3, R.S. 2517.
98. Ibid., Swarupkati Thana, vol. 1, R.S. 177.

cation they can easily take the life of another. Criminal breach of peace is a daily occurrence here. The people are so irreligious that to take revenge from a man they never hesitate to bring false criminal case against a man. . . . The river dacoits [bandits] of Bish Khali river are none others than the inhabitants of this village and of neighboring other villages, too.[99]

Refractory or unruly as they may have appeared to law-and-order-minded British officials, these men—or, more correctly, their ancestors—were in fact the primary agents of the extension of agriculture in much of eastern Bengal. As one officer remarked in 1902 concerning another Bakarganj village, "The population are almost all Mohammedans, who have been trying their best to bring the waste lands into cultivation. In fact, the jungles have now been mainly cleared."[100] Or again: "There are a good many petty tenures in this mauza [settlement], all of which have been created for bringing the lands under cultivation. The population are Muhammadan."[101]

Summary

Bengali literary and folk traditions dating from the sixteenth century are replete with heroes associated with taming the forest, extending the cultivable area, and instituting new religious cults. Typically, these heroes combined holy man piety with the organizational skills necessary for forest clearing and land reclamation; hence they were remembered not only for establishing mosques and shrines but also for mobilizing communities to cut the forests and settle the land. As this happened, people gradually came to venerate these men, who were usually Muslims. In the active delta, then, Islam was introduced as a civilization-building ideology associated both with settling and populating the land and with constructing a transcendent reality consonant with that process.

Enormously important environmental changes lay behind these developments. The main factors contributing to the emergence of new peasant communities in eastern Bengal—colonization, incorporation, and natural population growth—were all related to the shift of the active portion of the delta from the west to the east. First, this shift stimulated colonization of the active delta by migrants coming from the relatively less fertile upper delta or West Bengal, or even from North India and beyond. Second, as this happened, indigenous communities of fishermen and shifting cultivators became incorporated into sedentary communities that focused on the cha-

99. Ibid., Jhalakati Thana, vol. 3, R.S. 2471.
100. Ibid., Barisal Thana, vol. 1, R.S. 972.
101. Ibid., Jhalakati Thana, vol. 3, R.S. 2489.

risma and the organizational abilities of Muslim pioneers. And third, the shift of the delta's active portion to the south and east contributed to natural population growth, since the initiation or intensification of wet rice cultivation in this region dramatically increased local food supplies. Although East Bengal's growing fertility was too gradual to be noticed by contemporary observers, it is nonetheless witnessed in revenue demand statistics for the late sixteenth and mid seventeenth centuries, as well as in popular traditions that celebrated the leadership and labors of forest pioneers. The growth of a Muslim peasant society, such a striking development in the post-sixteenth-century eastern delta, thus appears to have been related to larger ecological and demographic forces.

Finally, the cultural and ecological-demographic changes of the post-sixteenth-century period must be seen in the context of the new political environment that accompanied these changes—namely, the advent of Mughal authority in the delta. By a coincidence of some note, the Ganges River completed its eastward shift into the Padma system at the very time—the late sixteenth century—when Mughal power was becoming consolidated in the region. In a sense, then, Mughal authority rode the back of the eastward-moving ecological movement, symbolized by the establishment of the Mughals' provincial capital in the heart of the active delta. To explore the impact of this new political atmosphere on cultural changes taking place in the region, we may examine contemporary Mughal documents concerning agrarian expansion and religious patronage. Fortunately, extensive Persian documentation of this kind has survived for critical sectors of the delta; it is to these that we turn our attention.

9 Mosque and Shrine in the Rural Landscape

> Once the land is brought under cultivation, the produce of the
> land must be used for the expenses of the mosque as well as
> the needs of himself, his descendants, and his dependents. And
> he must assiduously pray for the survival of the powerful state.
>
>   *Sanad* in Chittagong under the seal of Aurangzeb (1666)

The Mughal State and the Agrarian Order

From the reign of Akbar onward, the Mughals sought to integrate Indians
into their political system at two levels. At the elite level they endeavored
to absorb both Muslim and non-Muslim chieftains into the imperial service, thereby transforming potential state enemies into loyal servants.
They also sought to expand the empire's agrarian base, and hence its
wealth, by transforming forest lands into arable fields and the semi-
nomadic forest-dwelling peoples inhabiting those lands into settled farmers. "From the time of Shah Jahan [1627–58]," records an eighteenth-
century revenue document,

> it was customary that wood-cutters and plough-men used to accompany
> his troops, so that forests may be cleared and land cultivated. Ploughs
> used to be donated by the government. Short-term *pattas* [documents
> stating revenue demand] were given, [and these] fixed government de-
> mand at the rate of 1 anna per bigha during the first year. *Chaudhuris*
> [intermediaries] were appointed to keep the *ri'aya* [peasants] happy
> with their considerate behaviour and to populate the country. They
> were to ensure that the *pattas* were issued in accordance with Imperial
> orders and the pledged word was kept. There was a general order that
> whosoever cleared a forest and brought land under cultivation, such
> land would be his zamindari. . . . Ploughs should also be given on behalf
> of the State. The price of these ploughs should be realised from the za-
> mindars in two to three years. Each *hal mir* (i.e., one who has four
> or five ploughs) should be found out and given a *dastar* [sash or tur-
> ban; i.e., mark of honor] so that he may clear the forests and bring
> land into cultivation. In the manner, the people and the *ri'aya* would
> be attracted by good treatment to come from other regions and *subas*

[provinces] to bring under cultivation wasteland and land under forests.[1]

An undated order by Shah Jahan's successor, Aurangzeb (1658–1707), reveals a similar concern with increasing arable acreage, adding that should any peasant flee the land, the local revenue officers (*'āmil*) "should ascertain the cause and work very hard to induce him to return to his former place."[2] Such an appeal hardly suggests a state bargaining from a position of strength. In fact, it points to the chronic surplus of land over labor that obtained in premodern India generally, and in Bengal until as late as the mid nineteenth century.[3]

If such extracts reflect policy, how was it implemented in Bengal? In the older, more settled parts of the province, meaning the western and northwestern sectors, Mughal officials collected the land tax from a predominantly Hindu peasantry at the usual, full rates, through the existing class of Kayasthas and other *zamīndārs*. In the relatively uncultivated forest and marshlands of the east and south, however, the government promoted the founding of new agrarian colonies focusing on individuals considered to possess local influence. The basis of this influence was most often religious, since the government sought to patronize persons attached to stable, and hence reliable, institutions. At local levels, the most typical building blocks of Mughal authority were mosques or shrines.

The Rural Mosque in Bengali History

As the focus of public prayer, the mosque has always been the principal public institution in Islamic civilization. Whether a grand edifice or a hum-

1. *Ḥaqīqat-i Ṣūba Bihār* (Persian MS.). Soon after 1765, when the English East India Company acquired revenue-collecting rights in Bengal, Company officials launched inquiries into the origin of land tenure rights in Bengal and Bihar. One of several documents that emerged from those inquiries, this manuscript was cataloged under the title *Kaifīyat-i Ṣūba Bihār* in Wilhelm Pertsch, *Handschriften-Verzeichniss der Königlichen Bibliothek zu Berlin* (Berlin: A. Asher, 1888), Persische Handschriften, No. 500, 4: 484. From the old Royal Library in Berlin, it was subsequently shifted to the University of Marburg Library. It is summarized, and extracts from it translated, by S. Nurul Hasan in his "Three Studies of Zamindari System," in *Medieval India — A Miscellany*, vol. 1 (Bombay: Asia Publishing House, 1969), 237–38.
2. Jadunath Sarkar, "The Revenue Regulations of Aurangzeb," *Journal of the Asiatic Society of Bengal*, n.s., 2, no. 6 (June 1906): 234–35. Sarkar's translation.
3. A study of rural Comilla District, in the southeastern delta, found that until the mid nineteenth century, the people in that district were still nomadic in nature and, "land being available, [they] could exercise free choice in selecting and reselecting habitation." S. A. Qadir, *Village Dhanishwar: Three Generations of Man-Land Adjustment in an East Pakistan Village* (Comilla: Pakistan Academy for Rural Development, 1960), 46.

ble thatched hut, the mosque conceptually conflates Islam's macro-
community of the *umma*—the worldwide body of believers—into a
microcommunity of fellow villagers or fellow city-dwellers, affording
them the physical space to articulate their collective response to the word
of God. As such the mosque is the physical embodiment of the social reality of Islam, and hence the paramount institution by which community
identity and solidarity are expressed. This is especially true of the "Friday"
or "congregational" mosque (*jāmi' masjid*), in which Muslims gather once
a week for a sermon read by one of its functionaries. Such mosques—
unlike personal, or private, mosques—were generally intended for the
male Muslim population of settled communities and were constructed as
soon as any local society had achieved a sufficient number of Muslims to
warrant one.

As is seen in table 1 (see p. 67), a total of 188 dated mosques built in
the course of six hundred years of Muslim rule in Bengal have survived
into the present. Of these fully 117, or 62 percent of the total, were built
in the relatively short span of a hundred years, from 1450 to 1550. Most
are located in the western portion of the delta, especially near the old Muslim capitals of Gaur and Pandua; almost a third of the total are in the
present-day Malda and Murshidabad districts. Conversely, eastern districts
like Comilla, Rangpur, Khulna, Jessore, and Bakarganj have only a few
mosques each, and Faridpur and Noakhali have none at all. There is thus
a negative correlation between the location of dated mosques and the distribution of Muslims in the delta: surviving mosques predominate in western Bengal, whereas Muslim society came to predominate in the east. And
whereas the vast majority of dated mosques appeared between 1450 and
1550, the first recorded evidence of substantial rural Muslim communities
appears only from the very end of the sixteenth century. How, then, can
we reconcile the contradiction between the appearance of these mosques,
both in time and in space, and the appearance of a predominantly Muslim population?

The answer is that the mosques recorded in table 1 include only those
bearing inscriptions. Endowed by men in command of considerable resources—rulers or other wealthy patrons—these were typically monumental structures built of durable materials like brick or stone, which
explains why they have survived into the present. On the other hand,
there were many more smaller and humbler mosques that have not physically survived into the present, and that were not endowed with dated
inscription tablets. Built of ordinary bamboo and thatching, and patronized not by the court but by local gentry, hundreds of such mosques
appeared in the seventeenth and eighteenth centuries, especially in east-

ern Bengal.[4] Since the appearance of these institutions correlates positively with that of majority Muslim communities, both in time and place, one may hypothesize that such humble mosques, and not the monumental works of art endowed by the wealthy, played the more decisive role in the Islamization of the countryside (see figs. 22–24).

Why and how were such institutions built? We have seen that in the empire generally, Mughal policy aimed at expanding the agrarian basis upon which the state's wealth rested, and at creating loyal constituencies among local elites and their dependents. Although these aims were manifestly economic and political in nature, a characteristic means of achieving them, especially in frontier regions where new lands were being brought into cultivation, was by promoting the establishment of durable agrarian communities focused on religious institutions. Thus, in eastern Bengal, the state oversaw the establishment of both Hindu and Muslim institutions as new lands were opened up for cultivation. Of these, the Muslim institutions proved by far the more numerous and influential, and from them Islamic values, attitudes, terminology, and rituals gradually diffused over the countryside in the course of the sixteenth, seventeenth, and eighteenth centuries. Contemporary state documents mention, in passing, that at such institutions new Friday assemblies or circles of believers had been established (*iqāmat-i ḥalqa-yi jum'a*).[5]

Such remarks take on special significance when it is recalled that throughout the delta the fundamental unit of social organization is not and never has been the *mauza'*, or "village." Nucleated settlement patterns such as are typical in North India never existed in the delta proper, even though the Mughals, and later the British, continued to use the term *mauza'* as though they did.[6] Rather, homesteads are strung out in lines along the banks of past or existing creeks. Or, more often, they are stippled

4. The same is true of *madrasas*, or schools. Although remnants of a few stone or brick schools of the sultanate period survive today, schools made of humbler materials have perished altogether. For example, in 1609 a traveler passing through Bagha, in modern Rajshahi District, recorded seeing a *madrasa* with grass-thatched roofs and mud-plastered walls. Inside, a host of pupils studied under a certain Hawadha Mian, a teacher of that locale. The government had granted the revenues of the countryside surrounding Bagha for the maintenance of the shaikh and his college. Today the structure no longer stands, however, and it was evidently not endowed with a foundation tablet and dedicatory inscription that would testify to its former existence. See Jadunath Sarkar, "A Description of North Bengal in 1609 A.D.," *Bengal Past and Present* 35 (1928): 144.
5. "Kanun Daimer Nathi," Chittagong District Collectorate Record Room, No. 64: bundle 78, case no. 5027; No. 7: bundle 62, case no. 4005.
6. Peter J. Bertocci, "Elusive Villages: Social Structure and Community Organization in Rural East Pakistan" (Ph.D. diss., Michigan State University, 1970), 11–14.

throughout the rural countryside, dispersed in amorphous clusters. A pair of rural sociologists have described the East Bengali countryside as "one vast, seamless village. People build on high ground to avoid floods, and since high ground usually lies along slight ridges or hillocks, their houses are dispersed, with no clear demarcation between one village and the next."[7] The geographers O. H. K. Spate and A. T. A. Learnmonth remark: "Over large areas there is no real 'pattern' at all, so homogeneous is the environment."[8]

As the Bengali physical landscape was for the most part flat and homogeneous in all directions, so also the social order lacked natural nodes of authority. To be sure, kin groups (*baṃśa, goṣṭhī*) sharing common patrilineal descent are found in Bengali society. But these do not have the same cohesiveness or social significance as the endogamous *barādarī*s among Muslims of Upper India, much less the endogamous *jāti*s of fully developed Hindu caste society.[9] In such a circumstance, especially where centralized political authority was weak, as in the hinterland of Mughal Bengal, maintaining social order could be a serious problem. "In lawless communities," writes Eric Hobsbawm, "power is rarely scattered among an anarchy of competing units, but clusters round local strong-points. Its typical form is patronage, its typical holder the private magnate or boss with his body of retainers and dependents and the network of 'influence' which surrounds him and causes men to put themselves under his protection."[10]

In Mughal Bengal, lacking tightly organized units such as nucleated villages or dominant clans through which authority might be exercised and social control maintained, local networks of patronage coalesced around locally defined centers of authority. The religious basis of these networks is noted by Ralph Nicholas:

> Social order is a serious problem in frontier society everywhere. The people of the lower delta are known to be tough and independent. They are famous for their skill with the lathi ["staff," "cudgel"], which is of-

7. Betsy Hartmann and James Boyce, *A Quiet Violence: A View from a Bangladesh Village* (London: Zed Press, 1983), 17.
8. O. H. K. Spate and A. T. A. Learnmonth, *India and Pakistan: A General and Regional Geography*, 3d ed. (London: Methuen, 1967), 590. See the map of typical Bengali settlement patterns on p. 580.
9. E. A. Gait, "The Muhammadans of Bengal," in *Census of India, 1901*, vol. 6, *The Lower Provinces of Bengal and Their Feudatories*, pt. 1, "Report" (Calcutta: Bengal Secretariat Press, 1902), 441.
10. Eric Hobsbawm, *Primitive Rebels: Studies in Archaic Forms of Social Movement in the 19th and 20th Centuries* (New York: Norton, 1959), 32. Similarly, in Morocco's Atlas Mountains, lineages of charismatic saints have developed networks of patronage and influence among local pastoral tribes. See Ernest Gellner, *Saints of the Atlas* (Chicago: University of Chicago Press, 1969), chs. 3–5.

ten the only means of establishing a claim to a plot after a flood has
changed the location of agricultural land. For centuries, in the lower
delta, authority was poorly organized, centers of officialism were few
and widely scattered. It seems likely that Islam and Vaisnavism functioned to provide authority in anarchic frontier society, and that they
did so through loosely constituted religious organizations. The Vaisnava
form of this organization is called a mandali (circle, congregation), it is
organized around a particular guru, who may be called a gosvai by his
followers, and is frequently constituted of persons of more than one
village.

The Muslim equivalent of the *maṇḍalī*, Nicholas continues, is called a *millat* (Arabic for "sect," "party," or "religious group") or simply *samāj*, "society," and is organized around a particular *mullā*, who may also be called
a *pīr* by his followers.[11] In the southeastern delta the typical *millat* is composed of from eighty to four hundred members, who dine together during
festivals, celebrate rites of passage together (circumcision, marriage,
death), and pray together in times of community stress. The *mullā* who
provides the group with religious leadership is maintained by a monthly
payment from each family in the *millat*.[12]

Similar structures of authority are found among rural Muslim communities in central and northern Bengal. In the central deltaic district of
Pabna, the anthropologist John Thorp notes, a group whose members share
mutual "feasting obligations" and who celebrate life-cycle rituals together
is locally called a *samāj*, whereas a group that prays together in a single
mosque is known as a *jamā'at*. In practice, the *jamā'at* may be coterminous
with the *samāj*; alternatively, it may be composed of several *samājes*.[13] In

11. Ralph W. Nicholas, "Vaisnavism and Islam in Rural Bengal," in *Bengal: Regional Identity,* ed. David Kopf (East Lansing: Asian Studies Center, Michigan State
University, 1969), 44.
12. Ibid. For observations on this point so far as concerns western Comilla District
in modern Bangladesh, see Robert Glasse, "La Société musulmane dans le Pakistan
rural de l'est," *Etudes rurales* 22–24 (1968): 202–4. Here, religious and non-
religious authority appear to be divided between the *mullā* and a leader known as
a *mātabbar*. The latter, who owes his position to his force of character and social
prestige, resolves disputes, levies fines for petty infractions, and represents the
group vis-à-vis the outside world.
13. The latter occurs as a result of natural population growth. According to John
Thorp, when the effective *jamā'at* reaches around five hundred, it is ready for a
split, since any number over that is too cumbersome for effective group action. At
this point, two *samājes* might emerge, though members of both would remain
members of the same *jamā'at* and the same mosque. In the region studied by
Thorp, the total *jamā'at* community was composed of two *samājes*, making up
some eighty households, or approximately six hundred people. But this larger
group prayed together only in celebration of the 'Id holiday. On ordinary Fridays,
only some 10 to 20 percent of the *jamā'at* community actually came to the mosque
and prayed together. John Thorp, personal communication, May 13, 1985.

any event, here as in the southeastern delta, it is the mosque and its socio-religious constituency, and not the "village" or the clan, that serves as the focus of identity and the effective vehicle for social mobilization. In neighboring Rajshahi District, two rural sociologists identified the *jamā'at*, a community of some fifty to sixty scattered households drawn to the same rural mosque, as the closest analog of the North Indian nuclear village.[14] The same is true further north. "In many villages," wrote Karunaketan Sen in a 1937 study of rural Dinajpur District, "there were huts which were places of worship and were called the 'Jumma-ghars.' Where there were more than one in a village, the local Muhammedan population was very often divided into factions, *each attached to one of the Jumma-ghars.*"[15] Whatever Sen may have meant here by a "village," his remarks confirm that in rural Dinajpur, as in rural Rajshahi, Pabna, and Comilla, the mosque (*masjid, jum'a-ghar*) was the effective unit of social organization among Muslims.

The continuing social significance of the mosque in today's rural Bengali society is a legacy of a time when a religious gentry of *'ulamā* and *pīrs*—and in their institutionalized form, mosques and shrines—first emerged as nodes of authority around which new peasant communities originally coalesced, and in relation to which such communities were understood as "dependents" (*vā bastagān*). Such people were attracted to the religious gentry not only as devotees of a religious leader but as groups of client peasants who had formerly been local fishermen and shifting cultivators beyond the pale of Hindu society. Islamization in Bengal, then, was but one aspect of a general set of transformations associated with an expanding economic frontier, which took place most dramatically in the Mughal period. We may scrutinize these processes more closely by examining the exceptional Persian documentation that has survived in two districts on the eastern edge of the delta, Chittagong and Sylhet.[16]

The Growth of Mosques and Shrines in Rural Chittagong, 1666–1760

The estuary of the Karnafuli River, where the city of Chittagong is located, was settled at least as early as the thirteenth century.[17] Although briefly

14. See Hartmann and Boyce, *Quiet Violence*, 11.
15. Karnaketan Sen, "Notes on Rural Customs of Dinajpur District," *Journal of the Asiatic Society of Bengal* 3 (1937), 38. Emphasis mine.
16. Because the towns of Sylhet and Chittagong are located on prominent hills, the District Collectorate buildings there stand high and dry, and their records are remarkably well preserved. Lower-lying districts, subject to the destructive floods that are endemic in the delta, have not been so fortunate in this respect.
17. See Nani Gopal Majumdar, *Inscriptions of Bengal*, vol. 3 (Rajshahi: Varendra Research Society, 1929), 158–63.

part of the independent sultanate of Bengal in the early fifteenth century, and sporadically in the sixteenth,[18] for most of the two centuries after 1459 the city and its hinterland were dominated by the kings of Arakan, a predominantly Buddhist coastal kingdom, whose capital was Myohaung, some 150 miles down the coast.[19] For long the city has been a window on the Indian Ocean; when under the control of the sultans, it served as a principal port for Muslim pilgrims and for the export of manufactured goods. From the mid sixteenth century on, Chittagong was inhabited by many Portuguese renegades, who, finding in it a haven beyond the reach of the Portuguese viceroy at Goa for their private commercial and military enterprises, effectively merged with Bengali society.[20]

Prior to the Mughal conquest in 1666, Chittagong's hinterland remained agriculturally undeveloped—a dense, impenetrable jungle. In 1595 Abu'l-fazl described the city of Chittagong as "belted by woods."[21] In 1621,

18. For the history of Chittagong's changing masters in this period—Gaur, Tripura, and Arakan—see M. A. Rahim, "Chittagong under the Pathan Rule in Bengal," *Journal of the Asiatic Society of Bengal* 18, no. 1 (1952): 21–30, and Suniti Bhushan Qanungo, "Chittagong during the Afghan Rule, 1538–1580," *Journal of the Asiatic Society of Bangladesh* 21, no 2 (1976): 54–75.

19. Independent of Burmese authority since 1433, the kings of Arakan, although Buddhist, absorbed a good deal of Muslim influence from the Bengal sultanate: they styled themselves "sultan," they issued medallions bearing the Muslim confession of faith, and they adopted Muslim names alongside their Buddhist names. They lived not so much from the land as from the sea, engaging especially in raiding the Bengal delta for slaves. In this activity, which eventually provoked the Mughal invasion and annexation of Chittagong in 1666, the Arakanese were often joined by renegade Portuguese adventurers and soldiers. But whereas the Portuguese seem to have sold their prisoners to points beyond the delta, the kings of Arakan acquired their slaves as a form of tribute from dependent subordinates and settled them on the land as cultivators. Most were Muslims. Godfrey E. Harvey, *History of Burma from the Earliest Times to 10 March 1824* (1925; reprint, London: Frank Cass & Co., 1967), 139–40, 144; Jadunath Sarkar, "The Conquest of Chatgaon, 1666 A.D.," *Journal of the Asiatic Society of Bengal* 3 (1907): 415, 417; D. G. E. Hall, *Burma* (London: Hutchinson's University Library, 1950), 57–62.

20. François Pyrard, who visited the city in 1607, noted: "A large number of Portuguese dwell in freedom at the ports on this coast of Bengal; they are also very free in their lives, being like exiles. They do only traffic, without any fort, order, or police, and live like natives of the country; they durst not return to India [i.e., Goa], for certain misdeeds they have committed, and they have no clergy among them. There is one of them named Jean Garie, who is greatly obeyed by the rest; he commands more than ten thousand men for the king of Bengal, yet he makes not war against the Portuguese, seeing they are friends." Pyrard, *Voyage*, 1: 334.

21. Abu'l-fazl 'Allami, *Ā'īn-i Akbarī* (Lucknow ed.), 2: 79; trans., 2: 137. "For practical purposes," recorded the Chittagong District *Gazetteer* in 1908, "the revenue history of Chittagong may be said to begin with the Muhammadan conquest of 1666. Previous to that date the district consisted for the most part of uncleared jungle, but here and there immigrant squatters had made small settlements." L. S. S. O'Malley, *Eastern Bengal District Gazetteers: Chittagong* (Calcutta: Bengal Secretariat Book Depot, 1908), 136.

wrote Mirza Nathan, Mughal troops proceeded through the present Chittagong District below the Karnafuli River along "a jungle route which was impassable even for an ant."[22] And a contemporary chronicler of the 1665–66 Mughal expedition to Chittagong, Shihab al-Din Talish, recorded that before embarking on the expedition, Mughal commanders in Dhaka supplied their troops with thousands of axes, for the army had literally to hack its way through the dense jungle down the Chittagong coast from the Feni to the Karnafuli rivers, an area described by Shihab al-Din as an "utterly desolate wilderness."[23]

The Chittagong interior was at that time inhabited by indigenous peoples described as having dark skin and little or no beard.[24] In other words, from the Mughal—that is, Turko-Iranian—racial perspective, they were distinctly alien. And their religion, wrote Abu'l-fazl, "is said to be different to that of the Hindus and Muhammadans. Sisters may marry their own twin brothers, and they refrain only from marriage between a son and his mother. The ascetics, who are their repositories of learning, they style *Wali* whose teaching they implicitly follow."[25] Thus the Islamization of Chittagong did not occur among peoples who had already been integrated into a Hindu social order, but among indigenous peoples practicing cults that, from a Mughal perspective, were recognizably neither Hindu nor Muslim. Their marriage customs would constitute incest from either a Muslim or a Hindu perspective, suggesting little contact with either civilization. Their predisposition to follow holy men (*walī*) is significant, for, as we shall see, the earliest representatives of Islamic civilization in the Chittagong forests were pioneers locally understood as holy men.

The material culture of these people was based on *jhūm*, or shifting cultivation, as described by Francis Buchanan, a servant of the English East India Company who toured the region in 1798. The "Joom," wrote Buchanan,

> is a species of cultivation peculiar, I believe, to the rude tribes inhabiting the hills east from Bengal. During the dry season, the natives of these places cut down to the root all the bushes growing on a hilly tract. After drying for some time the bush wood is set on fire, and by its means as much of the large timber as possible is destroyed. But if the trees are large, this part of the operation is seldom very successful. The whole surface of the ground is now covered with ashes, which soak in with the first rain, and serve as a manure. No sooner has the ground been soft-

22. Nathan, *Bahāristān*, trans. Borah, text, fol. 272b; trans., 2: 632.
23. Jadunath Sarkar, "Shaista Khan in Bengal (1664–66)," *Journal of the Asiatic Society of Bengal*, n.s., 2, no. 6 (June 1906): 409–11.
24. Abu'l-fazl, *Ā'īn-i Akbarī* (Lucknow ed.), 2: 74; trans., 2: 132.
25. Ibid., text, 2: 74–75; trans., 2: 132.

ened by the first showers of the season than the cultivator begins to plant. To his girdle he fixes a small basket containing a promiscuous mixture of the seeds of all the different plants raised in Jooms. These plants are chiefly rice, cotton, Capricum, indigo, and different kinds of cucurbitaceous fruits. In one hand the cultivator then takes an iron pointed dibble with which he strikes the ground, making small holes at irregular distances, but in general about a foot from each other. Into each of these holes he with his other hand drops a few seeds taken from the Basket as chance directs, and leaves the further rearing of the crop to nature. . . . Next year the cultivator for his Joom selects another spot covered with wood, for in such a rude kind of cultivation the ashes are a manure necessary to render the soil productive. When the wood on the former tract has grown to a proper size, the cultivator again returns to it, and then there being no large trees standing, the operation of cutting down is easier, and the ground is more perfectly cleared.[26]

As lands under *jhūm* cultivation were not permanently cleared, this kind of cultivation did not require intensive labor. Nor could it produce quantities of grain sufficient to support dense populations. Here as elsewhere, the shift from *jhūm* to field agriculture, involving the adoption of the plow, draft animals, and rice-transplanting techniques, led to dramatic increases in population. All of these swiftly followed the Mughal conquest of 1666.

In 1665 the Mughal court ordered the governor of Bengal, Shaista Khan, to outfit an expeditionary force to seize Chittagong, from whose harbor Arakanese and Portuguese freebooters had been raiding and plundering the waterways of lower Bengal. Departing Dhaka in December 1665, a force of 6,500 under the command of Buzurg Umid Khan hacked its way though the jungly coastal corridor in January 1666, moving in tandem with a naval force of 288 war vessels. Reaching the port of Chittagong a month later, the Mughals subjected the Arakanese to a three-day siege, taking the citadel on January 26, 1666.[27] The city was at once made the headquarters of a new Mughal *sarkār*, or district, headed by a military commander (*faujdār*) in charge of administrative affairs and a chief revenue officer ('*āmil*). A large number of Hindu immigrants also settled in the district at this time, some as traders, who came in the train of the invading army, and some as clerks, for the Mughals here as elsewhere relied heavily on Hindu bureaucratic expertise.[28] Most of the 6,500 troops in the expeditionary force remained garrisoned in the area to protect the

26. Francis Buchanan, "An Account of a Journey Undertaken by Order of the Bd. of Trade through the Provinces of Chittagong and Tipperah in Order to Look Out for the Places Most Proper for the Cultivation of Spices, March–May 1798" (British Museum, London, Eur. MSS. Add. 19286), 46–47.
27. Jadunath Sarkar, "Shaista Khan," 257.
28. O'Malley, *Eastern Bengal District Gazetteers: Chittagong*, 53.

frontier from land or sea invasion by the Arakanese. In return for their military service, these men were given small, rent-free patches of land, which they were at liberty to bring under cultivation. Later, when considerations of military security were no longer paramount, these lands were repossessed by the Chittagong government, and the troopers, or their descendants, became petty landholders, *zamīndārs*, charged with collection of the lands' revenues.[29] These men did not themselves undertake clearing operations, however. Instead, they remained hereditary chieftains over territorially defined parcels of forest, authorizing more energetic souls to undertake the arduous task of organizing the clearing and cultivation of the land.

Soon after the Mughal conquest, mosques and shrines began proliferating throughout the Chittagong hinterland. In 1770 a British report found that fully two-thirds of the district's best lands were "held by charity sunnuds" issued since 1666.[30] These documents, or *sanads*, had been issued in the name of the Mughal emperor by Chittagong's chief revenue officer and were addressed to the petty clerks (*mutasaddī*) posted in the smallest units of revenue collection, the *parganas*. The documents attest to the systematic transfer of jungle territory from the royal domain to members of an emerging religious gentry who had built and/or managed hundreds of mosques or shrines (*dargāh*) dedicated to Muslim holy men. The documents were not called *waqf* grants—that is, lands denied to personal use and reserved for the support of religious Muslim institutions such as mosques, schools, hospitals, shrines, and so on. Rather, they granted tax-free lands directly to the trustees (*mutawallī*) of mosques or shrines and guaranteed that the grantee's heirs would continue to enjoy such grants. Hence the grantees became the de facto and de jure landholders of territories alienated for the support of institutions under their administrative control.[31] The grants thus set in motion important social processes in this

29. H. J. S. Cotton, *Memorandum on the Revenue History of Chittagong* (Calcutta: Secretariat Press, 1880), 3–4.
30. Ibid., 13.
31. These grants exhibit elements of both the Islamic *waqf* and personal grants. The former were in principle institutional and permanent in nature, whereas grants such as *in'ām* or *madad-i ma'āsh* grants were personal and revocable. In practice, however, this pure distinction tended to break down. As Gregory Kozlowski has observed, "even an endowment for a mosque or school had a personal dimension, since the staff obtained their livings from it." Thus the grants we are considering resembled *waqf* grants inasmuch as they were institutional and permanent in nature, and *in'ām* or *madad-i ma'āsh* grants inasmuch as they were personal and inheritable by the grantee's descendants. See Kozlowski, *Muslim Endowments and Society in British India* (Cambridge: Cambridge University Press, 1985), 24–25.

part of the delta: forest lands became rice fields, and indigenous inhabitants became rice-cultivating peasants, at once both the economic and the religious clients of a new gentry.

Between 1666 and 1760, a total of 288 known tax-free grants in jungle land were given to pioneers by Mughal authorities in Chittagong for the purpose of clearing forests and establishing permanent agricultural settlements.[32] These included grants to trustees of mosques, to trustees of the shrines (*dargāhs*) of Muslim holy men, to pious Muslims not attached to any such institution, to trustees of Hindu temples, and to Brahman communities (see table 6). Of the total, 262, or 91 percent, were given to Muslims, and of the total forested area transferred from royal to private domain, Muslims received 11,195.4 acres, or 87 percent. The single most important type of grant was that endowing a rural mosque, typically a humble structure of bamboo, straw thatch, and earth, of the types illustrated in figures 22–24.[33] The period in which the appearance of these village mosques became statistically significant was the 1720s, when fifty such structures appeared, scattered throughout the Chittagong hinterland.

Map 6, which indicates the geographical distribution of these grants as of 1720, 1730, 1745, and 1760, shows how mosques and shrines, and to a lesser extent Hindu institutions, spread out from the Chittagong metropolis and onto the low-lying plains cradled by the ranges of hills north and

32. The only Mughal records still preserved in the Chittagong District Collectorate are documents pertaining to *lā-kharāj*, or rent-free, grants. These survived because when the East India Company rule commenced in 1760, the British declared they would honor rent-free tenures authorized by the previous regime, meaning that those who possessed Mughal documents proving such tenure had a powerful motive to keep them. Indeed, so powerful was this motive that, as the British discovered to their dismay, some enterprising Bengalis contrived to invent such claims by forging their own "Mughal" documents. This discovery led to a series of hearings by the deputy collector of Chittagong inquiring into the validity of all such grants, with the aim of reclaiming those judged invalid. In the course of these "Resumption Hearings," held sporadically between 1819 and 1848, the British collected and examined Mughal land records scattered throughout the district. The total of 288 grants herein analyzed represents only those that survived the scrutiny of the hearings and were declared valid. Many of the original *sanads* conferring such grants were probably lost during the many years since their original issuance. Nonetheless, the surviving *sanads* represent a sizeable body of primary data. For details on the Resumption Hearings, see *Correspondence on the Settlement of the Noabad Lands in the District of Chittagong* (Calcutta: Bengal Secretariat, 1871), 1: 20–21, 59–61, and Cotton, *Memorandum*. For a study of the Resumption Hearings, including their background in English political economy theory, their implementation, and the storm of protest they provoked in the early nineteenth century, see Abu Mohammad Waheeduzzaman, "Land Resumption in Bengal, 1819–1846" (Ph.D. diss,, University of London, 1969).
33. These diagrams were included in the files pertaining to the Resumption Hearings by the deputy collector of Chittagong between 1819 and 1848.

Table 6. Distribution of Tax-free Land Grants in *sarkār* Chittagong, 1666–1760

	Mosques		Muslim Shrines		Muslim Charity		Hindu Temples or Brahman Communities	
	Number	Acres	Number	Acres	Number	Acres	Number	Acres
1666–1699	1	166	—	—	2	262.6	—	—
1700–1709	2	38.4	1	89.6	1	16.6	—	—
1710–1719	4	288.3	1	256	9	517	1	209.6
1720–1729	50	1,583	11	391.8	11	111.6	3	392
1730–1739	30	1,118	14	281.6	5	82	3	78.4
1740–1749	31	1,606.4	16	386	11	237.2	5	139.6
1750–1760	32	3,120.5	20	428	10	214.8	14	817.6
Total	150	7,920.6	63	1,833	49	1,441.8	26	1,637.2

Note: The original sources give these figures in a land area unit called the *dūn*, of which there were two kinds. A *mogī dūn* was equal in area to 6.4 acres, whereas a *shāhī dūn* was four times as large as the former, equal in area to 25.6 acres. In either system, a *dūn* is made up of sixteen subunits called *kānī*. See J. B. Kindersley, *Final Report on the Survey and Settlement Operations in the District of Chittagong* (Alipore: Bengal Government Press, 1938), 17.

south of the Karnafuli valley. They show the growth pattern not only of Islamic institutions but also of agrarian society, since the establishment of each institution involved the cutting and clearing of forest. Even the terms used in the *sanad*s to identify the lands show how religious institutions spearheaded the eastward march of the economic frontier: whereas grants located near settled areas were often identified in terms of human geography,[34] those in the hinterland were identified in terms of natural geography.[35] Some *sanad*s located grant areas with reference to other grants. Thus, a Sufi shrine of Hathazari Thana built in 1723 was supported with

34. For example, a 1754 *sanad* conferring a grant of fourteen acres in a relatively settled area near Chittagong city, identified the granted area as "east of the royal highway, west of the tall mountains, south of the lands and gardens of Nur Khan, and north of the road and tank of Muhammad Khan." "Kanun Daimer Nathi," Chittagong District Collectorate Record Room, No. 208, bundle 64, case no. 4122.
35. A 1746 grant for the support of a mosque in the frontier region of Banskhali Thana identified the granted area as "east of the sea, south of Kulkhali *nāla* (Beng., *nālā*, "tributary"), west of Hamtala *nāla*, and north of Khatkhali *nāla*." Ibid., No. 182, bundle 33, case no. 2188.

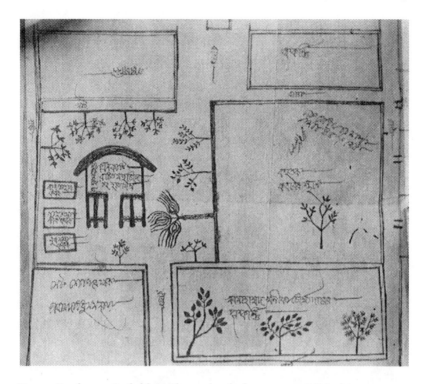

Fig. 22. Sundarpur, Fatikchhari Thana, thatched mosque established in 1759. "Kanun Daimer Nathi," Chittagong District Collectorate Record Room, bundle 62, case no. 4005.

a grant of 25.6 acres of jungle located "east of the endowment [*khairat*] of Manik Daulat, north of the endowment of Muhammad Reza, and south of the endowment of 'Abd al-Ghufur."[36] The identification of grant areas in terms of other grants points to their relative density, and also to the absence of prior settlements in the Chittagong hinterland. Finally, it can be seen that by mapping the land in this way, the *'āmil* of Chittagong and his staff imposed a distinctively Mughal sense of space and social order on Bengal's formerly forested landscape.[37]

36. Ibid., No. 45, bundle 56, case no. 3626.
37. Whether defined in terms of human or natural geography, these grants show that Mughal administrators recognized land as a spatial category, possessing fixed boundaries. Although some modern scholars have argued that such territorially defined notions of power were first introduced in India by the English, it is clear from these data that concern with land as spatial territory, and not just the "village grain heap," predated British rule. See W. C. Neale, *Economic Change in Rural India* (New Haven: Yale University Press, 1962), 5–7, 20–34.

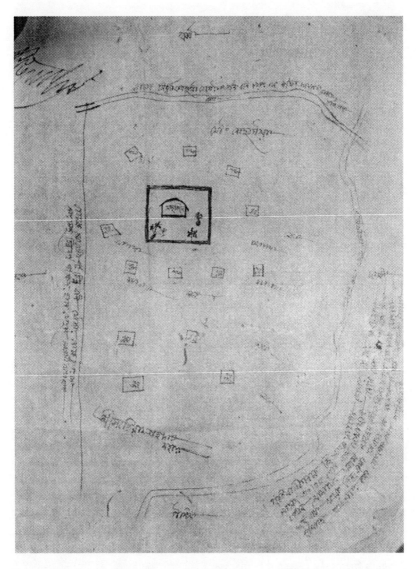

Fig. 23. Lohagara, Satkania Thana, thatched mosque established in 1720, diagram dated 1843. "Kanun Daimer Nathi," Chittagong District Collectorate Record Room, bundle 29, case no. 1808.

Fig. 24. Dabna, Hathazari Thana, thatched mosque established in 1766. "Kanun Daimer Nathi," Chittagong District Collectorate Record Room, bundle 51, case no. 3329.

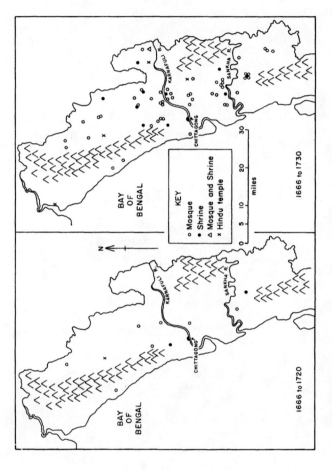

Map 6. Growth of Muslim institutions in *sarkār* Chittagong, 1666–1760

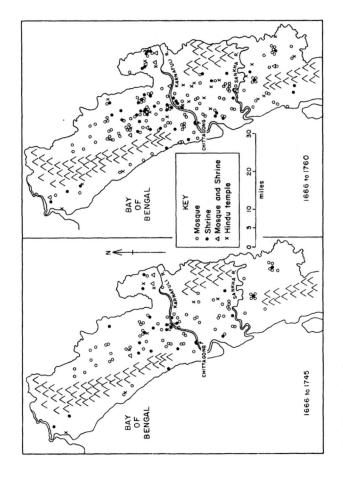

Map 6 (*continued*)

The social processes set in motion by these grants are seen in a *sanad* dated September 2, 1666, the earliest such document issued in Chittagong:

Clerks [*mutaṣaddī*], assessors [*muʿāmil*] past and present, headmen [*chaudhurī*], accountants [*qānūngō*], and peasants [*raʿāyā, muzāriʿ*] of the revenue circles [*pargana*] of Sarkar Islamabad [i.e., Chittagong], know that:

Shah Zain al-ʿAbidin has made it known that he has many dependents and has built a mosque, where a great many *faqīr*s and inhabitants come and go. But, as he has no means of maintaining the mosque, he is hopeful that the Government will bestow some land on him.

Having investigated the matter, the revenue department has fixed the sum of six *shāhī dūn* and eight *kānī* [i.e., 166.4 acres] of jungle land, lying outside the revenue rolls, and located in villages Nayapara and others of *pargana* Havili Chittagong, as a charity for the expenses of the mosque as well as a charity for the person mentioned above. Once the land is brought under cultivation, the produce of the land must be used for the expenses of the mosque as well as the needs of himself, his descendants, and his dependents. And he must assiduously pray for the survival of the powerful state. He and his descendants are not required to pay any land revenue or non-land revenue, highway taxes, bridge taxes, special cesses, or any other assessments issuing from either the administrative or the revenue branches of government. Nor is he bound to seek a fresh *sanad* each year. Take great care to execute this order. Dated 2 Rabi I 1077.[38]

The economic aim of these grants, to expand the empire's agrarian base, is evident from a phrase contained in nearly every *sanad*: "It is agreed that having brought the land into cultivation . . . ," followed by a statement of the particular ways the recipient was expected to use the fruits of the land's harvests.[39] The religious aim of grants for mosques and shrines was to promote Islamic piety in the countryside. In most cases this meant supporting simple, rural mosques and the petty functionaries and clerics who served them. For example, a 1721 *sanad* concerning the establishment of a mosque in Kadhurkhil, Boalkhali Thana, specified that in addition to expenses for carpets and lamps, the mosque's tax-free lands were to be used to pay the reader of the sermon (*khaṭīb*), the prayer-leader (*imām*), the caller to prayer (*muʾażżin*), pious men and preachers (*muṣallīān*), leaders in special prayers (*fātiḥa ʿabdīn*), and a sweeper (*jārūb-kesh*).[40] Other sa-

38. Chittagong District Collectorate Record Room, "Kanun Daimer Nathi," No. 1, bundle 59, case no. 3863.
39. Ibid., No. 54, bundle 40, case no. 2545. *Muqarrar numūda shud ki ābād va taraddud numūda . . .*
40. Ibid., No. 31, bundle 77, case no. 4971.

nads made provisions for repairs (*tarmīm*) to the mosque, or mentioned special religious festivals earmarked for support, such as the major Muslim 'Id holidays.[41] Still others supported Islamic ideals even when no institutional base was involved, as in the case of a grant of eight acres of jungle given in 1715 to Muhammad Munawwar and Shaikh Muhammad Ja'far on condition that they read the Qur'an in Bakkhain, Patiya Thana.[42] Similarly, in 1748 Shaikh Imam Allah was granted 14.4 acres in Hulain, in the same *thāna*, for reading the Qur'an and performing prayers (*fātiḥa*).[43]

Politically, the grants aimed at deepening the roots of Mughal authority on the frontier. The condition that the grantee "must assiduously pray for the survival of the powerful state," as in the 1666 *sanad* cited above, established a direct link between the government and the grantee, in addition to an indirect link between the government and God. Not one document failed to mention this condition of government patronage. Less apparent, though no less important, was the state's interest in securing the loyalty of those persons described as the grantee's dependents (*vā bastigān*). These were people who, having assisted the grantee in clearing the forests and building the institution, continued to serve it by cultivating the lands attached to it, and were therefore its clients. Some documents explicitly stated that the purpose of the grant was to support the followers of this or that holy man, as in a 1725 grant to Taj al-Din and Zia al-Din, who received a patch of jungle in Hathazari Thana in order that its produce might support their children and "dependents."[44] In 1745 three men—Mir Sa'id Allah, Ghulam Husain, and Afzal Khalifa—declared that they had many dependents whom they could not support. For the maintenance of these persons, the state granted them 30.4 acres in the same *thāna*.[45] Other grants stated that after the expenses of maintaining the mosques or shrines had been met, the balance of the land's produce should go to support the grantee's dependents.[46] In sum, the government recognized mosques and shrines as the foci of sociopolitical activity on the frontier and sought to form them into a dependent clientele, just as those institutions had already formed dependent clienteles of their own.

41. Ibid., No. 85, bundle 68, case no. 4314.
42. Ibid., No. 12, bundle 30, case no. 1937.
43. Ibid., No. 193, bundle 71, case no. 4526. See also No. 238, bundle 27, case no. 1628, and No. 265, bundle 62, case no. 4002.
44. Ibid., No. 54, bundle 40, case no. 2545.
45. Ibid., No. 165, bundle 28, case no. 1751.
46. Such was the case with Shaikh Ahmad Shah, who in 1720 constructed a thatched mosque in the hinterland of Patiya Thana. Ibid., No. 26a, bundle 69, case no. 4404.

The Rise of Chittagong's Religious Gentry

By supporting frontier mosques and shrines, Mughal authorities in Chittagong established ties with political systems that functioned at a very local level. This was logical, for it was on the frontier itself, and not in district offices in Chittagong city, far less at the provincial or imperial levels, that the manpower and organization requisite for the arduous task of clearing the thickly wooded interior were to be found. The government did no more than legitimate and support an enterprise whose initiative was located at the grass roots. A 1798 survey, undertaken several decades after the English East India Company had occupied Bengal, is suggestive of how the Chittagong hinterland was reduced to the plow in Mughal times. "The following process for clearing new land is that here adopted by the Bengalese," wrote Francis Buchanan:

> A man of some consequence, a diwan, a phausdar [*faujdār*], or the like, gets a grant of some uncleared district. Different persons, who have a little stock, apply to him for pottahs [*pāṭṭā*] or leases, of certain portions, and in clearing their portions these men are often assisted by the Zemeendar, or possessor of the original grant, with a little money, as a temporary support. But this money becomes a debt which they are obliged to repay when they are able.
>
> In the cold season the operation commences by cutting down the bushes and smaller trees. After drying a few days these are burned and at the commencement of the rains the ground is ploughed, as well as the strength of the cattle and the resistance of the roots will admit. Rice is then sown, and a small crop is produced. The sirdar [*sardār*] or overseer, and three labourers, are supposed to be able to perform this operation with eight kanays [i.e., 3.2 acres] of ground. The second year's operation consists in cutting down the greater part of the large trees, in burning them, and digging out the roots of the bushes and underwood, from the remains of which, after the first year's ploughing, many shoots have then formed. The ground is again sown at the beginning of the rains, and yields a better crop. One sirdar and two labourers are reckoned equal to the performance of this work, on eight kanays [*kānī*].
>
> In the third year the operation is concluded by again cutting down such brushwood as may have shot up, and by digging out and burning all the roots of the large trees that have been felled. The same number of persons are employed as in the second year. The ground in the fourth year is reckoned perfectly clear, and pays the usual rent. For the first three years nothing is exacted. Two men and two bullocks are reckoned equal to the cultivation of eight kanays, which here are the usual extent of one grist's possession. All over Chittagong the cow is employed with the plough as well as the bullock.[47]

47. Buchanan, "Account of a Journey," 37–38.

It is clear, first, that the initiative for clearing the land lay with local men of enterprise, and not with the government. Second, we see the role played by cash money advanced to laborers by the *zamīndār*, or primary landholder. And third, we find the equally important role played by "some local man of some consequence," who, having acquired a grant of uncleared land, apportioned it among laborers, who in turn became shareholders beneath him.

If we apply to data from the early eighteenth century the same mechanisms that Buchanan described at the end of that century, the categories used in Mughal *sanads* become readily intelligible. The "local man of some consequence" mentioned by Buchanan in 1798 corresponds to the man named in the Mughal *sanads* who organized local labor into work gangs to clear the forest and commence cultivation. The documents do not identify where these "men of consequence" came from, though the titles that occasionally accompany their proper names provide clues to their social origins. These included, in order of frequency, *shaikh* (23), *chaudhurī* (11), *khwāndkār* (9), *hājī* (8), *ta'alluqdār* (7), *shāh* (4), *faqīr* (4), *saiyid* (3), *darvīsh* (3), and *khān* (3). The twenty-one men identified as *chaudhurī*, *ta'alluqdār*, and *khān* were evidently members of the rural landholding aristocracy before they acquired these grants, and in all likelihood they built or supported mosques or shrines as a means of obtaining tax-free rights to their lands. The rest were associated with either formal or informal Islam. The largest category, "shaikh," could have referred either to informal holy men or to members of the *'ulamā*. Those styled *khwāndkār*, a Persian term meaning generally "one who reads," were originally associated with public Qur'an reading. *Hājīs* were men who had performed the pilgrimage to Mecca, and *saiyids* were those claiming genealogical descent from the Prophet Muhammad. The remainder of the titles—*shāh*, *faqīr*, and *darvīsh*—all refer to *pīrs*, or holy men.

Whatever their origins, these men played central roles in transforming the jungle to paddy, in introducing Mughal and Islamic culture into the forests, and in integrating forest communities into that culture. They were also entrepreneurs, arranging on the one hand to get necessary authorization from a local *zamīndār* to clear the forest, while on the other hand arranging with local laborers to work the land as shareholders. These latter persons, who in Buchanan's account were lease-holding cultivators, correspond to the "dependents" (*vā bastigān*) named in the Mughal *sanads*. And finally, at the top of the local structure, both Buchanan's account and the Persian documents mention the *zamīndār*, or the primary landholder from whom the organizer of field operations acquired the right to commence clearing.

From Buchanan's account it appears that by 1798 the Islamization and peasantization of the native peoples of Chittagong's uplands had made little progress, for he describes the tribal peoples of the Sitakund mountains in northern Chittagong as still practicing shifting, or *jhūm*, cultivation, growing cotton, dry rice, ginger, "and several other plants which they sell to the Bengalese in return for salt, fish, earthen ware, and iron."[48] He also noted among these peoples some worship of Śiva.[49] Nor had Mughal or European notions of property rights yet extended to these still-forested lands. "The woods," Buchanan wrote, "are not considered as property; for every ryot [cultivator] may go into them and cut whatever timber he wants."[50] We may contrast this attitude with the keen sense of proprietorship among Mughal grantees. In 1734, for example, the servants of the shrine of a certain Shah Pir received over sixty acres of jungle in Satkania Thana in order to maintain the shrine and meet the expenses of travelers. Some time later, the shrine's trustee [*mutawallī*] filed a complaint in the court of the local *qāzī* alleging that a certain Tej Singh had unlawfully established a market on the lands belonging to the shrine and insisting that the market be removed.[51] To the Mughals, settling the frontier entailed the establishment of legally defined notions of property backed by state power.

If the agrarian frontier had not yet reached the Chittagong highlands by the end of the eighteenth century, in the low country Buchanan noted that natural forest lands had recently been replaced by cultivated fields. "The stumps of trees still remaining on several of those [valleys] which I today passed," he wrote referring to southern Satkania Thana, "show how lately they have been cleared." Or again, referring to northern Chakaria Thana: "It is only 13 or 14 years since the upper part of this valley began to be cultivated. New land is still taking in, and the stumps of trees remain everywhere in the fields."[52] The domain of field agriculture ended only in the extreme south, for he remarked that "the whole country to the south [of the Ramu River] is an immense forest, utterly impenetrable without the assistance of a hatchet."[53]

Buchanan also observed "that most of the new cultivated lands belong

48. Ibid., 15. Their rice, he wrote, "would no more grow on low ground than the rice of the jeel would on the hills." Ibid., 50.
49. The low hills east of Sitakund, he wrote, "are occupied by small tribes of Mugs and Tiperahs, who cultivate Jooms, and at the temple on the hill adore the god of generation." Ibid., 20.
50. Ibid., 36.
51. "Kanun Daimer Nathi," Chittagong District Collectorate Record Room, No. 121, bundle 51, case no. 3320.
52. Buchanan, "Account of a Journey," 29, 31.
53. Ibid., 52.

to Hindoos, who by acting as officers about the Courts of the Judges and collectors, and by possessing greater . . . economy than the Mohammedans, are very fast rooting these out. The great body of the people, however, in the province of Chittagong, is still composed of the Mohammedan persuasion."[54] The latter observation was later confirmed in the earliest (1872) census, which showed Muslims comprising 78.2 percent of Satkania Thana and 78 percent of Cox's Bazar Subdivision, in which both Chakaria and Ramu Thanas are located.[55] As to Buchanan's remarks about Hindus, in Chittagong as in Dhaka and Bakarganj, the apex of the social hierarchy was dominated by absentee Hindu *zamīndārs*. Although these played a key role in the task of land reclamation, their lines of patronage did not lie with the cultivators below, but with the ruling class above—those in "the Courts of the Judges and collectors."[56] Once having acquired their *zamīndārī* rights, these men adopted the ritual style of kings vis-à-vis their agricultural tenants, for Buchanan went on to add, referring to Bengal generally, that "every Hindoo Zemeendar of the least note is called a Rajah, and every such person by his ryots and servants is commonly called Maha-raj, or the Great Prince. . . . As a *zemeendar* the Rajah is amenable to our courts, but within his own country he is absolute, and possesses the uncontrolled power of life and death."[57]

In sum, the structure of land tenure as described in 1798 consisted of three tiers beneath Chittagong's chief revenue officer. At the apex was the *zamīndār*, aloof from the actual process of forest clearing or field agriculture, typically Hindu, and given to the ceremonial style of a petty raja. Next was Buchanan's "local man of some consequence," the pivotal figure who secured from the *zamīndār* a grant to clear jungle land and hired laborers to accomplish the task. This would be either a member of the religious gentry itself or a petty landholder who supported a religious institution to obtain tax-free status. Typically enterprising entrepreneurs, and usually Muslim, these were the men who mobilized local manpower and oversaw clearing operations. Finally, there was the mass of laborers, who after four years of clearing forest lands were ready to begin regular field agriculture. It is significant that Buchanan describes the inhabitants of the uncleared jungle as non-Muslim tribal peoples who practiced some

54. Ibid., 36.
55. H. Beverly, *Report on the Census of Bengal, 1872* (Calcutta: Secretariat Press, 1872), lxvi.
56. This alliance of Hindu *zamīndārs* with government on the one hand, and Muslim cultivators with their immediate patrons on the other, foreshadowed a polarization that in the nineteenth and twentieth centuries was to take on a communal coloring, eventually culminating in the Partition of 1947.
57. Buchanan, "Account of a Journey," 162, 163.

form of Śiva worship, whereas the cultivators of lands already cleared he describes as Muslims. This suggests that peasantization and Islamization proceeded hand in hand among the peoples of Chittagong's arable low country.

There were three discernible means by which the religious gentry acquired their land rights: donation, purchase, and pioneering. The first method corresponds to what Buchanan found at the end of the eighteenth century, when men produced documents showing that some legitimate local authority had donated land to them. Described in Mughal documents as *sardār* (chieftain), *chaudhurī* (headman), or most frequently *zamīndār* (landholder), the Muslims among these authorities were most likely descendants of the Mughal troopers who had accompanied Buzurg Umid Khan's expedition to Chittagong in 1666. The Hindus among them were probably descendants of the clerks or revenue agents who had also accompanied that expedition and, in a manner described by Buchanan for the late eighteenth century, used their proximity to the governing authorities to get new lands made over to them in their own names. By authorizing a petitioner to clear the jungle and build a mosque or shrine, these local authorities became patrons of the petitioners named in the *sanad*s. It is also evident that by the mid eighteenth century the patronage system had not hardened along communal lines: some Hindu *chaudhurī*s patronized mosques and some Muslim *chaudhurī*s patronized temples. As early as 1705, at the close of Aurangzeb's long and turbulent reign, Thakur Chand, a Hindu *chaudhurī* in Fatikchari Thana, donated 17.5 acres of jungle land for the construction and support of a village mosque built by a local *qāzī*.[58] In 1740 Manohar and Jagdish, two Hindu *chaudhurī*s in Rauzan Thana, donated 76.8 acres to Shikur Muhammad Pahlawan to cover the expenses of a mosque the latter had built in the forest.[59] Conversely, in 1740 Mir Ibrahim, a Muslim *chaudhurī* in Rangunia Thana, donated 3.2 acres to a certain Mukundaram in the way of a *devottar*, a tax-free land grant for the support of a temple or image.

Acquisition by donation generally involved a Muslim pioneer with a religious title like "shaikh" going into the jungle and, having secured a document of authorization from a local chieftain, building a mosque or shrine with local labor. The document attested that the chieftain had donated a certain portion of undeveloped jungle land to the shaikh. The latter would then produce this document to local Mughal authorities in a formal request for legal recognition of tenurial rights over jungle lands that he

58. "Kanun Daimer Nathi," Chittagong District Collectorate Record Room, No. 7, bundle 62, case no. 4005.
59. Ibid., No. 138, bundle 63, case no. 4044.

either proposed to bring under cultivation in order to support those institutions, or that he had already brought under cultivation. After investigating to verify the petitioner's claim, the Chittagong revenue authorities would issue a *sanad* in the name of the chief revenue officer of Chittagong *sarkār* and bearing the seal of the reigning Mughal emperor, thereby extending government recognition of the petitioner's trusteeship (*tauliyat*) of the institution and the lands supporting it. In this process the petitioner moved from de facto to de jure landholdership, enjoying the rights to the produce of the land subject to his support of the institution specified in the *sanad*.[60] Actually, chieftains who in this way donated portions of their jungle territory to such shaikhs were adhering to an ancient model of Indian patronage. In Buddhist, Jain, and Hindu contexts laymen had gained religious merit by donating lands to monastic or Brahmanic establishments, a practice that served to reinforce the cultural bonds between donating clients and receiving patrons.[61]

Some members of the religious gentry acquired their tenure by purchasing undeveloped forest from the chieftains or headmen who were its legally recognized holders. In such instances, the transfer of land did not reinforce cultural ties between donors and receivers according to classical models of Indian patronage. On the contrary, the use of cash enabled people to bypass traditional modes of patronage and deal with groups of people of different cultures. For example, in 1725 Shaikh 'Abd al-Wahhab of *pargana* Panchkhain in Rauzan Thana purchased 16.4 acres of untaxed and undeveloped jungle land from the *pargana* headman, Jagdish Chau-

60. An example will illustrate how this process worked. On A.H. 2 Ramazan 1145 (corresponding to A.D. February 16, 1733), a *sanad* was issued in favor of a certain Darwish Muhammad, confirming him as the trustee of both a mosque and the shrine of a holy man located in Gomdandi, Boalkhali Thana, and granting him sixteen acres of jungle land to meet the expenses of the two institutions. In the first half of the *sanad*, which normally consists of the petitioner's plea, we learn that Darvish Muhammad had originally been given trusteeship over the mosque and shrine by a certain 'Abd al-Majid, the *chaudhuri*, or headman, of *pargana* Ya'qubnagar, which was the revenue circle in which these institutions were located. In his petition, Darwish Muhammad stated that 'Abd al-Majid had given him a document, or *khairat-nāma*, conferring on him the trusteeship of the mosque and the shrine, as well as the sixteen acres of land. What the petitioner now requested was Mughal recognition and confirmation of this grant. As the *sanad* concluded, "On examining the *qānūngū*'s records and the above-mentioned documents, it is found that the above-mentioned amount of land is fixed for the expenses of the mosque and the shrine." In short, the headman (*chaudhuri*) of the *pargana* initiated the grant, the *pargana* accountant (*qānūngū*) verified it, and the Mughal authorities in Chittagong eventually confirmed it. Ibid., No. 110, bundle 17, case no. 632.

61. See Barbara S. Miller, ed., *The Powers of Art: Patronage in Indian Culture* (New Delhi: Oxford University Press, 1992), 1–8, 19–167.

dhuri, a Hindu. The new owner then donated the land to Muhammad Khan, whose father had built a mosque on it.[62] Here both donation and purchase were operating, as a Hindu landholder had sold jungle land to a Muslim intermediary patron, who in turn donated it to the builder of the mosque. There are also numerous instances of chaudhurīs selling jungle land directly to the trustees of mosques or shrines. In 1748 Shaikh Muhammad Akbar and Muhammad 'Abbas notified Mughal authorities that they had purchased 38.4 acres from the headmen (chaudhurīs and ta'alluqdārs) of their locality and had built a mosque there. As more land was necessary to meet the expenses of maintaining the mosque, however, they requested additional jungle land for clearing, preparatory to cultivation, and they were given 19.2 acres for this purpose.[63] Ten years later, Muhammad Sardar of Fotika, Hathazari Thana, notified the Mughal authorities that he had purchased 16 acres of land from the headmen (chaudhurīs) and landholders (zamīndārs) of his pargana in order to support a preacher and prayer-leader, and to meet the expense of celebrating the 'Id festivals of a mosque and the commemorative festivals ('urs) for a saint buried in a shrine there. He now wanted government recognition of the tax-free status of these lands.[64]

Such cases suggest how a cash-based economy facilitated the movement of men and resources in the forest, the clearing of land, and the expansion of mosque-centered settlements in formerly forested areas. Silver had, of course, been in widespread circulation as currency in Bengal ever since the Turks had established their rule in the thirteenth century. Already in the late sixteenth century, the poet Mukundaram had linked mobile cash with the process of forest clearing and agricultural operations.[65] In the seventeenth and eighteenth centuries, however, both European and Asian merchant-investors greatly expanded the volume of money circulating in Bengal, making possible transactions such as the case cited above in which a Hindu chaudhurī sold forest land to Muslims for development. Moreover, the monetization of Bengali society allowed people to attach new meanings to land. What had formerly been a ritual item, appropriate for

62. "Kanun Daimer Nathi," Chittagong District Collectorate Record Room, No. 55, bundle 38, case no. 2431.
63. Ibid., No. 188, bundle 57, case no. 3736.
64. Ibid., No. 222, bundle 78, case no. 5026.
65. In the Caṇḍī-Maṅgala, the goddess Chandi orders the poem's hero, Kalaketu, to sell a valuable ring and use the money thus obtained to clear the forest so that a city may be built in her honor. Once the land was prepared for agriculture, Kalaketu was to advance his men rice, seeds, and cash, thereby facilitating their establishment on newly claimed lands. Mukundaram, Kavikaṅkaṇa Caṇḍī, 290, 295–96, 354–55. See also Bhattacharya, "La Déesse," 33.

acquiring religious merit in the context of Buddhist or Brahmanical gifting (*dāna*), had now become a freely transferable commodity.

The third and most common mode of land acquisition among the grantees was that of men and their dependents clearing the jungle in territories apparently unclaimed by superior *zamīndārs*. In these cases, land was acquired neither by donation nor by purchase, but by primary settlement by pioneers who claimed, and whose descendants would also claim, a tax-free tenure called *jangal-burī maurūthī*, or "jungle-cutting inheritance." Thus we read of a certain Muhammad Sadiq, son of Shaikh Mumin, who informed the Mughal authorities in 1722 that he and his dependents had cleared 57.6 acres of jungle in what is now Rauzan Thana, where they had built a mosque. Noting that the land he held was "occupied by established custom," Sadiq claimed tenurial rights of *jangal-burī maurūthī*. Now he requested Mughal confirmation of his claim so that he would be able to support his dependents.[66] In the absence of any superior landholder, Sadiq himself became the de facto *zamīndār* of this territory.

If the political identity of these pioneers was based on their integration with the Mughal state through ties specified in the grants, their religious identities rested on different footings. Some were local holy men popularly redefined as Muslim holy men, some were Muslim holy men further redefined as Sufis, and still others were popularly accorded a Middle Eastern origin. Some seem to have been the very sort of indigenous Bengali *walīs* that the native population of the Chittagong hinterland had revered from pre-Muslim times, as noted by Abu'l-fazl.[67] For example, in 1723 and 1733, 25.6 acres of jungle were given to the dependents and local shrine of a "dervish" named Kali Shah, whose name associates him with the goddess Kali.[68] The same is true of a certain Shaikh Kali, who built a mosque in

66. "Kanun Daimer Nathi," Chittagong District Collectorate Record Room, No. 37, bundle 39, case no. 2513.
67. The appropriation of saints by different religious traditions in this part of the delta was observed by the British ethnographer R. C. Temple. Writing in 1925 of the cult of Badr 'Alam, Temple noted: "To the Buddhists, he is a *nat*; to the Hindus a *deva* or inferior god, to the Muhammadans a saint, to the Chinese a spirit. His worship is precisely that which is common all over the East to spirits or supernatural beings, believed in by the folk irrespective of their particular form of professed belief, and it points, in just the same way as do all other instances, to the survival of an old animistic worship in 'pre-religious' days. As in all other similar cases, one of the contending local professed religions has chiefly annexed this particular being to itself, and he is pre-eminently a Muhammadan saint, legendarily that saint best known to the bulk of the Muhammadan seafaring population, namely Pir Badr of their own chief town of Chittagong." Temple, "Buddermokan," *Journal of the Burma Research Society* 15 (1925): 9.
68. "Kanun Daimer Nathi," Chittagong District Collectorate Record Room, "Kanun Daimer Nathi," No. 45, bundle 56, case no. 3626.

Rauzan Thana in 1760.[69] In 1725 a shrine appeared in Charandip, Boalkhali Thana, in honor of a certain Jangal Pir, whose name identifies him as a holy man of the forest.[70] In such cases, local *walīs* or saints of the Chittagong forest became integrated into the Mughal religio-political system as petty clients at the bottom of a vast patronage network extending clear to the emperor's palace in Delhi. Yet their affiliation with mosques and shrines also cast them in the role of representatives of Islamic civilization.

In short, the tendency of Chittagong's forest-dwelling peoples to follow the teachings of charismatic holy men allowed an outsider to be situated in this category and to find acceptance among the populace as one of their own. Later, the charismatic authority of such foreign holy men became routinized when they or their descendants merged with the revenue bureaucracy as petty landholders, as had happened to the sons of Pir 'Umar Shah, who became the *zamīndārs* of the area in Noakhali cleared by their holy man father. The very first grant in the Chittagong collection of *sanads* illustrates the process. In 1666 Shah Muhammad Barbak Maghribi, whose name associates the saint with northwest Africa, settled in the forests of Chittagong, where he and his followers built a mosque and cleared the 166.4 acres of jungle given by the Mughals for its support. A century later, the descendants of his followers claimed revenue-free rights to the lands on the grounds that they were descended from the original jungle-clearers and thus held a legally recognized form of inheritance (*jangal-burī maurūthī*).[71] In another instance, in 1717 a Sufi named Shah Lutf Allah Khondkar had been given 108.8 acres in Satkania Thana as personal charity (*madad-i ma'āsh*). By 1740 the village founded by him had acquired the name "Mun'imabad," or "the benefactor's cultivated area," and the descendants of the Sufi's followers claimed rights to the land on the grounds that their ancestors had originally cleared the jungle.[72] Thus, too, in 1726 a local preacher (*khaṭīb*) named 'Abd al-Wahhab Khondkar built a brick mosque in Patiya Thana, and just over a decade later his grandson, 'Inayat Muhammad, emerged not only as the heir to the lands attached to the mosque but also as the region's *chaudhurī*.[73] Such developments illustrate Max Weber's notion of the "routinization of charismatic authority": the descendants of persons credited with charismatic religious authority came to assume proprietary rights over the land.[74]

69. Ibid., No. 248, bundle 79, case no. 5099.
70. Ibid., No. 56, bundle 71, case no. 4503.
71. Ibid., No. 1, bundle 59, case no. 3863.
72. Ibid., No. 20, bundle 44, case no. 2792.
73. Ibid., No. 70, bundle 51, case no. 3321.
74. *Max Weber: The Theory of Social and Economic Organization*, ed. Talcott Parsons (London: Free Press of Glencoe, 1964), 363–81.

If holy men or their descendants could become landlords, the reverse was also true; such was the malleability of social status on the Bengal frontier. Reversing Weber's "routinization of charismatic authority," one also finds a "sanctification of bureaucratic authority," as enterprising developers or even government officials came to be locally regarded as saints capable of interceding with divine power.[75] We have noted the case of Khan Jahan 'Ali, the fifteenth-century Turkish officer remembered for clearing the jungles of Khulna and Jessore, later popularly elevated to the position of one of the great saints of southern Bengal. In Chittagong there is the case of a certain Shaikh Manik. Described in contemporary sources as the *zamīndār* of *pargana* Fathapur, Shaikh Manik in 1715 notified government authorities that he had built a mosque in Paschimpati, Hathazari Thana. Complaining that he had insufficient means to maintain the institution, he appealed for some forest land to cultivate. The state gave him 54.5 acres and recognized him as the mosque's legitimate trustee. By 1755, forty years after the construction of the mosque, a shrine had been built over the grave of the late Shaikh Manik, and his son, Ja'far Muhammad, had emerged as the shrine's manager. By 1755 the shrine had become so institutionalized that—in ways mimicking any bureaucratic government—it had begun issuing documents stamped with its own stylized seal: "Shrine [*dargāh*] of Shaikh Manik."[76]

In such cases the vocabulary of popular Sufism stabilized in popular memory those persons who had been instrumental in building new communities. There is no evidence that either Khan Jahan or Shaikh Manik, both of them pioneers and developers, had any acquaintance with, far less mastery of, the intricacies of Islamic mysticism. Nor will their names be found in any of the great pan-Indian hagiographies. Yet from the culture of institutional Sufism came the asymmetric categories of *pīr* and *murīd*, or shaikh and disciple, which rendered Sufism a suitable model for channeling authority, distributing patronage, and maintaining discipline—the very requirements appropriate to the business of organizing and mobilizing labor in regions along the cutting edge of state power. It is little wonder that Sufis appeared along East Bengal's forested frontier.

75. As noted in the *Gazetteer* for Chittagong, compiled in 1908, "In a district which has been so recently reclaimed from jungle that memories of the arduous labour involved in reclamation are fresh in men's minds, and find expression in such titles as *jungalburi* (clearer of jungle), *talukdar*, *abadkar* (original cultivator) and the like, it is natural that great respect should attach to the title of the original reclaimer and of his successors." O'Malley, *Eastern Bengal District Gazetteers: Chittagong*, 153.
76. "Kanun Daimer Nathi," Chittagong District Collectorate Record Room, No. 15, bundle 68, case No. 4317.

The Religious Gentry of Sylhet

Located in Bengal's northeastern corner, Sylhet, like Chittagong, was densely forested at the time of its conquest by Muslims. A royal grant of the mid seventh century had described parts of this region as "outside the pale of human habitation, where there is no distinction between natural and artificial; infested by wild animals and poisonous reptiles, and covered with forest out-growths."[77] Many of the southern tracts of what are now Sylhet and Mymensingh districts were inundated with water and inhabited by communities of non-Aryan fishermen, prominently the Kaivartas.[78] In fact, the central and southwestern part of present-day Sylhet District once formed part of a huge lake. But from the late tenth century to the early twelfth, a dynasty of semi-independent Hindu kings emerged to rule over the principality of Śrihatta in the northern part of the district.[79] Its most powerful king, Govinda-Kesava (fl. ca. 1050), built a lofty Krishna temple of stone in his capital city—probably identifiable with the north and northeastern part of Sylhet town—where he amassed a force of "innumerable" war boats, infantry, cavalry, and elephants.[80] Yet the process of Brahmanization had by this time made little headway among the native communities (Kaivarta, Das, Nomo) in the region's forested and marshy hinterland.

By the time Ibn Battuta visited Sylhet in 1345, some forty years after the Turkish conquest of the region, the large river valleys had become settled by a stable and flourishing Hindu population. "Along the banks of the (Meghna) river," recalled the Moroccan traveler,

> to the right as well as to the left, there are water wheels, gardens and villages such as those along the banks of the Nile in Egypt. The inhabitants of *Habanq* [ten miles south of Habiganj] are infidels under protection (*dhimma*) from whom half of the crops which they produce is taken; besides, they have to perform certain duties. For fifteen days we sailed down the river passing through villages and orchards as though we were going through a mart.[81]

For the next several centuries little is known of Muslim rule in Sylhet, a distant frontier town, which throughout the sultanate period did not even possess a mint. When Akbar conquered western Bengal in the late six-

77. Niyogi, *Brahmanic Settlements*, 41.
78. K. N. Gupta, "On Some Castes and Caste-Origins in Sylhet," *Indian Historical Quarterly* 7 (1931): 725–26.
79. Kamalakanta Gupta, *Copper-plates of Sylhet*, vol. 1 (Sylhet: Lipika Enterprises, 1967), 196–97.
80. Ibid., 190, 199 n.
81. Ibn Battuta, *Rehla*, trans. Mahdi Husain, 241.

teenth century, the hilly and forested tracts of southern Sylhet District became a refuge area for Afghan chieftains fleeing advancing Mughal armies. Even after the Mughals annexed Sylhet in 1612, the region seems to have remained Bengal's "Wild East," as we hear only sporadic reports of a Mughal presence there.[82]

From 1660 on, however, there is clear evidence of the agrarian growth that was quietly taking place in the region. Tables 7 and 8, which summarize the grants approved by the Sylhet *faujdār's* office between 1660 and 1760, indicate the amount of jungle area transferred from state to private hands in this period. Although only one of the twenty-six *faujdārs* in this period was a Hindu,[83] a significant share of government patronage was extended to Hindu institutions. Indeed, the *brahmottar*, a tax-free land grant to a Brahman as a reward for his sanctity or learning, constituted the largest category of transfer, each one averaging 22.9 acres in size. As in Chittagong, it was not the Mughal authorities in the Sylhet headquarters who initiated these grants; Mughal *faujdārs* in Sylhet only confirmed agreements already concluded between local *zamīndārs* and Sylhet's religious gentry. For example, a 1721 *sanad* confirmed a document previously drawn up by local *zamīndārs* who had donated 39 acres (10 *qulba*s) of jungle lands to a certain Mahadev Bhatacharjee, a Brahman (*zunnārdār*) "possessing consummate skills in the Hindu sciences."[84] Most *brahmottar* grants were justified in terms of the Brahman's poverty and his reputed mastery of Hindu knowledge.[85]

The second most common type of grant to Hindus or Hindu institutions was the *devottar*, a tax-free transfer made over to the caretakers of a Hindu temple or image. One such grant, dated December 8, 1720, reads:

82. In 1636 Muhammad Zaman Tehrani, the *faujdār* of Sylhet, was summoned to accompany a Mughal expedition to Kamrup, "as he had resided for years in the country and was well acquainted with every particular regarding it." Inayat Khan, *Shah Jahan Nama*, trans. A. R. Fuller, ed. W. E. Begley and Z. A. Desai (Delhi: Oxford University Press, 1990), 235.

83. S. N. H. Rizvi, ed., *Bangladesh District Gazetteers: Sylhet* (Dacca: Bangladesh Government Press, 1975), 68–71.

84. "'Ilm-i hindawī istiʿdād-i kamāl dārad." The *sanad* stipulated that the lands be handed over to Bhatacharjee's possession, that after they were brought into cultivation, their produce must be used to meet his needs, and that he must pray assiduously for the long life of the state. Sylhet District Collectorate Record Room, "Register of Sanads," 17: 60.

85. A grant issued in 1744 described a certain Mahadev Chakravarti as a "master of Hindu knowledge" ("'ilm-i hindawī mahārat-i tamām dārad"), who, however, had no means of subsistence. The grant instructed local agents to confirm the Brahman's "possession" (*ba taṣarruf-i ū*) of 1.95 acres of jungle that local *zamīndārs* had deeded him. Ibid., 19: 317.

Table 7. Distribution of Jungle Land in Tax-free Grants in *sarkār* Sylhet, 1660–1760, by Number of Grants

				Madad-i Ma'āsh		
Brahmottar	Devottar	Vishnottar	Śivottar	Hindu	Muslim	Chirāghī
Aurangzeb (1658–1707)						
4	1	—	—	23	8	1
Shah 'Alam (1707–1712)						
1	—	—	—	—	—	—
Farrukh Siyar (1713–1719)						
—	—	—	—	2	—	—
Muhammad Shah (1719–1748)						
337	54	2	3	22	55	39
Ahmad Shah (1748–1754)						
91	27	1	1	6	35	13
'Alangir II (1754–1759)						
95	25	1	—	3	38	20
Total						
528	107	4	4	56	136	73

Table 8. Distribution of Jungle Land in Tax-free Grants in *sarkār* Sylhet, 1660–1760, by Area in Acres

Reign	Brahmottar	Devottar	Vishnottar	Śivottar	Madad-i Maʿāsh		
					Hindu	Muslim	Chirāghī
Aurangzeb (1658–1707)	39	3.9	—	—	760.5	1,248	195
Shah ʿAlam (1707–1712)	39	—	—	—	75	—	—
Farrukh Siyar (1713–1719)	—	—	—	—	42.9	—	—
Muhammad Shah (1719–1748)	6,146.4	2,593.5	7.8	35.1	429	9,429.3	1,053
Ahmad Shah (1748–1754)	2,741.7	889.2	3.9	3.9	140.4	12,987	608.4
ʿAlamgir II (1754–1759)	3,143.4	1,205.1	15.6	—	132.6	8,455.2	1,579.5
Total	12,109.5	4,691.7	27.3	39	1,580.4	32,119.5	3,435.9
Average size	22.9	43.8	6.8	9.7	28.2	236.1	47.1

Note: The original sources give these figures in units of *qulba*, Arabic for "plow," equal in area to the Bengali *hāl*, also "plow." In Mughal Sylhet, a *qulba* was equal to 12 *kedār*, one *kedār* to 4 *poyā*, one *poyā* to 3 *jaṣṭi*, one *jaṣṭi* to one square *kāhan*, one *kāhan* to 2 *nal*, and one *nal* to 6.25 *dasta*. With one *dasta* equal to 21.625 inches, and with 43,560 square feet equal to one acre, one *qulba* works out to 3.9 acres. See Kamalakanta Gupta, *Śrīhaṭer Bhūmi o Rājasva Babasthā* (Sylhet: Śrīhaṭ Sāhitya Pariṣad, 1966), 26.

> In the home of Madhu Das Sen, a resident of Chakla Sylhet, there is an
> adorned image (*thākur*). But because of a lack of means to perform the
> worship of the deity, in order to provide for the Brahman priests [*pū-
> jārī*] there, and for the welfare of this illustrious place, it is requested
> that 70 *qulbas* [273 acres] of jungle lands lying outside the revenue reg-
> ister be given to Ram Das Sen as a *devottar*. The area having been
> brought under cultivation, its produce will support the aforesaid place
> and its Brahman priests.[86]

The Mughals of Sylhet also patronized Vaishnavas through grants called
vishnottar, and Śaivas through grants called *śivottar*. In 1725, for example,
the government granted four *qulbas* (15.6 acres) of jungle and a house to
Govind Das, a Vaishnava holy man (*bairāgī*) described as "worthy of
honor," *mustahaqq-i wājibu'r-ri'āyat*, an Arabo-Persian phrase that would
have befitted any accomplished Muslim scholar or Sufi.[87]

Grants called *chirāghī* were intended to support the shrines of Muslim
saints. In some cases, local revenue officials merely confirmed land transfers originally made by local *zamīndārs*.[88] In others, pioneers requested
government sanction to clear jungle with a view to using the land's harvests to support a shrine.[89] Still another category, *madad-i ma'āsh*, were
personal, tax-free grants typically awarded to men who had already
founded mosques, as was the case with the *sanad*s of Chittagong. In one
such grant, a certain Shaikh Muhammad built a mosque in the forest but
declared his inability to support its prayer-leader (*churgar*), preacher, and
caller to prayer, or to pay its other expenses. On July 25, 1749, the Sylhet
government responded by bestowing 390 acres (100 *qulbas*) of jungle "for
the expenses of Shaikh Muhammad's mosque and house, together with his
children."[90] The earliest-known grant made to the servants of the shrine
of the famous Shah Jalal in Sylhet city was also a *madad-i ma'āsh*. Dated
August 11, 1663, this document granted 78.2 acres (20 *qulbas*) of jungle
to the devotees at the shrine.[91] Henceforth, from the reign of Aurangzeb

86. Ibid., 17: 14.
87. Ibid., 10.
88. Thus in 1755 a *faqīr* named Rahman Bakhsh was given just over 21 acres (5.5
qulbas) of undeveloped jungle by local *zamīndārs* and *ta'alluqdārs* in support of
the reading of *fātiha* prayers at a local shrine and mosque. Ibid., 19, no. 607. The
same was true for Nasir 'Ali Faqir, to whom Hindu landholders in 1754 donated
3.9 acres for similar purposes. Ibid., 17: 215.
89. For example, on January 1, 1734 the government donated 13 acres of undeveloped jungle to Saiyid Mahdi, a servant of the shrine of Shaikh Ahmad Haji. The
government ordered that the land be made over to the saiyid's possession, and that
its revenues support the lighting of the shrine's candles and the reading of the
Qur'an there. Ibid., 11: 351.
90. Ibid., 21, no. 594.
91. Ibid., no. 353.

(1658–1707) through that of 'Alamgir II (1754–59), devotees of the shrine continued to receive Mughal patronage.[92]

It is known that in 1672–73 the conservative emperor Aurangzeb ordered that all *madad-i ma'āsh* granted to Hindus be repossessed, with future such grants reserved for Muslims only.[93] But Delhi, as the old Persian proverb went, "was still far away." During the emperor's reign, Mughal officers in Sylhet issued more *madad-i ma'āsh* to Hindus after the 1672–73 order than before that date.[94] Still, as is seen in table 7, the Hindu share of these grants steadily decreased in proportion to the Muslim share clear down to the reign of 'Alamgir II, when 38 of 41 *madad-i ma'āsh* grants were issued to Muslims. Moreover, for all reigns combined, such grants given to Muslims averaged nine times the size of those given to Hindus— 170.1 acres and 26.2 acres respectively.

As in Chittagong, the Sylhet grants combined political with economic objectives. A 1753 *sanad* stated that the considerable area of 4,387.5 acres (1,125 *qulbas*) of forest were to be "a *madad-i ma'āsh* for the prayer-leader and for the expenses of the students and those who come and go, and to the laborers and the good deeds of the organization of Maulavi Muhammad Rabi', together with his children."[95] Three years later another *sanad* ordered that an area of 975 acres (250 *qulbas*) of forest lying outside the revenue roll, but capable of being cultivated (*jangala-yi khārij-i jam', lā'iq al-zirā'at*) was to be issued to the same "organization" (*dastgāh*), but with important differences. It was to be used

> for the purpose of the expenses of a mosque, a house, a Qur'an school, the dependents, those who come and go, and the *faqīrs*. It is also a *madad-i ma'āsh* for the laborers and the good deeds of the organization of Maulavi Muhammad Rabi' and his children and dependents . . . It is agreed that once the aforesaid land is brought into cultivation, its produce shall be used to support the expenses of the mosque, the Qur'an school, those who come and go, the *faqīrs*, and his own needs, together

92. These included grants by Aurangzeb (ibid., 16: 388; 21, no. 353; 17: 338), Muhammad Shah (16: 9; 19, no. 639; 21, nos. 351 and 374), Ahmad Shah (21, no. 496), and 'Alamgir II (19, nos. 358 and 578).

93. Irfan Habib, *Agrarian System of Mughal India, 1556–1707* (Bombay: Asia Publishing House, 1963), 311.

94. Fourteen such grants were issued between 1673 and 1707, after the emperor's order, whereas eleven had been issued before his order (1658–72). Three others are of uncertain date. See "Register of Sanads," Sylhet District Collectorate Record Room, 17: 75, 243; 18, nos. 94, 154, 158, 279; 19, nos. 334, 618, 619; 20, nos. 851, 853, 959; 21, nos. 397, 400.

95. "Dar wajh-i madad-i ma'āsh-i churgarī va kharj-i ṭalaba va ṣādir-o-vārid ba fa'alat va karāmat-i dastgāh-i Maulavī Muḥammad Rabī' ma'ahu farzandān." Ibid., vol. 21, no. 608.

with those of his children and dependents, and that he shall busy himself in prayers for the long life of the State.[96]

In these documents, Maulavi Muhammad Rabi' emerges as a figure of considerable charismatic authority and organizational ability. We do not know the identity of the laborers belonging to his "organization," but he must have commanded considerable manpower in order to clear and cultivate stretches of forest the size of these two grants—a combined 5,363 acres. That Muhammad Rabi''s labor force, his mosque, and the Qur'an school were all to be supported by the harvested crops of the lands suggests that the field laborers were themselves affiliates of these Islamic institutions.

The founders of new villages in Sylhet, as in East Bengal generally, had an enormous impact in shaping the subsequent religious orientation of local communities. In 1898, a time when the colonization of some of the Sylhet forest was still within living memory, a Muslim gentleman of northern Sylhet recalled that whenever a new village was founded, a temple to the goddess Kali was built if the founding landlord were a Śākta Hindu, and a temple to Vishnu if he were a Vaishnava. If the majority of the villages were Vaishnava, they would build a shrine (ākhṛā) to Radha and Krishna. If the area were infested with snakes, the patron deity was the snake goddess Manasa, and if the village were founded by Muslims, a shrine to some Muslim pīr would be established.[97] In other words, grants made out to Hindus or Hindu institutions (brahmottar, devottar, vishnottar, śivottar) tended to integrate local communities into a Hindu-ordered cultural universe, while grants authorizing Muslims to establish schools, mosques, or shrines tended to integrate them into an Islamic-ordered cultural universe. Subsequent demographic patterns evolved from these earlier processes.

In Sylhet, although seventeenth- and eighteenth-century forest grants to Hindus outnumbered those to Muslims, two points offset this difference. First, the state alienated a considerably larger total of forest land to Muslims than to Hindus, as a result of which more indigenous peoples living in areas included in the grants would have been exposed to Muslim than to Hindu institutions. Second, grants made to Muslims often mentioned not only "dependents" of the grantee but also those institutional

96. "Dar wajh-i kharj-i masjid, khāna, va madrasa, va muta'alliqān va ṣādir-o-vārid va fuqarā; va madad-i ma'āsh-i fa'alat va karāmat-i dastgāh-i Maulavī Muḥammad Rabī' va farzandān va muta'alliqān-ish . . . muqarrar gashta, ki arāẓī-yi mażkūr-rā ābād sākhta, az muḥāsil-i ān kharji masjid va madrasa va ṣādir-o-vārid va fuqarā va mā-yaḥtāj-i khūd va farzandān va muta'alliqān-ish numūda, ba du'āgū-yi dawām-i daulat . . . [ishtighāl] bāshand." Ibid., no. 609.
97. P. N. Bhattacharjee, "Folkcustom and Folklore of the Sylhet District of India," Man in India 10, no. 1 (January–March 1930): 133.

structures that cleared the forest and maintained the workers' fixed and continued focus. The grants made out for the *dastgāh*, or "organization," of laborers working for Maulavi Muhammad Rabiʿ supported not only the laborers themselves but also the mosque and the Qurʾan school that would regularize the links between the laborers and formal Islam. Grants made over to Śākta Brahmans or Vaishnava *bairāgīs*, on the other hand, mentioned neither dependents nor the sort of community-building mechanisms found in the Muslim grants.

Thus Muslim grants explicitly connected state-sponsored public works projects with the establishment of Islamic institutions. In this way, the documented cases cited above confirm the process of religious and agrarian expansion alluded to in premodern Bengali poetry, in traditions collected by the British in eastern Bengal in the eighteenth and nineteenth centuries, and in traditions still found in the countryside today. Earlier traditions had celebrated men like Pir ʿUmar Shah, who, having come to Noakhali sometime in the eighteenth century, organized local Bengalis into labor teams and converted them to Islam (see pp. 211–12 above). Stories still circulate of how in Mughal times men came from the Middle East to the Habiganj region, where they organized the local population into groups to cut the jungle and cultivate rice. As such communities acquired an Islamic identity, they conferred on their leaders a sanctified identity appropriate to Islamic civilization, and especially to the culture of institutional Sufism, as witnessed by the growth of shrines over the graves of holy men throughout the Bengal frontier.

Summary

In the eastern delta, where settled agrarian life was far less advanced than in the west in the seventeenth and eighteenth centuries, Islam more than other culture systems became identified with a developing agrarian social order. As state-supported pioneers established Islamic institutions in formerly forested areas, three different kinds of frontier—the economic frontier separating field and forest, the political frontier separating Mughal from non-Mughal administration, and the religious frontier separating Islam and non-Islam—fused into one.

Yet Islamic institutions were by no means the only ones that grew with Bengal's advancing frontiers. In the forests of both Chittagong and Sylhet, new communities formed around pioneers and institutions associated with Hindu deities. In fact, the active delta was so ripe for cultural and economic development that even Christian pioneers made an impact, and this without the benefit of Mughal patronage. In 1713 the French Jesuit Père Barbier journeyed through Chittagong and into the interior of what is now

Noakhali District, where he encountered a community of Christian peasants organized around the authority of a local patriarch. "At five days' distance from *Chatigan* [Chittagong]," he wrote,

> we made a detour of one day to visit a Christianity [i.e., a Christian community] to be found in a place named *Bouloüa* [Bhallua, northwest of Noakhali town]. God maintains and directs it Himself immediately: for it is rare that any missionary goes to visit it. . . .
> The chief of these Christians is an old man who has five sons, all married. Their family, and the labouring folk who are gathered around them (for they have taken arable lands) form a village of three to four hundred persons. The laborious life which they lead, added to the vigilance and attention of the chief, keep them in the greatest innocence.[98]

The old man (*vieillard*) Barbier encountered and identified as "le chef de ces Chrétiens" was apparently not a European but a Bengali Christian, for the Frenchman had to employ an interpreter to communicate with him.[99] Evidently the man had managed to forge for himself a clientele from amongst the local population, in effect functioning as a petty *zamīndār* of a local community to which he gave both religious and economic leadership.[100] In this instance, it was neither a Muslim nor a Hindu institution but a fledgling Christian one that grew with agricultural development on the Bengal frontier.

Nonetheless, while Bengal's agrarian frontier accommodated Hindu and even Christian institutional growth, it was a Muslim gentry that received the lion's share of patronage from Mughal district revenue officers. It was they who acquired the greatest amount of state-recognized control over patches of virgin jungle, who attracted the most local labor for reducing the land to rice paddy, and who built the mosques or shrines that in turn served as nuclei for the economic and religious transformation of microregions. Greater patronage ultimately favored the growth of rural Muslim communities over the growth of communities professing other religious identities.

It would be wrong, however, to explain religious change here or else-

98. H. Hosten, S.J., "The Earliest Recorded Episcopal Visitation of Bengal, 1712–1715," *Bengal Past and Present* 6 (July–December 1910): 210. Trans. Hosten.
99. He may have been a renegade from Chittagong city, where there dwelled at that time a local Christian community of over two thousand persons converted by Portuguese missions. Ibid., 207.
100. That the chieftain had recruited his labor force from amongst the local population and did not bring it with him from outside Noakhali is suggested by the phrase "the labouring folk who are gathered around them (for they have taken arable lands)." The French original reads: "les gens de travail qui se sont rangés auprès d'eux (car ils ont pris des terres à cultiver)." *Lettres édifiantes et curieuses écrites des missions étrangères* (Paris: J. G. Merigot, 1781), 13: 282–83.

where as simply a cultural dimension of political or economic change, or to understand Islam itself as a timeless and fixed system of beliefs and rituals that the people of the delta passively accepted. For in the midst of the dramatic socioeconomic changes taking place in premodern Bengal, Islam creatively evolved into an ideology of "world-construction"—an ideology of forest-clearing and agrarian expansion, serving not only to legitimize but to structure the very socioeconomic changes taking place on the frontier. On the one hand, Islamic institutions proved sufficiently flexible to accommodate the non-Brahmanized religious culture of premodern Bengal. On the other, the religious traditions already present in eastern Bengal made accommodations with the amalgam of rites, rituals, and beliefs that were associated with the village mosques and shrines then proliferating in their midst. In the process, Islamic and Bengali worldviews and cosmologies became fused in dynamic and creative ways, a topic to which we now turn.[101]

101. "Creative adaptation" perhaps best describes this process. For my general approach to culture change, which stresses the active, creative role played by those undergoing it as opposed to the role of "missionaries" or other carriers, I acknowledge a great intellectual debt to my teacher, John R. W. Smail. Writing of Indonesian history, Professor Smail long ago observed, "Remembering that the essence of acculturation is the acceptance of change by the acculturating group—and hence that there can be no question, in the last analysis, of forced culture change—we can bring the problem of culture change in late colonial Indonesia under the more suggestive heading of creative adaptation." John R. W. Smail, "On the Possibility of an Autonomous History of Modern Southeast Asia," *Journal of Southeast Asian History* 2, no. 2 (July 1961): 91.

10   The Rooting of Islam in Bengal

Why are you afraid of demons, when you have got the
religious books?

> A *mullā* in Vijaya Gupta's poem *Padma*
> *Purāṇa* (1494)

From the perspective of Mughal authorities in Dhaka or Murshidabad, the
hundreds of tiny rural mosques and shrines established in the interior of
eastern Bengal served as agents for the transformation of jungle into arable
land and the construction of stable microsocieties loyal to the Mughal
state. From a religious perspective, however, these same institutions facilitated the diffusion of uniquely Islamic conceptions of divine and human
authority among groups under their socioeconomic influence. Government documents from the late seventeenth and early eighteenth centuries
note the establishment of new Friday assemblies or "circles" (*iqāmat-i
ḥalqa-yi jum'a*) at mosques or shrines patronized by the Mughal government, and refer to such communities as "dependents" (*vā bastagān*) of
those same institutions.[1]

In forest tracts recently cleared for cultivation, the appearance of such
assemblies coincided with the establishment of religious rites such as the
fātiḥa at rural mosques and shrines. Named after the opening verse of the
Qur'an, which would have been recited on the occasion, the *fātiḥa* was
a simple rite of remembrance of the dead, usually followed by a feast.
One type consisted of intercessory prayers offered to the Shi'a successors (*imām*) to the leadership of the Prophet Muhammad.[2] In another, the
fātiḥa-yi darvīshī, prayers were offered in memory of local *darvīsh*es, that
is, Muslim holy men.[3] Lists of persons supported by village mosques or

1. "Kanun Daimer Nathi," Chittagong District Collectorate Record Room, No. 64,
bundle 78, case no. 5027; No. 7, bundle 62, case no. 4005.
2. *Fātiḥa-yi imāmīn-i aiyām-i 'Āshūrā*. Ibid., No. 251, bundle 55, case no. 3568;
No. 127, bundle 63, case no. 4049; No. 232, bundle 30, case no. 1935.
3. For example, in 1749 the Mughal government granted Shaikh Jan Allah of Satkania Thana 25.6 acres of jungle so that he might perform *fātiḥa-yi darvīshī* at a
shrine entrusted to him. Ibid., No. 196, bundle 19, case no. 1093.

268

shrines frequently mention "leaders in *fātiḥa*," "readers of *fātiḥa*," or simply "Qur'an-readers."[4]

The cumulative effect of such simple observances was to promote the cult of Allah and associated lesser agencies in the religious universe of eastern Bengal. This process is usually glossed as "religious conversion," but the use of this phrase requires a precise understanding of both "religion" and "conversion." If one accepts the definition of religion proposed by the anthropologist Melford Spiro—"an institution consisting of culturally patterned interaction with culturally postulated superhuman beings"[5]—then it follows that, whatever other changes might occur, a society's acquisition of a new religious identity will involve a change in the identity of the superhuman beings postulated by that society. In tracing the process of Islamization in pre-modern Bengal, then, we need to focus on the increasing attention given to Allah, as well as to beings such as Iblis (Satan), Adam, Muhammad, the angel Gabriel, a host of minor spirits (*jinn*), and the many saints (*auliyā* or *pīrs*) who entered popular traditions as intermediaries between human society and Allah. The term *conversion* is perhaps misleading when applied to this process, since it ordinarily connotes a sudden and total transformation in which a prior religious identity is wholly rejected and replaced by a new one. In reality, in Bengal, as in South Asian history generally, the process of Islamization as a social phenomenon proceeded so gradually as to be nearly imperceptible.

Nonetheless, from the position of historical retrospect, one may discern three analytically distinct aspects to the process, each referring to a different relationship between Islamic and Indian superhuman agencies. One of these I am calling *inclusion;* a second, *identification;* and a third, *displacement.* By *inclusion* is meant the process by which Islamic superhuman agencies became accepted in local Bengali cosmologies alongside local divinities already embedded therein. By *identification* is meant the process by which Islamic superhuman agencies ceased merely to coexist alongside Bengali agencies, but actually merged with them, as when the Arabic name Allah was used interchangeably with the Sanskrit Niranjan. And finally, by *displacement* is meant the process by which the names of Islamic superhuman agencies replaced those of other divinities in local cosmologies. The three terms *inclusion, identification,* and *displacement* are of course only

4. *Muṣalliān-i fātiḥa,* or *fātiḥa-khwānī,* as in ibid., No. 31, bundle 77, case no. 4971; No. 40, bundle 47, case no. 3054. "Qur'an readers" were titled *Qur'ān-khwānī,* or *tilāwat,* as in No. 65, bundle 73, case no. 4677; No. 72, bundle 63, case no. 4100; No. 113, bundle 35, case no. 2296.
5. Melford E. Spiro, "Religion: Problems of Definition and Explanation," in *Anthropological Approaches to the Study of Religion,* ed. Michael Banton (London: Tavistock Publications, 1969), 96.

heuristic categories, proposed in an attempt to organize and grasp intellectually what was on the ground a very complex and fluid process.

Inclusion

In the corpus of premodern Bengali literature celebrating indigenous deities such as Manasa, Chandi, Satya Pir, Dharma, or Daksin Ray, one readily sees local cosmologies expanding in order to accommodate new superhuman beings introduced by foreign Muslims.[6] For example, we have seen that the *Rāy-Maṅgala*, a poem composed in 1686, celebrated both the Bengali tiger god Daksin Ray ("King of the South") and a Muslim pioneer named Badiʿ Ghazi Khan. According to this poem, conflict between the two was resolved, not by one defeating or displacing the other, but by the elevation of Badiʿ Ghazi Khan to the status of a revered saint, and by the peaceful coexistence of the two figures, who would thenceforth hold a dual religious authority over the Sundarban forests of southern Bengal. This dual authority was represented by the installation of the symbol of the tiger god's head at the burial mound of the Muslim saint. The two were not, however, fused into a single religious personage, but remained mutually distinct. A separation of the indigenous and the exogenous was also maintained at a higher level. The agent who resolved the conflict between Daksin Ray and Badiʿ Ghazi Khan was neither the Hindu god Krishna nor the Islamic prophet Muhammad, but a single figure represented as half Krishna and half Muhammad.[7] Islamic superhuman agencies were thus associated with indigenous agencies at two levels, though not yet fully identified with them.[8]

6. Bhattacharyya, "Tiger-Cult and Its Literature," 49–56; Tarafdar, *Husain Shahi Bengal,* 17–18, 164–66, 233–35; P. K. Maity, *Historical Studies in the Cult of the Goddess Manasā* (Calcutta: Punthi Pustak, 1966), 182. See esp. Asim Roy, *The Islamic Syncretistic Tradition in Bengal* (Princeton: Princeton University Press, 1983).
7. Bhattacharyya, "Tiger-Cult and Its Literature," 49–50.
8. In parts of Bengal this sort of easy inclusion has persisted down to modern times. In 1956 it was noted that fishermen in the West Bengal Sundarban forests, before putting their nets to water, typically performed *pūjā* to the forest goddess Bon Bibi (literally, "forest goddess") as a ritual intended to protect them from harm. For this purpose a small thatched and bamboo hut was constructed, in which was placed a clay image of Bon Bibi seated on a tiger. Flanking her on her right was an image of Daksin Ray, depicted as a strong, stout man standing with a sword. Behind him stood a bearded Muslim *faqīr* known as Ajmal, and in front of Daksin Ray lay the body and severed head of a young boy. Although the names and functions of the figures in the 1956 account differ from those of the seventeenth-century poem, the elements of both accounts—a tiger deity, a soldier, and a superhuman agent identified with Islam—have remained constant over the centuries, distinct from one another but included within a single religious cosmology. H. L. Sarkar, "Note

The inclusion of Muslim alongside local divinities is also seen in the rich tradition of folk ballads passed on orally by generations of professional bards. Since they were normally preceded by invocations (*bandanā*) in which Bengal's rustic bards invoked any and all divinities considered locally powerful, these ballads tell us much about the religious universe of the unlettered audience to whom they were sung. Here we may consider the opening lines of "Nizam Dacoit," a ballad of Chittagong District dating from the seventeenth or eighteenth centuries:[9]

> First of all I bow down to the Supreme Deity [Prabhu], and secondly to (the same Omnipotent Being conceived as) the Creator [Sirjan]; and thirdly to the benign Incarnation of Light. The Koran and other scriptural texts I regard as revelation—the sacred utterances of the Lord [Prabhu] himself.
>
> When the Lord was engrossed in deep meditation, the luminous figure of Mahomet flashed before His mind's eye, and as He gazed and gazed upon the vision, He began to feel a certain softening of the heart. So out of love, He created the prophet Mahomet and sent him down to the earth as the very flower of the Robikul (the solar race). He next created the entire universe. Had there been no incarnation of Mahomet, there would not have been established the seat of God [*arskors*, from Ar., 'arsh, "throne of God"] in all the three worlds.
>
> All reverence to Abdulla and to Amina; salutations at the feet of her, who bore in the womb Mahomet (the deliverer) of the earth. All honour to the city of Mecca in the west and to the Mahomedan saints; and further west, I do reverence to the city of Medina—the burial place of our Rosul [Prophet]. Bibi Fatemah, daughter of Rosul, honoured of all, was called "mother" by all excepting Ali.
>
> In the north, I offer my tribute of respects to the Himalayas, beneath whose snowy heights lies the entire universe. I bow down to the rising sun in the east, and also to the shrine of Vrindavan, together with Lord Krishna, the Eternal Lover of sweet Radha. I next do reverence to the milky rivers and the ocean, dashing against the two shores, with sandy shoals in the middle. In all the four directions, I tender my

---

on the Worship of the Deity *Bon Bibi* in the Sundarbans," *Journal of the Asiatic Society of Bengal* 22, no. 2 (1956): 211–12.

9. Dinesh Chandra Sen, who collected and published this sort of oral folk literature in the early twentieth century, dated this particular ballad to the fourteenth century. But a recent study of the collector's pioneering work concludes that "D. C. Sen, obviously influenced by his patriotic feelings, dated the ballads rather too far into the past; . . . unable to give other reasons than rather vague 'impressions of antiquity' or social aspects which, as known, can be very misleading in such cases. There are, no doubt, old or even ancient portions, but the whole treatment of the stories, their ideology and psychological approach, point rather to more recent times." Dusan Zbavitel, *Bengali Folk-Ballads from Mymensingh and the Problem of Their Authenticity* (Calcutta: University of Calcutta, 1963), 14.

respectful compliments to all the four sects of the Mussalmans. I pay homage to Mother Earth [Basumātā] below and to the heavens above.

I bow down to Mother Isamati in the village of Raunya and also to the mosque of the great Pir at Nawapara. I next make my *salam* to the hill of Kavalyamura to the right and the mosque of Hirmai to the left. The great upholders of truth are passed through these tracts. The river Sankha is also sacred. . . . Tendering my regards to all the sacred spots, I proceed onwards and arrive at Sita Ghat [Sitakund], where I offer my tribute of worshipful regards to that ideal of womanly virtue—Sita Devi—and also to her lord Raghunatha [Rama].[10]

Clearly, the religious culture of the area in which this ballad was sung included a broad spectrum of superhuman agencies, ranging from nearby *pīr*s and rivers to the distant Himalayas and even the sublime Absolute of Indian philosophy. Above all, the invocation illustrates how easily Islamic superhuman figures could be included in what appears to have been a fluid, expandable cosmology. As in the case of the poem *Rāy-Maṅgala*, moreover, the poet did not identify these powers with one another, but treated them as separate entities.

The poem also includes both indigenous and exogenous religious ideas. On the one hand, we see the tenacity of the Bengali emphasis on divine power as manifested in female agency—Mother Isamati, Mother Earth, Sita, and Radha. It is significant that this emphasis is extended to include prominent females of Islamic history: special reverence goes to Amina, the Prophet's mother, and Fatima, his daughter, is referred to as "mother" to all except her husband, 'Ali. On the other hand, the poem shows that themes wholly foreign to the delta had also infiltrated the religious universe of the Bengali countryside. The emphasis on Light, the association of Light with the Prophet Muhammad, and the creation of the world as the result of God's desire to see himself, all confirm what we know from Mughal government documents examined in previous chapters—that many of the men who played decisive roles in disseminating Islamic ideas in Bengal were steeped in Sufi metaphysics.

It is instructive to compare what these folk ballads have to say about the establishment of new mosques and shrines in eastern Bengal with what we know from the Mughal records discussed in chapters 8 and 9. Whereas government *sanads* describe the founding of local institutions from the perspective of the Mughal bureaucratic machine, the Bengali folk ballad tradition views the same process from the perspective of its rural clientele.

---

10. Dinesh Chandra Sen, ed. and trans., *Eastern Bengal Ballads*, 2: 283–84. The text is to be found in *Prācīn Pūrba Baṅga Gītikā*, ed. Ksitish Maulik (Calcutta: Mukherjee Publishers, 1972), 4: 308–10.

Listen to the sixteenth-century ballad "Kanka and Lila," set in what is now Mymensingh District. "At this time," goes the ballad,

> there came a Mahomedan *pir* to that village. He built a mosque in its outskirts, and for the whole day sat under a fig tree. The whole space he cleared with care so that there was not one tuft of grass left. His fame soon spread far and wide. Everybody talked of the occult powers that he possessed. If a sick man called on him he would cure him at once by dust or some trifle touched by him. He read and spoke the innermost thoughts of a man before he opened his mouth. He took a little dust in his hand and out of it prepared sugar balls to the astonishment of the boys and girls who gathered around him. They greatly relished these presents from him. Hundreds of men and women came every day to pay him their respects. Presents of rice, fruits, and other delicious food, goats, chickens and fowls came in large quantities to his doors. Of these offerings the *pir* did not touch a bit but freely distributed all amongst the poor.[11]

Although no known Mughal *sanads* pertain to this man or the mosque he built, it is likely that he, like the many *pīrs* and mosque functionaries discussed in the preceding chapters, had received government support in the form of a tax-free land grant intended for clearing jungle, establishing a rice-cultivating community, and building the mosque. In any event, it is evident that, by virtue of his charisma and his association with magic, the *pīr* of this ballad was understood as spiritually powerful. Villagers would likely have conferred on him an intermediate status between the human world and the transcendent power associated with his mosque.

Given that this part of Bengal was overwhelmingly Muslim by the time of the earliest census reports in the late nineteenth century, it is tempting to hypothesize that the holy man's intermediary status helped in easing the local community's transfer of religious allegiances from non-Islam to Islam. But what does that actually mean? One can by no means assume that the gap between "Islam" and "non-Islam" in sixteenth-century Mymensingh was the same as that of the late twentieth century. Indeed, the idea of Islam as a closed system with definite and rigid boundaries is itself largely a product of nineteenth- and twentieth-century reform movements, whereas for rural Bengalis of the premodern period, the line separating "non-Islam" from "Islam" appears rather to have been porous, tenuous, and shifting. Indeed, such boundaries seem hardly to have been present at all. Popular literature dating from the seventeenth century, such as the Mymensingh ballads cited above, evolved amongst communities of people who were remarkably open to accepting any sort of agency, human

11. Dinesh Chandra Sen, ed. and trans., *Eastern Bengal Ballads*, 1: 219–20; text, *Prācīn Pūrba Baṅga Gītikā*, ed. Maulik, 3: 33.

or superhuman, that might assist them in coping with life's everyday problems.

On this point we can profit from the insights of modern ethnographic research. Writing of religious change among the Yoruba of modern Nigeria, the anthropologist J. D. Y. Peel observes: "The more religion is regarded as a technique, whose effectiveness the individual may estimate for himself, the readier will the individual be to try out other techniques which seem promising. He will not be inclined to rely exclusively on one technique just for the sake of simplicity, nor will he prefer other techniques." [12] Similarly, Melford Spiro notes the ruthless pragmatism that the Ifaluk peoples of the Central Carolines (in the western Pacific Ocean) had toward superhuman power. "When I asked a group of Ifaluk men about the power of the spirit whose therapeutic intervention was being invoked in a healing ceremony, their response was 'We don't know if he is powerful or not; maybe he is, maybe he isn't. If he is not, we'll throw him away' (i.e., we will no longer concern ourselves with him)." [13] In the 1950s Igor Kopytoff remarked on the spirit of pragmatism with which the Suku of the Belgian Congo (now Zaire) assessed religious power. "There is a pervasive assumption in Suku culture," wrote Kopytoff,

> that somewhere, somehow, other methods exist for dealing with the culturally-given causes of misfortune—methods already known to others or as yet undiscovered. This instrumental orientation makes the system very much akin to a technology which is ever-receptive to innovation and trials of new means for the same ends. . . . Spectacular abandonment of old medicines does not mean disbelief in the old as much as the acceptance of the greater efficacy of the new, in somewhat the same way that the adoption of a diesel engine does not mean the rejection of the principles of steam power. When an innovation is seen to be a failure, a return to the old proven techniques is a logical step. [14]

It is this pragmatic attitude to religious phenomena that characterizes the phase of religious change in Bengal I am calling inclusion.

In sum, the worldview of the people here considered was the very opposite of a zero-sum-game cosmology, in which the addition of any one element requires the elimination of another. When Bengali communities be-

12. J. D. Y. Peel, "Syncretism and Religious Change," *Comparative Studies in Society and History* 10 (1967–68): 124–25.
13. Melford Spiro, "Religion and the Irrational," in *Symposium on New Approaches to the Study of Religion*, ed. June Helms (Seattle: American Ethnological Society, 1964), 110.
14. Igor Kopytoff, "Classifications of Religious Movements: Analytical and Synthetic," in *Symposium on New Approaches to the Study of Religion*, ed. June Helms (Seattle: American Ethnological Society, 1964), 78–79.

gan incorporating techniques or beliefs that we would call "Islamic" into their village systems, they did not consider these as challenging other techniques or beliefs already in the system, far less as requiring their outright abandonment. The holy man who appeared in sixteenth-century rural Mymensingh was locally believed to have brought something new to the village, some new access to superhuman power that the villagers had never before witnessed. Everyone spoke of his occult skills and of his ability to cure the sick and read the minds of others. But his arrival did not require a rejection of other cults—dedicated perhaps to the goddess Chandi or Manasa, the god Krishna, or a tiger god—that were locally familiar and known to be efficacious in tapping superhuman power. Nor did the saint come to the village proclaiming with great éclat that a New Age had dawned, a New World been ushered in. As Kopytoff writes of the Suku: "Instead of the promise of a new world, we have but the discovery of a new gimmick for handling the same old world."[15] This predisposition to accept new "gimmicks" to deal with old problems, while not itself constituting the full religious transformation that subsequent generations would call "conversion," was nonetheless a necessary first step along this road.

Identification

Analytically distinct from merely including Islamic with local superhuman beings in an expanding, accordionlike cosmology was the process of identifying superhuman beings with one another. A classic example of this is seen in a bilingual Arabic and Sanskrit inscription from a thirteenth-century mosque in the coastal town of Veraval in Gujarat. Dated 1264, the inscription records that an Iranian merchant from Hormuz named Nur al-Din Firuz sponsored the construction of a mosque there. The Arabic text refers to the deity worshiped in the mosque as Allah, and describes Nur al-Din as "the king (*sulṭān*) of sea-men, the king of the kings of traders," and "the sun of Islam and the Muslims." By contrast, the Sanskrit text of the same inscription addresses the supreme god by the names Viśvanātha ("lord of the universe"), Śunyarūpa ("one whose form is of the void"), and Viśvarūpa ("having various forms"). Moreover, it records that the mosque was built in the year "662 of the Rasūla Mahammada, the preceptor (*bō-dhaka*) of the sailors (*nau-jana*) devoted to Viśvanātha." The Sanskrit version thus identifies the deity worshiped in the mosque as Viśvanātha, and the prophet of Islam as a *bōdhaka*—that is, "preceptor," "elder," or "wise man." Similarly, it styles the mosque's builder, Nur al-Din Firuz, as a *dharma-bhāndaya*, or "supporter of *dharma*"—that is, cosmic/social order

15. Ibid., 80.

as understood in classical Indian thought.[16] So, while the Arabic text presents the worldview of the Muslim patron, the Sanskrit text reflects that of the proximate Indian population, which simply identified Islam's God with Viśvanātha, Islam's prophet with an Indian *bōdhaka*, and the Muslim patron of this particular mosque with a "supporter of *dharma*." In short, the local Gujarati population, while *looking at* a monument its patrons dedicated to Allah, *saw* one dedicated to Viśvanātha.

In Bengali literature dating from the sixteenth century—romances, epics, narratives, and devotional poems—we find identifications of a similar type.[17] The sixteenth-century poet Haji Muhammad identified the Arabic Allah with Gosāī (Skt., "Master"),[18] Saiyid Murtaza identified the Prophet's daughter Fatima with Jagat-jananī (Skt., "Mother of the world"),[19] and Saiyid Sultan identified the God of Adam, Abraham, and Moses with Prabhu (Skt., "Lord") or, more frequently, Niranjan (Skt., "One without color," i.e., without qualities).[20] Later, the eighteenth-century poet 'Ali Raja identified Allah with Niranjan, Iśvar (Skt., "God"), Jagat Iśvar (Skt., "God of the universe"), and Kartār (Skt., "Creator").[21] Even while forest pioneers on the eastern frontier were planting the institutional foundations of Islamic rituals, then, Bengali poets deepened the semantic meaning of these rituals by identifying the lore and even the superhuman agencies of an originally foreign creed with those of the local culture.

More than just translating Perso-Islamic romantic literature into the Bengali language, these poets attempted to adapt the whole range of Perso-Islamic civilization to the Bengali cultural universe.[22] This included Perso-

---

16. D. C. Sircar, "Veraval Inscription of Chaulukya-Vaghela Arujuna, 1264 A.D.," *Epigraphia Indica* 24 (1961–62): 141, 150.
17. From the thirteenth century on, Muslim Turks in Bengal built mosques with dedicatory Arabic inscriptions similar to that of the Veraval mosque. Unfortunately, though, no Bengali mosque has yet been found with a companion Sanskrit or Bengali text that might tell us how non-Muslims perceived such mosques and the deity worshiped there. It is only in premodern Bengali literature that we begin to see identifications of the type illustrated in the Veraval bilingual inscription.
18. Haji Muhammad, *Nūr Jamāl* (Dhaka University Library MS. No. 374, sl. 260), fol. 6 mc. Cited in Asim Roy, "Islam in the Environment of Medieval Bengal" (Ph.D. diss., Australian National University, 1970), 194.
19. Saiyid Murtaza, *Yoga-Qalandar* (Dhaka University Library MS. No. 547, sl. 394), fol. 1a. Cited in Roy, "Islam in the Environment," 299.
20. Saiyid Sultan, *Nabī-Baṃśa*, ed. Ahmed Sharif (Dhaka: Bangla Academy, 1978), 1: 1ff.
21. 'Ali Raja, *Jñāna-sāgara* (Dhaka University Library MS. No. 146b, sl. 9), fols. 109, 215, 216. Cited in Roy, "Islam in the Environment," 199, 202.
22. Actually, these literati were building on a long tradition of Persianization. As a result of prolonged contact between Persianized Turks and Bengalis since the early

Islamic aesthetic and literary sensibilities, as well as conceptions of divinity and superhuman agency. Thus the Nile river was identified with the Ganges, and a story set in biblical Egypt alludes to dark forests filled with tigers and elephants. The countryside in such stories abounds with banana and mango trees, peacocks and chirping parrots; people eat fish, curried rice, ghee, and sweet yogurt, and chew betel; women adorn themselves with sandal paste and glitter in silk saris and glass and gold bangles. Everywhere one smells the sweet aroma of fresh rice plants.[23]

The reasons poets employed this mode of literary transmission are not hard to find. Already exposed somewhat to Brahmanic ideas of the proper social order and its supporting ideological framework, the rural masses of the eastern delta's expanding rice frontier were familiar with the Hindu epics. One sixteenth-century poet wrote that "Muslims as well as Hindus in every home" would read the *Mahābhārata*, the great religious epic of classical India. Another poet of that century wrote of Muslims being moved to tears on hearing of Rama's loss of his beloved Sita in the epic *Rāmāyaṇa*.[24] In addition to such Vaishnava sympathies, the people of this period were also saturated with the *maṅgala-kāvya* literature that celebrated the exploits, power, and grace of specifically Bengali folk deities like Manasa and Chandi. It is hardly surprising, then, that romantic tales from the Islamic tradition drew on this rich indigenous substratum of religious culture. For example, an eighteenth-century Bengali version of the popular Iranian story of Joseph and Zulaikha employs imagery clearly recalling Radha's passionate love for Krishna, the central motif of the Bengali Vaishnava devotional movement. "Your face is as bright as the full moon," runs a description of the biblical Joseph,

> and your eyes are black as if bees are buzzing round them. Your eyebrows are like the bow of Kama [the Indian god of love] and your ears like lotuses which grow on shore. Your waist is as slim as that of a prowling tigress. Your step is as light as a bird's and when they see it even sages forget all else. Your body is as perfect as a well-made string

thirteenth century, many Persian words and phrases were absorbed into the Bengali language. These became so thoroughly indigenized that Bengalis today are often unaware of their foreign origin. In 1966 Shaikh Ghulam Maqsud Hilali published a lexicon of over nine thousand Bengali words and expressions of Persian origin. See Shaikh Ghulam Maqsud Hilali, *Perso-Arabic Elements in Bengali*, ed. Muhammad Enamul Haq (Dacca: Central Board for Development of Bengali, 1967).

23. See Mannan, *Emergence and Development*, 86–102; Roy, "Islam in the Environment," 315–21.

24. Asim Roy, "The Social Factors in the Making of Bengali Islam," *South Asia* 3 (August 1973): 29.

of pearls. A maid, therefore, cannot control herself and longs for your embrace.[25]

Similarly, the Sufi Saiyid Sultan, the epic poet of the late sixteenth-century Chittagong region, spares no detail in endowing Eve with the attributes of a Bengali beauty. She uses sandal powder and wraps her hair in a bun adorned with a string of pearls and flowers. She wears black eye paste, and a pearl necklace is draped around her neck. Adam was struck by the beauty of the spot (*sindur*) on her forehead "because it reminded him of the sun in the sky."[26]

The authors of this literature, Bengali Muslims, consciously presented Islamic imagery and ideas in terms readily familiar to a rural population of nominal Muslims saturated with folk Bengali and Hindu religious ideas.[27] Yet in doing so they felt a degree of anguish. Although certain that Arabic was the appropriate literary vehicle for the transmission of Islamic ideas, they could not use a language with which their Bengali audience was unfamiliar. Referring to this dilemma, the seventeenth-century poet 'Abd al-Nabi wrote, "I am afraid in my heart lest God should be annoyed with me for having rendered Islamic scriptures in Bengali. But I put aside my fear and firmly resolve to write for the good of common people."[28] Similar feelings were voiced by Saiyid Sultan, who lamented,

> Nobody remembers God and the Prophet;
> The consciousness of many ages has passed.
> Nobody has transmitted this knowledge in the local language.
> From sorrow, I determined
> To talk more and more about the Prophet.
> It is my misfortune that I was born a Bengali.
> None of the Bengalis understand Arabic,
> And so not one has understood any of the discourse of his own
>   religion.[29]

25. Mannan, *Emergence and Development*, 99. Mannan's translation.
26. Saiyid Sultan, *Nabī-Baṃśa*, 1: 115.
27. As we saw in Chapter 5, non-Bengali sources attest to the emergence by Saiyid Sultan's time of a rural Muslim community in the area in which that poet lived. In 1567 Cesare Federici found Muslims inhabiting Sondwip, a large island that is actually visible from Sitakund, in northern Chittagong District, where Saiyid Sultan lived and wrote some twenty years later.
28. 'Abd al-Nabi, *Vijay-Hamza*, quoted in Muhammad Enamul Huq, *Muslim Bāṅglā Sāhitya*, 2d ed. (Dacca: Pakistan Publications, 1965), 214–15. Translated by Rafiuddin Ahmed, "Conflict and Contradictions in Bengali Islam: Problems of Change and Adjustment," in *Sharī'at and Ambiguity in South Asian Islam*, ed. Katherine P. Ewing (Berkeley and Los Angeles: Universitiy of California Press, 1988), 122.
29. Cited in Ahmed Sharif, *Saiyid Sultān: Tār Granthābalī o tār Jūg* (Dhaka: Bangla Academy, 1972), 203.

Such expressions of tension between Bengali culture and the perceived "foreignness" of Islam were typical among those who were outsiders to the rural experience—whether they were members of Bengal's premodern Muslim literati, European travelers in Bengal, or modern-day observers.

But the rural masses do not appear to have been troubled by such tensions, or even to have noticed them. For them, an easy identification of the exogenous with the indigenous—that is, the "Arabic" with the "Bengali"—had resulted from prolonged cultural contact, in the course of which Allah and the various superhuman agencies associated with him gradually seeped into local cosmologies. What the anthropologist Jack Goody has written of modern West Africa applies equally to premodern Bengal: "I know of no society in West Africa which does not make an automatic identification of their own High God with the Allah of the Muslims and the Jehovah of the Christians. The process is not a matter of conversion but of identification. Nevertheless, it prepares the ground for change, here as elsewhere."[30] An excellent illustration of this is found in the earliest preaching of Christianity among the pagan Greeks. Addressing the council of Athens in the first Christian century, the apostle Paul declared:

> Men of Athens, I have seen for myself how extremely scrupulous you
> are in all religious matters, because I noticed, as I strolled round admiring your sacred monuments, that you had an altar inscribed: To an Unknown God. Well, the God whom I proclaim is in fact the one whom
> you already worship without knowing it.[31]

Instead of demanding outright rejection of the Athenian pantheon, Paul not only complimented the Greeks on their religious scruples but identified the Christian deity with an indigenous one, thereby making a transition from the "old" to the "new" both possible and acceptable.[32]

We see an instance of identification in premodern Bengal in the history of the cult of the legendary holy man Satya Pīr. Over a hundred manuscript works concerning this cult have been identified, most of them dating from the eighteenth century, with the earliest of them dating to the six-

30. Jack Goody, "Religion, Social Change, and the Sociology of Conversion," in *Changing Social Structure in Ghana*, ed. Goody (London: International African Institute, 1975), 103.
31. Acts 17:22–23.
32. "The Lo Dagaa [people of West Africa] did not initially think of the acceptance of Christianity as conversion, because the introduction of a new cult does not involve a displacement of other gods," Jack Goody notes ("Religion, Social Change, and the Sociology of Conversion," 103).

teenth century.[33] The emergence of the cult thus coincided chronologically with the growth of agrarian communities focused on the tiny thatched mosques and shrines that proliferated throughout rural East Bengal in the seventeenth and eighteenth centuries. The early literature written in praise of Satya Pir portrays a folk society innocent of hardened communal boundaries, and one that freely assimilated a variety of beliefs and practices that were "in the air" in Bengal's premodern religious environment. A text devoted to the cult composed by the poet Sankaracharya in 1664 identifies Satya Pir as the son of one of Sultan 'Ala al-Din Husain Shah's daughters, and hence a Muslim. Another version, composed by Krishnahari Das, begins with invocations to Allah and stories of the Prophet. Yet the same text portrays Satya Pir as born of the goddess Chandbibi and as having come into the world to redress all human ills in the Kali Yuga, the last and lowest Hindu epoch preceding a period of restored justice and harmony. Other texts explicitly identify this Satya Pir with the divinity Satya Narayan, understood as a form of the Brahmanic god Vishnu.[34]

Some scholars have understood the Satya Pir cult, and indeed Bengali folk religion generally, in terms of a synthesis of Islam and Hinduism.[35] But such thinking simply projects back into the premodern period notions of religion that became widespread in the colonial nineteenth and twentieth centuries, and that postulated the more or less timeless existence of two separate and self-contained communities in Bengal, adhering to two separate and self-contained religious systems, "Hinduism" and "Islam." Reinforcing this understanding was the objective polarization of colonial Bengali society into politically conscious groups drawn along communal lines. Thus it was at this time that Muslims ceased worshiping Satya Pir, while Satya Narayan became identified as an exclusively Hindu deity worshiped only by Hindus.[36] In reality, though, such polarized religious com-

33. Communication from Tony K. Stewart, July 1990. Although study of the Satya Pir cult has thus far been rudimentary, Stewart has begun a careful investigation with a view to translating representative samples of Satya Pir literature and to tracing the cult's evolution over time.
34. Dinesh Chandra Sen, *The Folk Literature of Bengal* (1920; reprint, Delhi: B.R. Publishing Corporation, 1985), 99–102.
35. Thus the modern folklorist D. C. Sen interpreted the Satya Pir cult as a hybrid cult synthesized by "Hindus" and "Muhammadans." "When two communities mixed so closely, and were so greatly influenced by one another," he wrote, "the result was that a common god was called into existence, worshiped by the Hindus and Muhammadans alike. His name was formed by compounding an Arabic [*sic*] word with a Sanskrit word. He was called Satya Pir." Dinesh Chandra Sen, *History of Bengali Language and Literature* (Calcutta: University of Calcutta, 1954), 677.
36. Ibid., 677–78. Sen, *Folk Literature,* 100–101. Sarat Chandra Mitra, "On the Worship of the Deity Satyanarayana in Northern India," *Journal of the Anthropological Society of Bombay* 9, no. 7 (1919): 768–77.

munities had evolved out of a time when religious identities at the folk level were far less self-conscious and religious systems were far more open-ended than in modern times.

It is not only during or since colonial times, however, that people have held to a polarized image of premodern Bengali religious culture. Even contemporary Europeans saw Bengali society through binary lenses. "Mahometans as well as Gentiles," wrote the French traveler François Pyrard in early 1607, "deem the water [of the Ganges River] to be blessed, and to wash away all offences, just as we regard confession."[37] Here the author's reference point is not twentieth-century Bengal, riven by its communal loyalties, but seventeenth-century Catholic Europe, riven by *its* communal loyalties. Considering France's long history of confrontational relations with nearby Arab Islam, Pyrard doubtless presumed a clear understanding of what constituted a "Mahometan," and respect for the sanctity of the Ganges River would certainly not have been included in that understanding. Imagining deltaic society to have been sharply divided into two mutually exclusive socioreligious communities, the Frenchman was naturally struck by the spectacle of "Muslims" participating in a "Hindu" rite.

To understand premodern Bengali society on its own terms requires suspending the binary categories typical of modern observers such as D. C. Sen,[38] of contemporary outsiders such as François Pyrard, and of members of the contemporary Muslim elite such as Saiyid Sultan, all of whom were informed by normative understandings of Islam. Instead of visualizing two separate and self-contained social groups, Hindus and Muslims, participating in rites in which each stepped beyond its "natural" communal boundaries, one may see instead a single undifferentiated mass of Bengali villagers who, in their ongoing struggle with life's usual tribulations, unsystematically picked and chose from an array of reputed instruments—a holy man here, a holy river there—in order to tap superhuman power. What Dusan Zbavitel has written of the ballads of premodern Mymensingh—that they were "neither products of Hindu or Muslim culture, but of a single Bengali folk-culture"[39]—may be justly said of premodern Bengali folk religion generally.

Displacement

A third dimension of the Islamization process—the displacement of Bengali superhuman agencies from the local cosmology and their replacement

37. Pyrard, *Voyage*, 2: 336.
38. See n. 35 above.
39. Zbavitel, *Bengali Folk-Ballads*, 133.

by Islamic ones—is clearly visible in the nineteenth and early twentieth centuries, when waves of Islamic reform movements such as the Fara'izi and the Tariqah-i Muhammadiyah swept over the Bengali countryside. These movements aimed to strip from Bengali Islam all the indigenous beliefs and practices to which folk communities had been accommodated, and to instill among them an exclusive commitment to Allah and the Prophet Muhammad.

The most influential nineteenth-century reform movement, the Fara-'izi, had been launched by Haji Shariat Allah (d. 1840), a man of humble rural origins who in 1799 made a pilgrimage to Mecca when only eighteen years of age. He then passed nineteen years in religious study in Islam's holiest city at a time when Arabia itself had fallen under the spell of a zealous reform movement, Wahhabism. Returning to Bengal in 1818, the *hājī* found that customs that had seemed natural to him before his pilgrimage now appeared as grotesque aberrations from Islam as practiced in Wahhabi Arabia. From 1818 until his death in 1840, he tirelessly applied himself to reforming his Bengali co-religionists. In time, he passed into legend as an almost super-historical figure, a savior of Islam in Bengal,[40] whose deeds a local bard versified around 1903–6:

> Where had you been
> > When Haji Shariat Allah came thither (to Bengal)?
> Who did abolish the custom of Fatihah,
> > The worship of shrines, and stop the corrupt Mullah?
> When he set his foot in Bengal
> > All *shirk* (polytheism) and *bid'at* (sinful innovation) were
> > > trampled down.
> All these *bid'at* were then abolished
> And the sun of Islam rose high in the sky.[41]

In 1894 James Wise characterized the nineteenth-century reform movement as one of "ignorant and simple peasants, who of late years have been casting off the Hindu tinsel which has so long disfigured their religion."[42] But as the above poem shows, more was involved in Haji Shariat Allah's movement than merely casting off "Hindu tinsel." References to the *hājī's* efforts to abolish the *fātiḥa* and the "worship of shrines," and to inhibit

---

40. Haji Shariat Allah was described on his tombstone as a "defender of religion against the menaces of the Shi'ahs and the disbelievers and against all misguidance, valiant fighter for righteousness against all falsehood and vanity, deliverer of Islam (which) was covered by darkness like the sun enveloped in clouds." Muin-ud-Din Ahmad Khan, *History of the Fara'idi Movement in Bengal (1818–1906)* (Karachi: Pakistan Historical Society, 1965), p. xxxiii.
41. Cited in ibid., 8.
42. Wise, "Muhammadans of Eastern Bengal," 61.

the influence of "corrupt" *mullās*, point to an attempt to eliminate the very instruments and institutions by which Islam had originally taken root in the delta. Without the shrines whose establishment had been authorized by seventeenth- and eighteenth-century provincial Mughal officials, there would have been no institutional basis for *mullās* and other members of the religious gentry to establish the *fātiḥa*—that is, readings from the Qur'an—in the newly created settlements of the eastern delta's expanding rice frontier.

Under the influence of the teachings of another Muslim reformist, Karamat 'Ali (d. 1874), boatmen of Noakhali District who had hitherto been addressing their prayers to the saint Badar and to Panch Pir (the "five *pīrs*"), were soon addressing their prayers to Allah alone.[43] Such activity on the divine level was paralleled by similar activity at the human level. Bengalis whose identity as Muslims had not previously been expressed in exclusivist terms now began adopting Arabic surnames, a sure sign of a deepening attachment to Islamic ideals. For example, the district gazetteer for Noakhali, published in 1911, notes that the "vast majority of the Shekhs and lower sections of the community are descended from the aboriginal races of the district," and that Muslims "with surnames of Chand, Pal, and Dutt are to be found in the district to this day."[44] But by 1956 it was observed that among Muslims of that district such names had practically disappeared and, owing to "the influence of reforming priests," had been replaced by Arabic surnames.[45]

There is, then, no denying that in the nineteenth and twentieth centuries, Bengali Muslims became increasingly aware of the beliefs and practices then current in the Arab heartland, and that they attempted to integrate those beliefs and practices into their identity as Muslims.[46] The factors contributing to this sense of awareness are well known: the assault on Islam mounted by Christian missionaries in India, the spread of reformist literature facilitated by print technology, political competition between Muslim and non-Muslim communities in the context of colonial

43. Risley Collection, "Reports on the Religious and Social Divisions amongst the Mahomedans of Bengal" (India Office Library, London, Eur. MSS. No. E 295), 9: 417.
44. Webster, *Eastern Bengal and Assam District Gazetteers: Noakhali*, 39.
45. A. K. Nazmul Karim, *Changing Society in India and Pakistan: A Study in Social Change and Social Stratification* (Dacca: Oxford University Press, 1956), 132.
46. For example, Muslim men were urged to grow long beards, women were discouraged from wearing saris or using henna to stain their feet and nails, and all were urged to eat grasshoppers on the grounds that Arabs ate locusts. See Wise, "The Muhammadans," 56; *The Cambridge History of Islam*, ed. P. M. Holt et al. (Cambridge: Cambridge University Press, 1970), 2: 77.

rule, steamship technology, and a quickened incidence of pilgrimage to Arabia. As the ethnographer H. H. Risley wrote in 1891: "Even the distant Mecca has been brought, by means of Mesrs. Cook's steamers and return-tickets, within reach of the faithful in India; and the influence of Mahomedan missionaries and return pilgrims has made itself felt in a quiet but steady revival of orthodox usage in Eastern Bengal."[47]

It would be wrong, however, to think of movements to purify local cosmologies as phenomena confined to the nineteenth or twentieth centuries, or as functions of, or responses to, the advent of "modernism."[48] Both in the original rise of Islam in Arabia and in the subsequent growth of Islam in premodern Bengal, one finds movements comparable both socially and theologically to those of the nineteenth and twentieth centuries. In all three instances—in early Arabia, in premodern Bengal, and in modern Bengal—lesser superhuman agencies came to be absorbed under or into the sovereignty of a single deity, a dynamic process Max Weber called "religious rationalization."[49]

The first of these, the rise of Islam in Arabia, established the model for the subsequent movements in Bengal, as in the Muslim world at large. Sources dating from the second through the seventh centuries reveal the gradual evolution of a monotheistic cult, heavily influenced by Jewish practice and Jewish apocalyptic thought, that in the time of Muhammad (d. 632) succeeded in absorbing neighboring pagan cults in the Arabian peninsula. As early as the second Christian century, a Nabataean inscription identified Allah as the patron deity of an Arab tribe in northwestern Arabia.[50] By the fifth century, two centuries before Muhammad, a Greek source reports Arab communities in northern Arabia practicing a religion that, although corrupted by the influence of their pagan neighbors, resembled the religion of the Hebrews up to the days of Moses. They prac-

47. H. H. Risley, *Tribes and Castes of Bengal* (reprint, Calcutta: Firma Mukhopadhyay, 1981), 1: xxx.

48. For a differing view, see Bruce B. Lawrence, *Defenders of God* (New York: Harper & Row, 1989), in which the author argues for the "modernness" of Islamic reform movements.

49. "The decisive consideration was and remains: who is deemed to exert the stronger influence on the individual in his everyday life, the theoretically supreme god or the lower spirits and demons? . . . The process of rationalization (*ratio*) favored the primacy of universal gods; and every consistent crystallization of a pantheon followed systematic rational principles to some degree, since it was always influenced by professional sacerdotal rationalism or by the rational striving for order on the part of secular individuals." Max Weber, *The Sociology of Religion*, trans. Ephraim Fischoff (Boston: Beacon Press, 1964), 20, 22.

50. See J. T. Milik, "Inscriptions grecques et nabatéennes de Rawwafah," appended to P. J. Parr, G. L. Harding, and J. E. Dayton, "Preliminary Survey in N.W. Arabia, 1968," *Bulletin of the Institute of Archaeology* 10 (1971): 54–58.

ticed circumcision like the Jews, refrained from eating pork, and observed "many other Jewish rites and customs." The source adds that these Arabs had come into contact with Jews, from whom they learned of their descent from Abraham through Ishmael and Hagar.[51] The earliest known biography of Muhammad, found in an Armenian chronicle dating from the 660s, describes the Arabian prophet as a merchant who restored the religion of Abraham among his people and led his believers into Palestine in order to recover the land God had promised them as descendants of Abraham.[52]

Between the second and seventh centuries, then, Allah had grown from the patron deity of a second-century Arab tribe to, in Muhammad's day, the high God of all Arabs, as well as the God of Abraham. This evolutionary process is also visible in the Qur'an. Before Muhammad's mission, the tribes of western Arabia were already paying increasing attention to Allah at the expense of lesser divinities or tribal deities. By the time Muhammad began to preach, Allah had become identified as the "Lord of the Ka'aba" (Qur'an 106:3), and hence the chief god of the pagan deities whose images were housed in the Meccan shrine. In some Qur'anic passages the existence of lesser divinities and angels was also affirmed, although their effectiveness as intercessors with Allah was denied.[53] In others, however, Arab deities other than Allah were specifically dismissed as nothing "but names which ye have named, ye and your fathers, for which Allah hath revealed no warrant."[54] This latter passage indicates the triumph of the monotheistic ideal, the end point of an evolutionary process in which divinities other than Allah were not merely dismissed as ineffectual but denied altogether.

Such a process of religious rationalization was repeated in premodern Bengal, as seen especially in the *Nabi-Baṃśa*, the ambitious literary effort of Saiyid Sultan. This poet and local Sufi of the Chittagong region flourished toward the end of the sixteenth century, a time when the forested hinterland of the southeastern delta was only beginning to be touched by plow agriculture and intense exposure to the Qur'an. Characterized as a "national religious epic" for Bengali Muslims,[55] the *Nabi-Baṃśa* is epic

51. *The Ecclesiastical History of Sozomen, Comprising a History of the Church from A.D. 324 to A.D. 440*, trans. Edward Walford (London: H. G. Bohn, 1855), 309–10.
52. Bishop Sebeos, *Histoire d'Héraclius*, trans. F. Macler (Paris: Imprimerie nationale, 1904), 94–96. Cited in Patricia Crone and Michael Cook, *Hagarism: The Making of the Islamic World* (Cambridge: Cambridge University Press, 1977), 6–7.
53. Qur'an 36:23, 43:86, 53:26.
54. Qur'an, 53:23.
55. Syed Sajjad Husain, ed. and trans., *A Descriptive Catalogue of Bengali Manuscripts in Munshi Abdul Karim's Collection*, by Munshi Abdul Karim and Ahmad Sharif (Dacca: Asiatic Society of Pakistan, 1960), xxiv.

not only in its size—the work contains over twenty-two thousand rhymed couplets—but also in one of its principal aims: to treat the major deities of the Hindu pantheon, including Brahma, Vishnu, Śiva, Rama, and Krishna, as successive prophets of God, followed in turn by Adam, Noah, Abraham, Moses, Jesus, and Muhammad.

In this respect we may compare Saiyid Sultan's overall endeavor with that of the mid-eighth-century Arab writer Ibn Ishaq (d. ca. 767), author of the earliest Islamic biography of the Prophet Muhammad. Both men aimed at writing a universal history that began with Creation and continued through the life of the Prophet Muhammad. To this end both divided their works into two large sections: a first part detailing the lives of all the prophets preceding Muhammad—which in Ibn Ishaq's work was entitled the *Kitāb al-Mubtada'*, "Book of Beginnings"—and a second part devoted exclusively to the Prophet Muhammad. This organization gave both works a powerful teleological trajectory. "By including all the world's history," writes the historian Gordon Newby, Ibn Ishaq's *Kitāb al-Mubtada'* "demonstrated that time's course led to Islam, which embraced the prophets and holy men of Judaism and Christianity, and finally produced the regime of the Abbasids, whose empire embraced Muslims, Christians, and Jews." Moreover, as a commentary on both the Bible and the Qur'an, the *Kitāb al-Mubtada'* "fosters the Muslim claim that Islam is the heir to Judaism and Christianity."[56] In like fashion, the *Nabī-Baṃśa*, by commenting extensively on Vedic, Vaishnava, and Śaiva divinities, in addition to biblical figures, fostered the claim that Islam was the heir, not only to Judaism and Christianity, but also to the religious traditions of pre-Muslim Bengal.

The structural similarity between the *Kitāb al-Mubtada'* and the *Nabī-Baṃśa* arises from the similar historical circumstances in which the two works emerged. Both authors lived in frontier situations where religious and social boundaries were very much in flux and where Islam, though politically dominant, was new and demographically dwarfed by a majority of adherents to much older creeds. In both cases, moreover, the religious and social identity of the Muslim community had not yet fully crystallized and was still very much in the process of formation. Such "frontier" circumstances fostered a climate conducive to literary creativity,[57] as both Ibn Ishaq and Saiyid Sultan felt it necessary to define the cultural identity of

56. Gordon Darnell Newby, *The Making of the Last Prophet: A Reconstruction of the Earliest Biography of Muhammad* (Columbia: University of South Carolina Press, 1989), 7, 3.

57. Cornell Fleischer made similar observations respecting the literary careers of the historians Ibn Khaldun (d. 1406) and Mustafa 'Ali (d. 1600), both of whom were greatly influenced by the frontier environments in which they lived and wrote. See Fleischer, "Royal Authority, Dynastic Cyclism, and 'Ibn Khaldunism'

their own communities in relation to larger, non-Muslim societies. Both endeavored to specify the historical and cosmic roles played by prophets who had preceded and foreshadowed the prophetic career of Muhammad. Such a strategy not only established vital connections between the larger community and their own but, more important, asserted their own claims to primacy over the majority communities.

Ibn Ishaq wrote the bulk of his *Kitāb al-Mubtada'* in Baghdad during the 760s. Located near the capital of the former Sasanian Persian dynasty, far to the north of what was then the Islamic heartland—Mecca and Medina in western Arabia—Baghdad in Ibn Ishaq's day was still in a cultural frontier zone, where a good deal of interaction between Muslims and non-Muslims could and did take place. At that time Muslims comprised less than 10 percent of the population of Iraq and Iran, the remainder being mainly Christian, Jewish, or Zoroastrian.[58] Since many figures from the Christian and Jewish scriptures also appear in the Qur'an, early Muslim scholars like Ibn Ishaq, desiring to form a fuller understanding of the Islamic revelation, took pains to collect lore concerning such biblical figures from representatives of the Jewish and Christian communities.[59] These extra-Islamic materials were then fitted into an evolving conception of community, history, and prophethood that linked the new Muslim community to the older communities, while at the same time distinguishing the new from the older communities.

Thus by the eighth century the most creative forces that served to forge an Islamic cultural identity were no longer to be found in Islam's original centers of Mecca and Medina, which had already become cities of shrines and reliquaries. Rather, the new religion's most creative energies had by then passed to the north, where Arab Muslims encountered, and had to come to terms with, much older civilizations. But Baghdad would not for long remain a frontier society. Ibn Ishaq happened to live there during the culturally formative and doctrinally fluid moment just before Abbasid power was consolidated, before the schools of Islamic Law had crystallized, and before Baghdad itself had passed from a frontier town to a sprawling metropolis at the hub of a vital and expanding Islamic civilization. At this point, when most of Iraq, Syria, and Iran converted to Islam, concern with

---

in Sixteenth-Century Ottoman Letters," *Journal of Asian and African Studies* 18, nos. 3–4 (1983): 216.

58. Richard Bulliet, *Conversion to Islam in the Medieval Period: An Essay in Quantitative History* (Cambridge, Mass., Harvard University Press, 1979), 44.

59. Newby, *Making of the Last Prophet*, 10. According to the early Muslim scholar al-Bukhari, in Muhammad's own day "Jews used to read the Torah in Hebrew and interpret [Arabic *fassara*] it to the people of Islam in Arabic." Quoted in ibid., 12.

pre-Islamic history slackened, and the part of Ibn Ishaq's work dealing with pre-Islamic prophets, the *Kitāb al-Mubtada'*, fell into disrepute, soon to disappear altogether from circulation.[60]

Although separated from the *Kitāb al-Mubtada'* by eight hundred years, Saiyid Sultan's *Nabī-Baṃśa* appeared during a similar phase in the evolution of a Muslim community's socioreligious self-consciousness. Hence we find in it a similar tendency simultaneously to associate Islam with earlier traditions and to dissociate it from them. Saiyid Sultan not only identified the God of Adam with the Sanskrit names Prabhu and Niranjan; he also identified the Islamic notion of a prophet (*nabī*), or a messenger sent down by God, with the Indian notion of an *avatār*, or an incarnation of a deity.[61] The poet lays out these ideas at the very beginning of the epic. "As the butter is hidden in the milk," he wrote, drawing on the rich imagery of India's Puranic literature, "that is how Prabhu was co-existent with the Universe. He manifested himself in the shape of Muhammad, as his *avatār*."[62] The author also juxtaposed Indian with Sufi notions of divine activity. After expressing the Vaishnava sentiment that Krishna had been created "in order to manifest love (*keli*) at Vrindavan," the poet expressed the Sufi sentiments that God ("Niranjan") used to enjoy his own self by gazing at his reflected image in a mirror, and that before creating the sky and the angels he had created the "Light of Muhammad" (*Nūr-i Muḥammad*).[63] Saiyid Sultan even understood the four Vedas as successive revelations sent down by God ("Niranjan," "Kartār"), each one given to a different "great person" (*mahājan*). Accordingly, Brahmans had been created in order to teach about Niranjan and to explain the Vedas to the people.[64] Rather than repudiating Bengal's older religious and social

60. See ibid., 8–14.
61. Although the identification of the Arabic *nabī* with the Sanskrit *avatār* was not unique to Saiyid Sultan, it is very rarely met with in the history of the Islamic encounter with Indian civilization. The earliest incidence of such an identification appears on coins minted by Sultan Mahmud of Ghazni in Lahore in 1027 and 1028 (A.H. 418 and 419). On these coins the sultan inscribed a Sanskrit translation of the Islamic confession of faith in which Muhammad was called the *avatār* of God, translated as Avyaktam, "the Unmanifested." This bold experiment at translating the most fundamental Islamic ideas into the Indian religious universe is unique in the history of Indian coinage, however, and it was never tried again. See D. C. Sircar, *Studies in Indian Coins* (Delhi: Motilal Banarsidass, 1968), 19. Isma'ili traditions dating perhaps to the fifteenth century also made use of the *avatār* notion, identifying the Prophet Muhammad's son-in-law 'Ali with the tenth of Vishnu's *avatārs*. See Azim Nanji, *The Nizari Isma'ili Tradition in the Indo-Pakistan Subcontinent* (Delmar, N.Y.: Caravan Books, 1978), 110–20.
62. Saiyid Sultan, *Nabī-Baṃśa*, 1: 2.
63. Ibid., 3, 4, 6.
64. Ibid., 24–25.

worlds, then, the epic served to connect Islam with Bengal's socioreligious past, or at least with that part of it represented in the high textual tradition of the Brahmans.

Indeed, the book's very title—*Nabī-Bamśa* means "the family of the Prophet"—points to the author's overall effort to situate Muhammad within a wider "family" of Bengali deities and Hebrew prophets. Like family members pitching in to solve domestic problems, Islamic figures in the *Nabī-Bamśa* occasionally appear for the purpose of resolving specifically Indian dilemmas or problematic outcomes. Even before creating man, wrote the poet, Niranjan created a prophet (*nabī*) to preach to the angels and demons because they had become forgetful of *dharma*, or "duty" as understood in classical Indian thought.[65] And Adam himself was created from the soil of the earth goddess Kṣiti, mother of Sita, as a device for resolving the problematic conclusion of the popular epic *Rāmāyaṇa*. Upon hearing Kṣiti's complaints concerning the shame suffered by her daughter Sita, whom people had falsely blamed for infidelity to Rama, Niranjan told the angels, "By means of Adam I will nurture Kṣiti; I will create Adam from the soil (*mātī*) of Kṣiti."[66]

But it would be wrong to consider the *Nabī-Bamśa* a basically "Hindu" epic with a few important Islamic personages and terms simply added to it, or as a "syncretic" work that merely identifies foreign deities with local deities. For on fundamental points of theology, the poet clearly drew on Judeo-Islamic and not on Indic thought. For example, his contention that each *nabī*/*avatār* of God (i.e., "Niranjan") had been given a scripture appropriate for his time, departed from the Indian conception of repeated incarnations of the divine and affirmed instead the Judeo-Islamic "once-only" conception of prophethood. Moreover, the epic did not subscribe to a view of cosmic history as oscillating between ages of splendor and ages of ruin in the cyclical manner characteristic of classical Indian thought. Rather, according to Saiyid Sultan, as religion in the time of each *nabī*/*avatār* became corrupt, God sent down later prophets with a view to propagating belief in one god, culminating in the last and most perfect *nabī*/*avatār*, Muhammad. Already in the four Vedas, the poet states, God ("Kartār") had given witness to the certain coming of Muhammad's prophetic mission.[67]

The epic thus presents a linear conception of religious time that is not at all cyclical, but moves forward toward God's final prophetic intervention in human affairs. It thus fully accords with the Qur'anic understanding of

65. Ibid., 11–12.
66. Ibid., 38.
67. Ibid., 25.

prophecy and of God's role in human history. It is, of course, true that the poet identifies Allah with Niraṇjan, and *nabī* with *avatār*. But the Prophet Muhammad is seen as standing at the end of a long chain of Middle Eastern prophets and Indian divinities, with whom he is in no way confused or identified. By proclaiming the finality and superiority of Muhammad's prophetic mission, then, Saiyid Sultan's work provides the rationale for displacing all other *nabī/avatār*s from Bengal's religious atmosphere. In this respect, Saiyid Sultan departed from the tradition of previous Bengali poets, who were content with merely including Allah in Bengali cosmologies, or with identifying Allah with deities in those cosmologies.

In fact, the poet explains the whole Hindu socioreligious order as it existed in his own day as the work of the fallen Islamic angel Iblis, or Satan. "The descendants of Cain," he wrote, "indulged in worshiping idols (*murti*) in the shape of men, birds and pigs—all taught them by Iblis."[68] And it was Iblis who, on discovering the Vedas, had deliberately created an alternative, corrupted text, which the Brahmans unwittingly propagated among the people.[69] On this basis, Brahmans were said to have misguidedly taught people, for example, to cremate their dead instead of returning them to the ground from which man was created.[70] And it was from such corrupted scriptures that Brahmans got the idea of wearing unstitched clothing (i.e, the *dhoti*) instead of stitched clothing.[71] For the use of stitched clothing had been taught by "Shish" (Seth in Genesis), the son of Adam and Eve after Abel's death, from whom were descended the righteous people of the earth, the Muslims.[72]

In short, far from describing Islamic superhuman agencies in Indian terms, the *Nabī-Baṃśa* does just the opposite: while Brahmans are portrayed as the unwitting teachers of a body of texts deliberately corrupted by Iblis, the rest of the Hindu social order is portrayed as descended from Cain, the misguided son of Adam and Eve. It was only from Adam and Eve's other son, Shish, that a "rightly guided" community, the Muslim *umma*, would descend. The epic thus reflects a level of consciousness that had come to understand Islam as more than just another name for an already dense religious cosmology, and "Allah" as more than just another name for a familiar divinity. Rather, Saiyid Sultan, like the early Arab writer Ibn Ishaq, understood the advent of Islam as the inevitable result of a unique cosmic and historical process.

68. Ibid., 181.
69. Ibid., 242–43.
70. Ibid., 244.
71. Ibid., 252.
72. Ibid., 132–33.

Literacy and Islamization

Although the growth of Islam in Bengal witnessed no neat or uniform progression from inclusion to identification to displacement, one does see, at least in the eastern delta, a general drive toward the eventual displacement of local divinities. In part, one can explain this in terms of Bengal's integration, since the late sixteenth century, into a pan-Indian, and indeed, a global civilization. Akbar's 1574 conquest of the northwestern delta established a pattern by which the whole delta would be politically and economically integrated with North India. What was unique about the east, however, was that prior to the late sixteenth century, its hinterland had remained relatively undeveloped and isolated as compared with the west; hence the expansion of Mughal power there was accompanied by the establishment of new agrarian communities and not simply the integration of old ones. Composed partly of outsiders—emigrants from West Bengal or even North India—and partly of newly peasantized indigenous communities of former fishermen or shifting cultivators, these communities typically coalesced around the many rural mosques, shrines, or Qur'an schools built by enterprising pioneers who had contracted with the government to transform tracts of virgin jungle into fields of cultivated paddy.

It was mainly in the east, moreover, that political incorporation was accompanied by the intrusion and eventual primacy of Islamic superhuman agencies in local cosmologies. Contributing to this was the very nature of Islamic religious authority, which does not flow from priests, magicians, or other mortal agents, but from a medium that is ultimately immortal and unchallengeable—written scripture. The connection between literacy and divine power in Islam is perfectly explicit.[73] Moreover, well before their rise to prominence in Bengal, Muslims had already constructed a great world civilization around the Qur'an and the vast corpus of literature making up Islamic Law. It is therefore not coincidental that Muslims have described theirs as the "religion of the Book."

It is true, of course, that the Hindu tradition is also scripturally based. As living repositories of Vedic learning, or at least of traditions that derive legitimacy from that learning, Brahmans "represent" scriptural authority in a way roughly analogous to the way Muslim men of piety mediate, and thus "represent," the Qur'an. By the time of the Turkish conquest, a scripturally based religious culture under Brahman leadership had already become well entrenched in the dense and socially stratified society of the

73. This fundamental point is repeatedly proclaimed in the Qur'an itself—e.g., "And We have sent down on thee the Book making clear everything, and as a guidance and a mercy, and as good tidings to those who surrender." *The Koran Interpreted*, trans. Arthur J. Arberry (New York: Macmillan, 1970), Sura 16:91.

western delta. In this context, the intrusion of another scripturally defined religious culture, Islam, failed to have a significant impact. But the coherence of the Brahmanic socioreligious order progressively diminished as one moved from west to east across the delta, rendering the preliterate masses of the east without an authority structure sufficient to withstand that of Islam. Among these peoples the rustic shrines, mosques, and Qur'an schools that we have been examining introduced a type of religious authority that was fundamentally new and of greater power relative to what had been there previously. "In non-literate societies," writes J. D. Y. Peel, a scholar of religious change in modern West Africa,

> the past is perceived as entirely servant of the needs of the present, things are forgotten and myth is constructed to justify contemporary arrangements; there are no dictionary definitions of words. . . . In religion there is no sense of impersonal or universal orthodoxy of doctrine; legitimate belief is as a particular priest or elder expounds it. But where the essence of religion is the Word of God, where all arguments are resolved by an appeal to an unchangeable written authority, where those who formulate new beliefs at a time of crisis commit themselves by writing and publishing pamphlets . . . religion acquires a rigid basis. "Structural amnesia" is hardly possible; what was thought in the past commits men to particular courses of action in the present; religion comes to be thought of as a system of rules, emanating from an absolute and universal God, which are quite external to the thinker, and to which he must conform and bend himself, if he would be saved.[74]

In eastern Bengal, where Brahmans were thinly scattered, the analog to Peel's "particular priest or elder" was typically a local ritualist who was neither literate nor a Brahman. True, the mosque builders, rural *mullās*, or charismatic *pīrs* who fanned out over the eastern plains may also have been illiterate; moreover, the basis of their authority, like that of indigenous non-Muslim ritualists, was often charismatic in nature. But what is important is that these same men patronized Qur'an readers and "readers of *fātiḥa*," who, even if themselves only semi-literate in Arabic, were seen as representing the authority of the written word as opposed to the ad hoc, localized, and transient authority of indigenous ritualists.[75] Therefore, with the introduction of Qur'an readers, Qur'an schools, and "readers of *fātiḥa*" into the delta, the relatively fluid and expansive cosmology of pre-

---

74. Peel, "Syncretism," 139–40. See also Jack Goody, *The Logic of Writing and the Organization of Society* (Cambridge: Cambridge University Press, 1986), 1–44.
75. In the case of Qur'an schools (*madrasas*), of course, the government's support of literate Islam was explicit. In one 1732 *sanad*, for example, 390 acres of forest in Sylhet were granted in the expectation that the land, once cleared and cultivated, would support the students of a Qur'an school (*kharj-i ṭālibān-i madrasa*). "Register of Sanads," Sylhet District Collectorate Record Room, 20, no. 932.

Muslim eastern Bengal began to resolve into one favoring the primacy of Allah and the Prophet Muhammad. As Peel puts it, religion began to acquire "a rigid basis."

Further facilitating the growth of this "religion of the Book" in Bengal was the diffusion of paper and of papermaking technology. Introduced from Central Asia into North India in the thirteenth century by Persianized Turks, by the fifteenth century the technology of paper production had found its way into Bengal, where it eventually replaced the palm leaf.[76] Already in 1432, the Chinese visitor Ma Huan remarked that the Bengalis' "paper is white; it is made out of the bark of a tree, and is as smooth and glossy as deer's skin."[77] And by the close of the sixteenth century the poet Mukundaram noted the presence of whole communities of Muslim papermakers (*kāgajī*) in Bengali cities.[78] The revolutionary impact that the technology of literacy made on premodern Bengali society is suggested in the ordinary Bengali words for paper (*kāgaj*) and pen (*kalam*), both of which are corrupted loan words from Perso-Arabic. It is also significant that on Bengal's expanding agrarian frontier, the introduction of papermaking technology coincided with the rise of a Muslim religious gentry whose authority structure was ultimately based on the written word—scripture. While it would be the crudest technological determinism to say that the diffusion of paper production simply *caused* the growth of Islam in Bengal or elsewhere, it is certainly true that this more efficient technology of knowledge led to more books, which in turn promoted a greater familiarity with at least the idea of literacy, and that this greater familiarity led, in turn, to the association of the written word with religious authority.

Serving to check the growth of the "religion of the Book," however, was the fact that the book in question, the Qur'an, was written in a language unknown to the masses of Bengali society. Moreover, since the Qur'an had been revealed in Arabic, in Bengal as elsewhere fear of tampering with the word of God inhibited its outright translation. As we have seen, Bengali Muslims were extremely reluctant to translate even Islamic popular lore into Bengali. Of course, they could have done what many other non-Arab Muslims did—that is, retain their own language for writ-

76. Losty, *Art of the Book*, 10–12, 113.
77. Rockhill, "Notes on the Relations," 440. See also S. A. K. Ghori and A. Rahman, "Paper Technology in Medieval India," *Indian Journal of the History of Science* 2 (November 1966): 136. For a history of the diffusion and technology of papermaking in the premodern Muslim world generally, see Johannes Pedersen, *The Arabic Book*, trans. Geoffrey French, ed. Robert Hillenbrand (Princeton: Princeton University Press, 1984), 59–67.
78. Mukundaram, *Kavikaṅkaṇa Caṇḍī*, 346.

ten discourse but render it in the Arabic script, as happened in Iran (modern Persian) and North India (Urdu). The transliteration of any language into Arabic script not only facilitates the assimilation of Arabic vocabulary but fosters a psychological bond between non-Arab and Arab Muslims. In the seventeenth century, in fact, attempts were made to do the same for Bengali. The Dhaka Museum has a manuscript work composed in 1645 entitled *Maqtul Husain*—a tract treating the death of Husain at Karbala—written in Bengali but using the Arabic, and not the Bengali, script.[79] Although subsequent writers made similar such literary attempts,[80] it is significant that the effort never took hold, with the result that Bengali Muslims remain today the world's largest body of Muslims who, despite Islamization, have retained both their language and their script.[81]

Since Islamic scripture was neither translated nor transliterated in premodern Bengal, it not surprisingly first entered mass culture in a magical, as opposed to liturgical, context. In Ksemananda's *Manasā-Mangala*, a work composed in the mid seventeenth century, we hear that in the house of one of the poem's Hindu figures (Laksmindhara, son of Chand), a copy of the Qur'an was kept along with other charms for the purpose of warding off evil influence.[82] From the remarks of Vijaya Gupta, a poet of East Bengal's Barisal region, who wrote in 1494,[83] we find an even earlier reference to the same use of Muslim scripture. In this instance, the written word appeared not in a Hindu household but in the hands of a *mullā*. A group of seven weavers, evidently Muslims, since they resided in "Husain-hati," were bitten by snakes unleashed by the goddess Manasa and went to the court of the *qāzī* seeking help. Wrote the poet:

> There was a teacher of the Qāḍī named Khālās . . . who always engaged himself in the study of the Qur'an and other religious books. . . . He said, if you ask me, I say, why are you afraid of demons [*bhūt*], when you have got the religious books. Write (extracts) from the book and hang it down the neck. If then also the demons (implying snakes) bite, I

79. Muhammad Khan, *Maqtul Husain*, Dhaka Museum MS. No. 2826, Acc. No. 6634.
80. For example, Shaikh Muttalib, *Kifayat al-Mussalin*, Dhaka Museum MS. No. 2825, composed in 1856.
81. As recently as 1967, a judge on the Supreme Court of Pakistan suggested that, in the interests of fostering unity between Pakistan's eastern and western wings, Bengali, like Urdu, be rendered in the Arabic script. But this was resisted by the Bengalis themselves, who several years later wrested their independence from Pakistan. See Golam Morshed, "Cultural Identity of Former East Pakistan and Conflicting State Policies," *Journal of the Institute of Bangladesh Studies* 3 (1978): 69.
82. Dinesh Chandra Sen, *History of Bengali Language and Literature*, 674.
83. Zbavitel, *Bengali Literature*, 161–62.

shall be held responsible. The Qāḍī accepted what the *Mullā* said and all present took amulet[s] from him (the *Mullā*).[84]

Here we see a Muslim ritualist mediating on the people's behalf with a class of ubiquitous spirits, *bhūt*, that pervaded (and still pervades) the folk Bengali cosmology.[85] Moreover, the *mullā* clearly used the scripture in a magical and not a liturgical context, for it was not by reading the holy book that he dealt with evil spirits but by having his clients wear written extracts from it around their necks—a usage that enjoyed the endorsement of the state-appointed Muslim judge, or *qāzī*.[86] In modern times, too, one finds ritualists employing the magical power of the Qur'an for healing purposes in precisely the manner that *mullā*s had done three centuries earlier. In 1898 an *ojhā*, a local shamanlike ritualist, was observed in a village in Sylhet District using Qur'anic passages in his treatment of persons possessed by *bhūt*s.[87] And in recent years *ojhā*s among the non-

84. Karim, *Social History of the Muslims in Bengal*, 171. Karim's translation. Cf. Viyaya Gupta, *Padma Purāṇa* (Calcutta: University of Calcutta, 1962), 140.
85. For an excellent summary of how the belief in *bhūt* permeates contemporary Bengali Muslim life, especially among women in rural society, see Thérèse Blanchet, *Meanings and Rituals of Birth in Rural Bangladesh* (Dhaka: University Press, 1984), 50–63.
86. Toward the end of the sixteenth century, Mukundaram wrote that *mullā*s also performed life-cycle rituals for Muslims and collected from their clients regular payments for their services, paralleling in this respect the functions of Brahmans in Hindu society: "The *Mullā*s perform the ceremony of the *nikā* [wedding] and get a reward of four annas and bless the couple by reading the *Kalimah*. He [the *mullā*] takes a sharp knife, kills the fowl, and gets a reward of ten *gaṇḍā*s of cowri. For butchering a she-goat, the *mullā* gets six *buri*s of cowri, and also the head of the animal killed." Mukundaram, *Kavikaṅkana Caṇḍī*, 344. Karim, *Social History of the Muslims in Bengal*, 172. Karim's translation.
87. The report read: "A circle is described round the affected person with a stick, charms being recited at the same time; a verse from the Koran is read over a quantity of mustard oil, and a wick smeared with the oil thus charmed is burnt and the smoke out of it is thrust into the nostrils of the affected person. To the *bhut* this is unbearable and so it speaks through the possessed. The sorcerer (Ojha) then asks the *bhut* his name and whereabouts and how he came to have possession of the person, and he gives replies. The sorcerer then makes the *bhut* promise in the name of Suleman Badshah, the sovereign of *bhut*, that it would never more enter the body and then, when he is satisfied, he cuts the magic circle and the *bhut* goes away." Bhattacharjee, "Folkcustom and Folklore," 19–20. Relevant in this regard are Thérèse Blanchet's remarks on *bhūt* as a fundamental category in Bengali folk belief: "*Bhut* are said to originate from the north, in the mountains. *Bhut* used to be masters of the land, before, when there was no civilization. But then came the 'great religions.' These had powerful gods who could dominate the *bhut*. Their learned men, or priests, could pronounce the words that keep *bhut* at bay. Indeed both Sanskrit and Arabic incantations (*montro*) are effective against *bhut*. Their written words have the same effect (i.e. *tabij*). Civilized ways did not penetrate everywhere however and *bhut*, even after the advent of the 'great religions' still

Muslim Chakma tribesmen of the Chittagong Hill Tracts have been integrating Muslim scripture and Islamic superhuman agencies into their healing rituals, indicating the continued penetration of Islamic religious culture beyond the delta and into the adjacent mountains.[88]

On the other hand, European observers noted that Bengali *mullās* also used the Qur'an in purely liturgical, as opposed to magical, contexts. In 1833 Francis Buchanan observed that in rural Dinajpur, *mullās* "read, or repeat prayers or passages of the Koran at marriages, funerals, circumcisions, and sacrifices, for no Muslim will eat meat or fowl, over which prayers have not been repeated, before it has been killed. . . . According to the Kazis, many of these Mollas cannot read, and these only look at the book, while they repeat the passages."[89] Although the *mullās* observed by Buchanan were themselves unable to read, they were nonetheless understood by their village clients to be tapping into a transcendent source of power, the written word, fundamentally greater and more permanent than those known to local ritualists. In the same way, it was reported in 1898 that Muslim villagers in Sylhet "employ Mullahs *to read Koran Shariff* and allow the merit thereof to be credited to the forefathers"[90]—an apparent reference to the same kind of *fātiḥa* rituals that *sanad*s of the late seventeenth and early eighteenth centuries had authorized for rural mosques and shrines.

All of this points to a progressive expansion in the countryside of the culture of literacy—that is, a tendency to confer authority on written reli-

---

played tricks on men, but even more on women. *Bhut* are believed to be numerous in the jungle or where habitations are sparse (on the *chor*). They are few in towns." Blanchet, *Meanings and Rituals*, 54.
88. In 1986 it was reported that an *ojhā* had healed a mentally deranged Chakma woman by "using all the abusive words to the evil spirit who was believed to have possessed this village woman. His whole body began to shake and tremble. He then recited some incantations taken from the religious books of the Muslims and the Hindu community. He was using names of Allah, Hari, Muhammad, Krishna, Kalima, Fatima, and deities in Kamakhya, a place in Assam noted for its magic, and made a circle around the woman. He then made mild strokes on the body and poured hot mustard oil into the nostrils of the patient. The attendant of the Ojha was beating a tin can. The Ojha then burnt incense and asked the patient to bend over it and to inhale the smoke." When the ceremony was concluded and the woman fully recovered, the *ojhā* asked the patient's guardians to make a sacramental sacrifice at the *mazār*, or shrine, of a certain *pīr*. Anwarul Karim, "Shamanism in Bangladesh," *Bangladesh Observer*, February 7, 1986. The last detail is significant, as it shows that the healing ceremony was specifically linked to the agency of a local Muslim saint, thereby associating Islam in the villagers' minds with physical or psychic health.
89. Buchanan, *Geographical, Statistical, and Historical Description*, 92.
90. Bhattacharjee, "Folkcustom and Folklore," 139. Emphasis mine.

gious texts and on persons associated with them (whether or not they could read those texts). This expanding culture of literacy naturally facilitated the growth of the cult of those superhuman agencies with which that culture was most clearly identified. In short, as the idea of "the book-as-authority" grew among ever-widening circles of East Bengal's rural society—a development clearly traceable from the sixteenth century—so too did the "religion of the Book," with its emphasis on the cosmological supremacy of Allah.

Gender and Islamization

The evolution of Islam in Bengal illustrates the complex relationship between economic base and ideological superstructure, a perennial issue amongst theorists of social change. It is evident that the incorporation of indigenous peoples of the eastern delta into an expanding peasant society paved the way for their gradual Islamization, and in this respect a changing economic base did indeed shape the resultant ideological superstructure, or Islam. Yet it is also true that the Islamic vision of the proper society as sustained by "the Book," together with the corpus of Perso-Islamic popular lore that swept over premodern Bengal, served to pattern the subsequent evolution of Muslim culture in the delta. Nowhere is this more visible than in the changing status of women in Bengali Muslim communities.

In moral terms, the Qur'an, which refers repeatedly to "believing men," "believing women," and to "Muslim men and Muslim women," places the two sexes in a position of absolute equality before God (Qur'an 33:35). But in social terms, women are subordinate to men. In the context of seventh-century Arabia, it is true, Qur'anic injunctions respecting women doubtless constituted a progressive force: the Qur'an emphasizes the just treatment of women, it prohibits female infanticide and the inheritance of female slaves, and it provides legal protection for women in matters like inheritance or divorce. But women inherit only half of what men do, and they are generally understood as requiring male supervision, as indicated in the following Qur'anic verse:

> Men are in charge of women, because Allah hath made the one of them to excel the other, and because they spend of their property (for the support of women). So good women are the obedient, guarding in secret that which Allah hath guarded. As for those from whom ye fear rebellion, admonish them and banish them to beds apart, and scourge them. Then, if they obey you, seek not a way against them.[91]

91. *The Glorious Koran: A Bilingual Edition with English Translation, Introduction and Notes,* trans. Marmaduke Pickthall (London: George Allen & Unwin, 1976), Sura 4:34.

Underlying the content of this passage is a structural hierarchy of authority connecting Allah, men, and women. Whereas God and men are grammatical subjects and actors, women are objects of action; indeed, much of the chapter entitled "Women" (Sura 4:1–43) consists of God's instructions to men as to what they should do in respect to women.

These scriptural norms were gradually translated into social reality in most societies that became formally Islamic—including, eventually, in Bengal. They also seem to have merged with social practices current among non-Arab civilizations with which early Muslims came into contact. Thus, in the seventh century, when pastoral Arabs conquered the agrarian societies of Iraq and Syria, Muslim conquerors absorbed a wide spectrum of Greek and, especially, Iranian culture. This included what became known as the purdah system, or the seclusion of a woman from all men but her own—in private apartments at home, and behind a veil if she walked abroad—which had long been a mark of privilege in upper-class Byzantine and Sasanian society.[92] By the second half of the eighth century, the seclusion of women and the wearing of the veil had become official policy at the Abbasid court in Baghdad. Soon urban Muslims of all social classes followed the court's example, with the result that by the fourteenth century, women had effectively disappeared from public life throughout the Arab Muslim world. But this was not yet the case beyond the Arab world, among Turkish, Indian, and West African peoples who had been only recently Islamized. Thus the great Arab traveler Ibn Battuta (d. 1377) expressed shock at seeing unveiled Muslim women in southern Anatolia, Central Asia, the Maldive Islands, and the western Sudan.[93] The Moroccan was especially astonished by the unrestrained social movement of Turkish women in Central Asia.[94]

In Bengal, both before and during the rise of Islam, outsiders made similar observations. In 1415, before Islam had become a force in the countryside, the Ming Chinese ambassador to Bengal noted with apparent reference to wet rice field operations that "men and women work in the fields or weave according to the season."[95] Toward the end of the following cen-

---

92. Marshall Hodgson, *Venture of Islam*, 1: 342. The wearing of the veil would have inhibited the sort of manual labor associated with the lower classes, in much the same way as did the practice of footbinding among upper-class women of China between the eleventh and twentieth centuries. The wearing of the veil also appears to find support in the Qur'an (Sura 24:31, 33:59).

93. *Ibn Battuta: Travels in Asia and Africa*, trans. H. A. R. Gibb (London: Routledge & Kegan Paul, 1929), 124, 146–47, 243–44, 321.

94. Ibid., 146–47.

95. Rockhill, "Notes on the Relations," 443. Hou Hsien would have seen a good bit of the interior delta, as he traveled from Chittagong to Pandua via Sonargaon.

tury, around 1595, Abu'l-fazl recorded in his entry for Chittagong that "it is the custom when a chief holds a court, for the wives of the military to be present, the men themselves not attending to make their obeisance." Referring to Bengal generally, he remarked that "men and women for the most part go naked wearing only a cloth (*lungi*) about the loins. The chief public transactions fall to the lot of the women."[96] Although Muslim communities were just beginning to appear in the Bengal countryside when Abu'l-fazl wrote these lines, his remarks suggest that neither the veiling nor the seclusion of women had yet taken hold.

Still, the normative vision of a segregated society undeniably formed part of scriptural Islam, and pressure to realize that vision increased to the extent that Islamic literary authority sank roots in Bengali popular culture. The earliest reference to a normative gendered division of labor is found in a Bengali version of the story of Adam and Eve dating from the late sixteenth century. In Saiyid Sultan's epic poem *Nabī-Baṃśa*, the angel Gabriel gives Adam a plow, a yoke, seed, and two bulls, advising him that "Niranjan has commanded that agriculture will be your destiny."[97] Adam then planted the seed and harvested the crop. At the same time, Eve is given fire, with which she learns the art of cooking.[98] In short, a domestic life would be Eve's destiny, just as Adam's vocation would be farming.

By around 1700 the process of Islamization had proceeded to the point where romantic literature set in the Bengali countryside now included Muslim peasants as central characters. Yet the gendered division of labor and female seclusion, long entrenched in the Islamic heartlands, had still not appeared in the Bengali Muslim countryside. The *Dewana Madina*, a ballad composed by Mansur Bayati around 1700 and set in the town of Baniyachong in southern Sylhet, tells of a Muslim peasant woman's lament for her deceased husband. "Oh Allah," she sobbed,

> what is this that you have written in my forehead? . . . In the good month of November, favoured by the harvest-goddess, we both used to reap the autumnal paddy in a hurry lest it should be spoilt by flood or hail-storm. My dear husband used to bring home the paddy and I spread them in the sun. Then we both sat down to husk the rice. . . . In December when our fields would be covered with green crops, my duty was to keep watch over them with care. I used to fill his *hooka* with water and prepare tobacco;—with this in hand I lay waiting, looking towards the path, expecting him! . . . When my dear husband made the fields soft and muddy with water for transplanting of the new rice-plants, I used to cook rice and await his return home. When he busied

96. Abu'l-fazl, *Ā'īn-i Akbarī* (Lucknow ed.), 2: 75, 76. English trans., 2: 132, 134.
97. Saiyid Sultan, *Nabī-Baṃśa*, 1: 107–8.
98. Ibid., 110.

himself in the fields for this purpose, I handed the green plants over to
him for replanting. . . . In December the biting cold made us tremble in
our limbs; my husband used to rise early at cock-crow and water the
fields of *shali* crops. I carried fire to the fields and when the cold became
unbearable, we both sat near the fire and warmed ourselves. We reaped
the *shali* crops together in great haste and with great care. How happy
we were when after the day's work we retired to rest in our home.[99]

If one compares today's Bengali Muslim society with that depicted in
this early ballad, one sees how far the purdah system has become a reality.
Whereas the ballad depicts men and women both reaping the rice paddy,
spreading it for drying, and transplanting young seedlings, today only
men perform these operations, while women's work is confined to post-
harvest operations—winnowing, soaking, parboiling, husking—all of
which are done within the confines of the farmyard.[100] In the eastern delta
the principal drive behind the domestication of female labor, according to
recent studies, has been the popular association of proper Islamic behavior
with the purdah system—that is, the very system of female seclusion that
became normative in Muslim Arab societies from the eighth century on.[101]
In the predominantly Hindu western delta, by contrast, rural women do
participate in pre-harvest field operations.[102] Similarly, among *jhūm* culti-

99. Dinesh Chandra Sen, trans. and ed., *Eastern Bengal Ballads*, 1, pt. 1: 307–8.

100. Analysis of how the purdah system restrains women from participating in
economic activities outside the house is found in Mahmuda Islam, "Social Norms
and Institutions," in *Situation of Women in Bangladesh*, ed. Mahmuda Islam et
al. (Dacca: UNICEF, 1979), 225–64.

101. "Traditional village religious figures and specially esteemed preachers, who
are brought to the village from time to time, always stress the religious obligation
men have to keep their women inside." Tahrunnessa A. Abdullah and Sondra A.
Zeidenstein, *Village Women of Bangladesh: Prospects for Change* (New York: Per-
gamon Press, 1982), 56. For a study of the rigidity with which the purdah system
is practiced by women from different socioeconomic classes, see Florence McCar-
thy, *The Status and Condition of Rural Women in Bangladesh* (Dacca: Ministry
of Agriculture and Forests, 1978).

102. Using indices such as life expectancy, literacy rates, undernourishment, and
mortality ratios, the economist Pranab Bardhan has noted that the status of females
is higher in West Bengal, Assam, and Orissa than in Punjab and Rajasthan. Bardhan explained this difference not in terms of culture or religion, but in terms of
the different economy of eastern India as opposed to northern and northwestern
India. In the east (and also the south), he argued, "the predominant crop is paddy
which—unlike wheat and other dry-region crops—tends to be relatively intensive
in female labour. Transplantation of paddy is an exclusively female job in the paddy
areas; besides, female labour plays a very important role in weeding, harvesting
and threshing of paddy." From this Bardhan concluded that "the social and economic value of the woman is likely to be related to the ecological conditions and
production relations of a particular region." It is true that in predominantly Hindu

vating populations of the Chittagong Hill Tracts to the immediate east of the delta, where Mughal administration, Muslim pioneers, and wet rice agriculture did not penetrate, women are also active in field operations—planting, weeding, harvesting, winnowing—and are in general socially unconstrained.[103]

This suggests that among communities that had become nominally Muslim from the sixteenth century on, there was a time lag between the appearance of a normative vision that separated male and female labor and the eventual realization of that vision. As with the increasing attention given to Islamic superhuman agencies, this seems to have resulted from the gradual diffusion of men or institutions associated with religious literacy—that is, the idea that the written word exerts a compelling authority over one's everyday life.

Summary

In 1798 Francis Buchanan, an English explorer and servant of the East India Company, toured the hilly and forested interior of Chittagong District on official business, and incidentally made important observations about the religions of the peoples he encountered. Among the "Arakanese" peoples of the Sitakund mountains, for example, Buchanan noticed some worship of Śiva.[104] In central Chakaria, he found forest-dwelling Muslims who made their living collecting oil, honey, and wax.[105] Further south, among the *jhūm* cultivators of Ukhia, he found a form of Buddhism that he said "differs a good deal from that of the orthodox Burma": their priests

---

West Bengal women are active in transplanting, weeding, and harvesting, and that their social status is higher there than in northern or northwestern India. But in predominantly Muslim East Bengal, where the economic base is identical with that of the western delta, women do not generally take part in these operations. In other words, contrary to Bardhan's hypothesis, the region's economic base does not dictate the social value of women. On the other hand one important cultural variable, Islam, does correlate with relatively low female status in the Bengal delta, as it does, too, in northern and northwestern India. See Pranab K. Bardhan, "On Life and Death Questions," *Economic and Political Weekly*, August 1974, 1302–4.

103. Lucien Bernot, *Les Paysans arakanais du Pakistan oriental* (Paris: Mouton, 1967), 249–64. As the author notes: "Après quelques jours passés dans les plaines des environs de Chittagong, en milieu bengali, où les femmes, surtout les musulmanes, sont invisibles, le voyageur européen est toujours surpris de rencontrer dès les premiers villages des collines, des groupes de femmes bavardes, interrompant les conversations de leurs époux, nullement effrayées par la venue de l'étranger, lui demandant où il va, quel est son nom, s'il parle marma, lui offrant spontanément un cigare ou des fruits, de l'eau fraîche ou du bétel." Ibid., 16.

104. Buchanan, "Account of a Journey," 20.

105. Ibid., 36.

Table 9. Religious Aspects of Islamization in Bengal

A = indigenous high god   B = Islamic high god
a = indigenous lesser agency   b = Islamic lesser agency

A		A B		A-B
a		a b		a-b
a		a b		a-b
a		a b		a-b

INDIGENOUS   INCLUSION   IDENTIFICATION
COSMOLOGY

B		B
b	
b	
b	

DISPLACEMENT   MONOTHEISTIC IDEAL

---

were styled *"pungres,"* and their chief god was Maha Muni, worshiped in the form of a great copper image.[106] On the other hand, in the Cox's Bazar region the Englishman was unable to find evidence of religious ideas of any sort. "They said they knew no god (Thakur) and that they never prayed to Maha Muni, Ram, nor Khooda"[107]—that is, deities associated respectively with the Buddhist, Hindu, and Muslim traditions. Clearly, by the end of the eighteenth century, scripturally legitimated religions had as yet gained only a tenuous foothold, if any at all, among the *jhūm* population of Bengal's extreme eastern edge. Here Allah—or his Persian equivalent, Khudā—was only one among several high gods in current circulation.

Like François Pyrard before him, Buchanan seems to have brought into Bengal's interior an understanding of religions as static, closed, and mutually exclusive systems, each with its own community and its own superhuman beings. For Pyrard, these were "Mahometans" and "Gentiles"; for Buchanan, followers of "Maha-moony" (i.e., Buddhists), "Mohammedans," and "Hindoos." But what Pyrard and Buchanan encountered were systems of religious beliefs and practices that at the folk level were strikingly porous and fluid, bounded by no clear conceptual frontiers. In fact, it was precisely the fluidity of folk Bengali cosmology that allowed

106. Ibid., 62–63.
107. Ibid., 67.

Bengalis to interact creatively with exogenous ideas and agencies, as is summarized in table 9. Both indigenous and the Islamic cosmologies comprised hierarchies of superhuman agencies that included at the upper end one or another high god (or goddess) presiding over a cosmos filled with lesser superhuman agencies. Allah was identified as the Islamic high god, followed by a host of lesser superhuman agencies, including the Prophet Muhammad at the upper end and various charismatic *pīrs* at the lower end. Initially, superhuman agencies identified with contemporary Perso-Islamic culture were simply included in local cosmologies alongside indigenous powers already there. In time, these became identified with those in the indigenous cosmology; still later, they were understood to have displaced the latter altogether.

As with that of any other exogenous agency, however, the advance of Islamic superhuman agencies in Bengali cosmologies was always inhibited by the perception that they were alien. To be widely accepted, a deity had to be perceived not only as powerful and efficacious but as genuinely local.[108] Thus the success of Islam in Bengal lay ultimately in the extent to which superhuman beings that had originated in Arab culture and subsequently appropriated (and been appropriated by) Hebrew, Greek, and Iranian civilizations, succeeded during the sixteenth through eighteenth centuries in appropriating (and being appropriated by) Bengali civilization. Initially, this involved the association or identification of Islamic with Bengali superhuman beings. But when figures like Adam, Eve, and Abraham became identified with central leitmotifs of Bengali history and civilization, Islam had become established as profoundly and authentically Bengali.

---

108. Around the turn of the twentieth century a Chittagong beggar, in explaining why he had renounced his earlier conversion to Christianity, declared that "a local Krishna is better than a foreign Krishna." Risley Collection, "Reports on the Religious and Social Divisions," 9: 286–87.

11   Conclusion

Like the strata of a geologic fossil record, place names covering the surface of a map silently testify to past historical processes. In Bengal they betray a major theme of the delta's history—the advance of agrarian civilization over the forest. Names of villages and cities alike speak of clearing marsh or forest, establishing markets, and founding urban centers. Suffixes meaning "city" (Beng., -nagar, -pur) refer to an endpoint in this process, as in Krishnanagar or Faridpur. Suffixes meaning "market" (Beng., -hāṭ; Pers., -bāzār) or "storehouse" (Pers., -ganj) indicate the monetized and commercial basis of the movement, as in Bagerhat, Cossimbazar, or Bakarganj. Suffixes meaning "cultivated area" (Pers., -ābād) point to earlier stages in the process (e.g., Murshidabad), while suffixes meaning "clearing" echo its very earliest phase. Such is the case with -kāṭi, cognate with the English "cut," found in numerous settlements in the eastern delta— for example, Swarupkati or Jhalakati in Barisal District.[1]

The other great theme of the premodern period was the establishment and evolution of Islamic society and culture in Bengal. It would be wrong, however, to view Islam as some monolithic agency that simply "expanded" across space, time, and social class, in the process assimilating great numbers of people into a single framework of piety. Rather, the religion was itself continuously reinterpreted as different social classes in different periods became its dominant carriers. Thus, in the thirteenth century, Islam had been associated with the ruling ethos of the delta's Turkish conquerors, and in the cities, at least, such an association persisted for several centuries, sustained especially by Sufi shaikhs of the Chishti order.

1. H. Beveridge, *The District of Bakarganj: Its History and Statistics* (London: Trubner, 1876), 223.

Somewhat later, the Mughal conquest permitted an influx of a new elite class of *ashrāf* Muslims—immigrants from points west of the delta, or their descendants—who were typically administrators, soldiers, mystics, scholars, or long-distance merchants. For them, a rich tradition of Persian art and literature served to mediate and inform Islamic piety, which most of them subordinated to the secular ethos of Mughal imperialism. By the seventeenth and eighteenth centuries, however, the dominant carriers of Islamic civilization in Bengal were not the urban *ashrāf*, but peasant cultivators of the eastern frontier, who in extraordinary ways assimilated Islam to their agrarian worldview.

These two interrelated themes of Bengal's premodern period—agrarian growth and Islamization—were products of various forces. Certainly, the cultural accommodation achieved during the two and a half centuries between 1342 and 1599 contributed to the ultimate Islamization of the delta. This period opened with Sultan Shams al-Din Ilyas Shah's founding of Bengal's first independent Muslim dynasty and closed with the death of 'Isa Khan, the delta's last effective independent ruler prior to the Mughal age. Cut off from North India and deprived of fresh military or administrative recruits from points west, Bengal's rulers in this period found their political moorings in local society and culture, especially after the Raja Ganesh revolution of 1410–15. It was at this time, too, that the delta was drawn into an Indian Ocean commercial network permeated by an Islamic ethos. This was a "world system" not just in Immanuel Wallerstein's narrowly economic sense of the phrase[2] but in the wider sense of an arena for the circulation of shared texts and values sustained by Sufis, pilgrims, merchants, adventurers, scholars, and soldiers. Both the nature of that system and Bengal's inclusion in it are seen in Ibn Battuta's 1345 visit to Sylhet: the famous world traveler had gone there not to engage in trade but to gain the spiritual blessings of a renowned holy man, Shah Jalal.

Yet the political accommodations that characterized the sultanate period and the delta's inclusion in the Indian Ocean culture system were not, of themselves, sufficient to bring about the emergence of Islam as a mass religion. This outcome occurred in the context of other historical forces, among them the shift of the epicenter of agrarian civilization from the western delta to the eastern hinterland. This in turn was a function of a long-term eastward movement of the great river systems that bore the silt and fresh water necessary for wet rice agriculture—a chronologically deep ecological process corresponding to Fernand Braudel's understanding of

2. See Immanuel Wallerstein, *The Modern World-System: Capitalist Agriculture and the Origins of the European World-Economy in the Sixteenth Century* (New York: Academic Press, 1974).

structure or *longue durée*.[3] A decisive moment was reached in the late six-teenth century when the Ganges River linked up with the Padma, as a consequence of which the Ganges's main discharge flowed directly into the heart of the eastern delta. By momentous coincidence, this happened about the time that Akbar launched efforts to incorporate the entire delta into the Mughal Empire, thereby ending Bengal's two and a half centuries of political isolation from North India. As a result, the Ganges carried the Mughal conquerors straight into what had been for the Bengal sultans a distant, forested hinterland. There the new rulers planted their provincial headquarters.

To be sure, Dhaka was selected as the Mughals' provincial capital for strategic reasons: Raja Man Singh and Islam Khan needed a staging site for subduing independent-minded chieftains who had taken refuge in the eastern hinterland. However, the choice of Dhaka had far-reaching impli-cations, since it concentrated the Mughals' political energies on the part of the delta that, having just become its most active sector ecologically, was ripest for agrarian expansion. Once recalcitrant chieftains had submitted to imperial authority, Mughal officers in Dhaka endeavored to deepen the roots of that authority at more local levels. In the western delta, where a functioning agrarian order had long been in place, the Mughals simply overwhelmed or coopted existing elites (*zamīndārs*) much as they had al-ready done with those of the upper Gangetic Plain. But the eastern hinter-land—virtually the whole delta east of the Karatoya and south of the Padma—was, in the early seventeenth century, still largely undeveloped, a region covered by marsh or forest. Here the problem was not so much winning over the local gentry as creating one, and at the same time creat-ing an agrarian base.

In the east, then, agrarian and political frontiers collapsed into one. From Sylhet through Chittagong the government fused the political goal of deepening its authority among dependent clients rooted on the land, with the economic goal of expanding the arable land area. A principal in-strument for achieving these goals was the land grant that aimed at the agricultural development of the forested hinterland. Data for the entire delta are not available, but those for the modern-day districts of Dhaka, Bakarganj, Sylhet, and Chittagong suggest the general movement. Al-though Vaishnava temples, Śaiva temples, and individual Brahmans re-ceived numerous forest grants, the bulk of these went to members of Is-

3. See Fernand Braudel, *La Méditerranée et le monde méditerranéen à l'époque de Philippe II* (Paris: A. Colin, 1949). Translated by Sian Reynolds as *The Mediterra-nean and the Mediterranean World in the Age of Philip II* (New York: Harper & Row, 1972).

lam's religious gentry—petty *mullās*, pilgrims returned from Mecca, preachers, and holy men (*pīrs*)—men who had overseen, or had undertaken to oversee, the clearing of forest and the construction of mosques or shrines. Although humble in physical appearance, these institutions became the nuclei of new communities, attracting local or distant labor for clearing the forest and working the rice fields included in the grants. These institutions also possessed considerable cultural influence, becoming the nuclei for the diffusion of Islamic ideals along the eastern frontier. In this way Islam gradually became associated with economic development and agricultural productivity.

In short, Bengal's eastern zone was not only an agrarian and political frontier, but also a cultural one, as Islam became locally understood as a civilization-building ideology, a religion of the plow. According to the *Nabī-Baṃśa*, Saiyid Sultan's epic poem composed in the late sixteenth century, the father of the human race, Adam, had made his earthly appearance on Sondwip Island, off Bengal's southeastern coast. There the angel Gabriel instructed him to go to Arabia, where at Mecca he would construct the original Ka'aba.[4] When this was accomplished, Gabriel gave Adam a plow, a yoke, two bulls, and seed, addressing him with the words, "Niranjan [God] has commanded that agriculture will be your destiny (*bhāl*)." Adam then planted the seeds, harvested the crop, ground the grain, and made bread.[5] Present-day Muslim cultivators attach a similar significance to Adam's career. Cultivators of Pabna District identify the earth's soil, from which Adam was made, as the source of Adam's power and of his ability to cultivate the earth. In their view, farming the earth successfully is the fundamental task of all mankind, not only because they themselves have also come from (i.e., were nurtured by the fruit of) the soil, but because it was God's command to Adam that he reduce the earth to the plow. It was by farming the earth that Adam obeyed God, thereby articulating his identity as the first man and as the first Muslim. Hence all men descended from Adam, in this view, can most fully demonstrate their obedience to God—and indeed, their humanity—by cultivating the earth.[6]

Similar ideas are found in Saiyid Sultan's treatment of Abraham, the

4. Saiyid Sultan, *Nabī-Baṃśa*, 1: 88, 98, 103.
5. Ibid., 107–9. To Adam's wife Eve, meanwhile, Gabriel gave fire, with which she mastered the art of cooking. Boiling some milk, Eve made *sandeś*—a famous Bengali sweet that, the poet observes, has no equal. Ibid., 110.
6. John P. Thorp, "Masters of Earth: Conceptions of 'Power' among Muslims of Rural Bangladesh" (Ph.D. diss., University of Chicago, 1978), 40–54. Although Adam's career as a tiller of the soil is also found in the Book of Genesis (3:23), such an association is not made in the Qur'an. In the Muslim world, the perception of Adam as the first cultivator, and of his taking up cultivation at the command of

supreme patriarch of Judeo-Christian-Islamic civilization. Born and raised in a forest, Abraham traveled to Palestine, where he attracted tribes from nearby lands, mobilized local labor to cut down the forest, and built a holy place, Jerusalem's Temple, where prayers could be offered to Niranjan.[7] It is obvious that the main themes of Abraham's life as recorded by Saiyid Sultan—his sylvan origins, his recruitment of nearby tribesmen, his leadership in clearing the forest, and his building a house of prayer—precisely mirrored the careers of the hundreds of pioneering *pīrs* and petty *'ulamā* who, during the sixteenth to eighteenth centuries, mobilized local clients in the Bengali countryside for just such activities.

The religious authority possessed by the hundreds of tiny mosques and shrines that sprang up along the eastern frontier was enhanced by, among other things, the simultaneous diffusion of papermaking technology. Traceable to the fifteenth century and unmistakably identified with Islamic civilization—the Bengali for "paper" and "pen" are both Perso-Arabic loan words—the new technology fostered attitudes that endowed the written word with an authority qualitatively different from oral authority. With the proliferation of books and the religious gentry in the countryside, a "culture of literacy" began to spread far beyond the state's bureaucratic sector or the delta's urban centers. Contemporary government sources confirm that Qur'an readers were attached to rural mosques and shrines as part of their endowments, while Bengali sources dating from the fifteenth century refer to the magical power popularly attributed to the Qur'an. In particular, the culture of literacy endowed the cult of Allah with a kind of authority—that of the unchangeable written word—that preliterate forest cults had lacked. For, apart from those areas along the older river valleys where Hindu civilization had already made inroads among indigenous peoples, most of the eastern hinterland was populated by communities lightly touched, if touched at all, by Hindu culture. In the east, then, Islam came to be understood as the religion, not only of the ax and the plow, but also of the book.

Moreover, the frontier folk of the eastern delta do not appear to have perceived Islam as alien, or as a closed, exclusive system to be accepted or rejected as a whole. Today one habitually thinks of world religions as self-contained "culture-boxes" with well-defined borders respecting belief and practice. But such a static or fixed understanding of religion does not apply to the premodern Bengal frontier, a fluid context in which Islamic superhu-

---

God, may be a uniquely Bengali variant. On the other hand, the notion that God fashioned Adam from clay is common to both Genesis (2:7) and the Qur'an (15:26).
7. Saiyid Sultan, *Nabī-Baṃśa*, 1: 348, 420–21.

man agencies, typically identified with local superhuman agencies, gradually seeped into local cosmologies that were themselves dynamic. This "seepage" occurred over such a long period of time that one can at no point identify a specific moment of "conversion," or any single moment when peoples saw themselves as having made a dramatic break with the past. To a greater degree than elsewhere in India, Islam in Bengal absorbed so much local culture and became so profoundly identified with Bengal's long-term process of agrarian expansion, that in its formative years the cultivating classes never seem to have regarded it as "foreign"—even though some Muslim and Hindu literati and foreign observers did.[8] As late as the early twentieth century, Muslim cultivators retained indigenous names like Chand, Pal, and Dutt.[9] In the context of premodern Bengal, then, it would seem inappropriate to speak of the "conversion" of "Hindus" to Islam. What one finds, rather, is an expanding agrarian civilization, whose cultural counterpart was the growth of the cult of Allah. This larger movement was composed of several interwoven processes: the eastward movement and settlement of colonizers from points west, the incorporation of frontier tribal peoples into the expanding agrarian civilization, and the natural population growth that accompanied the diffusion or the intensification of wet rice agriculture and the production of surplus food grains.

Because this growth process combined natural, political, economic, and cultural forces, we find in eastern Bengal a remarkable congruence between a socioeconomic system geared to the production of wet rice and a religious ideology that conferred special meaning on agrarian life. It is thus hardly surprising that in the twentieth century, Bengali Muslim villagers have been found to refuse, whenever possible, to engage in non-cultivating occupations. A 1913 village survey in Dhaka District noted that the Muslims "entirely fall upon agriculture as their only source of income, and unless driven to the last stage of starvation they never hire themselves for any kind of service, which is looked upon with contempt on their part."[10] In 1908 the gazetteer for Khulna District noted that the Muslim masses "are descendants of semi-Hinduized aborigines, principally Chandals and Pods" who "do not, however, know or admit that they are the descendants of converts to Islam; according to them they are the tillers of the soil."[11]

8. In the nineteenth and twentieth centuries, British imperialists and both Hindu and Muslim reformers stressed Islam's "foreignness," each for their own reasons. But this should not blind us to the situation before the advent of British colonial rule.
9. Webster, *Eastern Bengal and Assam District Gazetteers: Noakhali*, 39.
10. Dhaka District Collectorate Record Room, "Mauza Notes," Rupganj Thana, Mauza Agla, No. 1063.
11. O'Malley, *Eastern Bengal District Gazetteers, Khulna*, 65.

Such attitudes, however, were not and are not shared by the *ashrāf*, the small but influential class of mainly urban Muslims who perpetuated the Mughals' ruling-class mentality, cultivated Urdu and Persian, and typically claimed ancestral origins west of the delta. If the rural masses saw themselves as good Muslims *because* they cultivated the soil, the *ashrāf* disdained the plow and refused to touch it.[12] Members of this social class typically viewed their ancestors as men who had come to India to administer a vast empire, and not to join indigenous peasants as fellow cultivators. Herein lay the basis of a social cleavage between rural Muslims and noncultivating *ashrāf* that would further widen in the context of the political and religious movements of the nineteenth and twentieth centuries.[13]

The findings summarized above refute stereotypes found in both Indian historiography and Islamic studies. One of these is the tendency to see the Mughal Empire in the eighteenth century as hopelessly mired in decline, disorder, chaos, and collapse. In part, this view grew out of a British imperial historiographical tradition serving to legitimize the European conquest and occupation of India by contrasting the alleged dynamism of "modern" (i.e., British imperial) India with the alleged chaos or stagnation of "traditional" (i.e., pre-British) India. In part, too, the view of the eighteenth century as one of endemic decline and disorder grew out of a centrist bias common to both British imperial and Mughal schools of historiography. Viewed from the parapets of the imperial Red Fort in Delhi, things did indeed look bad throughout most of the eighteenth century: revenue failed to arrive from the provinces, rebellions sprang up everywhere, and governors acted independently of central authority.[14] Written by courtiers steeped in a "Red Fort view" of India, contemporary court chronicles naturally reflected a centrist perspective, as did subsequent histories based on such materials.

Original sources for the history of premodern Bengal reveal a very different picture, however. In place of a stagnant or decadent society, one sees one characterized by physical expansion and religious integration, a picture of both Mughal and Islamic ascendancy. Here, however, one must distinguish between the empire as centralized imperial power—the ability of

12. As a 1901 survey of Muslims of Nadia District reported, the *ashrāf* "will not adopt cultivation for their living. They consider cultivation to be a degraded occupation and they shun it for that reason." Risley Collection, "Reports on the Religious and Social Divisions," 88.
13. See Rafiuddin Ahmed, *Bengal Muslims*.
14. A good summary of the historiography of Mughal decline, and a fresh view of it from the perspective of two provinces, Punjab and Awadh, is found in Muzaffar Alam, *The Crisis of Empire in Mughal North India: Awadh and the Punjab, 1707–48* (Delhi: Oxford University Press, 1986).

officials in Delhi to elicit obedience on the political periphery—and the empire as a bureaucratic and ideological framework, as a cultural system. It is the latter vision of the Mughal empire that this study has emphasized. For, even while central power in Delhi declined, rendering Bengal effectively independent from the second decade of the eighteenth century on, the ideological and bureaucratic structure of Mughal imperialism continued to expand in the Bengal delta.[15] Beginning in the seventeenth century and continuing right up to the advent of British power in 1760, including the period from around 1712 when central imperial authority visibly disintegrated, eastern Bengal experienced unparalleled growth, as vast stretches of forest were cut and its land cleared for cultivation. Settlers moving into these areas gave religious and political direction to newly established agrarian communities, into which local peoples were absorbed, while provincial officials carved new revenue units around these agrarian settlements, thereby integrating them into the Mughal bureaucratic and ideological framework. Thus the local history of Bengal, like those of eighteenth-century Awadh and Punjab as studied by Muzaffar Alam,[16] or of Maharashtra as studied by André Wink,[17] demonstrates the degree of provincial growth that took place under the banner of Mughal imperialism even while the imperial center experienced visible decline.

Secondly, European colonialists have long stereotyped the Muslim clergy, or *'ulamā*, as a conservative class of men obstinately hostile to "change." Aware that North Africa, India, and Indonesia had all been ruled by Muslims prior to the rise of European imperialism, French, British, and Dutch colonial officials anxiously suspected Muslim resentment of their rule in those regions. In 1871 W. W. Hunter published an influential book that portrayed India's *'ulamā* as stagnant, unprogressive, disenfranchised, and potentially seditious—a stereotype that lingered long after the close of the colonial era.[18] Evidence presented in this study, however, has pointed to the dynamic role played by Bengal's religious gentry in advancing the

15. The decline of central power is usually dated from the death of Aurangzeb (1707), although it was after the death of Shah 'Alam (1712) that the disintegration of central power is most dramatically seen, as in palace revolutions and in the emergence of independent provincial dynasties in places like Hyderabad and Lucknow. Bengal's own de facto independence from centralized Mughal authority dated from the governorship of Murshid Quli Khan (1713–27). See Jadunath Sarkar, ed., *History of Bengal*, 405–13.
16. See Alam, *Crisis of Empire*.
17. See Wink, *Land and Sovereignty in India*.
18. William Wilson Hunter, *The Indian Musalmans: Are They Bound in Conscience to Rebel against the Queen?* (London: Trubner, 1871).

frontiers of both the Mughal political-ideological system and the Islamic world.

A stereotype common among Islamicists is the understanding of Islam as an essentially "urban" religion: a religion of shopkeepers and artisans focused on the city or town bazaar, or of administrators and scholars focused on *madrasas*, mosques, and courts of law. All these were natural orientations of members of the *ashrāf* who cultivated administration and education, wrote books, and claimed to speak on behalf of Bengali Muslims generally. Men like Khondkar Fuzli Rubbee and Abu A. Ghuznavi, discussed in Chapter 5, illustrate both the perspective and the intellectual influence of this social class. But the association of Islam with urban culture, assumed by *ashrāf* Muslims, has led scholars to ignore the overwhelmingly rural nature of Islam in the Bengal delta. This study has sought to correct this by drawing attention to the agrarian basis of the ethnogenesis of the vast majority of Bengali Muslims.

Finally, from a world history perspective, the Bengali experience with religious growth was perhaps not at all unique. There is at least one other case—western Java—in which Islam grew in tandem with deforestation, agrarian expansion, and the establishment of small mosques on lands granted by the state.[19] A better-known parallel is found in the history of Christianity in northern Europe. From the sixth century and especially between the eleventh and thirteenth centuries (*"l'âge des grands défriche-ments,"* according to French writers), monastic orders like the Benedictines and the Cistercians actively planted monasteries in wooded regions, where they took the lead in clearing forests, converting unbelievers, and extending agriculture. Especially noteworthy are the religious aspects of this process: the desacralization of the forest, the Christianization of native peoples, and the sanctification of pioneering monks.[20] "As they pushed into the woodlands and felled the trees," writes Richard Koebner, monks

19. Between the sixteenth and nineteenth centuries, *hājīs* backed with tax-free, state-supported land grants pioneered new rice-cultivating agrarian communities in formerly forested regions of the sultanate of Banten, on the western tip of Java. Sartono Kartodirdjo, *The Peasants' Revolt of Banten in 1888: Its Conditions, Course and Sequel* (The Hague: Martinus Nijhoff, 1966), 34–61.

20. A dramatic example of this is seen in the activities of Wilfred Boniface, an eighth-century saint who preached in the forests of what is now Germany. In the presence of a great crowd of pagans, Boniface personally chopped down a sacred and exceptionally large oak tree known to the German peoples as the "Oak of Jupiter." On witnessing this, the crowd formally accepted the Christian cult, while Boniface built an oratory from the felled timber and dedicated it to St. Peter. Wilhelm Levison, *England and the Continent in the Eighth Century* (Oxford: Clarendon Press, 1946), 45–46.

"helped to dispel that religious awe which the Germans had to overcome before they would attack thick forest. The attraction of the Church's miraculous powers was transferred to the holy men in the woods, and brought the laity to settle near them."[21] Although the early movement's austere pioneers were succeeded by rich landlords who managed wealthy estates, we should not ignore the civilization-building role that monastic establishments had earlier played in the forests of northern Europe.

Viewed historically, religious systems are created, cultural artifacts, and not timeless structures lying beyond human societies. As such they are continuously reinterpreted and readapted to particular sociocultural environments. Yet even while this happens, religious traditions transform those environments in creative ways. Herein lies, perhaps, the secret of the successful world religions, for when they are not flexible or adaptable, they tend to ossify into hollow shells, and survive only in museums or forgotten texts. Christianity would never have flourished—and perhaps not even have survived—had it not absorbed a great part of both the imperial culture and the Germanic popular culture of the late Roman Empire.[22]

This is no less true of Islam and the Bengal frontier. In the "success stories" of world religions, and the story of Islam in Bengal is surely among these, the norms of religion and the realities of local sociocultural systems ultimately accommodate one another. Although theorists, theologians, or reformers may resist this point, it seems nonetheless to be intuitively

21. Richard Koebner, "The Settlement and Colonization of Europe," in *The Cambridge Economic History of Europe*, vol. 1, *The Agrarian Life of the Middle Ages*, ed. M. M. Postan, 2d ed. (Cambridge: Cambridge University Press, 1966), 45. A description of twelfth-century Cistercian activities in northern Germany runs as follows: "The abbot was with the workers when they started to fell the trees for making the arable. In one hand he had a wooden cross, in the other a vessel of holy water. When he arrived in the center of the woods, he planted the cross in the earth, took possession of this untouched piece of earth in the name of Jesus Christ, sprinkled holy water around the area, and finally grasped an axe to cut away some shrubs. The small clearing made by the abbot was the starting point for the monks' work. One work group (*incisores*) cut down the trees, a second (*exstirpatores*) took out the trunks, a third (*incensores*) burnt up the roots, boughs, and the undergrowth." Cited in Clarence J. Glacken, *Traces on the Rhodian Shore: Nature and Culture in Western Thought from Ancient Times to the End of the Eighteenth Century* (Berkeley and Los Angeles: University of California Press, 1967), 309. Glacken writes of the "exaltation in changing nature" found throughout the Middle Ages, citing a phrase repeatedly encountered in Carolingian texts, "horridae quondam solitudines ferarum, nunc amoenissima diversoria hominum"—that is, what formerly were frightful wastelands suited only for beasts have now become most pleasant abodes for man. Ibid., 312.
22. See Judith Herrin, *The Formation of Christendom* (Oxford: Basil Blackwell, 1987), esp. pt. 1, 19–127; Robin Lane Fox, *Pagans and Christians* (New York: Knopf, 1987).

grasped by common folk. A famous proverb, known throughout Bengal and northern India and uttered usually with a smile, implicitly links social status with Islamically legitimated titles:

> The first year I was a Shaikh, the second year a Khan;
> This year if the price of grain is low I'll become a Saiyid.[23]

What made Islam in Bengal not only historically successful but a continuing vital social reality has been its capacity to adapt to the land and the culture of its people, even while transforming both.

23. The proverb's Persian form is:

> Shaikh būdam sāl-i auwal; Khān shudam sāl-i dīgar.
> Ghalla gar arzān shavad, imsāl Saiyid mīshavam.

Census of India, 1931, 5, pt. 1, "Bengal and Sikkim" (Calcutta, 1933), 422.

Mint Towns and Inscription Sites under Muslim Rulers, 1204–1760

No.	Site	Mint Town (x) or Inscription Site (o)	District	Reference	Earliest Date of Site

GOVERNORS, BALBANI RULERS, SHAMS AL-DIN FIRUZ, AND SUCCESSORS
(1204–81; 1281–1300; 1301–22; 1322–42; SEE MAP 2A)

No.	Site	Mint/Insc.	District	Reference	Earliest Date
1	Siwan	o	Birbhum	10	1221
2	Naohata	o	Rajshahi	19: no. 3	1229–30
3	Lakhnauti (Gaur)	x	Malda	2	1236
4	Bihar	o	Patna	1: 1	1242
5	Gangarampur	o	W. Dinajpur	1: 4	1249
6	Sitalmat	o	Rajshahi	19: no. 6	1254
7	Mahesvara	o	Monghyr	1: 11	1292
8	Lakhisarai	o	Monghyr	1: 12	1297
9	Devikot	o	W. Dinajpur	1: 15	1297
10	Tribeni	o	Hooghly	1: 18	1298
11	Mahasthangarh	o	Bogra	1: 21	1300
12	Bang	x	Eastern Bengal, location uncertain	2	1302
13	Sylhet	o	Sylhet	1: 24	1303
14	Sonargaon	x	Dhaka	2	1305

No.	Site	Mint Town (x) or Inscription Site (o)	District	Reference	Earliest Date of Site
15	Wazir-Beldanga	o	Rajshahi	19: no. 17	1322
16	Ghiyathpur	x	Mymensingh	2	1322
17	Satgaon	x	Howrah	2	1328
18	Firuzabad (Pandua)	x	Malda	2	1341

ILYAS SHAHI AND RAJA GANESH DYNASTIES
(1342–1414; 1415–33; SEE MAP 2B)

No.	Site		District	Reference	Earliest Date of Site
19	Calcutta	o	Twenty-four Parganas	1: 31	1342
20	Kamru	x	Northern Bengal, location uncertain	2	1357
21	Mu'azzamabad	x	Dhaka	2	1358
22	Pandua	o	Malda	1: 35	1369
23	Mulla Simla	o	Hooghly	1: 38	1375
24	Chittagong	x	Chittagong	2	1415
25	Fatehabad	x	Faridpur	6	1418
26	Rotspur (probably Rohtas)	x	Shahabad	2	1423
27	Mandra	o	Dhaka	1: 44	1427
28	Sultanganj	o	Rajshahi	1: 46	1432

RESTORED ILYAS SHAHIS, ABYSSINIAN KINGS AND HUSAIN SHAHIS
(1433–86; 1486–93; 1493–1538; SEE MAP 2C)

No.	Site		District	Reference	Earliest Date of Site
29	Baliaghata	o	Murshidabad	1: 49	1443
30	Bhagalpur	o	Bhagalpur	1: 51	1446
31	Balanagar	o	Birbhum	1: 52	1450
32	Ghagra	o	Mymensingh	1: 54	1452
33	Navagram	o	Pabna	15	1454
34	Malda	o	Malda	1: 55	1455
35	Dhaka	o	Dhaka	1: 57	1456
36	Ghazipur	o	Ghazipur, U.P.	19: no. 59	1459–74
37	Tejpur	o	Mymensingh	19: no. 43	1459
38	Bagerhat	o	Khulna	1: 64	1459
39	Barbakabad (Mahisantosh)	o	Rajshahi	1: 73	1459
40	Dinajpur	o	Dinajpur	1: 71	1460
41	Bhanga	o	Cachar	1: 76	1463

No.	Site	Mint Town (x) or Inscription Site (o)	District	Reference	Earliest Date of Site
42	Deotala	o	Malda	1: 77	1464
43	Peril	o	Dhaka	1: 79	1465
44	Mirzaganj	o	Bakarganj	1: 81	1465
45	Basirhat	o	Twenty-four Parganas	1: 88	1466
46	Gurai	o	Mymensingh	1: 83	1467
47	Hathazari	o	Chittagong	1: 91	1474
48	Birol	o	Dinajpur	1: 128	1475
49	Chhota Pandua	o	Hooghly	1: 97	1477
50	Bandar	o	Dhaka	1: 113	1481
51	Muhammadabad	x	Jessore	4, 7: 44	1481–86
52	Dhamrai	o	Dhaka	1: 117	1482
53	Bikrampur (Rampal)	o	Dhaka	1: 118	1483
54	Mandaran	x	Hooghly	5	1483
55	Rohanpur	o	Rajshahi	19: no. 81	1486
56	Garh Jaripa	o	Mymensingh	1: 134	1486–89
57	Kalna	o	Burdwan	1: 138	1489
58	Chunakhali	o	Murshidabad	1: 140	1490
59	Nawabganj	o	Malda	1: 147	1492
60	Depara	o	Hooghly	9	1494
61	Chandrabad (Chandpur)	x	Comilla	2	1493–1519
62	Raikha	o	Burdwan	11	1493–1519
63	Suata	o	Burdwan	11	1496
64	Kheraul	o	Murshidabad	1: 152	1495
65	Monghyr	o	Monghyr	1: 153	1497
66	Kusumba	o	Rajshahi	1: 155	1498
67	Margram	o	Murshidabad	1: 154	1499
68	Mahalbari	o	Dinajpur	15	1500
69	Babargram	o	Murshidabad	1: 156	1500
70	Arashnagar	o	Khulna	15	1501
71	Machain	o	Dhaka	1: 159	1501
72	Ismailpur	o	Saran	1: 157	1501
73	Hemtabad	o	W. Dinajpur	17: 84	1501
74	Bonahra	o	Bhagalpur	16: 104	1502
75	Suti	o	Murshidabad	1: 162	1503
76	Chirand	o	Saran	1: 163	1503
77	Narhan	o	Saran	16: 108	1503

No.	Site	Mint Town (x) or Inscription Site (o)	District	Reference	Earliest Date of Site
78	Azimnagar	o	Dhaka	1: 167	1504
79	Jhilli	o	Murshidabad	1: 171	1505
80	Ulipur	o	Rangpur	12	1506
81	Atiya	o	Mymensingh	1: 180	1507
82	Mangalkot	o	Burdwan	1: 184	1510
83	Nawadah	o	Patna	1: 187	1510
84	Patna	o	Patna	16: 110	1510
85	Sakulipur	o	Birbhum	11	1510
86	Kaitahar	o	Bogra	13	1510
87	Kherur	o	Murshidabad	1: 193	1515
88	Khalifatabad (Bagerhat)	x	Khulna	2	1516
89	Suri	o	Birbhum	11	1516
90	Bholahat	o	Malda	1: 195	1517
91	Nusratabad (Ghoraghat)	x	Dinajpur	2	1518
92	Barabazar	o	Jessore	14	1519
93	Kantaduar	o	Rangpur	1: 202	1493–1519
94	Chakdah	o	Nadia	1: 205	1493–1519
95	Matihani	o	Monghyr	16: 114	1519–32
96	Bagha	o	Rajshahi	1: 212	1523
97	Bandel	o	Hooghly	1: 214	1524
98	Ashrafpur	o	Dhaka	3: 68	1524
99	Navagram	o	Pabna	1: 218	1526
100	Sikandarpur	o	Azamgarh	1: 221	1527
101	Murshidabad	o	Murshidabad	1: 227	1529
102	Santoshpur	o	Hooghly	1: 229	1530
103	Dhorail	o	W. Dinajpur	1: 236	1533
104	Jowar	o	Mymensingh	1: 239	1534
105	Purnea	o	Purnea	16: 116	1536
106	Shahpur	o	Malda	1: 239	1536

AFGHANS AND MUGHALS
(1538–75; 1575–1760; SEE MAP 2D)

No.	Site		District	Reference	Earliest Date of Site
107	Sherpur	o	Bogra	1: 248	1552
108	Rajmahal	o	Santal Parganas	1: 241	1556
109	Kumarpur	o	Rajshahi	1: 244	1558
110	Burdwan	o	Burdwan	1: 256	1562

No.	Site	Mint Town (x) or Inscription Site (o)	District	Reference	Earliest Date of Site
111	Chatmohar	o	Pabna	1: 259	1581
112	Barar Char	o	Comilla	19: no. 218	1591
113	Nayabari	o	Dhaka	19: no. 217	1591–92
114	Dohar	o	Dhaka	19: no. 219	1591–92
115	Brahmanbaria	o	Comilla	15	1600
116	Karatia	o	Mymensingh	19: no. 223	1610
117	Sarail	o	Comilla	15	1615
118	Kesiari	o	Midnapur	8	1622
119	Sherpur	o	Birbhum	1: 271	1632
120	Rajshahi	o	Rajshahi	1: 271	1634
121	Nawadah	o	Murshidabad	1: 277	1642
122	Egarasindhur	o	Mymensingh	1: 278	1652
123	Hajo	o	Kamrup	1: 280	1657
124	Durgapur	o	Bogra	19: no. 251	1675
125	Masjidpara	o	Mymensingh	18: 99	1699
126	Inchlabazar	o	Burdwan	1: 292	1703
127	Shanbandi (Dinanath)	o	Hooghly	1: 296	1723

Sources
EIAPS = *Epigraphia Indica, Arabic and Persian Supplement.*
JVRM = *Journal of the Varendra Research Museum.*

1. Shamsud-Din Ahmed, *Inscriptions.*
2. Karim, *Corpus of the Muslim Coins,* table II.
3. Dani, *Bibliography of the Muslim Inscriptions.*
4. M. Mir Jahan, "Mint Towns of Medieval Bengal," *Pakistan History Conference, Proceedings 1953* (3d session): 238.
5. G. S. Farid, "Madaran, a New Mint of Fath Shah of Bengal, dated 887/1483," *Indo-Iranica* 33, nos. 1–4 (March–December 1980): 143–45.
6. Ahmad Hasan Dani, "The House of Raja Ganesa of Bengal," *Journal of the Asiatic Society* 18, no. 2 (1952): 145.
7. Habib, *Atlas of the Mughal Empire.*
8. W. H. Siddiqi, "Three Mughal Inscriptions from Kesiari, West Bengal," *EIAPS* (1961): 69–73.
9. M. F. Khan, "Three New Inscriptions of 'Alau'd-Din Huasin Shah," *EIAPS* (1965): 23–28.
10. Z. A. Desai, "An Early Thirteenth Century Inscription from West Bengal," *EIAPS* (1975): 6–12.
11. S. S. Hussain, "Some More New Inscriptions of Husain Shah from West Bengal," *EIAPS* (1975): 31–38.
12. A. K. M. Yakub Ali, "An Inscription of Ala'-ddin Husayn Shah," *JVRM* 2 (1973): 67–70.

13. A. K. M. Yakub Ali, "An Inscription of Sultan as-Salatin," *JVRM* 4 (1975–76): 63–69.
14. Sohrabuddin Ahmed, "Antiquities of Barabazar," *JVRM* 4 (1975–76): 71–80.
15. Habiba Khatun, "The Tomb of Arifail in Comilla District," *JVRM* 7 (1981–82): 183–86.
16. Qeyamuddin Ahmad, *Corpus.*
17. Asher, "Inventory."
18. Hasan, *Muslim Monuments.*
19. Siddiq, *Arabic and Persian Texts.*

Principal Rulers of Bengal, 1204–1757

Note: Some governors later became sultans, and in the process changed their names or titles. In the following table, such changes are indicated by arrows.

Governor	Sultan	Dates
DELHI SULTANATE (1206–1526)		
Muhammad Bakhtiyar		1204–6
Muhammad Shiran Khan		ca. 1206–7
Husam al-Din 'Iwaz ─────────────┐		ca. 1207–8
'Ali Mardan ──────────────↴ │		ca. 1208–10
	'Ala al–Din ↴	1210–1213
	Ghiyath al-Din 'Iwaz	1213–27
Nasir al-Din Mahmud		1227–29
Daulat Shah		1229
Malik 'Ala al-Din Jani		1229
Saif al-Din Aibek		1229–33
'Izz al-Din Tughral Tughan Khan		1233–44
Malik Qamr al-Din Tamar Khan		1244–46
Malik Ikhtiyar al-Din Yuzbak ──────↴		1246–55
	Mughith al-Din Yuzbak	1255–57
Malik 'Ala al-Din Mas'ud Jani		1257–58
'Izz al-Din Balban		1258–60
Muhammad Arsalan Khan		1260–ca. 1265
Sher Khan		uncertain
Amin Khan		uncertain
Mughith al-Din Tughral ────────↴		1268–ca. 1275
	Mughith al-Din Tughral	ca. 1275–1281

Governor	Sultan	Dates
Bughra Khan ─────────────┐		1281–87
BALBANI DYNASTY (1287–1301) ↓		
	Nasir al-Din Mahmud	1287–91
	Rukn al-Din Kaikaus	1291–1300
FIRUZ SHAHI DYNASTY (1301–42)		
	Shams al-Din Firuz Shah	1301–22
	Jalal al-Din Mahmud	ca. 1304–9
	Shihab al-Din Bughday Shah	1317–18
	Ghiyath al-Din Bahadur	1310–12, 1322–25
Nasir al-Din Ibrahim		ca. 1324–26
Ghiyath al-Din Bahadur		1328–33
Qadar Khan (Lakhnauti)		uncertain
'Izz al-Din Yahya (Satgaon)		uncertain
Bahram Khan (Sonargaon)		1328–38
	Fakhr al-Din Mubarak Shah (Sonargaon)	1338–49
	Ikhtiyar al-Din Ghazi Shah (Sonargaon)	1349–52
	'Ala al-Din 'Ali Shah (Lakhnauti)	1341–42
ILYAS SHAHI DYNASTY (1342–1415)		
	Shams al-Din Ilyas Shah	1342–57
	Sikandar Shah	1357–89
	Ghiyath al-Din A'zam Shah	1389–1410
	Saif Hamzah Shah	1410–11
	Shihab al-Din Bayazid Shah	1411–14
	'Ala al-Din Firuz Shah	1414
RAJA GANESH DYNASTY (1415–33)		
	Jalal al-Din Muhammad Shah	1415–32
	Shams al-Din Ahmad Shah	1432–33
RESTORED ILYAS SHAHI DYNASTY (1433–86)		
	Nasir al-Din Mahmud I	1433–59
	Rukn al-Din Barbak Shah	1459–74

Governor	Sultan	Dates
	Shams al-Din Yusuf Shah	1474–81
	Sikandar	1481
	Jalal al-Din Fath Shah	1481–86

ABYSSINIANS (1486–93)

	Barbak Shah-zadah	1486
	Saif al-Din Firuz Shah	1486–90
	Shams al-Din Muzaffar Shah	1490–93

HUSAIN SHAHI DYNASTY (1493–1538)

	'Ala al-Din Husain Shah	1493–1519
	Nasir al-Din Nusrat Shah	1519–32
	'Ala al-Din Firuz Shah	1532
	Ghiyath al-din Mahmud Shah	1532–38

SHER SHAH SUR AND SUCCESSORS (1538–64)

	Sher Shah Sur	1538
	(Emperor Humayun)	(1538–39)
	Sher Shah Sur	1539–45
	Islam Shah	1545–53
	Shams al-Din Muhammad Shah	1553–55
	Ghiyath al-Din Bahadur Shah	1556–60
	Ghiyath al-Din II	1560–63
	Ghiyath al-Din III	1563–64

KARRANI DYNASTY (1564–75)

	Taj Khan Karrani	1564–65
	Sulaiman Karrani	1565–72
	Bayazid Karrani	1572
	Daud Karrani	1572–75

MUGHAL DYNASTY (1526–1858)

Mun'im Khan		1574–75
Husain Quli Beg		1575–78
Muzaffar Khan Turbati		1579–80
Mirza 'Aziz Koka		1582–83
Shahbaz Khan		1583–85

Governor	Sultan	Dates
Sadiq Khan		1585–86
Wazir Khan		1586–87
Sa'id Khan		1587–94
Man Singh		1594–1606
Qutb al-Din Khan Koka		1606–7
Jahangir Quli Beg		1607–8
Islam Khan Chishti		1608–13
Qasim Khan Chishti		1613–17
Ibrahim Khan		1617–24
Mahabat Khan		1625–26
Mukarram Khan		1626–27
Fidai Khan		1627–28
Qasim Khan Juyini		1628–32
'Azam Khan Mir Muhammad Baqar		1632–35
Islam Khan Mashhadi		1635–39
Prince Muhammad Shuja'		1639–60
Mu'azzam Khan (Mir Jumla)		1660–63
Shaista Khan		1664–78
Fidai Khan		1678
Prince Muhammad 'Azam		1678–88
Khan Jahan Bahadur Khan		1688–89
Ibrahim Khan		1689–97
Prince 'Azim al-Din ('Azim al-Shan)		1697–1712
Murshid Quli Khan (Ja'far Khan)		1713–27
Shuja' al-Din Muhammad Khan		1727–39
Sarfaraz Khan		1739–40
Aliwardi Khan		1740–56
Siraj al-Daula		1756–57

Select Bibliography

PRIMARY SOURCES

Persian or Arabic

'Abd al-Latif. "Safar-nāma." In "A Description of North Bengal in 1609 A.D." Translated by Jadunath Sarkar. *Bengal Past and Present* 35 (1928): 143–46.

'Abd al-Razzaq. "Matla' al-sa'dain." Extracts in *The History of India as Told by Its Own Historians*, translated and edited by H. M. Elliot and John Dowson, 4: 89–126. 8 vols. Allahabad: Kitab Mahal, 1964.

Abu'l-fazl 'Allami. *Ā'īn-i Akbarī*. 3 vols. Lucknow: Nawal Kishor, 1869. English edition: vol. 1 translated by H. Blochmann, edited by D. C. Phillott; vols. 2 and 3 translated by H. S. Jarrett, edited by Jadunath Sarkar. 2d ed. Calcutta: Asiatic Society of Bengal, 1927. Reprint. New Delhi: Oriental Books Reprint Corp., 1977–78.

———. *Akbar-nāma*. Edited by Abdur Rahim. 3 vols. Calcutta: Asiatic Society of Bengal, 1873–87. Translated by Henry Beveridge. 3 vols. Calcutta: Asiatic Society of Bengal, 1897–1921. Reprint. New Delhi: Ess Ess Publications, 1979.

Ahbar as-Sin wa al-Hind: Relations de la Chine et de l'Inde. Translated by Jean Sauvaget. Paris: Société d'édition "Les Belles Lettres," 1948.

Ansari, 'Abd al-Samad. *Akhbār al-aṣfiyā*. Khuda Bakhsh Library, Patna. Persian MS. No. 188. Compiled 1645.

Askari, S. H. "New Light on Rajah Ganesh and Sultan Ibrahim Sharqi of Jaunpur from Contemporary Correspondence of Two Muslim Saints." Letters of Shaikh Nur Qutb-i 'Alam and Ashraf Jahangir Simnani. Translated by S. H. Askari. *Bengal Past and Present* 57 (1948): 32–39.

Baḥr al-ḥayāṭ. India Office Library, London. Persian MS. No. 2002.

Balkhi, Mahmud b. Amir Wali. *The Bahr ul-Asrar: Travelogue of South Asia.* Edited by Riazul Islam. Karachi: University of Karachi, 1980.

Balkhi, Muzaffar Shams. *Maktūbāt-i Muẓaffar Shams Balkhī*. Persian MS. Khuda Bakhsh Oriental Public Library, Patna. Acc. No. 1859.

Barani, Zia al-Din. *Tārīkh-i Fīrūz Shāhī*. Edited by Saiyid Ahmad Khan. Calcutta: Asiatic Society of Bengal, 1862. Extracts in *The History of India as Told by Its*

Own Historians, translated and edited by H. M. Elliot and John Dowson, 3: 93–268. 8 vols. Allahabad: Kitab Mahal, 1964.

Chishti, 'Abd al-Rahman. Mirāt al-asrār. Khuda Bakhsh Library, Patna. Persian MS. No. 204. Compiled 1654.

Dani, Ahmad Hasan. Bibliography of the Muslim Inscriptions of Bengal, Down to A.D. 1538. Appendix to the Journal of the Asiatic Society of Pakistan 2. Dacca: Asiatic Society of Pakistan, 1957.

Dastūr al-'amal-i 'Ālamgīrī. Persian MS. British Library, London. Add. 6599. Copy at Aligarh Muslim University, Aligarh, Department of History. Rotograph No. 53.

Desai, Z. A. "Correct Attribution of the Two So-called Inscriptions of Nasirud-din Mahmud Shah II of Bengal." Epigraphia Indica, Arabic and Persian Supplement (1973): 26–35.

———. "An Early Thirteenth-Century Inscription from West Bengal." Epigraphia Indica, Arabic and Persian Supplement (1975): 6–12.

———. "The So-Called Chunakhali Inscription of Nasirud-din Mahmud Shah II of Bengal." Epigraphia Indica, Arabic and Persian Supplement (1973): 36–43.

Dihlavi, 'Abd al-Haq Muhaddis. Akhbār al-akhyār. Deoband, U.P.: Kitab Khana-yi Rahimia, 1915–16.

Fakhr al-Din Razi. Jāmi' al-'ulūm. Edited by Muhammad Khan Malik al-Kuttab. Bombay, A.H. 1323 [A.D. 1905].

Firdausi, Shaikh Shu'aib. Manāqib al-aṣfiyā. Calcutta: Nur al-Afaq, 1895.

Firishta, Muhammad Qasim. Tārīkh-i Firishta. 2 vols. Lucknow: Nawal Kishor, 1864–65. Translated by John Briggs under the title History of the Rise of the Mahomedan Power in India. 4 vols. London, 1829. Reprint. 3 vols. Calcutta: Editions Indian, 1966.

Haidar, Maulvi Muhammad Nasir al-Din. Suhail-i Yaman, or Tārīkh-i Jalālī. Persian MS. Muslim Sahitya Samsad, Sylhet. Compiled A.H. 1277 [A.D. 1860–61].

Hussain, S. S. "Some More New Inscriptions of Husain Shah from West Bengal," Epigraphia Indica, Arabic and Persian Supplement (1975): 31–38.

Hujwiri, 'Ali b. 'Uthman al-Jullabi al-. The Kashf al-Mahjūb: The Oldest Persian Treatise on Sufiism. Translated by Reynold A. Nicholson. 1911. 2d ed. 1936. Reprint. London: Luzac, 1970.

Ibn Battuta, The Rehla of Ibn Battuta. Translated by Mahdi Husain. Baroda: Oriental Institute, 1953.

Ibn Hajar al-'Asqalani. Inbā' al-ghumr bi-anbā al-'umr. 3 vols. Cairo: al-Majlis al-A'lā li-l-Shu'ūn al-Islāmiyah, 1969.

Ikram, S. M. "An Unnoticed Account of Shaikh Jalal of Sylhet." Journal of the Asiatic Society of Pakistan 2 (1957): 63–68.

Inayat Khan. Shah Jahan Nama. Translated by A. R. Fuller. Edited by W. E. Begley and Z. A. Desai. Delhi: Oxford University Press, 1990.

Jahangir. The Tūzuk-i-Jahāngīrī, or Memoires of Jahāngīr. Translated by Alexander Rogers. Edited by Henry Beveridge. 2d ed. 2 vols. in 1. New Delhi: Munshiram Manoharlal, 1968.

Jamali, Maulana. Siyar al-'ārifīn. Delhi: Matba' Rizvi, 1893.

"Kanun Daimer Nathi." Persian and Bengali MSS. Chittagong. Chittagong District Collectorate Record Room.

Karim, Abdul. *Corpus of the Muslim Coins of Bengal, down to* A.D. *1538.* Asiatic Society of Pakistan Publication No. 6. Dacca: Asiatic Society of Pakistan, 1960.
———. "Nur Qutb Alam's Letter on the Ascendancy of Ganesa." In *Abdul Karim Sahitya-Visarad Commemoration Volume,* edited by Muhammad Enamul Haq, 335–43. Dacca: Asiatic Society of Bangladesh, 1972.
Kazim b. Muhammad Amin, Munshi Amin (d. 1681). *'Ālamgīr-nāma.* Edited by Khadim Husain and 'Abd al-Hai. Calcutta: Asiatic Society of Bengal, 1868.
Mas'udi. *Les Prairies d'or [Murūj al-dhahab].* Translated by Barbier de Meynard and Pavet de Courteille. Corrected by Charles Pellat. Vol. 1. Paris: Société asiatique, 1962.
Minhaj-ud-Din Abu'l-'Umar-i-'Usman, Maulana. *Ṭabakāt-i-Nāṣirī: A General History of the Muhammadan Dynasties of Asia, Including Hindustan (810–1260).* Translated by H. G. Raverty. Calcutta: Asiatic Society of Bengal, 1881. Reprint. 2 vols. New Delhi: Oriental Books Reprint Corp., 1970.
Muhsin Fani. *Dabistān-i mażāhib.* Edited by Nazir Ashraf and W. B. Bayley. Calcutta, 1809.
Nathan, Mirza. *Bahāristān-i ghaibī.* Paris: Bibliothèque nationale. Sup. Pers. MS. No. 252. Photostat copies: Dhaka University Library, Dhaka; National Library, Calcutta, Sarkar Collection No. 60, Acc. No. 1327.
———. *Bahāristān-i-ghaybī: A History of the Mughal Wars in Assam, Cooch Behar, Bengal, Bihar and Orissa during the Reigns of Jahāngīr and Shāhjahān, by Mīrzā Nathan.* Translated by M. I. Borah. 2 vols. Gauhati, Assam: Government of Assam, 1936.
Ni'mat Allah, Khwajah. *Tārīkh-i Khān Jahān wa makhzan-i Afghān.* Edited by S. M. Imam al-Din. 2 vols. Asiatic Society of Pakistan Publication No. 4. Dacca: Asiatic Society of Pakistan, 1960.
Nizamuddin Ahmad, Khwajah. *The Ṭabaqāt-i-Akbarī.* Edited by Brajendranath De and M. Hidayat Hosein. 3 vols. Calcutta: Bibliotheca Indica, 1931–35. Translated by B. De. 3 vols. Calcutta: Bibliotheca Indica, 1927–39.
Nur Qutb-i 'Alam, Shaikh. *Maktūbāt-i Shaikh Nūr Qutb-i 'Alam.* Persian MS. Aligarh Muslim University, Aligarh, Maulana Azad Library. Subhan Allah No. 297671/18. Copy in the Indian National Archives, New Delhi. Or. MS. No. 332.
———. *Mu'nis al-fuqarā'.* Asiatic Society of Bengal, Calcutta. Persian MS. No. 466.
Nurul Hasan, S. "Three Studies of Zamindari System." In *Medieval India—A Miscellany,* vol. 1, edited by K. A. Nizami, 233–39. Bombay: Asia Publishing House, 1969.
Qeyammudin Ahmad. *Corpus of Arabic and Persian Inscriptions of Bihar (*A.H. *640–1200).* Patna: K. P. Jayaswal Research Institute, 1973.
Rajgiri, Imam al-Din. *Manāhij al-shaṭṭār.* Khuda Bakhsh Library, Patna. 2 vols. Persian MSS. Nos. 1848, 1848-A.
"Register of Sanads." Persian MSS. Sylhet: Sylhet District Collectorate Record Room.
Sakhavi, Muhammd. *al-Zau' al-lāmi' li-ahl al-qarn al-tāsi'.* 12 vols. Beirut: Maktabat al-Hayat, 1966. Vols. 2 and 8.
Salim, Ghulam Hussain. *Riyāzu-s-Salātīn: A History of Bengal.* Translated by Abdus Salam. 1903. Reprint. Delhi: Idarah-i Adabiyat-i Delli, 1975.

Salimullah, Munshi. *Tarīkh-i-Bangālah.* Edited by S. M. Imamuddin. Dacca: Asiatic Society of Bangladesh, 1979.

Sarwani, ʿAbbas Khan. *Tārīkh-i Śēr Śāhī.* Translated by B. P. Ambashthya. Patna: K. P. Jayaswal Research Institute, 1974.

Shams-i Siraj ʿAfif. *Tārīkh-i Fīrūz Shāhī.* Edited by Maulavi Vilayat Husain. Calcutta: Asiatic Society of Bengal, 1891. Extracts in *The History of India as Told by Its Own Historians,* translated and edited by Henry Elliot and John Dowson, 3: 269–373. 8 vols. Allahabad: Kitab Mahal, 1964

Shamsud-Din Ahmed, ed. and trans. *Inscriptions of Bengal.* Vol. 4. Rajshahi: Varendra Research Museum, 1960.

Shattari, Muhammad Ghauthi. *Gulzār-i abrār.* Asiatic Society of Bengal, Calcutta. Persian MS. No. 259. Compiled 1613. Translated into Urdu by Fazl Ahmad Jiwari. Lahore: Islamic Book Foundation, 1975.

Shihab al-Din Talish. *Faṭhiyah-i ʿibriyah.* Persian MS. Bodleian Library, Oxford. MS Bodl. Or. 589. Extracts translated by H. Blochmann in "Koch Bihar, Koch Hajo, and Assam in the 16th and 17th Centuries, According to the Akbarnamah, the Padshahnamah, and the Fathiyah i ʿIbriyah," *Journal of the Asiatic Society of Bengal* 41, no. 1 (1872): 49–101. Extracts translated by Jadunath Sarkar in "The Conquest of Chatgaon, 1666 A.D.," *Journal of the Asiatic Society of Bengal* 3 (1907): 405–17; "Assam and the Ahoms in 1660 A.D.," *Journal of the Bihar and Orissa Research Society* 1, no. 2 (1915): 179–95; and "Shaista Khan in Bengal (1664-66)," *Journal of the Asiatic Society of Bengal,* n.s., 2, no. 6 (June 1906): 257–67.

Siddiq, Mohammad Yusuf. *Arabic and Persian Texts of the Islamic Inscriptions of Bengal.* Watertown, Mass.: South Asia Press, 1991.

Simnani, Shaikh Ashraf Jahangir. *Maktūbāt-i ashrafī.* Persian MS. Aligarh Muslim University History Department, Aligarh. MS. No. 27. Copy in the British Library, London. Or. MS. No. 267.

Yusuf Husain. "Haud al-hayat: La Version arabe de l'Amratkund." *Journal asiatique* 113 (October–December 1928): 291–344.

Bengali or Sanskrit

Gupta, Kamalakanta. *Copper-plates of Sylhet.* Vol. 1. Sylhet: Lipika Enterprises, 1967.

Huq, Muhammad Enamul, ed. *Muslim Bāṅglā Sāhitya.* 2d ed. Dacca: Pakistan Publications, 1965.

Husain, Syed Sajjad, ed. and trans. *A Descriptive Catalogue of Bengali Manuscripts in Munshi Abdul Karim's Collection,* by Munshi Abdul Karim and Ahmad Sharif. Dacca: Asiatic Society of Pakistan, 1960.

Khan, Muhammad. *Maqtul Husain.* Dhaka Museum, Dhaka. MS. No. 2826. Acc. No. 6634.

Krsnadasa Kaviraja Goswami. *Śrī Caitanya-Caritāmṛta.* Abridged and edited by Sukumar Sen. New Delhi: Sahitya Akademi, 1977. Translated and edited by A. C. Bhaktivedanta Swami. 17 vols. New York: Bhaktivedanta Book Trust, 1973–75.

Majumdar, Nani Gopal. *Inscriptions of Bengal.* Vol. 3. Rajshahi: Varendra Research Society, 1929.

Maulik, Ksitish, ed. *Pracīn Pūrba Baṅga Gītikā.* 7 vols. Calcutta: Mukherjee Publishers, 1972.
Mukherji, Ramaranjan and Sachindra Kumar Maity. *Corpus of Bengal Inscriptions Bearing on History and Civilization of Bengal.* Calcutta: Firma K. L. Mukhopadhyay, 1967.
Mukundaram. *Kavikaṅkaṇa Caṇḍī.* Edited by Srikumar Bandyopadhyay and Visvapati Chaudhuri. Calcutta: University of Calcutta, 1974.
Muttalib, Shaikh. *Kifayat al-Mussalin.* Dhaka Museum, Dhaka. MS. No. 2825.
Roerich, George, trans. *Biography of Dharmasvamin (Chag lo-tsa-ba Chos-rje-dpal), a Tibetan Monk Pilgrim.* Patna: K. P. Jawaswal Research Institute, 1959.
Saiyid Sultan. *Nabī-Baṃśa.* Ca. 1584. Edited by Ahmed Sharif. 2 vols. Dhaka: Bangla Academy, 1978.
Sen, Dinesh Chandra, ed. and trans. *Eastern Bengal Ballads, Mymensing.* 4 vols. Calcutta: University of Calcutta, 1923–28.
Sen, Sukumar, ed. and trans. *Sekasubhodaya of Halayudha Misra.* Calcutta: Asiatic Society, 1963.
Sircar, D. C. *Some Epigraphical Records of the Medieval Period from Eastern India.* New Delhi: Abhinav Publications, 1979.
Vijaya Gupta. *Padma-Purāṇa.* Edited by Jayanta Kumar Dasgupta. Calcutta: University of Calcutta, 1962.
Vipra Das. *Manasā-Vijaya.* Edited by Sukumar Sen. Calcutta: Asiatic Society of Bengal, 1953.
Vishnu Pala. *Manasā-Maṅgala.* Edited by Sukumar Sen. Calcutta: Asiatic Society of Bengal, 1968.
Vrindavan Das. *Śrī-Śrī Caitanya Bhāgavat.* Calcutta: Dev Sahitya Kutar, 1980.

Chinese

Bagchi, P. C. "Political Relations between Bengal and China in the Pathan Period." *Visva-Bharati Annals* 1 (1945): 96–134.
Hsüan-tsang. *Chinese Accounts of India, Translated from the Chinese of Hiuen Tsiang.* Translated by Samuel Beal. 4 vols. Calcutta: Susil Gupta, 1958.
I-ching. *A Record of the Buddhist Religion as Practiced in India and the Malay Archipelago (A.D. 671–695).* Translated by J. Takakusu. Delhi: Munshiram Manoharlal, 1966.
Ma Huan. *Ying-yai Sheng-lan: "The Overall Survey of the Ocean's Shores."* Translated by J. V. G. Mills. Cambridge: Cambridge University Press, 1970.
Rockhill, W. W. "Notes on the Relations and Trade of China with the Eastern Archipelago and the Coast of the Indian Ocean during the Fourteenth Century." *T'oung Pao* 16, pt. 2 (1915): 61–73, 435–55.

European

Barbosa, Duarte. *The Book of Duarte Barbosa.* Translated by M. L. Dames. London: Hakluyt Society, 1921. Reprint. 2 vols. Nendoln/Liechtenstein: Kraus Reprint, 1967.
Bernier, François. *Travels in the Mogul Empire, A.D. 1656–68.* Translated by Archibald Constable. 2d ed. New Delhi: S. Chand & Co., 1968.

Buchanan, Francis. *A Geographical, Statistical, and Historical Description of the District, or Zila, of Dinajpur, in the Province, or Soubah, of Bengal.* Calcutta: Baptist Mission Press, 1833.

———. "An Account of a Journey Undertaken by Order of the Bd. of Trade through the Provinces of Chittagong and Tipperah in order to look out for the Places most Proper for the Cultivation of Spices (March–May, 1798)." British Library, London. Eur. MSS. Add. 19286.

Dagh-Register gehouden int Casteel Batavia vant passerende daer ter plaetse als over geheel Nederlandts-India. 30 vols. Batavia: C. Kolff, 1887–1931.

Federici, Cesare. "Extracts of Master Caesar Frederike his Eighteene Yeeres Indian Observations." In *Hakluytus Posthumus, or Purchas his Pilgrimes,* by Samuel Purchas (1625), 10: 83–143. 20 vols. Glasgow: James MacLehose & Sons, 1905.

Fitch, Ralph. "The Voyage of Master Ralph Fitch Merchant of London to Ormus, and so to Goa in the East India, to Cambaia, Ganges, Bengala. . . . " In *Hakluytus Posthumus, or Purchas his Pilgrimes,* by Samuel Purchas (1625), 10: 165–204. 20 vols. Glasgow: James MacLehose & Sons, 1905.

Generale missiven van gouverneurs-generaal en raden aan Heren XVII der Verenigde Oostindische Compagnie. The Hague: Martinus Nijhoff, 1971.

Hosten, H. "The Earliest Recorded Episcopal Visitation of Bengal, 1712–1715." *Bengal Past and Present* 6 (July–December 1910): 200–227.

———. "Jesuit Letters from Bengal, Arakan and Burma (1599-1600)." *Bengal Past and Present* 30 (1925): 52–78.

Khan, Shafaat Ahmad, ed. *John Marshall in India: Notes and Observations in Bengal, 1668–1672.* London: Oxford University Press, 1927.

Lettres édifiantes et curieuses écrites des missions étrangères. 36 vols. Paris: J. G. Merigot, 1781.

Manrique, Fray Sebastien. *Travels of Fray Sebastien Manrique, 1629-1643.* Translated by E. Luard and H. Hosten. Hakluyt Society Publications, 2d ser., nos. 59, 61. 2 vols. Oxford: Hakluyt Society, 1927.

Pires, Tome. *Suma Oriental of Tome Pires.* Translated by A. Cortesão. Hakluyt Society Publications, 2d ser., nos. 89–90. 2 vols. London: Hakluyt Society, 1944.

Pyrard, François. *The Voyage of François Pyrard of Laval to the East Indies, the Maldives, the Moluccas and Brazil.* Edited and Translated by Albert Gray. 2 vols. Hakluyt Society Publications, 1st ser., nos. 76, 77, 80. 1887–90. Reprint. 2 vols. in 3 parts. New York: Burt Franklin, n.d.

Sen, Surendranath, ed. *Indian Travels of Thevenot and Careri.* New Delhi: National Archives of India, 1949.

Tavernier, Jean Baptiste. *Travels in India.* Translated by V. Ball. 2 vols. London: Macmillan, 1889. Reprint. Lahore: Al-Biruni, 1976.

Varthema, Ludovico di. *The Travels of Ludovico di Varthema in Egypt, Syria, Arabia Deserta and Arabia Felix, in Persia, India, and Ethiopia, A.D. 1503–1508.* Translated by John W. Jones. Edited by George P. Badger. Hakluyt Society Publications, 1st ser., no. 32. 1863. Reprint. New York: Burt Franklin, n.d.

Voyage dans les deltas du Gange et de l'Irraouaddy: Relation portugaise anonyme (1521). Translated and edited by Genevieve Bouchon and Luis Filipe Thomaz. Paris: Centre culturel portugais, 1988.

Yule, Henry, and Henri Cordier, trans. and eds. *The Book of Ser Marco Polo*. 3d ed. 2 vols. Amsterdam: Philo Press, 1975.

SECONDARY SOURCES

Abid Ali Khan, M. *History and Archeology of Bengal, or Memoirs of Gaur and Pandua*. Edited and revised by H. E. Stapleton. Calcutta: Bengal Secretariat, 1931. Reprint. New Delhi: Asian Publication Services, 1980.

Ali, Muhammad Mohar. *History of the Muslims in Bengal*. Vol. 1A–B. Riyadh: Imam Muhammad Ibn Sa'ud Islamic University, 1985.

Arasaratnam, S. "The Rice Trade in Eastern India, 1650–1740 ." *Modern Asian Studies* 22, no. 3 (1988): 531–49.

Ascoli, F. D. *Final Report on the Survey and Settlement Operations in the District of Dacca, 1910 to 1917*. Calcutta: Bengal Secretariat Book Depot, 1917.

Asher, Catherine B. "Inventory of Key Monuments." In *The Islamic Heritage of Bengal*, edited by George Michell, 37–140. Paris: UNESCO, 1984.

———. "The Mughal and Post-Mughal Periods." In *The Islamic Heritage of Bengal*, edited by George Michell, 193–212. Paris: UNESCO, 1984.

Askari, S. H. "The Correspondence of Two Fourteenth-Century Sufi Saints of Bihar with the Contemporary Sovereigns of Delhi and Bengal." *Journal of the Bihar Research Society* 42, no. 2 (1956): 177–95.

———. *Maktub and Malfuz Literature as a Source of Socio-Political History*. Patna: Khuda Bakhsh Oriental Public Library, 1981.

———. "The Mughal-Magh Relations Down to the Time of Islam Khan Mashhadi." In *Indian History Congress, Proceedings*, 22d session (Gauhati, 1959), 201–13. Bombay: Indian History Congress, 1960.

———. "New Light on Rajah Ganesh and Sultan Ibrahim Sharqi of Jaunpur from Contemporary Correspondence of Two Muslim Saints." *Bengal Past and Present* 57 (1948): 32–39.

Bagchi, Kanangopal. *The Ganges Delta*. Calcutta: University of Calcutta, 1944.

Beveridge, H. "The Antiquities of Bagura (Bogra)." *Journal of the Asiatic Society of Bengal* 47, no. 1 (1878): 88–95.

———. *The District of Bakarganj: Its History and Statistics*. London: Trubner, 1876.

Beverley, H. *Report on the Census of Bengal, 1872*. Calcutta: Secretariat Press, 1872.

Bhadra, Gautam. "Two Frontier Uprisings in Mughal India." In *Subaltern Studies II: Writings on South Asian History and Society*, edited by Ranajit Guha, 43–59. Delhi: Oxford University Press, 1983.

Bhattacharjee, P. N. "Folkcustom and Folklore of the Sylhet District of India." *Man in India* 10, no. 1 (January–March 1930): 116–49, 244–70.

Bhattacharya, France. "La Déesse et le royaume selon le Kālaketu Upākhyāna du Caṇḍī Maṅgala." In *Puruṣārtha*, vol. 5, *Autour de la déesse hindoue*, edited by Madeleine Biardeau, 17–53. Paris: Ecole des Hautes études en sciences sociales, 1981.

Bhattacharya, N. D. "Changing Course of the Padma and Human Settlements." *National Geographic Journal of India* 24, nos. 1 and 2 (March–June 1978): 62–76.

Bhattacharyya, Sudhindra Nath. *A History of Mughal North-east Frontier Policy.* Calcutta: Chuckervertty, Chatterjee & Co., 1929.

Bhattacharya, Swapna. *Landschenkungen und staatliche Entwicklung im frühmittelalterlichen Bengalen.* Wiesbaden: Franz Steiner Verlag, 1985.

Bhattacharyya, Asutosh. "The Early Bengali Saiva Poetry." *Dacca University Studies* 6, no. 2 (1944): 153–216.

———. "The Tiger-Cult and Its Literature in Lower Bengal." *Man in India* 27, no. 1 (March 1947): 44–56.

Bhattasali, Nalini Kanta. "Antiquity of the Lower Ganges and Its Courses." *Science and Culture* 7, no. 5 (1941): 233–39.

———. "Bengal Chiefs' Struggle for Independence in the Reigns of Akbar and Jahangir." *Bengal Past and Present* 35 (January–June 1928): 25–39.

———. *Coins and Chronology of the Early Independent Sultans of Bengal.* Cambridge: W. Heffer & Sons, 1922. Reprint. New Delhi: Indological Book Corporation, 1976.

Blochmann, H. "Contributions to the Geography and History of Bengal." *Journal of the Asiatic Society of Bengal* 42, no. 3 (1873): 209–73; 43, no. 3 (1874): 280–309.

Borah, M. I. "An Account of the Immigration of Persian Poets into Bengal." *Dacca University Studies* 1 (November 1935): 141–50.

Brown, Percy. *Indian Architecture, Islamic Period.* 5th ed. Bombay: D. B. Taraporevala, 1968.

Buchanan-Hamilton MSS: "List of Papers Respecting the District of Ronggopur." India Office Library, London. Eur. MSS. D 74. Vol. 1. Books 1 and 2.

Calkins, Philip B. "The Formation of a Regionally Oriented Ruling Group in Bengal, 1700–1740." *Journal of Asian Studies* 29, no. 4 (1970): 799–806.

———. "Revenue Administration and the Formation of a Regionally Oriented Ruling Group in Bengal, 1700–1740." Ph.D. diss., University of Chicago, 1972.

Campos, J. J. A. *History of the Portuguese in Bengal.* 1919. Reprint. New York: AMS Press, 1975.

Chatterjee, Anjali. *Bengal in the Reign of Aurangzeb, 1658–1707.* Calcutta: Progressive Publishers, 1967.

Chatterji, S. K. *Languages and Literatures of Modern India.* Calcutta: Bengal Publishers Private, 1963.

———. *Origin and Development of Bengali Language.* 3 vols. Calcutta: University of Calcutta Press, 1926.

Chaudhury, Sushil. "Merchants, Companies and Rulers: Bengal in the Eighteenth Century." *Journal of the Economic and Social History of the Orient* 31, no. 1 (February 1988): 74–109.

———. *Trade and Commercial Organization in Bengal, 1650–1720.* Calcutta: Firma K. L. M., 1975.

Chowdhury, Abdul Momin. *Dynastic History of Bengal, c. 750–1200 A.D.* Dacca: Asiatic Society of Pakistan, 1967.

Clark, T. W. "Evolution of Hinduism in Medieval Bengali Literature: Śiva, Caṇḍī, Manasā." *Bulletin of the School of Oriental and African Studies* 17, no. 3 (1955): 503–18.

Correspondence on the Settlement of the Noabad Lands in the District of Chittagong. Calcutta: Bengal Secretariat, 1871.

Cotton, H. J. S. *Memorandum on the Revenue History of Chittagong.* Calcutta: Secretariat Press, 1880.

Cunningham, Alexander. "Report of a Tour in Bihar and Bengal in 1879–80 from Patna to Sunargaon." In *Archaeological Survey of India, Report.* Vol. 15. Calcutta, 1882.

Dani, Ahmad Hasan. "The Bengali Muslim Society: Its Evolution." *Bengali Literary Review* 2 (1956): 4–9.

———. "Coins of the Chandra Kings of East Bengal." *Journal of the Numismatic Society of India* 24 (1962): 141–42.

———. "The House of Raja Ganesa of Bengal." *Journal of the Asiatic Society of Bengal: Letters* 18, no. 2 (1952): 121–70.

———. *Muslim Architecture in Bengal.* Dacca: Asiatic Society of Pakistan, 1961.

———. "Race and Culture Complex in Bengal." In *Social Research in East Pakistan,* edited by Pierre Bessaignet. 2d ed. Dacca: Asiatic Society of Pakistan, 1964.

———. "Shamsuddin Ilyas Shah, Shah-i Bangalah." In *Essays Presented to Sir Jadunath Sarkar,* edited by Hari Ram Gupta, 50–58. Vol. 2. Hoshiarpur: Punjab University, 1958.

Datt, Kalikinkal. "Relations between the Hindus and the Muhammadans of Bengal in the Middle of the Eighteenth Century (1740–1765)." *Journal of Indian History* 8 (1929): 328–35.

———. *Studies in the History of the Bengal Subah, 1740–70.* Vol. 1, *Society and Economy.* Calcutta: University of Calcutta, 1936.

Desai, Ziauddin. "Some New Data Regarding the Pre-Mughal Rulers of Bengal." *Islamic Culture* 32 (1958): 195–207.

Deyell, John S. "The China Connection: Problems of Silver Supply in Medieval Bengal." In *Precious Metals in the Later Medieval and Early Modern Worlds,* edited by J. F. Richards, 207–24. Durham, N.C.: Carolina Academic Press, 1983.

Digby, Simon. "The Sufi Shaikh as a Source of Authority in Mediaeval India." In *Puruṣārtha,* vol. 9, *Islam et société en Asie du sud,* edited by Marc Gaborieau, 57–77. Paris: Ecole des Hautes études en sciences sociales, 1986.

Dimock, Edward C., Jr. "Hinduism and Islam in Medieval Bengal." In *Aspects of Bengali History and Society,* edited by Rachel Van M. Baumer, 1–12. Honolulu: University Press of Hawaii, c. 1975.

——— and Ronald B. Inden. "The City in Pre-British Bengal." In *The Sound of Silent Guns and Other Essays,* by Edward C. Dimock, Jr., 113–29. Delhi: Oxford University Press, 1989.

——— and A. K. Ramanujan. "The Goddess of Snakes in Medieval Bengali Literature." *History of Religions* 3, no. 2 (Winter 1964).

Dutt, N. K. *The Origin and Growth of Caste in India.* 2 vols. Calcutta: Firma K.L.M., 1965.

Farid, G. S. "A New and Unique Ten Tankah Commemorative Coin of Jalaluddin Mohammad Shah of Bengal (818–837 A.H.)." *Journal of the Numismatic Society of India* 38 (1976): 88–95.

Friedmann, Yohanan. "A Contribution to the Early History of Islam in India." In

Studies in Memory of Gaston Wiet, edited by Myriam Rosen-Ayalon. Jerusalem: Institute of Asian and African Studies, 1977.

———. "Medieval Muslim Views of Indian Religions." *Journal of the American Oriental Society* 95 (1975): 214–21.

Gait, E. A. "The Muhammadans of Bengal." In *Census of India, 1901,* vol. 6, *The Lower Provinces of Bengal and Their Feudatories,* pt. 1, "Report," 165–81. Calcutta: Bengal Secretariat Press, 1902.

———. "Muhammadan Castes and Tribes." In *Census of India, 1901,* vol. 6, *The Lower Provinces of Bengal and Their Feudatories,* pt. 1, "Report," 439–51. Calcutta: Bengal Secretariat Press, 1902.

Ghoshal, Satyendranath. "The Beginning of Secular Romance in Bengali Literature." *Visva-Bharati Annals* 9 (1959): 1–300.

Ghuznavi, Abu A. "Notes on the Origin, Social and Religious Divisions and Other Matters Touching on the Mahomedans of Bengal and Having Special Reference to the District of Maimensing." India Office Library, London. N.d. Eur. MSS. E 295. Vol. 17.

Glasse, Robert. "La Société musulmane dans le Pakistan rural de l'Est." *Etudes rurales* 22–24 (1968): 188–205.

Grover, B. R. "Evolution of the Zamindari and Taluqdari System in Bengal (1576–1765 A.D.)." In *Bangladesh Itihas Parishad: Third History Congress, Proceedings,* 86–113. Dacca: Bangladesh Itihas Parishad, 1973.

Gupta, J. N. *Eastern Bengal and Assam District Gazetters: Bogra.* Allahabad: Pioneer Press, 1910.

Gupta, K. N. "On Some Castes and Caste-Origins in Sylhet." *Indian Historical Quarterly* 7 (1931): 716–26.

Gupta, P. L. "Nagari Legend on Horseman Tankah of Muhammad bin Sam." *Journal of the Numismatic Society of India* 35 (1973): 209–12.

———. "On the Date of the Horseman Type Coin of Muhammad bin Sam." *Journal of the Numismatic Society of India* 38 (1976): 81–87.

Habib, Irfan. *An Atlas of the Mughal Empire.* Delhi: Oxford University Press, 1982.

Halim, A. "An Account of the Celebrities of Bengal of the Early Years of Shahjahan's reign given by Muhammad Sadiq." *Journal of the Pakistan Historical Society* 1 (1953): 338–56.

Hambly, Gavin. "A Note on the Trade in Eunuchs in Mughal Bengal." *Journal of the American Oriental Society* 94, no. 1 (January–March 1974): 125–29.

Haq, Md. Enamul, trans. *Muslim Bengali Literature.* Karachi: Pakistan Publications, 1957.

Hasan, Perween. "Sultanate Mosques and Continuity in Bengal Architecture." *Muqarnas* 6 (1989): 58–74.

Hasan, Syed Mahmudul. *Muslim Monuments of Bangladesh.* 2d ed. Dacca: Islamic Foundation, Bangladesh, 1980.

Huntington, Susan L. *The "Pala-Sena" Schools of Sculpture.* Leiden: Brill, 1984.

Inden, Ronald. "The Ceremony of the Great Gift (Mahādāna): Structure and Historical Context in Indian Ritual and Society." In *Asie du sud: Traditions et changements,* edited by Marc Gaborieau and Alice Thorner, 131–36. Paris: Centre national de la recherche scientifique, 1979.

———. *Marriage and Rank in Bengali Culture: A History of Caste and Class in Middle-period Bengal.* Berkeley and Los Angeles: University of California Press, 1976.

Iqtidar Alam Khan. "The Nobility under Akbar and the Development of His Religious Policy, 1560–80." *Journal of the Royal Asiatic Society of Great Britain and Ireland,* pts. 1 and 2 (1968): 29–36.

Jack, J. C. *The Economic Life of a Bengal District: A Study.* 1916. Reprint. Delhi: Agam Prakashan, 1975.

———. *Final Report on the Survey and Settlement Operations in the Bakarganj District, 1900–1908.* Calcutta: Bengal Secretariat Book Depot, 1915.

———. *Final Report on the Survey and Settlement Operations in Faridpur District, 1904–14.* Calcutta: Bengal Secretariat Book Depot, 1916.

Jackson, Paul. "The Life and Teachings of a Fourteenth-Century Sufi Saint of Bihar (Sharfuddin Ahmed Maneri)." Ph.D. diss., Patna University, 1979.

Jafri, S. Z. H. "Rural Bureaucracy in Cooch Behar and Assam under the Mughals: Archival Evidence." In *Indian History Congress, Proceedings,* 49th session (Karnataka University, 1988), 277–86. Delhi: Indian History Congress, 1989.

Karim, Abdul. *Catalogue of Coins in the Cabinet of the Chittagong University Museum.* Chittagong: University Museum, 1979.

———. *Dacca, the Mughal Capital.* Dacca: Asiatic Society of Pakistan, 1964.

———. "'Khalifat Allah' Title in the Coins of Bengal Sultans." *Journal of the Pakistan Historical Society* 8, no. 1 (January 1960): 25–34.

———. *Murshid Quli Khan and his Times.* Dacca: Asiatic Society of Pakistan, 1963.

———. *Social History of the Muslims of Bengal (down to* A.D. *1538)* Dacca: Asiatic Society of Pakistan, 1959. 2d ed. Chittagong: Baitush Sharif Islamic Research Institute, 1985.

Karim, Khondkar Mahbubul. *The Provinces of Bihar and Bengal under Shahjahan.* Dacca: Asiatic Society of Bengal, 1974.

Kindersley, J. B. *Final Report on the Survey and Settlement Operations of the District of Chittagong, 1923–33.* Alipore: Bengal Government Press, 1938.

Klaiman, M. H. "Bengali." In *The World's Major Languages,* edited by Bernard Comrie, 490–513. New York: Oxford University Press, 1990.

Lahiri, Nayanjot. "Landholding and Peasantry in the Brahmaputra Valley, c. Fifth–Thirteenth Centuries A.D." *Journal of the Economic and Social History of the Orient* 33, no. 2 (June 1990): 156–68.

Lambton, Ann K. S. *State and Government in Medieval Islam.* New York: Oxford University Press, 1981.

Lowick, Nicholas W. "The Horseman Type of Bengal and the Question of Commemorative Issues." *Journal of the Numismatic Society of India* 35 (1973): 196–208.

McCutchion, David. "Hindu-Muslim Artistic Continuities in Bengal." *Journal of the Asiatic Society of Pakistan* 13, no. 3 (December 1968): 233–49.

MacPherson, D. *Final Report on the Survey and Settlement Operations in the Districts of Pabna and Bogra, 1920–29.* Calcutta: Bengal Secretariat Book Depot, 1930.

Maity, P. K. *Historical Studies in the Cult of the Goddess Manasā.* Calcutta: Punthi Pustak, 1966.

Majumdar, Gayatri Sen. *Buddhism in Ancient Bengal.* Calcutta: Navana, 1983.

Majumdar, R. C. *History of Ancient Bengal.* Calcutta: G. Bharadwaj & Co., 1971.
————. *History of Medieval Bengal.* Calcutta: G. Bharadwaj & Co., 1973.
————, ed. *History of Bengal.* 2d ed. Dacca: University of Dacca, 1963.
Majumdar, S. C. *Rivers of the Bengal Delta.* Calcutta: University of Calcutta Press, 1942.
Mannan, Qazi Abdul. *The Emergence and Development of Dobhasi Literature in Bengal up to 1855.* Dacca: University of Dacca, 1966.
"Mauza Notes." English MSS. Barisal: Barisal District Collectorate Record Room. Dhaka: Dhaka District Collectorate Record Room.
Michell, George, ed. *The Islamic Heritage of Bengal.* Paris: UNESCO, 1984.
————, ed. *Brick Temples of Bengal: From the Archives of David McCutchion.* Princeton: Princeton University Press, 1983.
Mitter, Rupendra Coomar. *The Decline of Buddhism in India.* Calcutta: Visvabharati, 1954.
Moosvi, Shireen. *The Economy of the Mughal Empire, c. 1595: A Statistical Study.* Delhi: Oxford University Press, 1987.
————. "The Silver Influx, Money Supply, Prices and Revenue-Extraction in Mughal India." *Journal of the Economic and Social History of the Orient* 30, no. 1 (February 1987): 47–94.
Morgan, James P., and William G. McIntire. "Quaternary Geology of the Bengal Basin, East Pakistan and India." *Bulletin of the Geological Society of America* 70 (March 1959): 319–42.
Morrison, Barrie M. *Lalmai, a Cultural Center of Early Bengal: An Archaeological Report and Historical Analysis.* Seattle: University of Washington Press, 1974.
————. *Political Centers and Cultural Regions in Early Bengal.* Tucson: University of Arizona Press, 1970.
————. "Social and Cultural History of Bengal: Approaches and Methodology." In *Nalini Kanta Bhattasali Commemoration Volume,* edited by A. B. M. Habibullah, 323–38. Dacca: Dacca Museum, 1966.
Mukerjee, R. K. *The Changing Face of Bengal: A Study of Riverine Economy.* Calcutta: University of Calcutta, 1938.
Mukhopadhyay, Somnath. *Candi in Art and Iconography.* Delhi: Agam Kala Prakashan, 1984.
Nazmul Karim, A. K. *Changing Society in India and Pakistan: A Study in Social Change and Social Stratification.* Dacca: Oxford University Press, 1956.
Nicholas, Ralph W. "Vaisnavism and Islam in Rural Bengal." In *Bengal: Regional Identity,* edited by David Kopf. East Lansing: Asian Studies Center, Michigan State University, 1969.
Nisar Ahmad. "Assam-Bengal Trade in the Medieval Period: A Numismatic Perspective." *Journal of the Economic and Social History of the Orient* 33, no. 2 (June 1990): 169–97.
Niyogi, Puspa. *Brahmanic Settlements in Different Subdivisions of Ancient Bengal.* Calcutta: R. K. Maitra, 1967.
————. *Buddhism in Ancient Bengal.* Calcutta: Jijnasa, 1980.
O'Connell, Joseph T. "Social Implications of the Gaudiya Vaisnava Movement." Ph.D. diss., Harvard University, 1970.
————. "Vaisnava Perceptions of Muslims in Sixteenth Century Bengal." In *Is-

lamic Society and Culture: Essays in Honour of Professor Aziz Ahmad, edited by Milton Israel and N. K. Wagle. New Delhi: Manohar, 1983.

O'Malley, L. S. S. *Eastern Bengal District Gazetteers: Chittagong*. Calcutta: Bengal Secretariat Book Depot, 1908.

———. *Eastern Bengal District Gazetteers, Khulna*. Calcutta: Bengal Secretariat Book Depot, 1908.

Prakash, Om. *The Dutch East India Company and the Economy of Bengal, 1630–1720*. Princeton: Princeton University Press, 1985.

———. "Bullion for Goods: International Trade and the Economy of Early Eighteenth Century Bengal." *Indian Economic and Social History Review* 13, no. 2 (April–June 1976): 159–88.

Qanungo, K. R. "How Local Custom Modifies Scripture (Personal Observation among Villagers of Chittagong Half a Century Ago)." *Bengal Past and Present* 70 (1951): 23–33.

Qanungo, Suniti Bhushan. "Chittagong during the Afghan Rule, 1538–1580." *Journal of the Asiatic Society of Bangladesh* 21, no. 2 (1976): 54–75.

Rahim, Muhammad Abdur. "Chittagong under the Pathan Rule in Bengal." *Journal of the Asiatic Society of Bengal* 18, no. 1 (1952): 21–30.

———. *History of the Afghans in India, A.D. 1545-1631*. Karachi: Pakistan Publishing House, 1961.

———. *Social and Cultural History of Bengal*. Vol. 1, *1201–1576*. Vol. 2, *1576–1757*. Karachi: Pakistan Publishing House, 1963, 1967.

Ray, Rajat and Ratna. "Zamindars and Jotedars: A Study of Rural Politics in Bengal." *Modern Asian Studies* 9, no. 1 (1975): 81–102.

Ray, Ratnalekha. "The Bengal Zamindars: Local Magnates and the State before the Permanent Settlement." *Indian Economic and Social History Review* 12, no. 3 (July 1975): 263–92.

———. *Change in Bengal Society, c. 1760–1850*. New Delhi: Manohar, 1979.

Ray, Niharranjan. "Medieval Bengali Culture." *Visva-Bharati Quarterly* 11, no. 2 (August–October 1945): 45–55, 87–95.

Raychaudhuri, Tapan. *Bengal under Akbar and Jahangir*. 2d ed. Delhi: Munshiram Manoharlal, 1966.

Risley Collection. "Reports on the Religious and Social Divisions amongst the Mahomedans of Bengal." India Office Library, London. Eur. MSS. E 295. Vol. 9.

Roy, Asim. "Islam in the Environment of Medieval Bengal." Ph.D. diss., Australian National University, 1970.

———. *The Islamic Syncretistic Tradition in Bengal*. Princeton: Princeton University Press, 1983.

———. "The Social Factors in the Making of Bengali Islam." *South Asia* 3 (August 1973): 23–35.

Rubbee, Khondkar Fuzli. *The Origin of the Musalmans of Bengal*. 2d ed. Dacca: Society for Pakistan Studies, 1970.

Sachse, F. A. *Final Report on the Survey and Settlement Operations for the District of Mymensingh, 1908–19*. Calcutta: Bengal Secretariat Book Depot, 1920.

Samiuddin, Saba. "The Nazims and the Zamindars of Bengal." In *Indian History Congress, Proceedings*, 45th session (Annamalainagar, 1984), 435–43. Delhi: Indian History Congress, 1985.

Sanyal, Hitesranjan. "Religious Architecture in Bengal (15th–17th Centuries): A Study of the Major Trends." In *Indian History Congress, Proceedings, 32d session* (Jabalpur, 1970), 1: 413–22. New Delhi: Indian History Congress, 1971.

———. "Regional Religious Architecture in Bengal: A Study in the Sources of Origin and Character." *Marg* 27, no. 2 (March 1974): 31–43.

———. "Social Aspects of Temple Building in Bengal: 1600 to 1900 A.D." *Man in India* 48, no. 3 (July–September 1968): 201–24.

———. "Transformation of the Regional *bhakti* Movement (Sixteenth and Seventeenth Centuries)." In *Bengal Vaisnavism, Orientalism, Society and the Arts*, edited by Joseph T. O'Connell. East Lansing: Michigan State University, 1985.

Sarkar, Jadunath, ed. *History of Bengal*. Vol. 2, *Muslim Period, 1200–1757*. 1947. Patna: Janaki Prakashan, 1977.

Sarkar, Jagadish Narayan. *Hindu-Muslim Relations in Bengal (Medieval Period)*. Delhi: Idarah-i Adabiyat-i Delli, 1985.

Sen, Dinesh Chandra. *The Folk Literature of Bengal*. Calcutta: University of Calcutta, 1920.

———. *History of Bengali Language and Literature*. 2d ed. Calcutta: University of Calcutta, 1954.

Sen, Karunaketan. "Notes on the Rural Customs of Dinajpur District." *Journal of the Asiatic Society of Bengal* 3 (1937): 33–38.

Sen, Sukumar. *History of Bengali Literature*. 3d ed. New Delhi: Sahitya Akademi, 1979.

Shahidullah, Muhammad. *Bāṅglā Sāhityer Kathā*. 2 vols. Dhaka: M. Safiyyullah, 1965.

Shamsul Alam, A. K. M. *Sculptural Art of Bangladesh, Pre-Muslim Period*. Dhaka: Department of Archaeology and Museums, 1985.

Sharif, Ahmed. *Bāṅgālī o Bāṅglā Sāhitya*. 2 vols. Dhaka: Bangla Academy, 1983.

———. *Saiyad Sultān: tār Granthābalī o tār Jūg*, Dhaka: Bangla Academy, 1972.

Sharma, Ram Sharan. *Material Culture and Social Formations in Ancient India*. New Delhi: Macmillan India, 1983.

Sidiq Khan, "A Study in Mughal Land Revenue System." *Islamic Culture* 12 (1938): 61–75.

Smith, William L. *The One-eyed Goddess: A Study of the Manasā-Maṅgal*. Oriental Studies, no. 12. Stockholm: Almquist & Wiksell, 1980.

Skelton, Robert. "The Iskandar Nama of Nusrat Shah." In *Indian Painting: Mughal and Rajput and a Sultanate Manuscript*, edited by Toby Falk, Ellen Smart, and Robert Skelton. London: P.& D. Colnaghi, 1978.

Stapleton, H. E. "Coins of Danujmardanna Deva and Mahendra Deva, Two Hindu Kings of Bengal." *Journal of the Asiatic Society of Bengal*, numismatic number, n.s., 26, no. 2 (1930): 5–13.

———. "Contributions to the History and Ethnology of North-eastern India." *Journal of the Asiatic Society of Bengal*, n.s., 18 (1922): 407–27.

Strickland, C. *Deltaic Formation, with Special Reference to the Hydrographic Processes of the Ganges and the Brahmaputra*. Calcutta: Longmans, Green, 1940.

Strong, F. W. *Eastern Bengal District Gazetteers: Dinajpur*. Allahabad: Pioneer Press, 1912.

Subrahmanyam, Sanjay. "Notes on the Sixteenth-Century Bengal Trade." *Indian Economic and Social History Review* 24, no. 3 (1987): 265–89.

Tarafdar, Momtazur Rahman. "The Bengali Muslims in the Pre-Colonial Period: Problems of Conversion, Class Formation, and Cultural Evolution." In *Puruṣārtha*, vol. 9, *Islam et société en Asie du sud*, edited by Marc Gaborieau, 93–110. Paris: Ecole des Hautes études en sciences sociales, 1986.

———. *Husain Shahi Bengal, 1494–1538 A.D.: A Socio-Political Study.* Dacca: Asiatic Society of Pakistan, 1965.

———. "Trade and Society in Early Medieval Bengal." *Indian Historical Review* 4, no. 2 (January 1978): 274–86.

Temple, R. C. "Buddermokan." *Journal of the Burma Research Society* 15 (1925): 1–33.

Thapar, Romila. *From Lineage to State: Social Formations in the Mid First Millennium B.C. in the Ganga Valley.* Bombay: Oxford University Press, 1984.

Thomas, Edward. "The Initial Coinage of Bengal." *Journal of the Asiatic Society of Bengal* 36 (1867): 1–73; 42 (1873): 343–64.

Thompson, W. H. *Final Report on the Survey and Settlement Operations in the District of Noakhali, 1914–1919.* Calcutta: Bengal Secretariat Book Depot, 1919.

Titly, Norah M. *Persian Miniature Painting and Its Influence on the Art of Turkey and India.* London: British Library, 1983.

Thorp, John P. "Masters of Earth: Conceptions of 'Power' among Muslims of Rural Bangladesh." Ph.D. diss., University of Chicago, 1978.

Waheeduzzaman, Abu Mohammad. "Land Resumption in Bengal, 1819–1846." Ph.D. diss., University of London, 1969.

Webster, J. E. *Eastern Bengal and Assam District Gazetteers: Noakhali.* Allahabad: Pioneer Press, 1911.

Westland, J. *A Report on the District of Jessore: Its Antiquities, Its History, and Its Commerce.* 2d ed. Calcutta: Bengal Secretariat, 1871.

Wink, André. "'Al-Hind': India and Indonesia in the Islamic World-Economy, c. 700–1800 A.D." In *Itinerario*, special issue, *The Ancien Régime in India and Indonesia*, 33–72. Leiden: Gravaria, 1988.

———. *Al-Hind: The Making of the Indo-Islamic World.* Vol. 1, *Early Medieval India and the Expansion of Islam, Seventh–Eleventh Centuries.* Leiden: E. J. Brill, 1990.

Wise, James. "The Hindus of Eastern Bengal." *Journal of the Asiatic Society of Bengal* 62, no. 3 (1893): 1–8.

———. "The Muhammadans of Eastern Bengal." *Journal of the Asiatic Society of Bengal* 63 (1894): 28–63.

———. "Note on Shah Jalal, the Patron Saint of Silhat." *Journal of the Asiatic Society of Bengal* 42, no. 3 (1873): 278–81.

———. *Notes on the Races, Castes and Traders of Eastern Bengal.* 2 vols. London: Harrison & Sons, 1883.

Wood, W. H. Arden. "Rivers and Man in the Indus-Ganges Alluvial Plain." *Scottish Geographical Magazine* 40, no. 1 (1924): 1–16.

Zbavitel, Dusan. *Bengali Literature.* Vol. 9, fasc. 3 of *A History of Indian Literature*, edited by Jan Gonda. Wiesbaden: Otto Harrassowitz, 1976.

———. *Bengali Folk-Ballads from Mymensingh and the Problem of Their Authenticity.* Calcutta: University of Calcutta, 1963.

Index

Bankura (district), 184n.67, 185
Barani, Zia al-Din (historian), 84
Barbier, Père (Jesuit missionary), 265–66
Barbosa, Duarte (Portuguese official), 99, 131–32
Barisal, 195n.1, 219. *See* Bakarganj (district)
Baudhāyana-Dharmasūtra, 118, 119
Begumpur mosque (Delhi), 37, 42, 45
Bengal: ancient subdivisions, 3; under Delhi sultanate, 32–38; diet and climate alien to Mughals, 167, 169–70; dominance of Hanafi legal school, 130; dynamics of religious change in, 268–70, 291–97, 301–03; as foreign colony under Mughals, 167–74; independent identity under sultans, 41; integration with world economy, 96–97, 202–04; kinship organization, 232; linguistic culture, 7n.17; Mughal origins of Orientalist views of, 168, 168n.29; nativist revolt in, 54–55; physical description, 3, 3n; 231–32; rainfall and vegetation, 19; revolts against Delhi Sultans, 38–40; settlement pattern in rural, 231–32; temple distribution in Mughal period, 185; in Vedic literature, 7. *See also* East Bengal, contrasts with West; Economy; Forest reclamation; Frontier; Indigenous communities; Islam; Mughal (dynasty)
Bengali language, 7n.17, 60, 66, 276n.22, 278, 293–94
Bengali literature, 66. *See also* 'Abd al-Nabi (*Vijay-Hamza*); 'Ali Raja (*Jñāna-sāgara*); Chandi Das (*Śrī Kṛṣṇa-Kīrtan*); Curamani Das (*Gaurāṅga-Vijaya*); Haji Muhammad (*Nūr Jamāl*); Jayananda (*Caitanya-Maṅgala*); Kavindra Parameśvara (*Mahābhārata*); Kirtivas Pundit (*Rāmāyaṇa*); Krishna Das (*Caitanya-Caritāmṛta*); Krishnaram Das (*Rāy-Maṅgala*); Ksemananda (*Manasā-Maṅgala*); Locan Das (*Caitanya Maṅgala*); Maladhara Basu (*Śrī Kṛṣṇa-Vijaya*); Muhammad Khan (*Maqtul Husain*); Mukundaram (*Kavikaṅkaṇa-Caṇḍī*); Saiyid Murtaza (*Yoga-Qalandar*); Saiyid Sultan (*Nabī-Baṃśa*); Shaikh Muttalib (*Kifayat al-Mussalin*); Vijaya Gupta (*Padma-Purāṇa*); Vijaya Pandita (*Mahābhārata*); Vipra Das (*Manasā-Vijaya*);

Vrindavan Das (*Śrī Caitanya Bhāgavat*)
Bernier, François (traveler), 201, 220n.83
Beverley, Henry, 120
Bhagirathi-Hooghly basin, 14, 18, 19
Bhallua, 191, 266
Bhati (East Bengal), 145–46, 146nn.30–31, 148, 150, 155, 189, 191, 194
Bhusna, 148, 153
Bhūt (spirits), 295
Bihar (city), 87
Bihar (region), 6, 7, 42, 138, 145
Birbhum District, 71, 184, 184n.67, 185
Bisu (Kuch raja), 187–88
Bogra District, 147n.35, 171, 179; distribution of Muslims, 120, 125; distribution of temples, 185; site of ancient Pundra, 4; social origin of Muslims, 125–26
Bon Bibi (goddess), 270n.8
Brahma (deity), 286
Brahmanism: Chandi cult and, 108; in eastern Bengal, 17–21, 76, 277; ideology, 9; reflected in art and temple patronage, 13, 13n.40, 184–86
Brahmans: according to Saiyid Sultan, 288, 290; on agrarian frontier, 221–22; appropriation of Goddess cults, 104–05, 108, 188; and Chaitanya, 111, 112; converts to Islam, 122; as court priests, 15–16, 17; as household priests, 14, 15; immigration patterns, 19, 292; model of gifting, 14, 253, 255; patronage of, 60n.80, 102, 259, 307; in relation to Hindu society, 103, 104, 117–19, 123, 124, 186; response to conquest, 102; role in civilizing Bengal, 10, 10nn.27–28, 18; and Śaiva cult, 103; and scriptural authority, 291; social ideology, 6; and theories of Islamization, 117. *See also* Brahmanism; Indo-Aryan culture
Brahmaputra River, 3, 77, 96n.2, 186, 187, 189, 194, 219
Buchanan, Francis (English official), 209, 236–37, 248–52, 296, 301–02
Buckler, F. W., 163–65
Buddhism, 76; in Arakan, 235n.19; architectural legacies, 62; colonizing role of monasteries, 18; decline, 10, 13, 13n.39, 14; diffusion, 12; emergence in Bengal, 9–10; among *jhūm* cultivators of Chittagong interior, 301; model of gifting, 14, 253, 255; noted by Chinese observers, 13n.39; patronized in Bengal, 10–12; so-

Economy (*continued*)
economic growth and price stability,
206; land-labor ratios, 229, 229n.3;
monetization, 204, 206–7, 253–55. *See
also* Exports and imports; Forest reclamation; Indian Ocean trading world;
Jāgīr; Land grants; Revenue and revenue systems; Silver; Textile manufacture
Eklakhi mausoleum, 61, fig.12
English East India Company, 151, 204,
236, 301
Eve, 278, 290, 299, 303, 308n.5
Exports and imports: commercial imports
of silver, 96, 204–05; to Dutch,
203n.25; rice exports, 201; silver imports in pre-Muslim period, 95n.2; textile exports, 11, 97, 97n.12, 202–03

Fa-hsien (Chinese Buddhist traveler),
13n.39
Fakhr al-Din Mubarak, Sultan, 96
Fara'izi (reform movement), 282
Farid al-Din Ganj-i Shakar, Shaikh, 83,
175
Faridpur (city), 54, 142, 147n.35, 153
Faridpur (district), 122, 148, 185, 195,
200n.7
Fatehabad, 54, 142, 147n.35, 153
Fatehpur Sikri, 143, 165, 171
Fātiḥa (Qur'anic readings), 247, 268–69,
282–83, 292, 296
Fatima (daughter of the Prophet Muham-
mad), 271–72, 276
Federici, Cesare (Venetian traveler), 96,
132, 198, 201, 278n.27
Fernandez, Francis (Jesuit missionary), 132
Firdausi (Persian poet), 28, 162, 165
Firdausi (Sufi order), 50, 82, 87, 88,
88n.48. *See also* Balkhi, Maulana Mu-
zaffar Shams; Maneri, Shaikh Sharaf
al-Din
Firishta, Muhammad Qasim (historian),
51, 52n.51, 55n.63
Firuzpuri, Shah Ni'mat Allah, 169,
169n.31
Firuz Tughluq (sultan of Delhi), 41, 42, 83,
87, 88
Fitch, Ralph (English traveler), 146–47,
201, 202
Forest reclamation: in ancient Gangetic
Plain, 6; associated with Muslim holy
men, 207–19; and cash economy, 206–

07, 249, 253–55; in Chittagong, 238,
240, 248–50; description of, 221, 248;
under Mughals, 137, 206–07; under sultans, 95, 95n.1, 207; in Sundarban forests, 223
Frontier: agrarian, xxi–xxii, 21, 95, 137,
150, 198–207, 212, 214, 218, 234, 240,
250, 257, 265, 307–08; dynamics of,
xxii–xxiii, 22, 207, 265; eastward movement of, 21, 194–202, 206–07, 226–27,
240; Islamic, xxi, xxii, 21, 71, 77, 218,
234, 251–52, 257, 265, 308; literary production on, 286, 286n.57; political, xxi,
22–23, 64, 71, 77, 96, 146, 149, 150,
183–84, 212, 237–38, 257, 307–08; Sanskritic, xxi, 6–7, 7nn.16–17, 187–88,
191; sociopolitical activity on, 247–48

Gabriel (angel), 269, 299, 308
Gait, E. A., 125
Gajapati (Orissa dynasty), 141
Ganesh. *See* Raja Ganesh
Ganga (goddess), 20n.60, 104
Ganga Sagar, 20, 68–69
Ganges River, 3, 38, 51, 179, 219; as "Adi
Ganga," 20; and coronation rituals
among sultans, 68; eastward diversion
of, 20, 144, 194–98, 227, 307; former
channel of, 20, 68; identified with Nile,
277; sanctity for Hindus, 19–20,
20n.60; sanctity for Muslims, 281;
Shaikh Tabrizi walks on, 216
Gangetic Plain, 5
Gangohi, Shaikh 'Abd al-Quddus, 78–79
Gaur, 143, 144n.22, 149, 150, 151, 158,
230; abandoned by Afghans, 142n.13;
abandoned by Mughals, 198; ancient
city, 18; capital of sultanate, 61, 82, 97;
court at, 64–65; description, 98, 131,
132, figs.14,15; export of textiles, 97;
long-distance merchants in, 99; plague
under Mughals, 144; ruin of, 144n.23;
as sacred center under Mughals,
176–77; seized by Sher Khan, 138. *See
also* Lakhnauti
Ghauth, Shaikh Muhammad, 79, 79n.27,
80, 81, 81n.30, 82
Ghazali, Abu Hamid al- (theologian), 29
Ghāzī, 72, 74, 77
Ghaznavid (Turkish dynasty), 28
Ghiyath al-Din A'zam Shah, Sultan, 47,
50, 51, 52, 86–89

Indo-Aryan culture (*continued*)
Gangetic Plain, 6; merger with indigenous cultures, 8
Iran, 23, 45–46, 72, 211, 287. *See also* Persian; Safavid (Persian dynasty); Sasanian (Persian dynasty)
Iranians, 165–66, 168, 275
'Isa Khan (chieftain), 149, 155, 170, 201, 306; defeats Mughal governors, 147, 148; diplomacy, 148n.37; as focus of anti-Mughal resistance, 146–48, 147n.35; legacy in history and folklore, 148n.43; use of gunpowder, 153
Isfahani, Muhammad Sadiq (*Ṣubḥ-i Ṣādiq*), 167–68
Islam: and an agrarian ethos, 308–10; as a closed, self-contained essence, 129, 273, 280–81, 302; local conceptions of, 272–74; and the Mughal state, 177–83; modern reform movements, 281–84, 283n.46; *nabī* and *avatār* identified, 288; Orientalist conceptions of, 113–14, 313; piety of Mughal *ashrāf*, 174–79; religious cosmology in, 16, 302–03; rise of in Arabia, 113–14, 284–85; and a ruling ethos, 305; social equality in, 117, 123–24; status of women in, 297–98; and world-construction, 267. *See also* Islamization; Mecca; Muslim society; Pilgrimage to Arabia; Religion; Sufis
Islamic law: as basis of legal arbitration, 100; formation of, 287; Hanafi tradition in Bengal, 130; and Persian political thought, 30, 32; and prominent Sufis, 89; role of in Islamic civilization, 291; schools of, 130
Islamization: conventional theories of, 113–19; dynamics of, 268–70, 291–97, 301–03; and economic growth, 219–27, 264–67; in legends of charismatic pioneers, 207–19; and liberation from caste system, 116–19, 120, 123–25; and literacy, 291–97, 309; and military force, 113–15; and socioeconomic patronage, 116; and status of women, 297–301
Islam Khan Chishti (Mughal governor), 164, 170, 175, 177, 307; annexes the southeast, 191–92; appointed governor, 150; career, 151; character, 150n.50, 151n.51; invades Kuch Bihar, 189–90; opposes religious conversion, 179, 182;

political rituals, 161, 165; political skills, 153–54; seeks Indian medical treatment, 166; subdues chieftains in the west, 184; ties with Chishti piety, 175
Islam Khan Mashhadi (Mughal governor), 133
Iśvar (*iśvara*), 68–69, 276

Jack, J. C., 219, 221, 222
Jadu. *See* Jalal al-Din Muhammad, Sultan
Jagannath temple, 140
Jagat Iśvar, 276
Jagat-jananī, 276
Jāgīr, 154–57, 179, 205n.37
Jāgīrdār, 154, 155, 161, 192
Jahangir (Mughal emperor), 150, 160, 160n.5, 163, 166, 176
Jahangirnagar, 156, 157. *See* Dhaka
Jalal al-Din Fath Shah, Sultan, 63n.88
Jalal al-Din Khalaji (sultan of Delhi), 40
Jalal al-Din Muhammad, Sultan, 63, 64, 91; Arab accounts of, 52; coinage, 54, 57; conversion to Islam, 52; installation as sultan, 52; patronage of Brahmans, 60n.80, 102; patronage of Chishti Sufis, 56; patronage of Islam, 57, 131; political ideology, 56–63; reconquest of eastern delta, 54, 96
Jalal al-Din Tabrizi, Shaikh, 73, 82n.34, 215–18
Jāti. See Caste
Jaunpur (sultanate), 53–54
Java, 313
Jayadeva (*Gīta Govinda*), 109
Jayananda (*Caitanya-Maṅgala*), 68, 111n.53
Jehovah, 279
Jessore (city), 210
Jessore (district), 147n.35, 153, 195; distribution of mosques, 230; distribution of temples, 185; Muslim pioneers in, 208; and Raja Pratapaditya, 154–55, 155n.73, 184
Jesus, 286
Jews and Judaism, 80, 284–5, 286, 287n.59
Jhūm, 5, 9, 236–37, 250, 250n.48, 300–302
Jihād, 72, 74
Jinn (minor spirits), 269

Ka'aba (Meccan shrine), 100, 285, 308
Kabuli, Ma'sum Khan (chieftain), 145, 147n.35, 148n.37, 148

with Bengal, 122–23, 144, 169–70; and
economic change, 137, 198–207, 238–
41; ethnic composition of nobility,
165–66; historiography of, 311,
311n.14; judicial practice, 179–83; military tactics, 142–43, 148; notions of
property and area, 241, 250; policy on
conversion, 178–79; policy toward non-
Muslims, 177–83; reign correlated with
Islamization, 132–34; stereotypes of
Bengal and Bengalis, 144, 168–71; weaponry, 151–53
—political rituals: affinities with Indian
culture, 165n.18; court ceremony, 159,
165; incorporation; 143, 143n.20; *jharokhā*, 161, 161n.5; *khil'at*, 164–65; salt,
162–64, 165, 165n.18, 177
—political theory and practice: of Akbar,
143, 159–61, 159n.1, 165, 166; diplomacy toward Bengali chieftains, 153–
56, 191–92; imperialism and architecture, 171–74; of Jahangir, 161n.5;
separation of church and state, 174–83;
strategic goals, 228. *See also* Akbar;
Aurangzeb; Babur; Humayun; Jahangir; *manṣabdārs;* Revenue and revenue systems; Shah Jahan
Muhammad (Prophet of Islam), 269, 284,
293; as *avatār* of Prabhu, 288; associations with Light, 272, 288; career compared with Shah Jalal's, 75; descendants
as gentry, 249; discussed by yogi and
qāzī, 79; in folk literature, 271; fusion
with Krishna, 270; Ibn Ishaq's biography of, 286–88; identification in Sanskrit inscriptions, 275; in Islamic cosmologies, 303; and modern reform
movements, 282; prophetic career, 285;
reliquaries in Arabia, 100; reliquaries
in Bengal, 177; in Saiyid Sultan's
thought, 289; and Satya Pir cult, 280;
spiritual master of Shah Jalal, 213n.63
Muhammad bin Tughluq (sultan of Delhi),
83, 86
Muhammad Ghuri, Mu'izz al-Din (sultan
of Delhi), 28, 33
Muhammad Khan (*Maqtul Husain*), 294
Mu'in al-Din Chishti, Shaikh, 175n.44
Mukunda Deva (raja), 140–41
Mukundaram (*Kavikaṅkaṇa-Caṇḍī*). Account of: cash economy on frontier,
206, 254; civilization-building on frontier, 214; Hindu communities, 103,

186; paper making, 293; role of Muslim pioneers in clearing forest, 214–15;
urban Muslims, 100, 101, 102; Vaishnavas, 112
Mullās: association with literacy, 292–93,
294–95; criticized by modern reformers, 282–83; ethnic origins of, 100; as
focus of authority on frontier, 233,
308; as lower-ranking clerics, 100; per-
formers of life-cycle rituals, 295n.86;
role in Islamization, 123; urge state to
favor Islam, 178, 178n.59
Munda, 5n.7
Mun'im Khan (Mughal governor), 142,
143, 144, 144n.22, 149, 152
Murshidabad (city), 220n.84, 224, 225
Murshidabad (district), 194, 195, 202, 230
Murshid Quli Khan (Mughal governor),
xxiii, 220n.84, 312n.15
Musa Khan (chieftain), 155–56, 170, 192
Muslim society: appearance in cities, 97–
102; appearance in countryside,
132–34; class-based attitudes toward
farming, 310–11; conversion and social
rank, 117–18; distribution in Bengal,
xx, 119–20, 192; distribution of dated
mosques, 230; distribution in India,
118, 119; emergence of cultivators,
222–27, 234, 249, 251–52; kinship in,
232; as minority community, 287; relation to textile industry, 101; social organization, 233–34; during sultanate, 97–
102. *See also Ashrāf* society; *Mullās;*
Qāzīs; Shekh (social class); Sufis
Musta'sim, al- (Abbasid caliph), 40
Muzaffar Shams Balkhi. *See* Balkhi, Maulana Muzaffar Shams
Mymensingh (district), 120, 122, 147n.35,
185; folk literature of, 273, 275, 281; as
refuge for Afghans, 149, 192; rustica-
tion of pre-Mughal architecture in, 173
Myohaung (Arakanese capital), 235

Nadia (city), 101, 110
Nadia (district), 195, 311n.12
Namasudra (indigenous community), 219,
225
Naraingarh, 180, 183
Narayan, Nara (Kuch king), 187
Narayan, Parikshit (Kuch king), 189
Nasir al-Din Nusrat Shah, Sultan, 63; coin-
age, 68; military tactics, 152–53; politi-

Nasir al-Din Nusrat Shah (*continued*)
cal rituals, 143n.20, 165; receives Afghans, 64, 138
Nathan, Mirza (Mughal officer) (*Bahāristān-i ghaibī*): complains of monsoon climate, 167; gets loans to finance campaigns, 157; his Sufi piety, 175–76, 177, 177n.52; loyalty of his Hindu subordinates, 177–78; relies on Indian medical therapy, 166, 166n.23
Navadwip (pilgrimage site), 20. *See also* Nadia (city)
Nicholas, Ralph, 232–33
Niranjan, 269, 276, 288, 289, 299, 309
Nizam al-Din Ahmad (historian), 51, 52
Nizam al-Din Auliya, Shaikh, 84
Noah, 286
Noakhali (district), 185; Christian community described, 266; distribution of Muslims, 119; Islamic reform in, 283; Muslim pioneers in, 211–12, 256, 265; Muslims described in, 133; social origin of Muslims, 125
Nomo (indigenous community), 258
Non-*ashrāf*, 101, 137
Nudiya (Sena city), xix, xixn, 21, 33
Nur al-Din Firuz (Iranian merchant), 275–76
Nur Qutb-i 'Alam, Shaikh: death date, 89n.52; mystical thought, 89n.52; patronizes Sultan Jalal al-Din, 56; protests rise of Raja Ganesh, 53, 89–91; tomb as state shrine, 91, 94, 177

Ojhā (folk exorcist), 295, 295n.87, 296n.88
Orientalist notions of: Bengali society and culture, 168, 168n.29, 170–71; caste system, 103; Islam and urbanism, 313; Islamic holy war, 72, 113–14; Mughal decline, 311; the 'ulamā, 312
Orissa, 42, 64, 140, 179, 181
Ottoman (Turkish dynasty), 72, 75, 75n.13, 116n.10, 151, 177

Pabna (district), 119, 125–26, 147n.35, 213, 233–34, 308
Padma River, 20, 21, 144, 150, 195–98, 227, 307
Paharpur (Buddhist monastery), 12, 61
Pāīk, 188, 190
Pakistan, xx, 127
Pala (Bengali dynasty), 51; assimilated into Kayasthas, 102; Buddhism in, 11–12,

12n.37; decline, 14; evolution of state under, 15; monetary system, 95–96; patronage of Brahmanism, 13
Panch Pir (cult), 283
Pandua, 18, 50, 87, 230, 298n.95; architecture at, 42–48, 61; coinage at, 53, 58, 86; description of court, 47–49, 131; as Ilyas Shahi capital, 41, 82, 97; and Jalal al-Din Tabrizi, 215–18; long-distance merchants in, 99; as sacred center under Mughals, 176–77; seized by Firuz Tughluq, 41; site of Adina mosque, 42; Sufis of, 56, 82n.34
Paper-making technology, 293
Partition of Bengal, 129
Parvati (deity), 188
Pathan, 122, 126. *See also* Afghans
Patna, 141, 201n.13
Patuakhali, 219, 223
Paul (apostle), 279
Peel, J. D. Y., 274, 292–93
Persian: art at court, 65n.97; customs regarding women, 298; ideals of kingship, 29–31, 47, 64–65; inscriptions under Mughals, 171; inscriptions under sultans, 47; language at court, 60; language cultivated by *ashrāf*, 311; renaissance, 28; treatises on Sufism, 30; vocabulary in Bengali, 276n.22
Pilgrimage to Arabia, 87, 100, 148n.37, 249, 282, 283–84
Pires, Tome (Portuguese official), 64, 97, 97n.12, 131, 131n.54
Pīrs, 269; clientele, 225; conflicts with government, 225; focus of authority on frontier, 233–34; in folk literature, 273; as gentry in Chittagong, 249; and healing, 273, 296n.88; in Islamic cosmologies, 303; and literacy, 292–93; role in settling frontier, 207–09, 211–12, 214–15, 218, 222, 224, 264, 308, 309
Pod (indigenous community), 118, 125, 310
Political rituals: of early Turkish rulers, 33; of later sultans, 64–66, 68–69, 143, 165; of Senas, 16–17, 38. *See also* Mughal (dynasty)—political rituals
Political theory: in Chandi mythology, 108–09; of early Delhi sultans, 28–32, 159, 165; of later Bengal sultans, 64–65, 68–69; Perso-Islamic, 29, 64–65, 161; of Razi, 29–30; Sena, 16–17; of Sufis, 30–31, 83–84, 88–91. *See also*

Yoga, 79–80
Yunani medicine, 166

Zafar Khan (commander), 37–38, 215n.66, fig.5
Zafar Mian (Muslim pioneer), 214–15
Zain al-'Abidin, Shah. *See* Maghribi, Shah Muhammad Barbak (Shah Zain al-'Abidin)
Zamīndārs (landholders), 157, 255; as absentee Hindus, 221–22, 223–24, 251–52, 251n.56; as descendants of holy

men, 211–12, 256; ideology of kingship, 251; initiate land transfers, 252–53, 259; integrated with sultanate's revenue system, 50–51, 102–03, 184; Muslim holy men transformed into, 212, 218–19, 224, 224n.96; patronize Hindu temples, 184–85, 186; position in Mughal revenue system, 221, 229; resist Mughals, 142, 142n.15, 145; role in settling frontier, 222, 223, 248–49, 251–52, 266. See also *Chaudhurī*
Zindah Ghazi (holy man), 209
Zulaikha, 277

Printed in the United States
108722LV00003B/65/A